Microsoft® Office 2000 For Windows® For Dummies®

Cheat Sheet

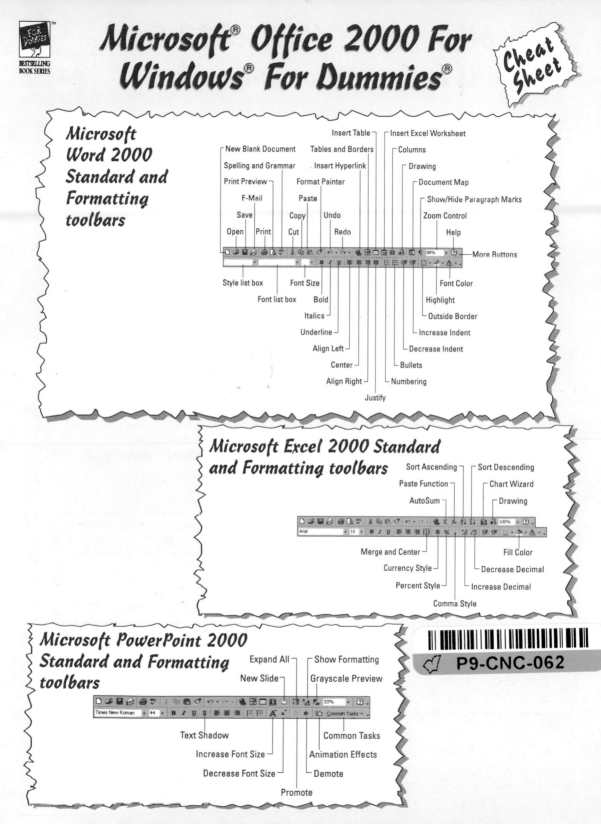

Microsoft Word 2000 Standard and Formatting toolbars

New Blank Document
Spelling and Grammar
Print Preview
F-Mail
Save
Open
Print

Insert Table
Tables and Borders
Insert Hyperlink
Format Painter
Paste
Copy
Cut
Undo
Redo

Insert Excel Worksheet
Columns
Drawing
Document Map
Show/Hide Paragraph Marks
Zoom Control
Help
More Buttons

Style list box
Font list box

Font Size
Bold
Italics
Underline
Align Left
Center
Align Right
Justify

Bullets
Numbering

Font Color
Highlight
Outside Border
Increase Indent
Decrease Indent

Microsoft Excel 2000 Standard and Formatting toolbars

Sort Ascending
Paste Function
AutoSum

Sort Descending
Chart Wizard
Drawing

Arial   10

Merge and Center
Currency Style
Percent Style
Comma Style

Increase Decimal
Decrease Decimal
Fill Color

Microsoft PowerPoint 2000 Standard and Formatting toolbars

Times New Roman   44

Expand All
New Slide

Show Formatting
Grayscale Preview

Text Shadow
Increase Font Size
Decrease Font Size
Promote

Common Tasks
Animation Effects
Demote

P9-CNC-062

...For Dummies®: Bestselling Book Series for Beginners

Microsoft® Office 2000 For Windows® For Dummies®

Cheat Sheet

Microsoft Office 2000 Shortcut Keys

Function	Keystroke
Copy	Ctrl+C
Cut	Ctrl+X
Find	Ctrl+F
Help	F1
Hyperlink	Ctrl+K
New	Ctrl+N
Open	Ctrl+O
Save	Ctrl+S
Paste	Ctrl+V
Print	Ctrl+P
Replace	Ctrl+H
Select All	Ctrl+A
Spell Check	F7
Undo	Ctrl+Z
Redo	Ctrl+Y

Online Resources for Microsoft Office 2000

Microsoft Internet Sites	URL Addresses
World Wide Web site	http:// www.microsoft. com
FTP site	ftp:// ftp.microsoft. com

Microsoft Newsgroups

microsoft.public.access

microsoft.public.excel

microsoft.public.frontpage

microsoft.public.office

microsoft.public.outlook

microsoft.public.powerpoint

microsoft.public.publisher

Microsoft Office 2000 Mouse Button Functions

Mouse Button Used	Action	Purpose
Left mouse button	Click	Moves the cursor, highlights an object, pulls down a menu, or chooses a menu command
Left mouse button	Double-click	Highlights a word or edits an embedded object
Left mouse button	Triple-click	Highlights a paragraph
Left mouse button	Drag	Moves an object, resizes an object, highlights text, or highlights multiple objects
Wheel mouse button	Click	Automatically scrolls a document
Right mouse button	Click	Displays a shortcut pop-up menu

Hungry Minds™

...For Dummies®: Bestselling Book Series for Beginners

TM

BESTSELLING BOOK SERIES

References for the Rest of Us!®

Are you intimidated and confused by computers? Do you find that traditional manuals are overloaded with technical details you'll never use? Do your friends and family always call you to fix simple problems on their PCs? Then the For Dummies® computer book series from Hungry Minds, Inc. is for you.

For Dummies books are written for those frustrated computer users who know they aren't really dumb but find that PC hardware, software, and indeed the unique vocabulary of computing make them feel helpless. For Dummies books use a lighthearted approach, a down-to-earth style, and even cartoons and humorous icons to dispel computer novices' fears and build their confidence. Lighthearted but not lightweight, these books are a perfect survival guide for anyone forced to use a computer.

> *"I like my copy so much I told friends; now they bought copies."*
> — Irene C., Orwell, Ohio

> *"Quick, concise, nontechnical, and humorous."*
> — Jay A., Elburn, Illinois

> *"Thanks, I needed this book. Now I can sleep at night."*
> — Robin F., British Columbia, Canada

Already, millions of satisfied readers agree. They have made For Dummies books the #1 introductory level computer book series and have written asking for more. So, if you're looking for the most fun and easy way to learn about computers, look to *For Dummies* books to give you a helping hand.

Hungry Minds™

1/01

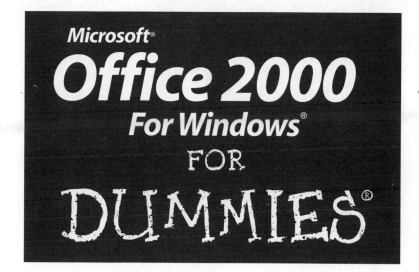

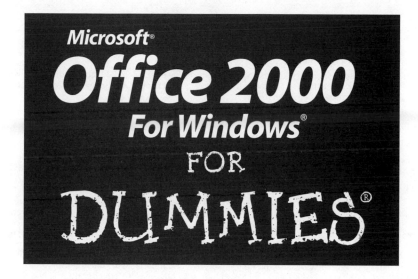

Microsoft® Office 2000 For Windows® FOR DUMMIES®

by Wallace Wang & Roger C. Parker

Hungry Minds™

Best-Selling Books • Digital Downloads • e-Books • Answer Networks • e-Newsletters • Branded Web Sites • e-Learning

New York, NY ◆ Cleveland, OH ◆ Indianapolis, IN

Microsoft® Office 2000 For Windows® For Dummies®

Published by
Hungry Minds, Inc.
909 Third Avenue
New York, NY 10022
www.hungryminds.com
www.dummies.com (Dummies Press Web site)

Library of Congress Catalog Card No.: 99-60744

ISBN: 0-7645-0452-5

Printed in the United States of America

15 14 13 12

1B/RY/QZ/QR/IN

Distributed in the United States by Hungry Minds, Inc.

Distributed by CDG Books Canada Inc. for Canada; by Transworld Publishers Limited in the United Kingdom; by IDG Norge Books for Norway; by IDG Sweden Books for Sweden; by IDG Books Australia Publishing Corporation Pty. Ltd. for Australia and New Zealand; by TransQuest Publishers Pte Ltd. for Singapore, Malaysia, Thailand, Indonesia, and Hong Kong; by Gotop Information Inc. for Taiwan; by ICG Muse, Inc. for Japan; by Intersoft for South Africa; by Eyrolles for France; by International Thomson Publishing for Germany, Austria and Switzerland; by Distribuidora Cuspide for Argentina; by LR International for Brazil; by Galileo Libros for Chile; by Ediciones ZETA S.C.R. Ltda. for Peru; by WS Computer Publishing Corporation, Inc., for the Philippines; by Contemporanea de Ediciones for Venezuela; by Express Computer Distributors for the Caribbean and West Indies; by Micronesia Media Distributor, Inc. for Micronesia; by Chips Computadoras S.A. de C.V. for Mexico; by Editorial Norma de Panama S.A. for Panama; by American Bookshops for Finland.

For general information on Hungry Minds' products and services please contact our Customer Care Department within the U.S. at 800-762-2974, outside the U.S. at 317-572-3993 or fax 317-572-4002.

For sales inquiries and reseller information, including discounts, premium and bulk quantity sales, and foreign-language translations, please contact our Customer Care Department at 800-434-3422, fax 317-572-4002, or write to Hungry Minds, Inc., Attn: Customer Care Department, 10475 Crosspoint Boulevard, Indianapolis, IN 46256.

For information on licensing foreign or domestic rights, please contact our Sub-Rights Customer Care Department at 650-653-7098.

For authorization to photocopy items for corporate, personal, or educational use, please contact Copyright Clearance Center, 222 Rosewood Drive, Danvers, MA 01923, or fax 978-750-4470.

For information on using Hungry Minds' products and services in the classroom or for ordering examination copies, please contact our Educational Sales Department at 800-434-2086 or fax 317-572-4005.

Please contact our Public Relations Department at 212-884-5163 for press review copies or 212-884-5000 for author interviews and other publicity information or fax 212-884-5400.

Hungry Minds™ is a trademark of Hungry Minds, Inc.

About the Authors

Wallace Wang

Before buying a book, many people like to know who the author is so they can determine whether the author's credentials may somehow make the book more pertinent or valuable in some obscure way. So to help you make a snap decision on whether to buy this book or not, here's a quick look at my resume.

Name: Wallace Wang

E-mail address: bothecat@home.com

Objective: To convince people that they're not stupid; it's the poorly designed computers and software that are.

Work and Education Experience

1979	Graduated from high school with absolutely no marketable skills or direction whatsoever. Support your local school system.
1983	Graduated from Michigan State University with an (appropriately abbreviated) Bachelor of Science degree in Materials Science, the only engineering major I could find that offered the most non-technical electives. Also pursued a dual degree in English that I never completed because I felt I already knew how to get a minimum wage job all by myself.
1983-1985	Worked as a technical writer for General Dynamics, home of the nuclear-tipped cruise missile. Got in trouble once for referring to General Dynamics as a "bomb factory," so from that point on I bought chocolate covered doughnuts for my boss, hoping to clog his arteries with cholesterol and induce a fatal heart attack. After turning in my resignation, I spent every day, for the final two weeks, taking home office supplies in shopping bags.
1985-1987	Worked as a computer programmer for the Cubic Corporation doing absolutely nothing at all. Spent many days sitting at a desk, staring out the window, and pretending I was the Vice-President of the United States.
1987-1991	Worked as a writer/editor for a San Diego computer magazine called *ComputorEdge*, where I met Dan Gookin (*DOS For Dummies*), Tina Rathbone (*Modems For Dummies*), and Andy Rathbone (*Windows For Dummies*). At one time, Dan Gookin and I got in trouble with the FBI for printing a fake FBI poster of myself, proclaiming that I was a criminal for buying a Macintosh computer.

1989	Spent a month teaching computer classes at the University of Zimbabwe in Harare, Zimbabwe. Took time off to visit Victoria Falls, canoe down the Zambezi River, and sleep in a hut where wild monkeys snuck up behind me and stole my breakfast.
1990-Present	Decided to pursue stand-up comedy and began performing in comedy clubs around San Diego and Los Angeles.
1993-Present	Got married and soon became the owner of four cats named Bo, Scraps, Tasha, and Nuit.
1994	Appeared on "A&E's Evening at the Improv."
1995	Became a columnist for *Boardwatch Magazine*.
1996	Finally ran out of office supplies that I had taken during my final two weeks working at General Dynamics 11 years ago.
1997	Tried to get another job with General Dynamics so I could steal another decade's worth of office supplies.
1998	Invented a solar-powered car. Unfortunately it stalls every time you try to drive under a bridge.
1999	Solved the Y2K millenium bug by turning back all the clocks in my house 100 years.
2000	Discovered the missing number that would solve Albert Einstein's Grand Unified Field Theory. That number is 4.
2001	Wrote to Arthur C. Clarke and told him his book was wrong.

Roger C. Parker

More than 750,000 desktop publishers and software users throughout the world own books by Roger C. Parker. In addition to frequently contributing to a variety of publications, including *Graphic Solutions, Publish, Technique,* and *x-height,* Roger has written numerous books on desktop publishing and design.

Roger has conducted presentations throughout the world for organizations such as the Consumer Electronics Show, Apple Computer, Creative Seminars, the State Street Bank, Yamaha Audio, and the University of Illinois. During the past few years, Roger has been the keynote speaker and the lead presenter at PageMaker conferences throughout the United States. He is active with the Boston Computer Society.

Roger's books for IDG Books Worldwide, Inc., include *Desktop Publishing & Design For Dummies, Harvard Graphics 2.0 For Windows For Dummies, WordPerfect 6.0 (DOS) SECRETS* (with David Holzgang), *WordPerfect 6.0 for Windows Power Techniques,* and *Freelance Graphics 2.1 For Dummies.*

Dedication

This book is dedicated to the following:

Roger Parker for laying the foundation for this book.

Brian Kramer (project editor extraordinaire) and Jim McCarter for doing a superb job of technical editing so this book doesn't make me look foolish.

Bo the Cat, Scraps the Cat, Tasha the Cat, Nuit the Cat, and Loons the Yellow Nape Amazon Parrot.

Patrick DeGuire, Dat Phan, Steve Pan, Leo Fontaine, Chris "the Zooman" Clobber, Karen Rontowski, Lamont Ferguson, Fred Burns, and Eric Schwandt for helping me weather the filthy nightclubs, the obnoxious audiences, and the horrible living conditions that all stand-up comedians have to face when playing comedy clubs around the country.

And to all the hecklers I've faced while performing stand-up comedy on stage. Your many taunts, insults, and racial slurs have only helped strengthen me as a human being. In the words of the famous philosopher Friedrich Nietzche, "That which does not kill you makes you stronger." As a result, hecklers everywhere have my eternal gratitude for their indirect contribution to my life. Of course, this dedication doesn't change the way I feel about hecklers in general. I still hate them.

Publisher's Acknowledgments

We're proud of this book; please send us your comments through our Online Registration Form located at www.dummies.com.

Some of the people who helped bring this book to market include the following:

Acquisitions, Editorial, and Media Development

Project Editor: Brian Kramer

Acquisitions Editor: Sherri Morningstar

Copy Editors: Kathleen Dobie, Stephanie Koutek, Donna Love

Technical Editor: Jim McCarter

Editorial Manager: Leah Cameron

Editorial Assistant: Beth Parlon

Production

Project Coordinator: Regina Snyder

Layout and Graphics: Kelly Hardesty, Angela F. Hunckler, Jane Martin, Brent Savage, Jacque Schneider, Janet Seib, Rashell Smith, Kate Snell, Michael A. Sullivan, Brian Torwelle

Proofreaders: Kelli Botta, Vickie Broyles, Jennifer Mahern, Rebecca Senninger, Ethel M. Winslow

Indexer: Donald Glassman

General and Administrative

Hungry Minds, Inc.: John Kilcullen, CEO; Bill Barry, President and COO; John Ball, Executive VP, Operations & Administration; John Harris, CFO

Hungry Minds Technology Publishing Group: Richard Swadley, Senior Vice President and Publisher; Mary Bednarek, Vice President and Publisher, Networking and Certification; Walter R. Bruce III, Vice President and Publisher, General User and Design Professional; Joseph Wikert, Vice President and Publisher, Programming; Mary C. Corder, Editorial Director, Branded Technology Editorial; Andy Cummings, Publishing Director, General User and Design Professional; Barry Pruett, Publishing Director, Visual

Hungry Minds Manufacturing: Ivor Parker, Vice President, Manufacturing

Hungry Minds Marketing: John Helmus, Assistant Vice President, Director of Marketing

Hungry Minds Online Management: Brenda McLaughlin, Executive Vice President, Chief Internet Officer

Hungry Minds Production for Branded Press: Debbie Stailey, Production Director

Hungry Minds Sales: Roland Elgey, Senior Vice President, Sales and Marketing; Michael Violano, Vice President, International Sales and Sub Rights

◆

The publisher would like to give special thanks to Patrick J. McGovern, without whom this book would not have been possible.

◆

Contents at a Glance

Cartoons at a Glance

By Rich Tennant

page 377

page 9

page 55

page 147

page 245

page 347

page 421

page 293

page 211

Fax: 978-546-7747
E-mail: richtennant@the5thwave.com
World Wide Web: www.the5thwave.com

Table of Contents

Introduction

· ·

*B*ack in the dark ages of computers, a single program cost several hundred dollars, worked entirely differently than any other program on your computer, and stored data in a special file format that no other program knew how to use. Not surprisingly, many people found these computer programs frustrating, intimidating, and downright hostile to use.

So in a desperate attempt to make computers easier to use, Microsoft developed a word processor (Microsoft Word), a spreadsheet program (Microsoft Excel), a presentation graphics program (Microsoft PowerPoint), a personal information organizer (Microsoft Outlook), and a database program (Microsoft Access). After they saw what they had created, they rested on the seventh day, and then went on to create a Web page design and management program (Microsoft FrontPage), a desktop publisher (Microsoft Publisher), and a photo-editing and illustrating program (Microsoft PhotoDraw).

With each version of each program, Microsoft tried to torture all of their programs to look and work the same so you can spend more time getting work done and less time trying to figure out how to use each individual program.

Then the marketing folks at Microsoft got really creative and decided to toss various Microsoft programs in one box, calling the whole thing an "office suite" with the name Microsoft Office 2000. (The previous version was called Microsoft Office 97, but Microsoft felt that calling this latest version Microsoft Office 00 didn't look as good in their advertisements.)

Microsoft Office *2000 For Windows For Dummies* helps you explore all the programs in the suite. Although this book won't make you an expert at using any single program, it does give you the basics for using each program in Microsoft Office 2000. The book also shows you how to use Microsoft Office 2000 as a single entity rather than as a rag-tag collection of programs packaged together.

After reading *Microsoft Office 2000 For Windows For Dummies,* you can get more specific information about the programs by reading *Word 2000 For Windows For Dummies,* by Dan Gookin; *Excel 2000 For Windows For Dummies,* by Greg Harvey; *Access 2000 For Windows For Dummies,* by John Kaufeld; *PowerPoint 2000 For Windows For Dummies,* by Doug Lowe; *Microsoft Outlook 2000 For Dummies,* by Bill Dyszel; *Microsoft Publisher 2000 For Dummies,* by Jim McCarter, Barrie Sosinsky, and Christopher Benz; and *Microsoft FrontPage 2000 For Dummies,* by Asha Dornfest; all published by IDG Books Worldwide, Inc.

Who Should Buy This Book

Everyone should buy this book because this sentence says that you should and you should believe everything you read. But you should especially buy this book if you have any of the following versions of Microsoft Office 2000:

- ✔ *Standard Edition:* Contains Microsoft Word, Excel, Outlook, and PowerPoint.
- ✔ *Small Business Edition:* Contains Microsoft Word, Excel, Outlook, Publisher, and Small Business Edition Tools.
- ✔ *Professional Edition:* Contains Microsoft Word, Excel, Outlook, Publisher, Access, and Small Business Edition Tools.
- ✔ *Premium Edition:* Contains Microsoft Word, Excel, Outlook, Publisher, Access, PhotoDraw, FrontPage, and Small Business Edition Tools.
- ✔ *Developer Edition:* Contains Microsoft Word, Excel, Outlook, Publisher, Access, PhotoDraw, FrontPage, Small Business Edition Tools, and special Developer Tools.

If you have any of these editions of Microsoft Office 2000 lurking on your hard disk like a computer virus that you can't get rid of, then you can use this book to help you figure out how to get started using Microsoft Office 2000 today.

This book provides a foundation that you can put to work immediately and then build on later by browsing through the other books in the popular *...For Dummies* series.

How This Book Is Organized

This book uses the time-tested method of binding pages and gluing them on one side to form a book. To help you find what you need quickly, this book is divided into nine parts. Each part covers a certain topic about using Microsoft Office 2000. Whenever you need help, just flip through this book, find the part that covers the topic you're looking for, and then toss this book aside and get back to work.

Part I: Getting to Know Microsoft Office 2000

Even though Microsoft Office 2000 looks like a bunch of unrelated programs thrown together by Microsoft, it is actually a bunch of unrelated programs that have been tortured over the years into working together.

All of the Microsoft Office 2000 programs provide similar menus, icons, and keystroke commands, so when you know how to use one program, you'll be able to quickly figure out how to use another Office 2000 program.

Part II: Working with Word 2000

Microsoft Word is the most popular word processor on the face of the earth. Although you can use Word just to write letters, proposals, or apologies, you can also use it to create reports, brochures, newsletters, and even Web pages that combine spreadsheet data and charts from Excel, artwork from PowerPoint, and addresses from Access.

If you can't type, don't like to write, or flunked spelling in second grade, you may be glad to know that you can use Word to turn your $2,000 computer into your personal secretary. With the Word spell checker, grammar checker, and outliner, you can turn your random thoughts into coherent words and sentences that even your boss can understand.

Part III: Playing the Numbers Game with Excel 2000

This part shows you how to design your very own spreadsheets by using Microsoft Excel. You discover what the heck a spreadsheet is, how you can plop numbers and labels into it, how to create your own formulas so that Excel calculates new results automatically, and how to format the whole thing to make it look pleasing to the eye.

After you get the basics of spreadsheet creation, the next step is to convert your raw data into eye-popping graphs, charts, and other colorful images that can amuse everyone from high-powered CEOs of Fortune 500 companies to children roaming around in a day-care center.

Part IV: Making Presentations with PowerPoint 2000

If Word helps you look good in print and Excel helps you convert numbers into attractive charts, Microsoft PowerPoint can help you create slide shows, overhead transparencies, and on-screen computer presentations that either enhance your information or hide the fact that you don't have the slightest idea what you're talking about in the first place.

Any time you need to make a presentation, let PowerPoint help you develop a dynamic presentation that includes visuals (which can be 35mm slides, overhead transparencies, or screen images), notes (to help you rehearse your presentation), and handouts (to give your audience something to look at instead of staring at you).

Part V: Getting Organized with Outlook 2000

Everyone seems busy all the time (even when doing absolutely nothing but waiting until it's time to go home). In today's fast-moving world where seconds count, you may want to keep track of your tasks, appointments, and schedule so you can effectively manage your time while your peers wander aimlessly through the corporate landscape.

To help you accomplish this task, Microsoft Office 2000 includes Microsoft Outlook, a program that combines the features of an appointment book, calendar, and to-do list in one screen. By managing your time with Microsoft Outlook 2000, you can plan your projects, ration out your time, and effectively squeeze every last productive second out of each day. Unless, of course, you don't turn on your computer that day.

Besides organizing your appointments and tasks, Microsoft Outlook can also organize all the e-mail that may flood you every day. From within Microsoft Outlook, you can write, reply to, send, and receive e-mail to and from your friends whether they're down the hall from you or on another continent.

Part VI: Storing Stuff in Access 2000

If you have the Professional, Premium, or Developer edition of Microsoft Office 2000, you have a bonus program called Microsoft Access. For those of you who like official definitions, Access is a relational database that lets you store and retrieve data, design reports, and actually create your own programs. If you don't have Microsoft Access in your edition of Microsoft Office 2000, you can always buy Access separately and install it on your computer so that this part of the book can be useful to you.

You may find Access handy for saving mailing lists as well as for storing more esoteric information, such as part numbers, Internet addresses, or credit card numbers. If you need to save and retrieve information at a later date, use Access to help you do it quickly and easily.

Part VII: Designing Pages with Publisher 2000

If you only have the Standard edition of Microsoft Office 2000, you may as well skip this part of the book. But owners of the other editions of Microsoft Office 2000 have a desktop publishing program called Microsoft Publisher 2000.

By using Microsoft Publisher, you can design your own newsletters, menus, brochures, flyers, and signs much faster and easier than trying to do the same task with Microsoft Word. If you need to create a visually interesting page to impress your boss or friends, then you need to know how to design and lay out text and graphics in Microsoft Publisher.

Part VIII: Creating Web Pages and Editing Photos

Owners of the Premium and Developer editions of Microsoft Office 2000 have additional bonus programs in the form of FrontPage and PhotoDraw. With FrontPage you can create or edit Web pages in much finer detail and with greater control than you can by using either Microsoft Word or Publisher. With PhotoDraw you can touch up, modify, and edit graphic images such as digitized photographs (perfect for pasting your dog's head on your neighbor's body) or graphic images for posting on your Web pages.

Both FrontPage and PhotoDraw are high-powered, heavyweight programs, so this book just gives you a gentle introduction to using these tools. By toying around with these programs, you can see whether you want to find out more about Web page creation and photo editing than you may have thought possible.

Part IX: The Part of Tens

For those people who just want to find shortcuts and tips for working more efficiently with Microsoft Office 2000 (so they can take the rest of the day off), this part of the book provides common keystrokes for using all the Microsoft programs.

In addition, you can find tips for making Microsoft Office 2000 seem a lot easier than the incomprehensible manuals may lead you to believe. Just remember if something in Microsoft Office 2000 doesn't make sense or confuses you, it's not your fault; it's Microsoft's fault, so feel free to blame the millionaire programmers in Redmond for failing to anticipate your needs and not selling you a more intuitive program.

How to Use This Book

You can use this book as a reference, a tutorial, or a weapon (depending on how hard you throw it at somebody). Unlike novels, this book isn't designed for someone to read from cover to cover (although you could if you wanted). Instead, just browse through the parts that interest you and ignore the rest.

If you plan to take full advantage of Microsoft Office 2000, read Part I first so you can acquaint yourself with the more common Microsoft Office 2000 features.

The other parts of this book are here for your reference and amusement. Though you may not care about making presentations with PowerPoint 2000 at first, one day you may want to play around with it just to see what it can do. To your surprise, certain programs you thought you would never use may turn out to be more useful than you ever imagined. Then again, the programs may really turn out to be useless after all, but you'll never find out until you try them.

Foolish assumptions

First of all, you should already have Microsoft Office 2000 installed on your computer. You should also be running Microsoft Windows 95, Windows 98, or Windows NT. If you don't feel comfortable with Windows 95 or Windows 98, you may want to buy *Windows 95 For Dummies,* 2nd Edition or *Windows 98 For Dummies,* by Andy Rathbone, published by IDG Books Worldwide, Inc. For more information regarding Windows NT, pick up a copy of *Windows NT 4 For Dummies,* by Andy Rathbone and Sharon Crawford, also published by IDG Books Worldwide, Inc.

Conventions

To get the most out of the information presented in this book, you need to understand the following:

- The *mouse cursor* appears either as an arrow or as an I-beam pointer (depending on the program you happen to be using at the time). Any time you lose track of the mouse cursor, start moving the mouse around until you see something flashing across your screen. Chances are that what you're seeing is the mouse cursor.

- ✔ *Clicking* refers to pressing the left mouse button once and then letting go. Clicking is how you activate buttons on the toolbar and choose commands from pull-down menus.

- ✔ *Double-clicking* refers to pressing the left mouse button twice in rapid succession. Double-clicking typically activates a command.

- ✔ *Dragging* refers to moving the mouse pointer while holding down the left mouse button. To drag an object, select the item by clicking it and then hold the left mouse button and move the item in the desired direction. When you release the mouse button, Windows places the item where you want.

- ✔ *Right-clicking* means clicking the button on the right side of the mouse. (Some mice have three buttons, so ignore the middle button for now.) Right-clicking usually displays a pop-up menu on the screen.

Note: If you're left-handed and you have changed your mouse settings so that you use your left hand to operate the mouse, *clicking* means pressing the right mouse button, and *right-clicking* means pressing the left mouse button.

Icons used in this book

Icons highlight useful tips, important information to remember, or technical explanations that you can skip if you want. Keep an eye open for the following icons throughout the book:

This icon highlights pieces of information that can be helpful (as long as you remember them, of course).

This icon marks certain steps or procedures that can make your life a whole lot easier when using Microsoft Office 2000.

Look out! This icon tells you how to avoid trouble before it starts.

This icon highlights information that's absolutely useless to know for operating Microsoft Office 2000 but could be interesting to impress your trivia buddies.

This icon points out new features found only in Office 2000. If you're already familiar with Office 97, look for this icon to discover what new surprises Office 2000 may offer you.

Keyboard shortcuts

Microsoft Office 2000 gives you two ways to choose commands:

- Clicking the mouse on a button or menu command
- Pressing a keystroke combination, such as Ctrl+S (which means that you hold down the Ctrl key, tap the S key, and then release both keys at the same time)

Most keyboard shortcuts involve holding down the Ctrl or Alt key (typically located to the left and right of the spacebar on your keyboard) in combination with one of the function keys (the keys labeled F1, F2, F3, and so on) or a letter key (A, B, C, and so on).

You can use whichever method you prefer, just as long as you know what you're doing. Some people swear by the mouse, some swear by the keyboard, and still others just swear at the computer.

Getting Started

By now, you're probably anxious to start trying out Microsoft Office 2000. Turn on your computer and get ready to jump miles ahead of the competition by having the foresight to use the world's most powerful and dominant programs bundled together in Microsoft Office 2000.

Part I

Getting to Know Microsoft Office 2000

The 5th Wave   By Rich Tennant

YES, MASTER?

In this part . . .

At first glance, Microsoft Office 2000 may seem like a sluggish beast that gobbles up megabytes of hard disk space and provides enough features to overwhelm even the most battle-hardened personal computer veteran. Only after you get over your initial impression (or fear) of Office 2000 that you may realize the elegant madness behind Office 2000's massive bulk.

Despite the fact that Microsoft Office 2000 contains more commands than any sane person would ever care to memorize, Office 2000 can be conquered. To guide you through the multitude of commands you may need to get your work done, Office 2000 provides the *Office Assistant* to answer your questions and provide support.

Want to know how to print mailing labels, save an Excel 2000 file in a Lotus 1-2-3 file format, or design your own newsletter in Word 2000? Just ask the friendly Office Assistant. Within seconds, the Office Assistant displays a list of topics that (hopefully) answer your question and get you back to doing productive work.

Besides showing you how to get help within Microsoft Office 2000, this part of the book also explains how to get the various programs of Office 2000 started in the first place. In addition, this part of the book provides information on using a special Office 2000 feature called the Office Shortcut Bar, which can load any Office 2000 program at the click of the mouse. (For those of you with a mischievous streak, you can also customize the Office Shortcut Bar to display and run non-Microsoft programs as well, such as Netscape Navigator, WordPerfect, and Lotus 1-2-3.)

Chapter 1

Starting Microsoft Office 2000

●●

●●

Microsoft Office 2000 contains a word processor (for writing), a spreadsheet (for manipulating numbers), a presentation graphics program (for creating slide shows and charts), a personal information organizer (for storing names, addresses, e-mail, and phone numbers), a database (for storing information for mailing lists or tracking inventories), a desktop publisher (for designing and laying out pages), a Web page creator (for designing your own Web pages), and a graphics editor (for editing images such as digitized photographs).

If this sounds overwhelming, relax. Microsoft thoughtfully made all their Office 2000 programs look and work alike. After you find out how to use one Microsoft Office 2000 program, you'll be able to figure out how to use any other Office 2000 program as well. (And if you *do* have trouble using a particular Office 2000 program, don't blame yourself; blame Microsoft for making programs that still aren't as easy to use as people would like.)

Getting Microsoft Office 2000 Started

Before you can use Microsoft Office 2000, you need to know how to start it. Otherwise, Office 2000 just sits around and takes up space like an unwanted houseguest. To give you the illusion of freedom and choice, Microsoft offers multiple ways to start Office 2000:

✔ Choose a Microsoft Office 2000 program to run from the Start button on the Windows 95/98/NT taskbar.

✔ Choose a Microsoft Office 2000 program to run from the Office Shortcut Bar.

✔ Run Windows Explorer and double-click a document created by a Microsoft Office 2000 program.

✔ Double-click the program's shortcut that you create and put on the desktop.

Microsoft gives you many ways to run Office 2000 programs so you can choose the way you like best. After you find a way to run a Microsoft Office 2000 program, you can ignore all the other ways to run an Office 2000 program if you want. Remember, you're the one in control, not your computer or any software monstrosity created by Microsoft.

Running Microsoft Office 2000 from the Taskbar

One way to run Microsoft Office 2000 is to choose the program that you want to run directly from the Windows 95/98/NT taskbar. Just to keep you amused, Microsoft Office 2000 provides two ways to load an Office 2000 program from the taskbar:

✔ Click the Start button on the taskbar, choose Programs, and choose the specific program (such as Word 2000) that you want to load.

✔ Click the Start button on the taskbar and choose New Office Document or Open Office Document.

Using the Programs pop-up menu

If you're one of those souls who don't mind wading through the (sometimes) cluttered appearance of the Programs pop-up menu, you can load and run a Microsoft Office 2000 program from the Windows 95/98/NT taskbar by following these steps:

1. **Click the Start button on the taskbar and choose Programs.**

   A pop-up menu appears, as shown in Figure 1-1.

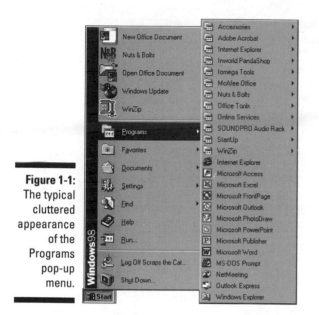

Figure 1-1:
The typical
cluttered
appearance
of the
Programs
pop-up
menu.

2. **Click the program that you want to use, such as Microsoft Word or Microsoft PowerPoint.**

   Your chosen program appears, ready for you to create a new file or open an existing one.

Clicking New Office Document on the taskbar

If your Programs pop-up menu contains so many programs that you can't find the one you want easily, here's a faster way of loading a Microsoft Office 2000 program:

1. **Click the Start button on the taskbar.**

   A pop-up menu appears.

2. **Click New Office Document.**

   The New Office Document dialog box appears, as shown in Figure 1-2.

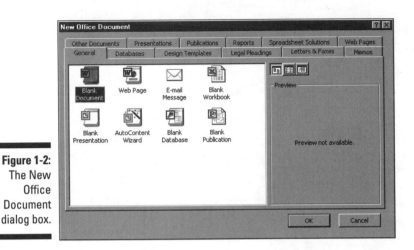

Figure 1-2:
The New
Office
Document
dialog box.

3. Click the General tab.

If you want to create a specific type of Microsoft Office 2000 file (such as a fax cover sheet or invoice), click on a different tab in this step, such as the Letters & Faxes tab or the Spreadsheet Solutions tab.

4. Click the type of document that you want to create.

For example, if you want to create a new Access database, choose Blank Database. If you want to create a new Word document, choose Blank Document.

5. Click OK.

Your chosen program appears, ready for you to start typing and creating valuable information that you can store on your hard disk.

You can skip Step 5 if you double-click on the file you want to create during Step 4.

Running Microsoft Office 2000 from the Microsoft Office Shortcut Bar

To give you still another way to run Office 2000, Microsoft created something called the Office Shortcut Bar. This Shortcut Bar displays icons for various Office 2000 programs. Just click the program icon that you want to run (such as Excel), and the Shortcut Bar obediently runs your chosen program.

Displaying the Microsoft Office Shortcut Bar

The Microsoft Office Shortcut Bar may be hiding from view like a frightened cat. To coax the Office Shortcut Bar into view so you can see and use it, follow these steps:

1. **Click the Start button on the taskbar.**

   A pop-up menu appears.

2. **Choose Programs Office Tools and then click Microsoft Office Shortcut Bar.**

   The Microsoft Office Shortcut Bar dialog box appears, asking if you want to load the Shortcut Bar automatically as soon as Windows loads.

3. **Click Yes (if you want the Shortcut Bar to appear automatically each time you turn on your computer) or click No (if you don't want the Shortcut Bar to load automatically).**

   The Microsoft Office Shortcut Bar appears, as shown in Figure 1-3.

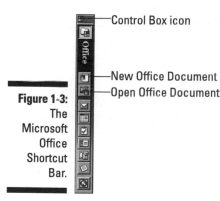

Control Box icon

New Office Document
Open Office Document

Figure 1-3:
The
Microsoft
Office
Shortcut
Bar.

4. **Click the New Office Document (or Open Office Document) icon in the Microsoft Office Shortcut Bar.**

   The New Office Document (or Open Office Document) dialog box appears.

5. **Double-click the file you want to open.**

Moving the Microsoft Office Shortcut Bar

The Microsoft Office Shortcut Bar can appear like a squashed dachshund smashed along one side of the screen (refer to Figure 1-3) or like a disembodied head floating in the middle of the screen as shown in Figure 1-4.

To move the Microsoft Office Shortcut Bar, follow these steps:

1. **Move the mouse pointer over the Microsoft Office Shortcut Bar. Make sure that the mouse pointer does not hover over any icons in the Shortcut Bar.**

2. **Hold down the left mouse button and drag the mouse in the middle of the screen or toward one side of the screen where you want to the Shortcut Bar to appear.**

   If you drag the Microsoft Office Shortcut Bar in the middle of the screen, the Shortcut Bar appears as a box, as shown in Figure 1-4.

Figure 1-4:
The Microsoft Office Shortcut Bar floating in the middle of the screen.

3. **Release the left mouse button.**

If you click the Minimize button or click on the Control Box icon and choose Minimize, you can make the Shortcut Bar disappear from the screen and appear in the Windows taskbar. Then you can click the Microsoft Office Shortcut Bar in the Windows taskbar to make it reappear again.

Resizing the Microsoft Office Shortcut Bar

If the Shortcut Bar appears in the middle of the screen (refer to Figure 1-4), you can resize it.

To resize the Microsoft Office Shortcut Bar, follow these steps:

1. **Move the mouse pointer over the left, right, or bottom edge of the Microsoft Office Shortcut Bar.**

   The mouse pointer turns into a double-pointing arrow.

2. **Hold down the left mouse button and drag the mouse.**

3. **Release the left mouse button when the Shortcut Bar is the size you want.**

You can only resize the Shortcut Bar if it appears in the middle of the screen. You can't resize the Shortcut Bar if it appears smashed against one side of the screen.

Modifying the icons on the Microsoft Office Shortcut Bar

The Microsoft Office Shortcut Bar contains icons for performing tasks such as creating a new Office document or opening an existing document. However, if you use Excel often, you may want to put the Excel icon on the Shortcut Bar. That way you can click the Excel icon and load Excel without going through the rather cumbersome step of clicking the New Office Document icon first and then double-clicking the Blank Workbook icon.

Adding an icon to the Shortcut Bar

The Shortcut Bar lets you load programs at the click of the mouse, but what if your favorite program (Word, Excel, Access, or whatever) doesn't appear on the Shortcut Bar? In that case, take some time to add an icon that represents your favorite program on the Shortcut Bar.

To add an icon to the Shortcut Bar:

1. **Click the control box of the Shortcut Bar.**

   A pull-down menu appears.

2. **Click Customize.**

   The Customize dialog box appears.

3. **Click the Buttons tab.**

   The Buttons tab of the Customize dialog box appears, as shown in Figure 1-5.

4. **Click the Add File button.**

   An Add File dialog box appears.

5. **Click the program that you want to add to the Shortcut Bar.**

   You may have to dig through folders to find the program icon you want, such as FrontPage or PhotoDraw. (Psst, you can even add non-Microsoft programs to the Office Shortcut Bar, including rival programs like WordPerfect, Lotus 1-2-3, and Paradox.)

Figure 1-5:
The
Customize
dialog box
shows you
all the won-
derful ways
you can
modify the
Shortcut
Bar.

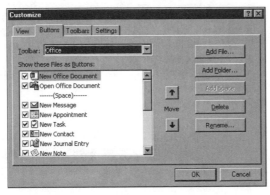

6. **Click Add.**

    Your chosen icon appears in the Customize dialog box. At this point, you can click the Up or Down Move arrow keys to move the position of your chosen button. You may also want to click the Rename button to give the button a more descriptive name.

7. **Click OK.**

If you want to delete a button from the Shortcut Bar, click the Delete button in Step 6.

Adding entire groups of programs to the Shortcut Bar

If you find the Shortcut Bar useful, you may want to add icons that represent entire groups of programs on the Shortcut Bar. The Shortcut Bar can display icons representing the following groups of programs:

- ✓ **Favorites:** Displays programs stored under the Favorites menu when you click the Start button on the Windows taskbar.

- ✓ **Programs:** Displays programs stored under the Programs menu when you click the Start button on the Windows taskbar. This option includes every single program installed on your computer.

- ✓ **Accessories:** Displays programs stored under the Accessories menu when you click the Start button on the Windows taskbar. This group of programs typically includes the Windows Calculator, Notepad, and Paint programs.

- ✓ **Desktop:** Displays programs whose icons appear on the Windows desktop.

To add a group of programs:

1. **Click the control box of the Shortcut Bar.**

   A pull-down menu appears.

2. **Click Customize.**

   The Customize dialog box appears.

3. **Click the Toolbars tab.**

   The Toolbars tab of the Customize dialog box appears, as shown in Figure 1-6.

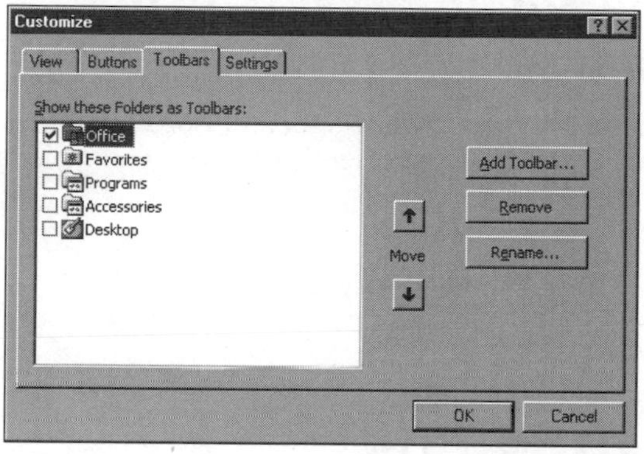

Figure 1-6:
The Toolbars tab in the Customize dialog box.

4. **Click in a check box (such as the Programs check box) so a check mark appears.**

5. **Click OK.**

   The Shortcut Bar now displays two toolbars inside the Shortcut Bar: an Office toolbar and a Programs toolbar, as shown in Figure 1-7.

Figure 1-7:
The Shortcut Bar displaying two toolbars you can use to choose which program to run.

The Shortcut Bar can only display one toolbar at a time. In Figure 1-7, the Shortcut Bar is displaying the Programs toolbar and tucking the Office toolbar to one side.

If you want to switch between toolbars, click the icon that appears next to the toolbar name. If you wanted to switch to the Office toolbar in Figure 1-7, you click the Office icon that appears directly above the words "Office" but underneath the title bar of the Shortcut Bar.

You can repeat these steps to remove a toolbar from the Shortcut Bar.

Getting rid of the Microsoft Office Shortcut Bar

In case you don't like the Microsoft Office Shortcut Bar hovering in your way and gobbling up valuable screen space, here's how you can make it go away:

- ✔ Press Alt+F4.
- ✔ Click the Control Box icon and choose Exit.

Opening an Existing File

Rather than create a brand-new file from scratch, you'll probably spend more time opening and editing existing files. Again, Microsoft Office 2000 bombards you with several different ways to open an existing file.

Clicking Open Office Document on the taskbar

The Windows taskbar provides the quickest way to open an existing Microsoft Office 2000 file. Just follow these simple steps:

1. **Click the Start button on the taskbar.**

   A pop-up menu appears.

2. **Click Open Office Document.**

   The Open Office Document dialog box appears.

3. **Click the file that you want to open.**

   If the file you want to open is buried in another folder, you may have to open that particular folder by clicking in the Look In list box.

4. **Click <u>O</u>pen.**

   Your chosen file appears, ready for you to start viewing and editing the information.

You can skip Step 4 if you double-click the file you want to open during Step 3.

Clicking Open Office Document on the Microsoft Office Shortcut Bar

If you can see the Microsoft Office Shortcut Bar on your screen, you may want use it to open an existing file by following these steps:

1. **Click the Open Office Document icon on the Shortcut Bar.**

   The Open Office Document dialog box appears (refer to Figure 1-3).

2. **Click the file that you want to open.**

   If the file you want to open is buried in another folder, you may have to open that particular folder by clicking in the Look in list box.

3. **Click <u>O</u>pen.**

   Your chosen file appears, ready for you to start viewing and editing the information.

You can skip Step 3 if you double-click on the file you want to open during Step 2.

Double-clicking in Windows Explorer

Perhaps the clumsiest (though still valid) way of opening an existing Office document is by using Windows Explorer and double-clicking the file you want to open. To do that, follow these steps:

1. **Click the Start button on the taskbar and choose <u>P</u>rograms.**

   A pop-up menu appears.

2. **Choose Windows Explorer.**

   The Windows Explorer program appears.

3. **Locate the document that you want to open.**

   You may have to double-click a folder (such as My Documents) to find the document you're looking for.

4. **Double-click the icon that represents the document that you want to open.**

   Microsoft Office 2000 opens your chosen document.

Taking a Shortcut

Rather than fiddle around with the clumsy Windows 95/98/NT taskbar, you may find that creating a desktop shortcut to your favorite Microsoft Office 2000 program is easier. That way, you can just double-click your shortcut and run the program right away.

A desktop shortcut is nothing more than an icon that represents a specific file. This file can be an actual program (such as Microsoft Word) or a file created by another program (such as your résumé written in Word). Shortcuts appear on your Windows desktop for easy access.

To place a shortcut to your favorite Microsoft Office 2000 program on the Windows desktop, follow these steps:

1. **Click the Start button on the taskbar and choose <u>P</u>rograms.**

   A pop-up menu appears.

2. **Choose Windows Explorer.**

   The Windows Explorer program appears.

3. **Double-click the Program Files folder.**

4. **Double-click the Microsoft Office folder.**

   The contents of the Microsoft Office folder appear.

5. **Click the Office folder.**

   The Office folder (buried within the Microsoft Office folder) opens, showing many of the files that make up Microsoft Office 2000, as shown in Figure 1-8.

6. **Right-click the program icon that you want.**

   For example, if you want to put a shortcut to Excel on the Windows desktop, right-click the Excel icon.

   A pop-up menu appears.

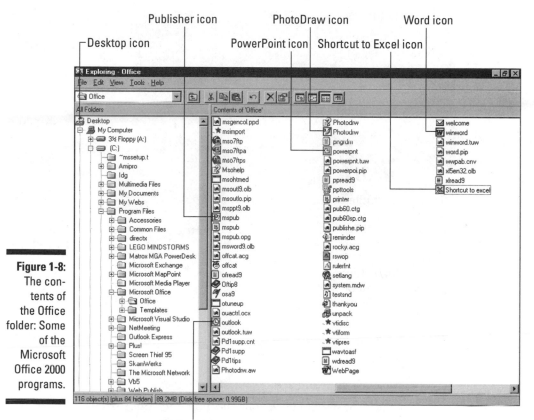

Publisher icon   PhotoDraw icon   Word icon

Desktop icon   PowerPoint icon Shortcut to Excel icon

Figure 1-8:
The con-
tents of
the Office
folder: Some
of the
Microsoft
Office 2000
programs.

Outlook icon

7. Click Create Shortcut.

The shortcut icon appears. (Refer to Figure 1-8.)

**8. Drag your chosen shortcut to the Desktop icon, which appears in the
left pane of the Windows Explorer near the top (directly above the My
Computer icon). (Refer to Figure 1-8.)**

9. Choose File➪Close.

The Windows desktop appears with your chosen shortcut, as shown in
Figure 1-9. Shortcuts are easy to spot because they have a little black and
white arrow in the lower-left corner of the icon.

Figure 1-9:
The Excel
shortcut
appears
on the
Windows
desktop.

10. Double-click your shortcut to run the program.

You may want to right-click your shortcut and choose Rename from the pop-up menu. That way, your shortcut icon doesn't have the silly name of "Shortcut to PowerPoint" or something equally annoying.

If you want to delete a shortcut icon from your desktop, right-click on it and choose Delete from the pop-up menu.

Exiting Microsoft Office 2000

No matter how much you may like Microsoft Office 2000, eventually you have to stop using it so you can go to sleep. Microsoft Office 2000 provides different ways to exit.

✔ If you want to close the current document but still keep the program running, choose File➪Close.

✔ If you want to exit the program completely, choose File➪Exit or click the close box of the program window. (The *close box* is a little gray box with an X in it, which appears in the upper right-hand corner of a program window.)

If you have made any changes since the last time you saved your file and you try to exit, Microsoft Office 2000 asks whether you want to save the changes and offers you the following options: Yes, No, Cancel, or Help.

- ✔ Click Yes to save your file.
- ✔ Click No if you don't want to save any recent changes.
- ✔ Click Cancel (or press the Esc key on your keyboard) if you suddenly don't want to exit after all.

The most drastic way to exit from Microsoft Office 2000 is to turn your computer off. But don't do this! If you turn off your computer without exiting from a Microsoft Office 2000 program first, you may lose your data. Even worse, if you turn off your computer before letting Windows 95/98/NT shut itself down, your computer may erase or wreck other files on your hard disk as well.

In case you forget how to shut down Windows 95/98/NT properly, click the Start button on the Windows taskbar and choose Shut Down. When the Shut Down Windows dialog box appears, click the Shut down option button and then click OK.

For more information about using Windows, pick up a copy of _Windows 95 For Dummies,_ 2nd Edition, _Windows 98 For Dummies,_ or _Windows NT 4 Workstation For Dummies,_ all by Andy Rathbone and published by IDG Books Worldwide, Inc.

Chapter 2

Getting Help from Microsoft Office 2000 and the Office Assistant

● ●

In This Chapter

▶ Using the Microsoft Office 2000 Assistant

▶ Customizing the Office Assistant

▶ Choosing a different Office Assistant

▶ Detecting and repairing problems with Microsoft Office 2000

● ●

Microsoft Office 2000 is a big program that can be confusing to use. But don't worry. You don't have to master every feature provided in the program; you just need to know the commands that you require to get your job done.

So what happens if you need help using Microsoft Office 2000? Before you panic, take some time to use the Office Assistant. The Office Assistant is a customizable little cartoon, and you can type in a question and have the Office Assistant (hopefully) display the answer you need.

Getting Acquainted with the Office Assistant

Computers frighten nearly everyone, including the people who design and program them. For that reason, Microsoft created the Office Assistant, which is an animated figure that provides a friendly face to an otherwise intimidating program.

Whenever you run any of the programs in Microsoft Office 2000 (such as Word, Excel, PowerPoint, and so on), you can make the Office Assistant pop up, as shown in Figure 2-1, by pressing F1.

Figure 2-1:
Rocky the dog, one of many Office Assistants, using a blowtorch to destroy unwanted data.

Neither FrontPage nor PhotoDraw provide a cartoon Office Assistant. However, you can still type in a question and have the programs display a list of possible answers just as if you were using a cartoon Office Assistant.

When you click an Office Assistant, a dialog box appears, as shown in Figure 2-2, which shows another of the many Office Assistant cartoons you can choose.

Figure 2-2:
Click an Office Assistant to display a dialog box where you can type your question.

> **What would you like to do?**
> ● Delete a file
> ● Delete an AutoText entry
> ● Delete a macro
> ● Remove arrowheads
> ● Delete a drawing object
> ▼ See more...
>
> [Options]   [Search]

Hiding and displaying the Office Assistant

For many people, leaving the Office Assistant on the screen may be amusing, but to others, the cartoon Office Assistants can be more annoying than helpful. If you want, you can hide the Office Assistant from view.

To hide the Office Assistant from view:

REMEMBER

  ✔ Choose Help⇨Hide the Office Assistant.
  ✔ Right-click the Office Assistant and choose Hide.

If you hide the Office Assistant, it doesn't appear again unless you press F1 or choose Help⇨Show the Office Assistant.

Choosing a new Office Assistant

In case you don't like the cartoon character that Microsoft Office 2000 has chosen for you, feel free to choose a different Office Assistant at any time.

To choose a new Office Assistant:

1. **Click the Office Assistant, press F1, or right-click the Office Assistant.**

   The Office Assistant dialog box appears. (Refer to Figure 2-2.)

2. **Click Options.**

3. **Click the Gallery tab.**

   A new window appears, letting you choose a different cartoon Office Assistant, as shown in Figure 2-3.

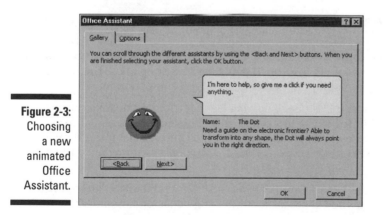

Figure 2-3:
Choosing
a new
animated
Office
Assistant.

4. **Click Back or Next to see the different animated Office Assistants available.**

   Picking an Office Assistant that you like is purely your choice. They all work the same; they just look different.

5. **Click OK when you find an Office Assistant you like.**

   You may need to insert the Office 2000 CD each time you choose to install a different Office Assistant.

Customizing the behavior of your Office Assistant

Besides changing the appearance of your Office Assistant, you can also specify the way it works. The two main features you can change about the Office Assistant are the way it responds and the type of help it displays.

The Office Assistant can respond in a variety of ways:

- ✔ **Use the Office Assistant:** If this check box is clear, Microsoft Office 2000 hides the cartoon Office Assistant from view and only displays a boring Help window in its place.

- ✔ **Respond to the F1 key:** If you clear this check box, pressing the F1 key displays a Help window without displaying the dialog balloon (refer to Figure 2-2) from the Office Assistant.

- ✔ **Move when in the way:** This option makes the Office Assistant move if you type or click the part of the screen that the Office Assistant is covering.

- ✔ **Help with wizards:** Provides help when you're using a wizard to accomplish a task, such as the Chart Wizard in Excel 2000.

- ✔ **Guess help topics:** Displays a list of likely topics that the Office Assistant thinks you may need help on. If you clear this check box, the Office Assistant just displays a box for you to type a question in.

- ✔ **Display alerts:** If this check box is clear, alert dialog boxes appear as standard Windows dialog boxes. If it is checked, alert dialog boxes appear as yellow dialog balloons near the Office Assistant. A typical alert dialog box resembles the one that appears when you try to close a document without saving it first.

- ✔ **Make sounds:** Turns sounds from the Office Assistant on or off, in case you don't like the Office Assistant making occasional noise while you're working.

- ✔ **Search for both product and programming help when programming:** Displays help topics in case you're writing macros using the Visual Basic for Applications (VBA) programming language.

You can also modify the tips the Office Assistant displays:

- ✔ **Using features more effectively:** Provides shortcut tips for using the various commands buried in Office 2000.

- ✔ **Only show high priority tips:** Displays tips that the Office Assistant thinks are the most important.

- ✔ **Using the mouse more effectively:** Provides tips for using the various buttons on your mouse to navigate around Office 2000.

- ✔ **Show the Tip of the Day at startup:** Displays a Tip of the Day dialog box as soon as you start Office 2000.

- ✔ **Keyboard shortcuts:** Offers hints for using cryptic keystrokes to get your work done faster.

- ✔ **Reset my tips:** Allows the Office Assistant to displays tips it may have shown you before in the Tip of the Day dialog box.

To customize the behavior of the Office Assistant:

1. **Click the Office Assistant, press F1, or right-click the Office Assistant.**

2. **Click Options.**

   The Office Assistant dialog box appears.

3. **Click the Options tab and click the check boxes to choose or disable the type of help you want the Office Assistant to provide.**

   The Office Assistant automatically checks most of the check boxes in the Office Assistant dialog box, as shown in Figure 2-4. You may want to experiment with changing different options to customize the Office Assistant to your liking.

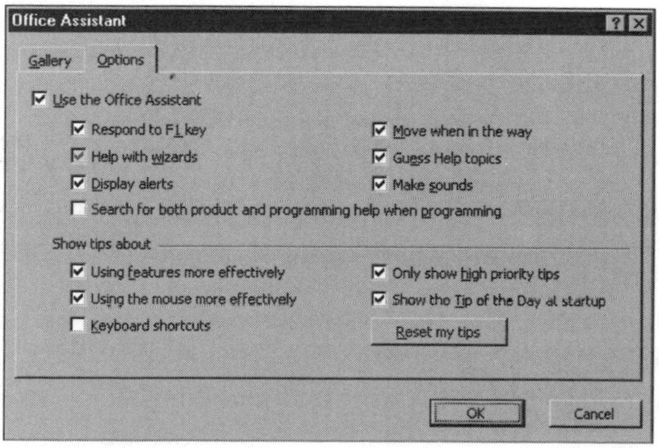

Figure 2-4:
Defining the way your Office Assistant works.

4. **Click OK when you're done making your choices.**

Animating your Office Assistant

If you get bored while using Office 2000 (which means it's probably time for you to get another job), you can animate your Office Assistant so it moves on the screen and provides a few seconds of amusement while you stare at the screen and pretend to be doing useful work. To animate your Office Assistant:

1. **Right-click the Office Assistant.**

2. **Click Animate!**

   The Office Assistant moves around the screen doing something cute and interesting, as shown in Figure 2-5.

Figure 2-5:
Your Office
Assistant
can move
around the
screen and
amuse you
with its
antics.

You can move the Office Assistant around the screen by moving the mouse pointer over the Office Assistant, holding down the left mouse button, and then dragging the mouse. If you need to type on the portion of the screen covered by the Office Assistant, the Office Assistant is smart enough to nudge itself out of your way by sliding to the side, top, or bottom of the screen.

Getting Help from the Office Assistant

The Office Assistant exists for your convenience. Whenever you need help, just click the Office Assistant. When the Office Assistant offers help, you have two choices:

- ✔ Click various help topics that the Office Assistant provides.
- ✔ Type a question into the Office Assistant and then click a displayed help topic.

If you have no idea what kind of help you need, clicking the help topics that the Office Assistant displays for you may be easier. When you get more experienced in using Office 2000, typing your questions directly into the Office Assistant can find you an answer much faster than endlessly clicking through multiple help topics.

Asking for help by clicking displayed help topics

When you click the Office Assistant or press F1, a yellow dialog balloon appears, listing various help topics that the Office Assistant thinks you may need help on.

If you clear the Guess Help Topics check box in the Options dialog box, the Office Assistant doesn't display a list of help topics as shown in Figure 2-6. Compare this Office Assistant with the one in Figure 2-7.

Figure 2-6:
The Office
Assistant
with its
Guess Help
Topics
check box
cleared.

To get help from the Office Assistant by clicking displayed help topics, follow these steps:

1. **Click the Office Assistant, press F1, or click the Help icon in the toolbar.**

   A yellow balloon (similar to a cartoon dialogue balloon) pops up, displaying a list of topics to choose from, as shown in Figure 2-7.

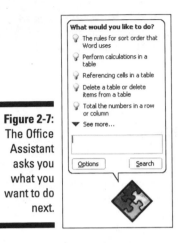

Figure 2-7:
The Office
Assistant
asks you
what you
want to do
next.

2. **Click a topic you'd like to get more help on.**

A Help window pops up on the right side of the screen, providing a list of topics related to your question, as shown in Figure 2-8.

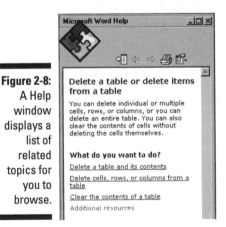

Figure 2-8:
A Help
window
displays a
list of
related
topics for
you to
browse.

3. **Click a subtopic that you hope will give you the answer you want.**

The Help window displays more detailed information about your chosen topic.

4. **Click the close box (the X in the window's upper-right corner) to get rid of the Help window.**

If you click the Print icon in the Help window, you can print a hard copy of the step-by-step instructions the Office Assistant provides. That way, you can save the instructions for future reference.

Typing a question for the Office Assistant

As a slightly faster way to get help, you can type questions directly into the Office Assistant. Then the Office Assistant displays a list of help topics related to your question.

When you ask for help by typing a question, the Office Assistant scans your sentence to look for relevant words that it can recognize, such as "format," "save," or "stylesheet." So, rather than type complete sentences such as "I want to know how to format a paragraph," just type "Format paragraph."

When you type a question, make sure you spell everything correctly; otherwise, the Office Assistant doesn't know what type of help you need.

To get help from the Office Assistant by typing a question:

1. **Click the Office Assistant, press F1, or click the Help icon in the toolbar.**

   A yellow balloon, similar to a cartoon dialog balloon, pops up. (Refer to Figure 2-7.)

2. **Type your question (such as Indent paragraph) and click Search.**

   The yellow dialog balloon displays a list of topics related to your question.

3. **Click the topic you want more help with.**

   A Help window appears, displaying more detailed information about your chosen topic.

4. **Click the close box (the X in the window's upper-right corner) to get rid of the Help window.**

If you click the Print icon in the Help window, you can print a hard copy of the step-by-step instructions the Office Assistant provides. That way, you can save the instructions for future reference.

Identifying the Office 2000 User Interface with the What's This? Command

Even though all the programs in Microsoft Office 2000 use similar menus, toolbars, and commands, you may still find the user interface cryptic, confusing, and completely mystifying. But don't worry, because Microsoft provides a handy What's This? command.

The What's This? command lets you point at any strange icon on the screen to have Office 2000 politely display a short description explaining the purpose of that particular icon.

To use the What's This? command:

1. **Choose Help⇨What's This? or press Shift+F1.**

   A question mark appears next to the mouse pointer. (In case you suddenly decide you don't want to use the What's This? command, press the Esc key.)

2. **Move the mouse pointer over a toolbar icon or menu command and click the mouse button.**

   Office 2000 displays a tiny window that provides a brief explanation about the toolbar icon or menu command you chose, as shown in Figure 2-9.

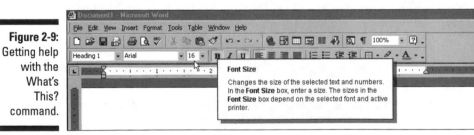

Figure 2-9: Getting help with the What's This? command.

3. **Press any key (such as the Esc key) or click the mouse to remove the tiny explanation window.**

Getting Help on the World Wide Web

Ever since the Internet blindsided Microsoft back in 1995, Microsoft has made every attempt to make sure the Internet remains an integral part of every Microsoft program.

So to provide you with the latest software updates, patches, bug fixes, program news, tips, and software add-ons, Microsoft runs its own Web site. To help you reach Microsoft's Web site quickly and easily, every Office 2000 program has a special Office on the Web command.

Before you can use this Office on the Web command, you must have an existing Internet account or be willing to create (and pay for) an Internet account.

For some odd reason, Microsoft Publisher and PhotoDraw don't have an Office on the Web command. Instead, they have a Microsoft Publisher Web Site command and a PhotoDraw on the Web command, respectively.

To access the Microsoft Web site, which is full of useful Microsoft Office 2000 information, software, news, or bug updates:

1. **Choose Help➪Office on the <u>W</u>eb.**

   Office 2000 starts up your Internet browser and loads the Microsoft Office 2000 Web page, as shown in Figure 2-10. (Microsoft sincerely hopes you're using Internet Explorer rather than the rival Netscape Navigator, but both work fine.)

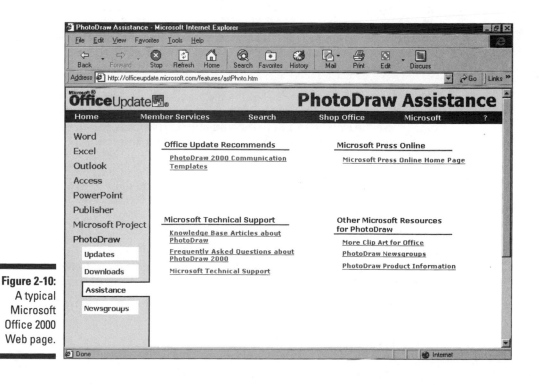

Figure 2-10:
A typical
Microsoft
Office 2000
Web page.

  2. **Browse the pages until you find the information you need.**

  3. **Choose File⇨Exit or click in the close box of your browser to make the browser go away.**

Exiting from your Web browser may not always disconnect you from the Internet.

Repairing Office 2000

In the old days, a program consisted of a single file, such as WORD.EXE. Nowadays, a program often consists of several files that work together to make up a single program.

Unfortunately, if you accidentally erase or modify one file, any programs that rely on that one file may refuse to work properly. If this happens to you, then you have to reinstall the entire program all over again and hope that you don't wipe out any important documents in the process.

But because erasing or damaging files is a fairly normal occurrence when using a buggy operating system like Windows 95/98/NT, Microsoft Office 2000 contains a special Detect and Repair command which (what else?) checks to make sure all those important files still exist on your hard disk and are in working order.

(Of course, the big problem is that if a file is missing or corrupted, you may not be able to run any Microsoft Office 2000 program in the first place in order to use the Detect and Repair command. In that case, you have to go back to reinstalling the entire program all over again and risk wiping out any important documents in the process.)

So the next time any Office 2000 program starts acting flaky, try to fix it by using the Detect and Repair command:

  1. **Run a Microsoft Office 2000 program (such as Word or PowerPoint).**

  2. **Choose Help⇨Detect and Repair. (You may have to click the downward-pointing arrow in the Help menu before you can see the Detect and Repair command.)**

  The Detect and Repair dialog box appears, as shown in Figure 2-11.

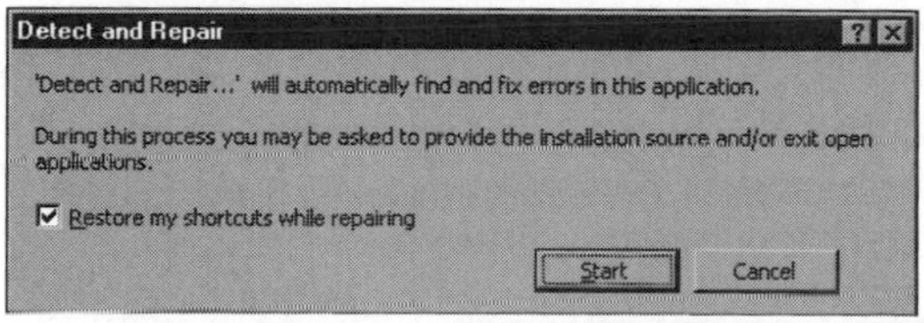

Figure 2-11:
The Detect
and Repair
dialog box.

3. **Click Start.**

   Follow the on-screen instructions as Microsoft Office 2000 valiantly tries
   to fix itself if it detects any problems. You may have to insert the
   Microsoft Office 2000 CD into your CD-ROM drive.

Chapter 3

Understanding Office 2000 Menus, Toolbars, and Windows

● ●

In This Chapter

▶ Using your menus

▶ Viewing your toolbars

▶ Working with multiple windows

● ●

Microsoft Office 2000 contains a variety of different programs, including a desktop publisher, a word processor, and a personal information manager. Using such diverse types of programs might be difficult at first, so Microsoft molded all their programs to look and work alike.

That means once you figure out how to use one program of Microsoft Office 2000, you should (theoretically) have little trouble figuring out any of the other Microsoft Office 2000 programs — the menus and toolbars look and act similarly.

The Incredible Changing Menus

Microsoft Office 2000 provides three ways to display menu commands on the screen, as shown in Figures 3-1, 3-2, and 3-3. You can

✔ Display every command possible (this is the old way previous versions of Microsoft Office work).

✔ Hide the more advanced commands from view (but you can still display the more advanced commands, such as using an auditing feature in Excel, by clicking the downward-pointing arrows at the bottom of the menu).

✔ Hide the more advanced commands from view but automatically display them as shaded after a few seconds.

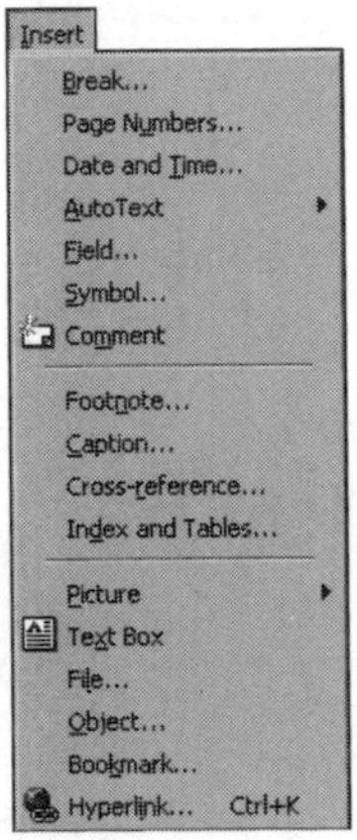

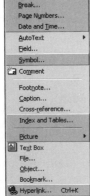

Figure 3-1: Displaying every command on the Insert menu.

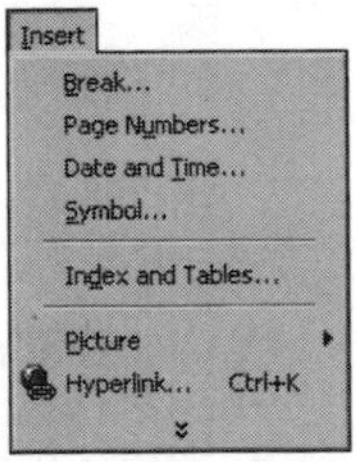

Figure 3-2: Hiding the more advanced commands on the Insert menu.

Figure 3-3: Displaying the more advanced commands as slightly shaded on the Insert menu.

REMEMBER

PhotoDraw is the only Microsoft Office 2000 program that displays all possible commands on every menu whether you like it or not.

Some people may find that hiding the more advanced commands from view can be disconcerting while others feel that displaying every possible command on a menu can be intimidating.

Try experimenting with the way Office 2000 displays your menus. That way you can customize the programs to work the way you like best.

To change the way menus work in Microsoft Publisher, you have to follow a slightly different procedure, as explained in later steps.

To change the way menus work in Word, Excel, PowerPoint, Access, and FrontPage:

1. **Choose View⇨Toolbars⇨Customize.**

   A Customize dialog box appears, as shown in Figure 3-4.

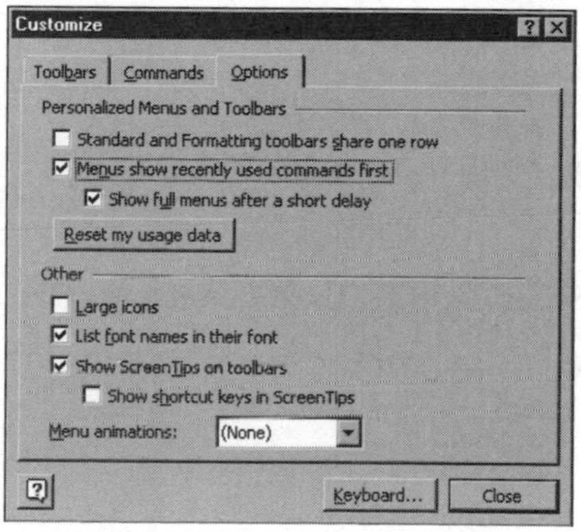

Figure 3-4:
The
Customize
dialog box
for
modifying
the way
your menus
work.

2. **Click the Options tab.**

3. **Click or clear one of the following check boxes:**

   • **Menus Show Recently Used Commands First:** If checked, this option shades the more advanced commands (refer to Figure 3-3).

   • **Show Full Menus After a Short Delay:** If checked, this option waits a few seconds before showing the more advanced commands on a menu. If this option is cleared, the menus appear as shown in Figure 3-2.

4. **Click Close.**

If you want Microsoft Office 2000 to hide the more advanced commands, regardless of whether you recently used them or not, click the Reset Usage Data button after Step 3.

To change the way menus work in Publisher only, follow these steps:

1. **Choose Tools⇨Options.**

   An Options dialog box appears, as shown in Figure 3-5.

2. **Click or clear the Menus Show Recently Used Commands First check box.**

   If checked, this option shades the more advanced commands (refer to Figure 3-3).

3. **Click OK.**

If you want Publisher to hide the more advanced commands, regardless of whether you recently used them or not, click the Reset Usage Data button after Step 2.

Viewing Your Toolbars

Toolbars contain *icons* that represent the most commonly used commands. The theory is that it's easier to click a toolbar icon to choose a command than it is to dig through a pull-down menu or press an obscure keystroke combination like Ctrl+Shift+D just to get something done.

Although every Microsoft Office 2000 displays different toolbar icons, they all work in similar ways and share icons that represent universal commands such as Save or Print.

Naturally, Microsoft Office 2000 lets you choose how to view your toolbars, where to place them on the screen, and even which icons you want to view.

Smashing (or stacking) the Standard and Formatting toolbars

The two most common toolbars in Microsoft Office 2000 are the Standard and Formatting toolbars. The *Standard toolbar* contains icons representing universal commands such as Save, Cut, or Paste. The *Formatting toolbar* contains icons representing text modifying commands, such as changing the font, font size, or underlining.

To save space, Microsoft Office 2000 can smash both the Standard and Formatting toolbars together as one toolbar. While this may tuck the toolbars out of the way, smashing two toolbars into one may look confusing. Figure 3-6 shows the Standard and Formatting toolbars smashed together as a single toolbar. Figure 3-7 shows the Standard and Formatting toolbars stacked one on top of the other.

Figure 3-6:
The Standard and Formatting toolbars smashed together as one.

Click the double-arrows to see additional toolbar icons.

Figure 3-7:
The Standard and Formatting toolbars stacked as two separate toolbars.

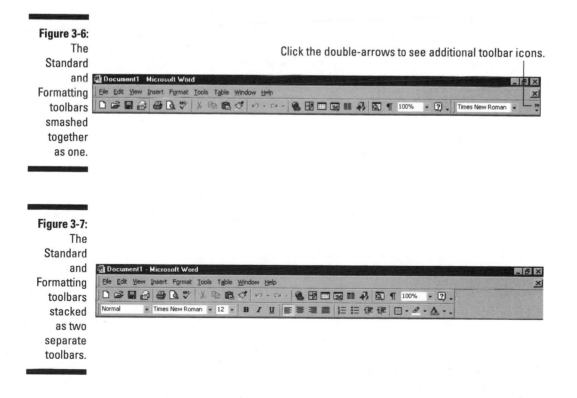

To smash together the Standard and Formatting toolbars in Publisher and PhotoDraw, you have to drag one toolbar on top of the other.

To combine or stack the Standard and Formatting toolbars:

1. **Choose View⇨Toolbars⇨Customize.**

   A Customize dialog box appears (refer to Figure 3-4).

2. **Click the Options tab.**

3. **Click or clear the Standard and Formatting Toolbars Share One Row check box.**

4. **Click Close.**

If you combine the Standard and Formatting toolbars to share one row, you may have to click the double-arrows on the toolbar to see a pull-down menu of the additional toolbar icons (refer to Figure 3-6).

Hiding and displaying toolbars

Another way to use toolbars is to hide them completely or display additional toolbars on the screen. For example, if you find yourself creating or editing Web pages frequently using Microsoft Office 2000, you may want to display the Web toolbar within Word. That way all Web page editing and creating commands are one click away.

To hide or display a toolbar:

1. **Choose View⇨Toolbars.**

   The Toolbars drop-down menu appears, as shown in Figure 3-8. Check marks appear next to those toolbars currently displayed.

2. **Click the toolbar that you want to display.**

   Or if you want a toolbar to disappear, click the toolbar that you want to hide.

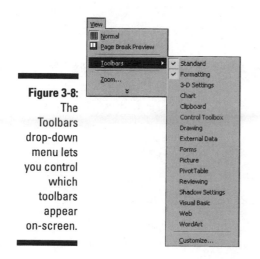

Figure 3-8:
The
Toolbars
drop-down
menu lets
you control
which
toolbars
appear
on-screen.

Moving a toolbar

While most people may be perfectly happy with their toolbars at the top of the screen, Microsoft 2000 gives you the option of moving them to the side, bottom, or in the middle of the screen if you like. See Figure 3-9.

Figure 3-9:
You can
move a
toolbar
anywhere
you like
on-screen.

To move a toolbar around the screen:

1. **Move the mouse pointer over the move handle of the toolbar you want to move.**

   Once over the move handle, the mouse pointer turns into a four-way pointing arrow, as shown in Figure 3-10.

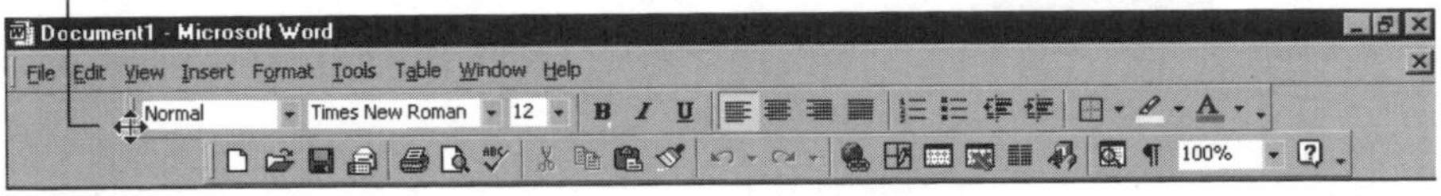

Figure 3-10:
The move
handle on
the toolbar
lets you
adjust the
toolbar's
position.

Move handle

2. **Hold down the left mouse button and drag the mouse.**

   The toolbar appears as a separate window (refer to Figure 3-9).

3. **Release the left mouse button when the toolbar window appears where you want it.**

   You can smash the toolbar to one side or to the bottom of the screen rather than letting it float in the middle of the screen.

If you leave the toolbar in the middle of the screen as a floating window, you can resize the toolbar window. Just move the mouse pointer over one edge of the toolbar window, wait until the mouse pointer turns into a double-pointing arrow, and then hold down the left mouse button and drag the mouse to resize the toolbar window.

Customizing your toolbars

Microsoft Office 2000 toolbars display the more commonly used buttons, but you may want to customize your toolbars so they display the commands you need most often. To customize a toolbar:

1. **Click the More Buttons button (it looks like a downward pointing arrow at the far right of the toolbar).**

   An Add or Remove Buttons menu appears, as shown in Figure 3-11.

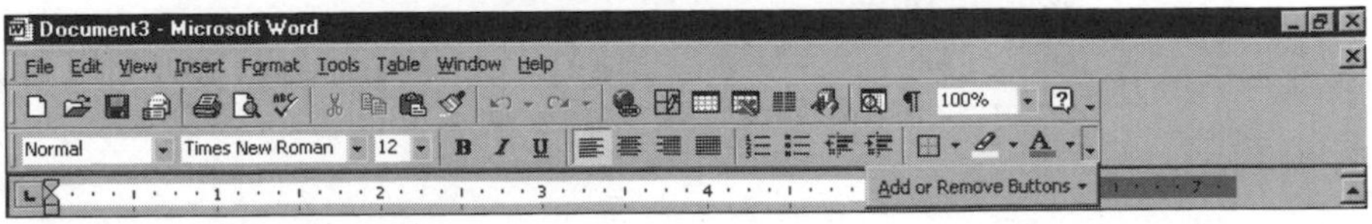

Figure 3-11:
The Add or
Remove
Buttons
menu.

2. **Move the mouse over the Add or Remove Buttons menu.**

   A list of buttons appears, as shown in Figure 3-12.

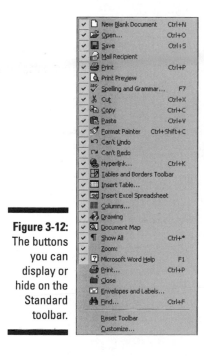

Figure 3-12:
The buttons you can display or hide on the Standard toolbar.

3. **Click to place or remove a check mark in the check box in front of the button you want to display (or hide).**

4. **Click anywhere in your document (do not click anywhere on the list of toolbar buttons).**

   The list of toolbar buttons disappears, and the toolbar now displays (or hides) the buttons you chose in Step 3.

If you want to reset your toolbar to their original, factory-installed settings, click the Reset Toolbar check box in Step 3.

Working with Multiple Windows

With each Microsoft Office 2000 program (except for Microsoft Publisher, Access, and Outlook), you can open two or more files, displayed in separate windows. By opening multiple files in separate windows, you can edit text in one window while reading text in another window.

While multiple windows let you edit and view the contents of two or more files at the same time, they also gobble up screen space, so each window displays less text.

Switching between multiple windows

Each time you open a file (by pressing Ctrl+O, clicking the Open icon on the toolbar, or choosing File➪Open), Microsoft Office 2000 opens another window.

To avoid cluttering up the screen, Microsoft Office 2000 only displays one window at a time. To switch between multiple windows:

1. **Click the Window menu.**

   A drop-down menu appears as shown in Figure 3-13.

2. **Click the window containing the file name that you want to view.**

Figure 3-13:
The
Window
menu lists
all of the
currently
open
windows.

Office 2000 displays a button on the taskbar for each window opened. Just click the appropriate button on the taskbar to switch to another window.

Arranging multiple windows

If you open two or more windows, you might want to see the contents of each window simultaneously. That way you can view the contents of one window while editing another.

Microsoft FrontPage and Publisher don't let you display two or more windows on the screen at the same time.

To display multiple windows on the screen:

1. **Choose Window⇨Arrange All.**

   All your currently open files arrange themselves on the screen as separate windows stacked one on top of the other.

2. **Click in the window that you want to edit.**

   The active window (the one you're currently editing) highlights its title bar while the other windows dim their title bar.

After a while, you may not want multiple windows cluttering up your screen. To close a window:

✔ Click the close box of all the windows you want to close. (The close box is that little X in the upper right-hand corner.)

✔ Click the minimize box of all the windows you want to keep open but hide out of view for the moment. (The minimize box has a little horizontal line.)

You can resize windows or move them by dragging the title bar of a window anywhere on the screen. By doing this, you can arrange your windows in any way you choose.

Saving and closing multiple windows

If you have two or more windows open, you may edit data in one or more windows. You can close windows individually (by clicking the close box of each window or choosing File⇨Close). But if you have several windows open, you can close and save windows more conveniently using the Save All and Close All commands.

The Save All and Close All commands are not available in PhotoDraw, Publisher, or FrontPage.

To save the files in every currently open window:

1. **Hold down the Shift key.**

2. **Choose File⇨Save All.**

   When you hold down the Shift key, the File menu changes the Save command to Save All.

To close every open window:

1. **Hold down the Shift key.**

2. **Choose File⇨Close All.**

   When you hold down the Shift key, the File menu changes the Close command to Close All.

Copy and Paste with the Office Clipboard

When you copy objects (such as text or graphics) in Windows, your computer stores the copied object on the *Windows Clipboard,* which is like an invisible place to store items temporarily.

The trouble with the Windows Clipboard is that it can only hold one item at a time. The moment you copy a second item, the Windows Clipboard erases anything currently stored on the Clipboard.

To avoid this problem, Microsoft Office 2000 comes with a special Office Clipboard, which works exactly like the Windows Clipboard except that the Office Clipboard can hold up to twelve (count them, 12) items at a time.

The major limitation of the Office Clipboard is that you can only use the Office Clipboard while working within one or more Office 2000 programs. This is Microsoft's subtle attempt to make rival programs like WordPerfect or Lotus 1-2-3 look obsolete.

Copying stuff to the Office Clipboard

You can only see the Office Clipboard from within Access, Excel, PowerPoint, or Word. However, you can copy objects from any Microsoft Office 2000 program to the Office Clipboard.

To copy an object to the Office Clipboard:

1. **Choose View⇨Toolbars⇨Clipboard.**

   The Office Clipboard appears. (You may have to switch to Access, Excel, PowerPoint, or Word to perform Step 1.)

2. **Highlight the text or graphic object that you want to copy.**

3. **Press Ctrl+C or click the Copy button on the Standard toolbar.**

   The Office Clipboard displays an icon that represents your copied object. This icon shows you the program where the object came from, so if you copy from Word, the Office Clipboard displays a Word icon; If you copy from Excel, the Office Clipboard displays an Excel icon; and so on, as shown in Figure 3-14.

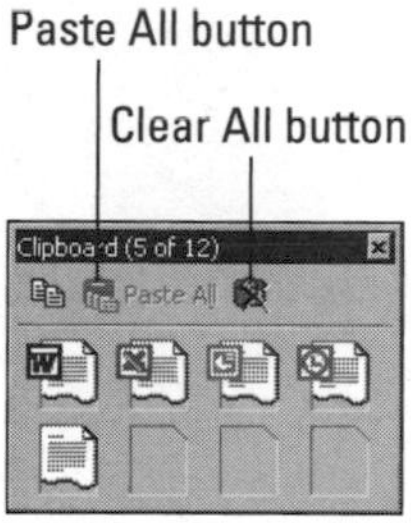

Figure 3-14:
The Office Clipboard displays icons representing the program where you copied the object.

Paste All button

Clear All button

Pasting stuff from the Office Clipboard

The Office Clipboard can only paste objects into Access, Excel, PowerPoint, and Word.

To paste an object from the Office Clipboard:

1. **Choose View➪Toolbars➪Clipboard.**

   The Office Clipboard appears. (Skip this step if the Office Clipboard is already visible.)

2. **Click where you want to paste the object from the Office Clipboard.**

3. **Click an icon in the Office Clipboard. (To paste all the objects from the Office Clipboard, just click the Paste All button in the Office Clipboard. Refer to Figure 3-14.)**

   If you move the mouse over an icon in the Office Clipboard, you can see the contents stored in that particular icon.

If you press Ctrl+V, choose Edit➪Paste, or click the Paste button on the Standard toolbar, you paste the last object that you cut or copied from another program, or the last object you pasted from the Office Clipboard, whichever action you did last.

Part II
Working with Word 2000

In this part . . .

To make your life easier, Microsoft has endowed Microsoft Word 2000 with powerful features to create resumes, reports, form letters, Web pages, or just plain notes to yourself.

In this part of the book, you discover how to write, edit, spell check, and grammar check your writing; how to format text to make it look really pretty; and how to use Word 2000 to create your own Web pages out of ordinary documents.

Word 2000 may seem like an ordinary word processor at first glance, but after you read this part of the book, you'll see that Word 2000 can help you write, create, and print your ideas as fast as you care to type them.

Chapter 4

Working with Word 2000 Documents

A s its name implies, Word 2000 lets you write words so that you can create letters, reports, proposals, brochures, newsletters, pink slips, ransom notes, and practically anything else that requires a rudimentary command of the written language.

Creating a New Word Document

Word gives you four ways to create a new document:

- ✔ When you first run Word, it automatically creates a new document, ready for you to start typing. (So stop reading this and start typing.)

- ✔ Click the New Blank Document button on the Standard toolbar.

- ✔ Choose File⇨New.

- ✔ Press Ctrl+N.

Opening a Previously Saved File

Rather than creating new documents, you will probably spend more of your time editing documents that you created earlier. To open a previously saved file, Word gives you four choices:

✔ Press Ctrl+O.

✔ Click the Open button on the Standard toolbar.

✔ Choose File➪Open.

✔ Choose one of the last four files you saved, which appear at the bottom of the File menu (as shown in Figure 4-1).

Figure 4-1: At the bottom of the File menu, Word displays the last four files you saved.

If you choose one of the first three opening methods, the Open dialog box appears. Just double-click the file that you want to open, and it should unfold before you in all its glory and greatness.

Viewing Microsoft Word Documents

Because word processing means staring at text for long periods of time, Word provides several different ways to view your documents so you don't strain your eyes looking at your words.

Some of the ways Word can make your text easier to read is by displaying your text in different views so you can see exactly how your writing will look when printed, enlarging the text, or revealing spaces and paragraph marks.

Choosing a different view of a document

Word lets you see your document from four perspectives, each offering a different appearance and amount of text and graphics displayed on-screen. To change the view of your document, choose View from the menu bar and then choose one of the following:

- ✔ **Normal:** Great when you want to write in a clean screen without worrying about headers, footers, or page numbers getting in your way.

- ✔ **Web Layout:** Shows you what your document looks like when displayed as a Web page.

- ✔ **Print Layout:** Shows you exactly how your document will look when printed, including headers and footers.

- ✔ **Outline:** Comes in handy when you don't have the slightest idea what to write and you want to create an outline to help organize your thoughts. While in Outline view (shown in Figure 4-2), you can organize your thoughts into topics and subtopics.

In case you really don't like the clutter of toolbars or pull-down menus, Word 2000 gives you the option of switching to the Full Screen view, which shows nothing but a blank screen and any text you type. To switch to the Full Screen view, choose View➪Full Screen.

As a quick way to switch document views, just click the Normal, Web Layout, Print Layout, and Outline View buttons that Word 2000 displays along the far left of the horizontal scroll bar (see Figure 4-2).

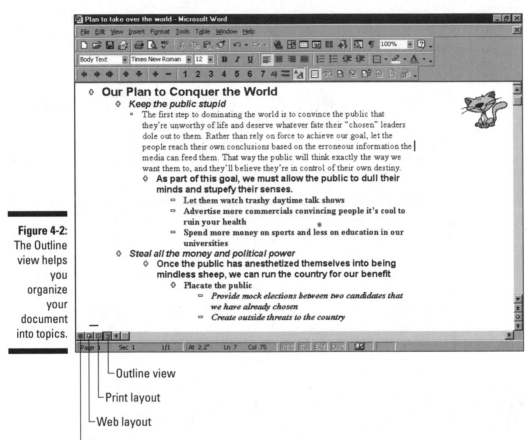

Figure 4-2:
The Outline view helps you organize your document into topics.

Outline view
Print layout
Web layout
Normal view

Hiding (or showing) the scroll bars

To give you a little bit more room on the screen to see your text, you can get rid of both the horizontal and vertical scroll bars. To hide the scroll bars:

1. **Choose Tools⇨Options.**

   The Options dialog box appears as shown in Figure 4-3.

2. **Click the View tab.**

3. **Click the check boxes next to Horizontal Scroll Bar and Vertical Scroll Bar.**

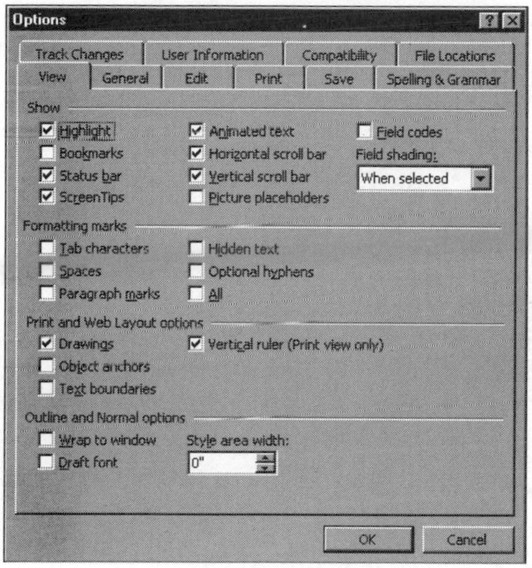

Figure 4-3:
The Options
dialog box
with the
View tab
displayed.

4. **Click OK.**

   Voilà! Word hides your scroll bars, giving you another few millimeters of
   space. If you later want to display your scroll bars, just repeat Steps 1
   through 4 and replace the check marks in the check boxes.

Changing screen magnification

Sometimes you get tired of seeing just a portion of your letter — you want to
see how the whole letter looks. Just adjust your screen's magnification so
that your entire document fits inside the screen. Likewise, if you want to get a
really good look at a particular paragraph, you can fiddle with the screen's
magnification until the paragraph fills the entire screen.

To change your screen's magnification, follow these steps:

1. **Choose View⇨Zoom.**

   The Zoom dialog box appears, as shown in Figure 4-4.

2. **Click one of the following option buttons in the Zoom To list:**

   - **200%:** Makes your text twice its normal size

   - **100%:** Makes your text the normal, default size

   - **75%:** Makes your text smaller

   - **Page Width:** Makes your text line just as wide as the currently
     open window displayed in Word

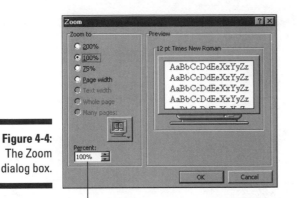

Figure 4-4:
The Zoom
dialog box.

Percent list box

• **Text width:** Blows up or squeezes the page so all the text fits on the screen (only available in Print Layout view)

• **Whole page:** Squeezes the whole page on the screen (only available in Print Layout view)

• **Many pages:** Shows miniature versions of all the pages of your entire document (only available in Print Layout view)

For you free spirits who absolutely must express your individuality, you can also specify a percent magnification to display your document by using the Percent list box. This list box lets you display your document in odd percentages, such as 57% , 93%, or 138%.

3. Click OK.

As another alternative, click the Zoom list box in the Formatting toolbar (see Figure 4-5) and choose a percentage between 500 and 10.

Showing spaces and paragraph marks

If your document ever exhibits strange word or paragraph spacing, you may need to know whether you inadvertently entered two spaces between words (or none at all) or pressed the Enter key twice after paragraphs. To make Word show spaces and paragraph marks in your document:

1. Click the Show/Hide Paragraph Marks button on the Standard toolbar.

Word displays the spaces (as dots), paragraph marks (those double-stemmed backwards Ps), and any hidden text in your document as shown in Figure 4-5.

Show/Hide Paragraph Marks button ┐ Zoom list box

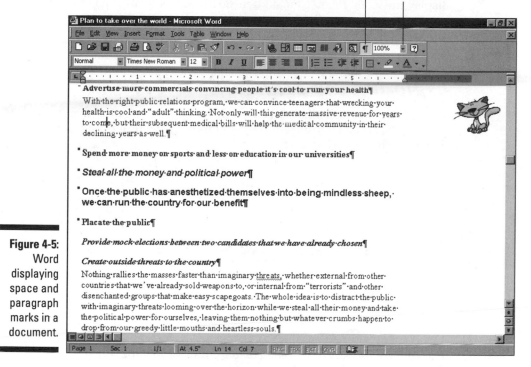

Figure 4-5:
Word
displaying
space and
paragraph
marks in a
document.

2. **Click the Show/Hide Paragraph Marks button again to hide spaces, paragraph marks, and any hidden text.**

Deciphering the Word Toolbars

Rather than force you to memorize obscure keystroke combinations or wade through multiple layers of pull-down menus, Word lets you choose common commands by clicking buttons stored on toolbars.

The two most common toolbars are the Standard and Formatting toolbars. (Word actually offers over a dozen different toolbars, but the Standard and Formatting toolbars are the main ones you use.) These two toolbars automatically appear when you first install and start Word. You can hide them later to make your screen less cluttered, if you want.

Unlike previous versions, Word can now automatically modify its toolbars to display the icons you use most often. So if your toolbar keeps looking different each time you use it, it's because Word is trying to display the icons representing the commands you use most often.

Exploring the Standard toolbar

The Standard toolbar offers access to the program's most frequently used commands, arranged from left to right in roughly the order of their frequency of use, as shown in Figure 4-6.

Figure 4-6:
All the pretty buttons on the Standard toolbar.

The commands featured on the Standard toolbar include:

- **New Blank Document:** Creates a new document
- **Open:** Opens an existing document
- **Save:** Saves your current document
- **E-mail:** Sends the current document as e-mail
- **Print:** Prints your current document
- **Print Preview:** Shows you what your document will look like when printed on your printer (as long as the printer doesn't jam)
- **Spelling and Grammar:** Checks the spelling and grammar in your document
- **Cut:** Moves the currently selected text to the *Clipboard,* the invisible Windows storage area
- **Copy:** Copies the currently selected text to the Clipboard
- **Paste:** Places in the current document whatever text is currently on the Clipboard
- **Format Painter:** Copies the formatting of the currently selected text so that you can apply that formatting to any text you select next
- **Undo:** Reverses the action of your last command
- **Redo:** The opposite of Undo — restores what the Undo command last did

✓ **Insert Hyperlink:** Creates a link to a Web page

✓ **Tables and Borders:** Displays the Tables and Borders toolbar

✓ **Insert Table:** Inserts a table in your document

✓ **Insert Microsoft Excel Worksheet:** Inserts a Microsoft Excel worksheet into your document

✓ **Columns:** Formats your documents into columns

✓ **Drawing:** Displays the Drawing toolbar at the bottom of the screen

✓ **Document Map:** Switches to Web Layout view

✓ **Show/Hide Paragraph Marks:** Shows or hides spaces, tabs, carriage returns, and hidden text in your document

✓ **Zoom Control:** Adjusts the magnification of your document

✓ **Microsoft Word Help:** Displays (or hides) the Office Assistant that you can click to get help with Word

✓ **More Buttons:** Displays or hides buttons on the Standard toolbar

To quickly find out what each button on the Standard toolbar does, point the mouse over a button and wait a second or two until the *ScreenTip* — a brief explanation of the button — appears.

Looking good with the Formatting toolbar

The Formatting toolbar contains commands to make your text look pretty with different fonts, type sizes, and typefaces (such as bold, italics, and underline). Figure 4-7 shows the Formatting toolbar.

Figure 4-7:
The
Formatting
toolbar.

| Normal | Times New Roman | 12 | **B** *I* U | 📋 📋 📋 📋 | 📋 📋 📋 📋 | 📋 · 🖉 · **A** · |

The buttons on the Formatting toolbar appear in the following order from left to right:

✓ **Style:** Controls the *style* — preset specifications for font, font size, paragraph spacing, and so on — of the currently selected text (or whatever paragraph the cursor is currently in)

✓ **Font:** Controls the *font* — the look of the letters — of the currently selected text

✔ **Font Size:** Controls the size of the currently selected text

✔ **Bold:** Makes selected text **bold**

✔ **Italic:** Makes selected text *italic*

✔ **Underline:** <u>Underlines</u> selected text

✔ **Align Left:** Makes the lines of the selected text line up on the left (with an uneven right margin)

✔ **Center:** Centers selected text between the left and right margins

✔ **Align Right:** Makes the lines of the selected text line up on the right (with an uneven left margin)

✔ **Justify:** Displays selected text with the left and right margins perfectly straight; unlike centering, justifying stretches full lines to extend to the margins

✔ **Numbering:** Adds (or removes) numbers from selected paragraphs

✔ **Bullets:** Adds (or removes) bullets from selected paragraphs

✔ **Decrease Indent:** Moves selected paragraph to the previous tab stop

✔ **Increase Indent:** Moves selected paragraph to the next tab stop

✔ **Outside Border:** Draws borders around selected paragraphs and tables

✔ **Highlight:** Displays selected text against a different color background

✔ **Font Color:** Displays selected text in a different color

✔ **More Buttons:** Displays or hides buttons on the Standard toolbar

To use any of the commands on the Formatting toolbar, just select the text that you want to format, and then click the appropriate button or the downward-pointing arrow of the list box on the Formatting toolbar. Chapter 5 explains how to select text so you can format it with the Formatting toolbar later.

Exploring the Word Ruler

The *ruler* defines the margins and tabs of your document. If you're creating a multicolumn document, the ruler also shows the column placement and the distance between the columns. By using the ruler, you can make margins wider (or smaller) and change the indentation of paragraphs.

Hiding and displaying the ruler

If you don't want to see the ruler on your screen (or if you want to display the ruler after you hide it), you can hide it (or display it) by choosing View⇨Ruler.

If you switch to Print Layout View, Word displays a vertical ruler along the left-hand side of the screen. To hide this vertical ruler, switch to a different view such as Normal or Web Layout View.

Setting tabs on the ruler

Word provides five different types of tabs (shown in Figure 4-8) that you can set on the ruler.

Left tab   Center tab

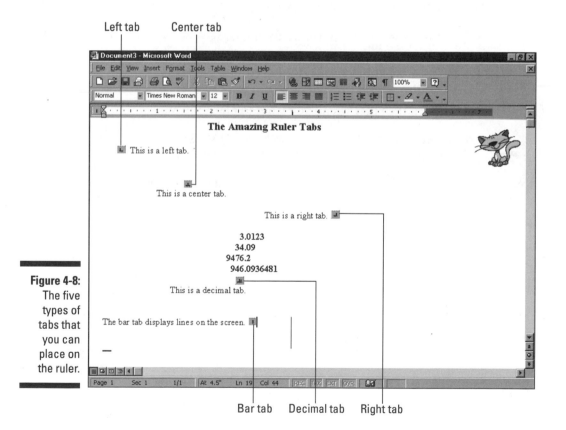

The Amazing Ruler Tabs

This is a left tab.

This is a center tab.

This is a right tab.

3.0123
34.09
9476.2
946.0936481

This is a decimal tab.

The bar tab displays lines on the screen.

Figure 4-8:
The five types of tabs that you can place on the ruler.

Bar tab   Decimal tab   Right tab

✔ **Left tab (looks like an L):** Moves text toward the right edge of the page as you type

✔ **Center tab (looks like an upside-down T):** Centers text around the tab

✔ **Right tab (looks like a backward L):** Moves text toward the left edge of the page as you type

✔ **Decimal tab (looks like an upside-down T with a dot next to it):** Aligns decimal numbers in a column on the decimal point, as in this example:

24.90

1.9084

58093.89

✔ **Bar tab (looks like a straight line like |):** Draws a vertical line on the document

To place a tab on the ruler, follow these steps:

1. **Click the cursor anywhere in the paragraph that you want to modify with a tab.**

2. **Click the Tab Selection button (which appears to the left of the ruler) until it displays the tab that you want to use.**

3. **Click the ruler where you want to place the tab.**

If you switch to Print Layout or Web Layout View, you can click in the location of your document where you want to insert a tab. To do this, move the mouse pointer until it turns into one of three icons as shown in Figure 4-9. Then double-click the left mouse button and start typing. This feature is known as Click and Type.

Figure 4-9:
The three
mouse
pointer
icons that
appear in
Print Layout
or Web
Layout
View.

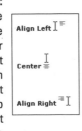

To move an existing tab on the ruler:

1. **Point the mouse on the tab that you want to move.**

2. **Hold down the left mouse button until you see a dotted line appear directly below the tab.**

3. **Move the mouse to where you want to move the tab.**

4. **Release the left mouse button.**

To remove a tab from the ruler:

1. **Point the mouse on the tab that you want to remove.**

2. **Hold down the left mouse button until you see a dotted line appear directly beneath the tab.**

3. **Move the mouse off the ruler.**

4. **Release the left mouse button.**

Indents on your ruler

To help you indent paragraphs, the Tab Selection button also displays two types of indentation icons, as shown in Figure 4-10.

- ✔ **First line indent (looks like an upside-down house):** Defines the left margin of the first line in a paragraph

- ✔ **Hanging indent (looks like a big U):** Defines the left margin of every line but the first line in a paragraph

To provide more indentation options, the ruler displays two indent icons that can indent your text left and right, as shown in Figure 4-10.

- ✔ **Left indent (does not appear in the Tab Selection button):** Defines the left margin of every line of a paragraph

- ✔ **Right indent (does not appear in the Tab Selection button):** Defines the right margin of every line of a paragraph

Figure 4-10:
Indenting
text with the
ruler.

Left indent
First line indent
Right indent
Hanging indent

The ruler can only display one First line, Hanging, Left, or Right indent per paragraph.

To indent paragraphs with the First Line Indent, Hanging Indent, Left Indent, and Right Indent markers, follow these steps:

1. **Select the paragraphs that you want to indent.**

   Skip this step if you haven't written any paragraphs to indent yet. Any indentation that you apply to a blank document affects the whole, future document.

2. **Point the mouse on a marker (First Line Indent, Hanging Indent, Left Indent, or Right Indent) and hold down the left mouse button.**

   Word displays a dotted vertical line directly under the marker.

3. **Move the mouse where you want to indent the paragraph; then release the mouse button.**

Instead of moving the indent markers on the ruler, you can also click the Tab Selection button until the First Line or Hanging Indent icon appears, and then click the ruler where you want to put the First Line or Hanging Indent marker.

Moving through a Word Document

You can navigate through a Word document by using the mouse or the keyboard. Although the mouse is easier to master, the keyboard can be more convenient to use — you don't have to keep reaching for the mouse when your fingers are already on the keyboard.

Using the mouse to jump around in a document

The mouse is often the quickest way to move around a document. When you use the mouse, you can use the vertical scroll bar, as shown in Figure 4-11.

- ✔ Click the up or down arrow to scroll up or down one line at a time.
- ✔ Drag the scroll box in the desired direction to jump to an approximate location in your document.
- ✔ Click in the scroll bar above or below the scroll box to page up or down one window at a time.
- ✔ Click the Previous page or Next page arrows at the bottom of the scroll bar to jump to the top of the previous or next page.

✔ Double-click the page number of the status bar so the Go To tab of the Find and Replace dialog box appears. Then type a page number as explained in the section "Using the Go To command."

✔ Click the Select Browse Object button and choose how you want to browse through your document, such as Browse by Heading as shown in Figure 4-12.

✔ Roll the middle wheel on your mouse. (If your mouse does not have a middle wheel in the middle, you can't use this option.)

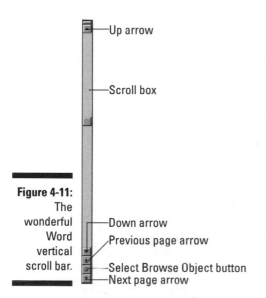

—Up arrow

—Scroll box

Figure 4-11:
The wonderful Word vertical scroll bar.

—Down arrow
—Previous page arrow
—Select Browse Object button
—Next page arrow

Using the keyboard to jump around in a document

For those who hate the mouse or just like using the keyboard, here are the different ways to jump around in your document by pressing keys:

✔ Press the ↓ key to move down one line in your document.

✔ Press the ↑ key to move up one line in your document.

✔ Hold down the Ctrl key and press ↑ or ↓ to jump up or down a paragraph at a time.

✔ Press the PgDn key (or Page Down, on some keyboards) to jump down the document one window at a time.

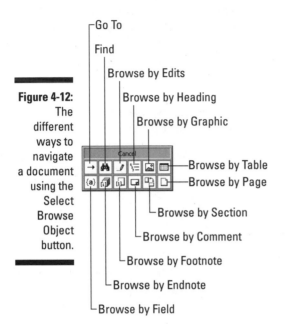

Go To

Find

Browse by Edits

Browse by Heading

Browse by Graphic

Figure 4-12:
The different ways to navigate a document using the Select Browse Object button.

Browse by Table

Browse by Page

Browse by Section

Browse by Comment

Browse by Footnote

Browse by Endnote

Browse by Field

- ✔ Press the PgUp key (or Page Up, on some keyboards) to jump up the document one window at a time.

- ✔ Hold down Ctrl and press the Home key to jump to the beginning of your document.

- ✔ Hold down Ctrl and press the End key to jump to the end of your document.

Using the Go To command

When you want to jump to a specific part of your document, the Go To command is a lot easier and faster than either the mouse or the keyboard. To use the Go To command:

1. **Choose Edit⇨Go To, press Ctrl+G, or click the Select Browse Object button and choose Go To.**

   The Go To tab of the Find and Replace dialog box appears, as shown in Figure 4-13.

2. **Type a page number and press Enter.**

3. **Click Close or press Esc.**

Figure 4-13:
Use the Go
To tab of the
Find and
Replace
dialog box
to jump to a
specific part
of the
document.

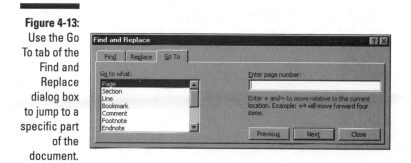

Saving Your Stuff

Obviously, if you're going to take the time and trouble to write something in Word, you probably want to save it so that you can use it again in the future. Word provides three ways to save your stuff.

Always save your work periodically in case your computer crashes, the power goes out, Windows 95/98/NT inexplicably freezes on you, or some jerk comes along and starts messing around on your computer.

Saving your document

To save your document, choose one of the following methods:

- ✔ Press Ctrl+S.
- ✔ Click the Save button on the Standard toolbar (the button that looks like a floppy disk).
- ✔ Choose File⇨Save.

If you have multiple documents open and want to save them all in one keystroke, hold down Shift and choose File⇨Save All.

If you're saving a document for the first time, Word asks you to choose a name. Ideally, you should make your filename as descriptive as possible, such as Letter To Dad or Hate Mail To Ex-Spouse, so that it jars your memory about the document's contents when you haven't looked at the file for a while.

The longest a filename can be is 255 characters. Filenames cannot include the forward slash (/), backslash (\), greater-than sign (>), less-than sign (<), asterisk (*), period (.), question mark (?), quotation mark ("), pipe symbol (|), colon (:), or semicolon (;).

Saving your document under a new name or as a different file type

Suppose you wrote a report that took five days to write and now you have to write a similar report, due on Monday. Rather than starting from scratch, you can open your old report, save it as a new document, and then edit this new document while leaving the original document intact.

To save your document under a different name, follow these steps:

1. **Choose File⇨Save As.**

   The Save As dialog box appears.

2. **Type a new name for your file in the File Name box.**

3. **(Optional) Click in the Save as Type list box and choose a file format to use, such as WordPerfect 5.0 or Works 4.0 for Windows.**

4. **Click Save.**

Word 2000 documents are compatible with Word 97 documents, but not with older versions of Word such as those created by Word 6.0. If you want to save a Word document so someone else can edit it using an older version of Word, choose the Save As command and choose Word 6.0/95 in the Save as Type list box of the Save As dialog box.

To insure maximum compatibility between Word 2000 documents and Word 97, turn off specific Word 2000 features that aren't supported by Word 97. To turn off these features, follow these steps:

1. **Choose Tools⇨Options.**

2. **Click the Save tab.**

   The Save tab in the Options dialog box appears as shown in Figure 4-14.

3. **Click the Disable Features Not Supported by Word 97 check box.**

4. **Click OK.**

Telling Word the file format to use

Word normally saves your documents in a special Word 2000 file format that's almost (but not quite) completely compatible with older Word 97 files. Rather than use the Save As command to tell Word which file format to use, you can define a default file format.

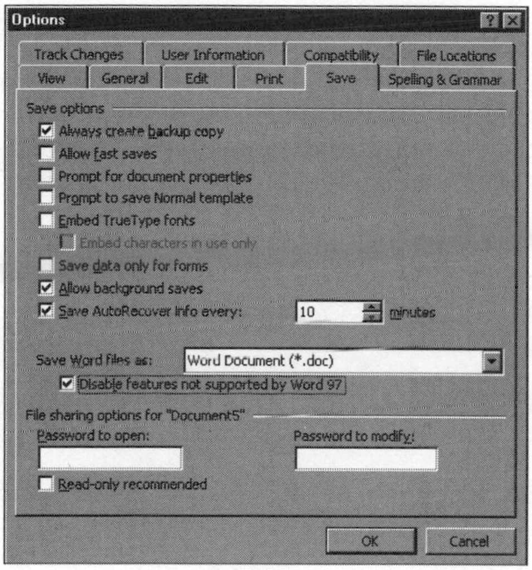

Figure 4-14:
The Save
tab of the
Options
dialog box.

This default file format tells Word, "Every time I save a file, use this file format unless I tell you otherwise." To define a default file format to use:

1. **Choose Tools⇨Options.**

2. **Click the Save tab.**

   The Save tab in the Options dialog box appears (refer to Figure 4-14).

3. **Click in the Save Word Files As list box.**

   A list of file formats appears.

4. **Click the file format you want Word to use from now on.**

5. **Click OK.**

Unless you regularly share files with people using different word processors or different versions of Word, you should stick with the Word Document (*.doc) file format.

Making backups of your file automatically

In case you're terrified of losing data (a completely justified fear, given penchant of Windows 95/98/NT for crashing), you may want to use Word's backup feature.

The *backup feature* creates a second copy (a backup) of your document every time you save your document. This backup file is called "Backup of (name of original document)." So if you save a document called "Plan for world domination," the backup file is called "Backup of Plan for world domination" and is stored in the same folder as your original document. (This also means if you accidentally wipe out the folder containing the original document, you also wipe out the backup copy as well.)

To turn on Word's backup feature, follow these steps:

1. **Choose Tools⇨Options.**

   The Options dialog box appears (refer to Figure 4-14).

2. **Click the Save tab.**

3. **Make sure a check mark appears in the Always Create Backup Copy check box.**

4. **Click OK.**

Saving automatically

Because few people ever listen to the advice urging them to save their documents periodically, Word can do it for you automatically. Essentially, this means that every few minutes, the program saves your document, whether you want it to or not.

If you tell Word to save files automatically, you may be typing away, and suddenly everything stops while Word saves your document, which could either get annoying once in a while or signal you that it's time to take another hour-and-a-half coffee break. But in general, having Word 2000 save your work is a good idea — that way, you don't lose valuable documents because of a power outage or some other disaster.

To tell Word to save your work automatically, follow these steps:

1. **Choose Tools⇨Options.**

   The Options dialog box appears (refer to Figure 4-14).

2. **Click the Save tab.**

   The Save tab of the Options dialog box appears.

3. **Click the Save AutoRecover Info Every check box.**

4. **Click in the Minutes scroll box and enter how many minutes (such as 10) you want Word to wait before saving your document automatically.**

5. **Click OK.**

Word also provides an Allow Fast Saves check box that you can click after Step 3. The Fast Saves option saves your files quickly (hence the name Fast Save) because it only stores any changes you make in a smaller, separate, temporary file on the disk. If you choose the Fast Saves option, you should clear the Allow Fast Saves check box periodically so Word consolidates all changes into a single file.

Saving Word documents as Web pages

Word gives you the additional option of saving documents as Web pages. That way you can create (or edit) your Web pages using the convenience of a word processor like Word, and then convert the whole thing into a Web page that you can post on the Internet so that everyone around the planet can read what you've written.

While Word won't substitute for a dedicated Web page creation program like Microsoft FrontPage, it can be easier and faster to use. When it comes to creating Web sites, you don't have to make them fancy just as long as they're functional and most importantly, informative.

To convert a Word document into a Web page:

1. **Choose File⇨Save as Web Page.**

   The Save As dialog box appears.

2. **Click the Change Title button.**

   A Set Page Title dialog box appears as shown in Figure 4-15.

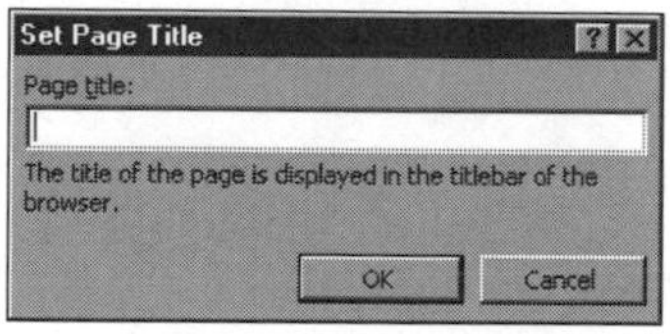

Figure 4-15:
The Set
Page Title
dialog box.

Set Page Title	? X
Page title:	
The title of the page is displayed in the titlebar of the browser.	
	OK Cancel

3. **Type the title that you want to appear at the top of your Web page and click OK.**

4. **Click Save.**

   Word immediately displays your document in Web Layout view. If you load your Web browser (such as Internet Explorer), you can load your newly created Web page to see how it looks in a real Web browser.

Previewing and Printing Your Masterpiece

To contribute to global deforestation, feel free to print every chance you get, just to see whether your documents are properly aligned. But if you're one of the growing crowd who cringe at the thought of wasting precious resources for the sake of unnecessary printing, use the Word Print Preview feature before actually printing out your work.

Putting Print Preview to work

Print Preview enables you to see how your document looks before you print it. That way, you can see things like whether your margins are aligned properly and your page numbers appear in the right place.

To use the Print Preview feature:

1. **Choose File➪Print Preview.**

   Word displays your document in minuscule print, as shown in Figure 4-16, and displays the cursor as a magnifying glass.

2. **Move the mouse cursor (the magnifying glass) over the document and click to view your document in its full size.**

3. **Click Close to close Print Preview.**

Defining your pages

Before you print your Word documents, you may want to define your page margins and paper size. To define your pages:

1. **Choose File➪Page Setup.**

   The Page Setup dialog box appears.

2. **Click the Margins tab and click the Top, Bottom, Left, or Right boxes to define the margins you want to set.**

   The Margins tab appears in Page Setup dialog box as shown in Figure 4-17.

3. **Click the Paper Size tab and click in the Paper Size list box to define the paper size (such as Legal or A4).**

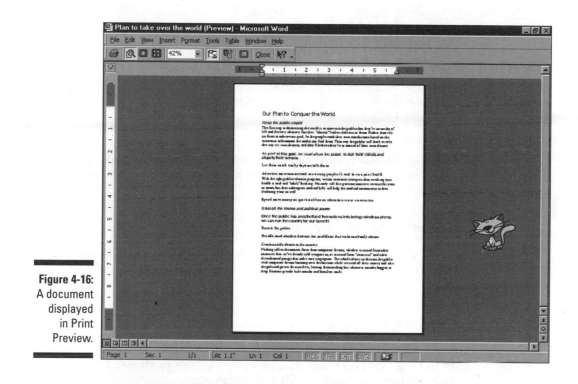

Figure 4-16:
A document
displayed
in Print
Preview.

You may also want to define the specific width and height of your pages or
change the paper orientation (Portrait or Landscape). *Portrait orientation*
prints text so that the page is taller than it is wide. This book's pages are
printed using Portrait orientation. *Landscape orientation* prints text so
that the page is wider than it is tall.

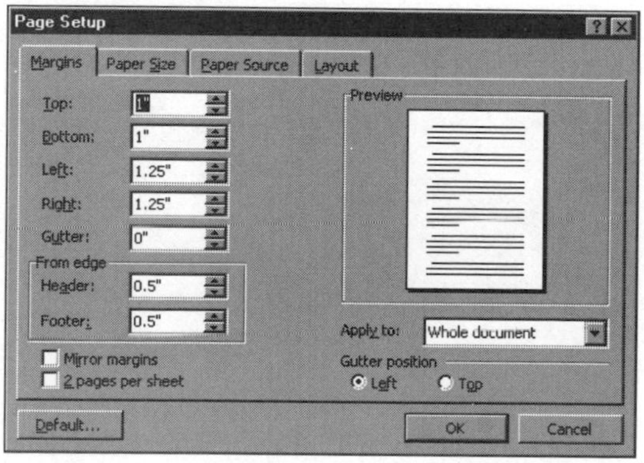

Figure 4-17:
The Page
Setup dialog
box lets
you define
margins and
paper size.

4. **Click the Paper Source tab to define the location of the paper you want to use for your printer.**

5. **Click the Layout tab.**

   The Layout tab lets you define if you want your headers and footers to appear differently on odd or even pages, or whether they should appear on the first page or not.

6. **Click OK.**

   After this exhaustive and tedious process of defining the paper you're going to use, you're ready to actually print your Word documents.

Printing your work

Eventually, you may need to print something that you created in Word. To print a Word document, follow these steps:

1. **Choose or press Ctrl+P.**

   The Page Setup dialog box appears as shown in Figure 4-18.

2. **Click the Name list box and choose the printer to use.**

3. **In the Page range group, click an option button to choose the pages you want to print, such as All or Current page.**

   If you click the Pages option button, you can selectively choose the pages you want to print, such as page 1, 3, and 5 through 12.

4. **Click the Number of Copies box and type the number of copies you want.**

Figure 4-18:
The Print dialog box enables you to choose what you want to print and where to print it.

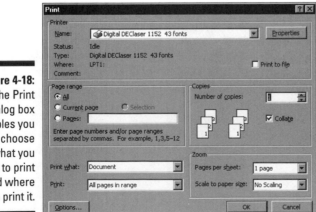

5. Click the Print <u>W</u>hat list box and choose what you want to print, such as your Document or any comments you've added to the document.

6. Click the P<u>r</u>int list box and choose what you want to print, such as Odd or Even pages.

7. Click OK.

When you click the Print button (the button that looks like a printer) on the Standard toolbar, Word immediately starts printing your entire document, bypassing the Print dialog box. If you want to print specific pages or a certain number of copies, go through the menu route instead (or press Ctrl+P).

Chapter 5

Manipulating Your Words

● ●

In This Chapter

▶ Highlighting your words

▶ Changing your text

▶ Correcting your grammar and spelling

▶ Finding old text and replacing it with the new

● ●

*E*ven the best writers in the world need to edit their writing once in a while to delete text, rearrange paragraphs, or check their spelling and grammar. Fortunately, Word can simplify (or even automate) most of these tasks for you. That way, you can concentrate on writing down your ideas rather than worrying about the trivial tasks of spelling and using grammar correctly.

Selecting Text

Before you can delete, move, copy, or format text, you must *select* it first. Selecting text tells Word, "See this text that I just highlighted? That's what I want you to change."

You have two ways to select text:

✔ Drag or click the mouse.

✔ Use the keyboard.

Dragging or clicking the mouse to select text

Dragging the mouse is the easiest and most intuitive way to select text (provided you're already comfortable using the mouse).

To select text with the mouse:

1. **Move the mouse pointer to the beginning (or end) of the text that you want to select.**

2. **Hold down the left mouse button and move the mouse to the other end of the text, highlighting all the text you want to select.**

3. **Release the left mouse button.**

If you trust your mouse-clicking abilities, try these other ways to select text with the mouse:

- Double-click a word (selects the word as well as the space that follows it).

- Hold down the Ctrl key and click inside a sentence to select the entire sentence.

- Triple-click inside a paragraph to select the entire paragraph.

- Click to the far left (where the cursor changes to an arrow) of the first word in a line to select the entire line.

- Double-click to the far left of a paragraph to select the entire paragraph.

- With your mouse to the far left of the text, vertically drag (that is, hold down the mouse button and move the mouse) to select multiple lines, whether those lines are part of a single paragraph or multiple paragraphs.

Using the keyboard to select text

Instead of reaching for the mouse, you may find one of the keyboard short-cuts shown in Table 5-1 easier for selecting text. If you repeat the key combination, you select more text in the direction indicated.

Table 5-1	Keyboard Shortcuts for Selecting Text
Pressing This	*Selects This*
Shift+→	Character to right of insertion point
Shift+←	Character to left of insertion point
Shift+Home	All the current line to the left of the insertion point
Shift+End	All the current line to the right of the insertion point
Shift+PgUp	A screenful of text from the insertion point up
Shift+PgDn	A screenful of text from the insertion point down
Ctrl+Shift+→	One word to the right of the insertion point
Ctrl+Shift+←	One word to the left of the insertion point

Pressing This	Selects This
Ctrl+Shift+Home	All text from the insertion point to the beginning of the document
Ctrl+Shift+End	All text from the insertion point to the end of the document
Alt+Ctrl+Shift+Page Down	All text from the insertion point to the end of the displayed window
F8 and an arrow key	From the insertion point in the direction of whichever arrow you choose. F8 puts you in selection mode, which you get out of by pressing Esc
Ctrl+Shift+F8 and an arrow key	Highlights a block of text (the size of the highlighted text varies depending on how many times you press the up/down or right/left arrow keys)
Ctrl+A	Entire document — all text, including footnotes (but excluding headers and footers); good for making a font change throughout the whole document

Editing Text

Not even the greatest authors can write their masterpieces in one draft. Most people need to edit their writing until it means exactly what they want to say. To make this (usually disagreeable) task easier, Word lets you edit text in several ways: deleting text, copying or moving text (even between different documents), using drag-and-drop editing, and spiking (which sounds like something horrible to do to text, but it's actually quite painless).

Deleting text

Two keys can delete individual characters and selected text:

- The Backspace key (typically gray, with an arrow pointing to the left), at the top of the keyboard, eliminates characters to the *left* of the insertion point.

- The Delete key, which you find in more than one place — below the Insert key (above the arrow keys) and below the 3 key on the numeric keypad — eliminates characters to the *right* of the insertion point.

Here are a few things to note:

- ✔ Choosing Edit➪Clear does the same thing as pressing the Delete key.
- ✔ You can delete entire blocks of text (or graphics) by selecting the text (or graphics) first and then pressing either the Backspace or Delete key.
- ✔ Rather than delete text and then type something new, you can delete and replace text at the same time by selecting the text and then typing your new text.

Avoid pressing the Insert key (or Ins, on some keyboards). The Word default mode is Insert mode, which means that when you type, your newly typed words push any existing words to the right. If you accidentally press the Insert key, you enter Overtype mode. When you're in Overtype mode, typing new text simply wipes out any existing text that gets in the way.

People have a tendency to change their minds (some more than others, especially politicians). In case you delete text (or do almost anything else, for that matter) and suddenly realize that you didn't want to perform that particular action after all, you have three options:

- ✔ Press Ctrl+Z.
- ✔ Choose Edit➪Undo.
- ✔ Click the Undo button on the Standard toolbar.

By choosing one of the three Undo options, Word takes back the last command. For example, if you delete a paragraph and suddenly realize you made a mistake, press Ctrl+Z and Word restores your text.

Copying and moving text

If you want to copy text and place the copy in a different part of the document, or simply move text from one place to another:

1. **Select the text that you want to copy.**

   Use the mouse or keyboard as explained in the "Selecting Text" section earlier in this chapter.

2. **Copy or cut the selected text.**

   Copying text lets you keep the original text in its current location but paste a copy of that text in another part of your document. To copy the text, you can do any of the following:

- Choose Edit➪Copy.
- Press Ctrl+C.
- Click the Copy button on the Standard toolbar.
- Press the right mouse button and choose Copy from the pop-up menu.

Cutting text removes text so you can move it to another part of your document. To cut the text, you can do any of the following:

- Choose Edit➪Cut.
- Press Ctrl+X.
- Click the Cut button on the Standard toolbar.
- Press the right mouse button and choose Cut from the pop-up menu.

3. **Move the cursor to where you want to place the copied or cut text.**

4. **Choose the Paste command in one of the following ways:**

- Choose Edit➪Paste.
- Press Ctrl+V.
- Click the Paste button on the Standard toolbar.
- Click the right mouse button and choose Paste from the pop-up menu.

Each time you copy or cut text, Windows stores this text on the Office Clipboard, which is a temporary storage place for holding up to 12 copied or cut objects. For more information about the Office Clipboard, see Chapter 3.

Discovering drag-and-drop editing

While *drag-and-drop* sounds like something you may do when shopping at the last minute during the holidays, it's actually a shortcut for cutting and pasting. Instead of copying or cutting text and pasting it somewhere else, drag-and-drop editing lets you drag text to a new location. Then you can drop the text by releasing the mouse button.

Drag-and-drop editing works within a document as well as between documents. If you have two documents open, you can simply drag and drop text between the two documents.

Drag-and-drop editing can be a bit tricky to master at first. You may want to experiment on a document that you can afford to mess up, such as your boss's resume. If you do make a mistake using drag-and-drop editing, you can always use the Undo command (press Ctrl+Z) to fix it.

To drag and drop selected text to a new location:

1. **Select the text to move by using the mouse or one of the keyboard commands.**

2. **Place the mouse pointer inside the selected text and hold down the left mouse button.**

   The mouse pointer displays a box underneath, and a gray, vertical dotted line shows you where Word will put your selected text when you let go of the left mouse button.

3. **Drag the text to the new location.**

4. **Release the left mouse button.**

If you'd rather copy text than move it, follow these steps:

1. **Select the text to copy by using the mouse or one of the keyboard commands.**

2. **Hold down the Ctrl key.**

3. **Place the mouse pointer on the selected text and hold down the left mouse button.**

4. **Drag the text to the new location.**

5. **Release the mouse button and the Ctrl key.**

Checking Your Grammar and Spelling

Some of the best writers in the world can't spell correctly — just look at all the weird spellings in Shakespeare's original plays. To make sure that your high-powered business presentation doesn't look like the scribblings of a 5-year-old, let Word check your grammar and spelling before you show your document to anyone else.

Checking grammar and spelling as you write

As you type, Word acts like a grammar-school teacher and immediately underlines possible problems to call them to your attention, putting a green, wavy line under possible grammar errors and a red, wavy line under possible spelling mistakes.

To address grammatical problems that Word underlined:

1. **Place the mouse pointer over the word underlined by a green wavy line.**

2. **Click the right mouse button.**

   A pop-up menu appears, as shown in Figure 5-1.

3. **Choose the boldface suggestion (or among the suggestions) Word provides, or click Grammar for more information.**

   If you click Grammar, the Grammar dialog box appears, as shown in Figure 5-2.

4. **Choose one of the following options, depending on your opinion of the matter in question:**

   - Click Ignore.

   - Click Ignore Rule.

   - Click a suggestion displayed in the Suggestions list box and click change.

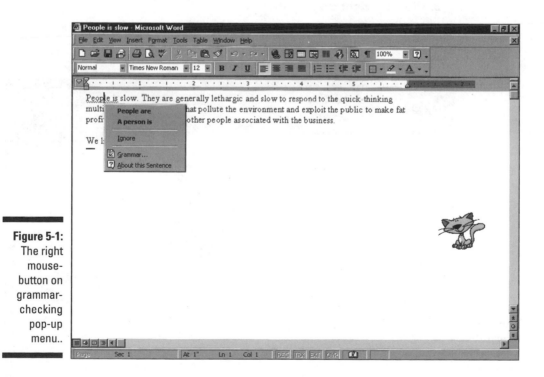

Figure 5-1:
The right mouse-button on grammar-checking pop-up menu..

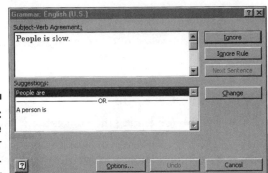

Figure 5-2:
The
Grammar
dialog box.

5. Click the close box in the upper-right corner of the window or press Esc to dismiss the Grammar dialog box.

To address spelling problems that Word underlines:

1. Place the mouse pointer over the word underlined by a red wavy line.

2. Click the right mouse button.

A pop-up menu appears, listing words that Word thinks you meant instead of the misspelled word, as shown in Figure 5-3.

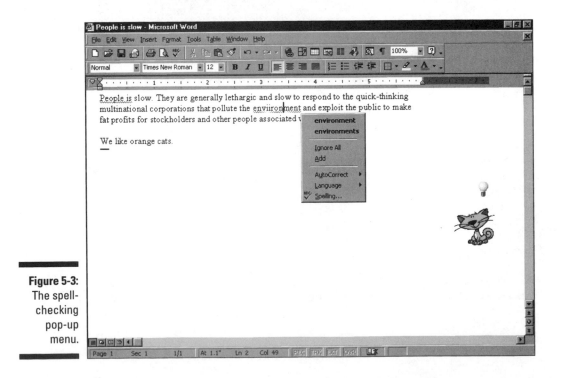

Figure 5-3:
The spell-
checking
pop-up
menu.

3. **Choose one of the following:**

   • Click one of the boldface words that Word suggests.

   • Click Add to add the underlined word to the dictionary so it won't be flagged as an error ever again.

   • Click Ignore All.

Ignore All makes Word bypass all future instances of this spelling in this document.

If having Word automatically check your spelling or grammar as you type gets on your nerves, you can turn it off by following these steps:

1. **Choose Tools⇨Options.**

   The Options dialog box appears.

2. **Click the Spelling & Grammar tab.**

3. **Click the Check Spelling as You Type or Check Grammar as You Type check box so that the check box is empty.**

4. **Click OK.**

Checking your entire document for spelling and grammar

No matter how clearly organized your ideas may be, poor spelling and grammar can destroy the credibility of your words. To check the spelling and grammar of your entire document:

1. **Choose one of the following:**

   • Choose Tools⇨Spelling and Grammar.

   • Press F7.

   • Click the Spelling and Grammar button on the Standard toolbar (the one with the check mark and the letters *ABC* on it).

   Each time Word finds a possible problem, it stops and displays the Spelling and Grammar dialog box, as shown in Figure 5-4.

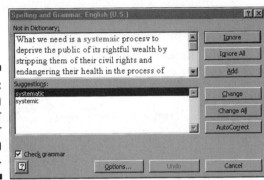

Figure 5-4:
Checking
your
grammar
and spelling
in Word.

2. **Choose one of the following, depending on your opinion of the matter at hand:**

   • Click Ignore.

   • Click Ignore All.

   • Click Add to add the underlined word to the dictionary so it won't be flagged as an error ever again.

   • Click a suggestion displayed in the Suggestions list box and click Change or Change All.

   After Word finishes checking your document, it displays the message The spelling and grammar check is complete.

3. **Click OK to return to your document.**

Instead of highlighting a suggested word from the Suggestions list box and clicking Change, you can accept a suggested word by double-clicking that word. As another alternative, just type your own correction directly in the Spelling and Grammar dialog box's top window.

The Word Spelling and Grammar dialog box offers several other important options:

✔ Click the Ignore button if the highlighted word in the document is correctly spelled — if the word is a proper noun, technical term, or four-letter word that you know is spelled correctly.

✔ Click Ignore All if you use the word in the document more than once and know that the spelling is correct. Thereafter, Word ignores that same word throughout the current document.

✔ Click Change All if you think that you misspelled the word in the document more than once. That way, Word just automatically corrects the spelling of future instances and doesn't flag the word every time.

✔ Click Add if you use the word in other documents. Word adds the word to a custom dictionary. (You can create additional dictionaries for specialized documents.)

✔ Click AutoCorrect to add the word to the AutoCorrect dictionary. Thereafter, Word corrects the word automatically as you type it. This procedure can save you a lot of time if you continually misspell the same words. (For more information about AutoCorrect, see "Saving time with AutoCorrect" later in this chapter.)

✔ Click Cancel after you tire of using the spell checker.

If you don't want Word to check your grammar while checking spelling, you can turn off just the grammar checker by following these steps:

1. **Choose Tools⇨Options.**

   The Options dialog box appears.

2. **Click the Spelling & Grammar tab.**

3. **Click the Check Grammar with Spelling check box so the check box is empty.**

4. **Click OK.**

Saving time with AutoCorrect

AutoCorrect contains a list of common typographical errors along with their corrections. The moment you type a word matching AutoCorrect's list of typographical errors (such as *teh* instead of *the,* or *adn* instead of *and*), AutoCorrect springs into action and corrects the misspelling right away (giving you the illusion that you actually spell everything correctly).

✔ You can add your own common spelling mistakes to the AutoCorrect dictionary so it corrects them automatically.

✔ If you use a lot of bizarre technical terms or proper names, you can store short-hand references in AutoCorrect. For example, instead of typing *Massachusetts Institute of Technology* each time, just store the letters *MIT* in AutoCorrect. Each time you type *MIT,* AutoCorrect automatically replaces it with *Massachusetts Institute of Technology.*

To modify AutoCorrect:

1. **Choose Tools⇨AutoCorrect.**

   The AutoCorrect dialog box appears, as shown in Figure 5-5.

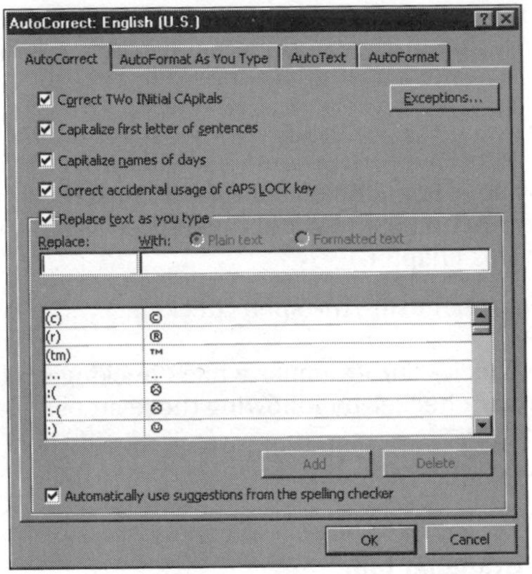

Figure 5-5:
The
AutoCorrect
dialog box.

2. **In the Replace box, type a word that you frequently misspell.**

   Or type a shorthand word to represent a longer word or phrase, such as *MIT.*

3. **Type the correct spelling of the word in the With box.**

   Or type the longer word or phrase that you want AutoCorrect to use, such as *Massachusetts Institute of Technology.*

4. **Click Add.**

5. **Click OK.**

If you enter a misspelled word in the With box, AutoCorrect misspells the word consistently (which goes to show you that computers aren't that smart after all).

To remove a word from AutoCorrect, follow these steps:

1. **Choose Tools⇨AutoCorrect.**

   The AutoCorrect dialog box appears (refer to Figure 5-5).

2. **In the two-column list box at the bottom of the dialog box, click the word that you want to remove from AutoCorrect.**

   Word highlights the entire row.

3. **Click Delete.**

4. **Click OK.**

If you want to turn off AutoCorrect so it doesn't annoy you as you write, follow these steps:

1. **Choose Tools⇨AutoCorrect.**

   The AutoCorrect dialog box appears.

2. **Click the AutoCorrect tab.**

3. **Click all the check boxes that currently have check marks. (The check boxes should appear empty when you're done.)**

4. **Click OK.**

Using Find and Replace

To find a certain word or phrase in your document, you can scroll through and examine the document line by line yourself, or you can do it the easy way and let Word find the word or phrase for you.

The Find and Replace feature can also come in handy when you want to replace certain words or phrases but don't feel like doing it yourself. For example, you may have a prenuptial agreement with the name *Frank* written everywhere. If you want to find all references to *Frank* and replace them with *Bob,* the Find and Replace feature can do it for you faster and more accurately than a high-priced lawyer (who probably uses the Find and Replace feature anyway).

Using the Find feature

To find a word or phrase, follow these steps:

1. **Choose Edit⇨Find or press Ctrl+F.**

   The Find and Replace dialog box appears, as shown in Figure 5-6.

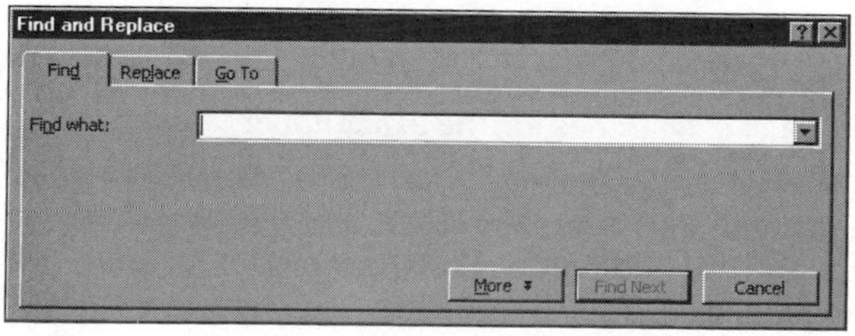

Figure 5-6:
The Find and Replace dialog box.

Find and Replace	? ×
Find Replace Go To	
Find what:	▼
	More ▼ Find Next Cancel

TIP

2. **Type the word or phrase that you want to find within your document in the Find What box.**

   If you're repeating a previous search, click the down arrow next to the Find What box to display a list of your last four searches.

3. **Click More to customize your search, or skip to Step 8 if you want to start your search right away.**

   The Find and Replace dialog box magically grows larger, as shown in Figure 5-7.

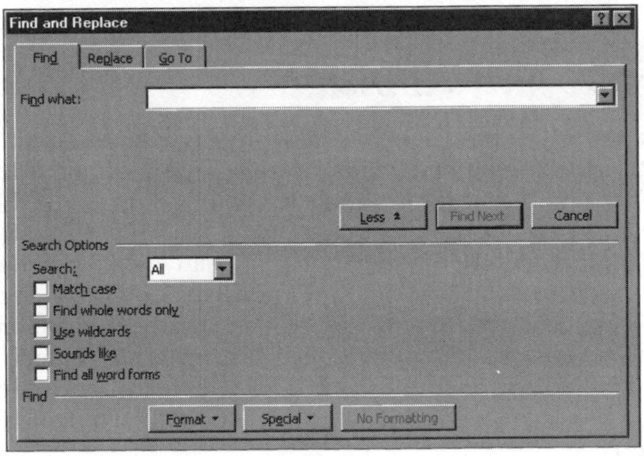

Figure 5-7:
The Larger
version of
the same
Find and
Replace
dialog box.

4. **Click the Search list box if you want to limit what part of the document Word checks. Choose from the following:**

   - **All:** Searches the entire document

   - **Down:** Searches from the current location of the cursor to the end of the document

   - **Up:** Searches from the current location of the cursor to the beginning of the document

5. **If you want to limit your search to specific criteria, check the appropriate check boxes:**

   - **Match Case:** Searches for the exact upper- and lowercase word or phrase that you type in the Find What box

   - **Find Whole Words Only:** Searches for complete words and doesn't flag words that contain the text you're searching for (for example, searching for *Ann* won't bring up *Anniversary*)

   - **Use Wildcards:** Lets you use wildcards in your search (such as *te to find all words that end with *te*)

- **Sounds Like:** Searches for words phonetically

- **Find All Word Forms:** Searches for different forms of a word (a search for *sing* would bring up *sang,* for example)

6. **Click Format if you want to search for words in a specified Font, Paragraph, Language, or Style.**

7. **Click Special if you want to search for particular punctuation marks or section breaks.**

8. **Start the search by clicking Find Next.**

9. **After reaching the first selection, click the Cancel button if you want to close the Find and Replace dialog box and work on your document. Or click Find Next again to search for the next occurrence of the object of your search.**

Using the Find and Replace feature

To find a word or phrase and replace it with another word or phrase, follow these steps:

1. **Choose Edit⇨Replace or press Ctrl+H.**

   The Find and Replace dialog box appears, as shown in Figure 5-8.

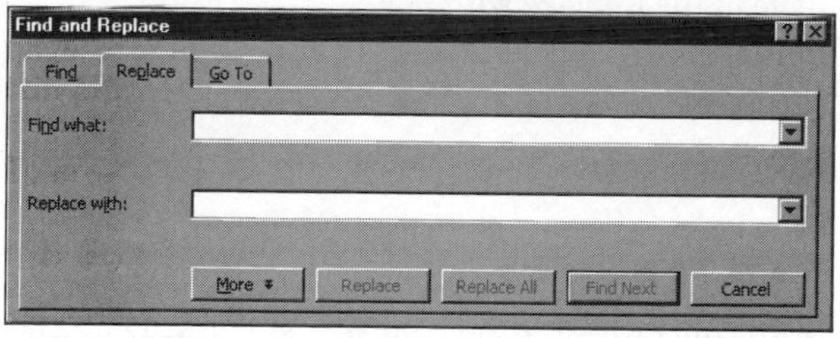

Figure 5-8:
The Find and Replace dialog box with the Replace tab selected.

2. **Type the word or phrase that you want to find within your document in the Find What box.**

3. **In the Replace With box, type the word or phrase that you want to use for replacing the Find What text.**

4. **Click More to customize your find and replace, or skip to Step 5 if you want to start finding and replacing text right away.**

   A larger version of the Find and Replace dialog box appears, as shown in Figure 5-9.

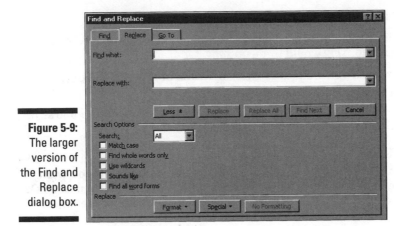

Figure 5-9:
The larger
version of
the Find and
Replace
dialog box.

For a description of all the options you have for narrowing your find and replace, refer to Steps 4 through 7 in the preceding section, "Using the Find feature."

5. **Start the search and replace by clicking Find Next.**

6. **When Word locates the desired word or phrase, choose one of the following options:**

   • To do nothing and continue searching, click **Find Next.**

   • Click **Replace** if you want Word to replace the found text with what you have in the Replace with box.

   • Click **Replace All** to replace every occurrence of the selected text with the replacement text. (This is known as trust.)

   • If you want to quit the search, click **Cancel**.

Be careful when choosing the Replace All command. To prevent Word from replacing words buried inside of other words (such as replacing the letters *can* inside the word *cannon*), click the Find Whole Words Only check box to put a check mark in it.

Chapter 6

Making Your Words Look Pretty

Words alone don't always sway an audience. Besides writing clearly (something you rarely see in most computer manuals), you also have to format your writing so that people want to look at it. The better-looking your document, the more likely that someone will take the time to read it.

Word gives you two ways to format text: by hand or by using something called a *style template* (explained later in this chapter, so don't worry about the exact meaning for now). Formatting text by hand takes longer but gives you more control. Formatting text using a style template is faster but may not format the text exactly the way you want, which means you still have to go back and format the text slightly on your own.

So which method should you use? Both. If you're in a hurry, use a style template. If you just need to do a little formatting, do it yourself.

Formatting Text Manually

To modify the appearance of your text, you can change one of the following options: the font and font sizes, the type *styles* (bold, italics, underline, and so on), and the color of the text.

Picking a font and font size

Your computer probably comes with a variety of fonts that you don't even know exist. Basically, a *font* defines the appearance of individual letters.

Depending on which fonts your computer has, you can make your text look like it was printed in a newspaper or written with a feather quill. Some examples of different fonts are:

- ✔ Times New Roman
- ✔ Courier
- ✔ Arial

When you click the Font list box on the Formatting toolbar, Word conveniently displays a list of all available fonts along with showing you what they look like, as Figure 6-1 shows.

Figure 6-1:
The Font list box shows you what all the different fonts installed on your computer look like.

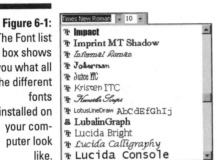

The font size makes your text bigger or smaller, regardless of the type of font you choose. Some fonts look better large, some fonts look pretty good small, and some fonts look horrible no matter what font size you choose.

If you're not sure whether or how to change the font or font size of your text, experiment with a few font and font size combinations to see whether they improve the readability of your text. To change the font and font size of text:

1. **Highlight the text that you want to modify.**

   If you need help highlighting text, see Chapter 5 and review the section on selecting text.

2. **Click the Font list box on the Formatting toolbar and choose a font.**

   Depending on how your toolbars look, you may have to click the double downward-pointing arrows on the Formatting toolbar to display the Font list box.

3. **Click the Font Size list box on the Formatting toolbar and choose a font size.**

   Word displays the selected text in your chosen font and font size.

If you choose a font and font size without selecting any text first, Word automatically uses your chosen font and font size on whatever text you type next.

Choosing a type style

Just to give you a little extra control over your text, Word also lets you display text as bold, italicized, or underlined, regardless of the font or font size you choose.

✔ **This sentence appears in bold.**

✔ *This sentence appears in italics.*

✔ This sentence is underlined.

✔ **This sentence shows that you can combine styles — bold and underlined *with italics*, for example.**

To change the type style of text, follow these steps:

1. **Highlight the text that you want to modify.**

2. **Choose one or more of the following, depending on how you want your text to look:**

   • Click the Bold icon on the Formatting toolbar or press Ctrl+B.

   • Click the Italic icon on the Formatting toolbar or press Ctrl+I.

   • Click the Underline icon on the Formatting toolbar or press Ctrl+U.

   Word displays the selected text in your chosen style.

If you choose a type style without selecting any text, Word automatically uses your chosen styles, such as italic or underline, on whatever text you type next.

Making a splash with color

Since the cost of color printers is falling as rapidly as the net worth of the United States government, you may want to experiment with using different colors to display text. (By the way, adding color doesn't have to be just an aesthetic choice. Color is very useful when you want to highlight portions of text or strain the eyes of the people forced to read your document.)

Depending on how your toolbars look, you may have to click the double downward-pointing arrows on the Formatting toolbar to display the Highlight and Font Color buttons shown in Figure 6-2.

Highlight Color button

Font Color button

Figure 6-2:
The
Highlight
Color and
Font Color
buttons.

To change the color of your text:

1. **Highlight the text that you want to modify.**

2. **Click the downward-pointing arrow to the right of the Highlight button on the Formatting toolbar.**

   A palette of different colors appears (refer to Figure 6-2).

3. **Click the color that you want to use on the background.**

   Word magically changes the background color of your text.

4. **Click the downward-pointing arrow to the right of the Font Color button on the Formatting toolbar.**

   A palette of different colors appears.

5. **Click the color that you want to use on the text.**

   Word changes the color of your text.

Painting text with the Format Painter

Suppose you have a chunk of text formatted perfectly — font, font size, type style, and so on. Do you have to go through the whole laborious process again to make another chunk of text look exactly the same? Of course not! Use the Format Painter.

The Format Painter tells Word, "See the way you formatted that block of text I just highlighted? I want you to use that same formatting on this other chunk of text."

By using the Format Painter, you don't have to format the individual characteristics of text yourself, saving you time so you can do something that's more important to you (like making plans for lunch or printing up your resume).

To use the Format Painter, follow these steps:

1. **Highlight the text containing the formatting that you want to use on another chunk of text.**

2. **Click the Format Painter button (it looks like a paintbrush and appears to the right of the Paste icon) on the Formatting toolbar.**

   The mouse cursor turns into an I-beam cursor with a paintbrush to the left. The paintbrush lets you know that Word automatically formats the next chunk of text that you select.

3. **Select the text that you want to format.**

   As soon as you release the left mouse button, Word formats the text with all the formatting characteristics of the text you selected in Step 1.

If the text that you select in Step 1 contains a variety of formatting characteristics, Word copies only the formatting characteristics that the entire chunk of selected text has in common. For example, if you select text that's in Times New Roman font with one sentence underlined, a second sentence in bold, and a third sentence with a yellow background, Word formats your new text with the only shared formatting characteristic — the Times New Roman font.

Aligning text to the right and the left

Word lets you choose an alignment for your text, which can be left, center, right, or justified, as shown in Figure 6-3. Most of the time you probably want to left-align text, but occasionally you may want to center a heading in the middle of the page or justify an entire paragraph. Don't worry too much about right-aligning text unless you like displaying your text in strange ways.

  ✓ **Left-align text:** The left margin is a straight line, and the right margin is uneven.

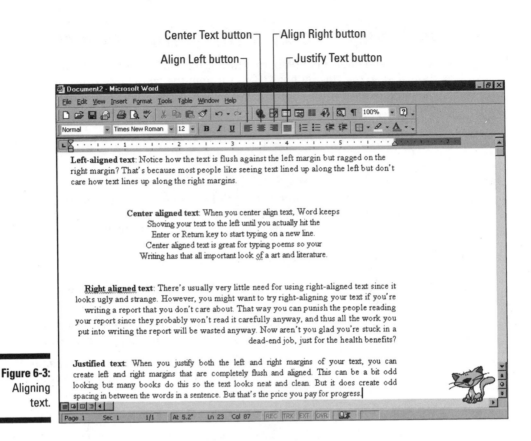

Figure 6-3:
Aligning
text.

✔ **Center text:** Each line is centered in the middle of the page. Consequently, both the left and right margins look ragged when you have several lines of unequal length centered.

✔ **Right-align text:** The right margin is a straight line, and the left margin is uneven.

✔ **Justify text:** Both the left and right margins are straight, and the letters in between look somewhat spaced apart.

To align text:

1. **Click anywhere inside the paragraph that you want to align.**

2. **Click the Align Left, Center, Align Right, or Justify button on the Formatting toolbar, depending on how you want the text to look.**

   As soon as you click a button, Word aligns your text.

If you choose an alignment without selecting any text first, Word applies your chosen alignment to whatever text you type next.

Formatting Your Document the Easy Way

If you really love using Word, you can format your text by using all the program's arcane commands. However, Word provides three shortcuts for changing the appearance of your documents:

- ✔ **Themes:** Define the color and graphical appearance of bullets, text, horizontal lines, and the background of a document

- ✔ **Style templates:** Provide one or more styles for creating common types of documents such as resumes, business letters, or fax cover pages

- ✔ **Styles:** Define the format for a paragraph using specific margins, font sizes, or underlining

Choosing a theme

A *theme* lets you choose the decorative appearance of your document. If you don't choose a theme, your text appears in boring black and white. Themes are mostly to make your document look pretty. If you don't care about appearances, you probably don't need to use themes.

To choose a theme, follow these steps:

1. **Choose Format⇨Theme.**

   The Theme dialog box appears, as shown in Figure 6-4.

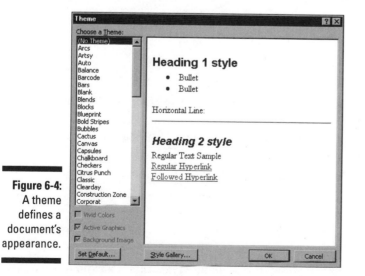

Figure 6-4: A theme defines a document's appearance.

2. **Click the theme you want to use in the Choose a Theme list.**

   Each time you click a theme, Word politely shows you a sample of how that theme can change the appearance of your document.

3. **Choose or clear one or more of the following check boxes:**

   - **Vivid Colors:** Adds (or removes) additional colors to text
   - **Active Graphics:** Adds (or removes) additional graphics to make bullets and horizontal lines look more interesting
   - **Background Image:** Adds (or removes) the background graphic

4. **Click OK after you find and define a theme to use.**

Choosing a style template

A *style template* provides formatting for common types of documents (faxes, reports, proposals, memos, and so on). So if you need to write a fax cover sheet or a business letter, you could write the whole thing from scratch and waste a lot of time in the process.

Or, you can use a special fax or business letter template that provides the formatting (styles) for creating a fax or business letter. Then all you have to do is type in the text and let Word worry about the formatting.

To choose a style template, follow these steps:

1. **Choose Format➪Theme.**

   The Theme dialog box appears (refer to Figure 6-4), showing you the theme used in your current document.

2. **Click the Style Gallery button.**

   The Style Gallery dialog box appears, as shown in Figure 6-5.

3. **Click one of the style templates listed in the Template box, such as Elegant Fax or Contemporary Report.**

   You can scroll up or down the list under the Template box to see more style templates.

4. **Click one of the following option buttons in the Preview group:**

   - **Document:** Shows what your current document looks like with the selected style template
   - **Example:** Shows how a typical document can look with the selected style template (refer to Figure 6-5)
   - **Style samples:** Shows the different styles that make up the style template

5. **Click OK after you find a style template that you want to use.**

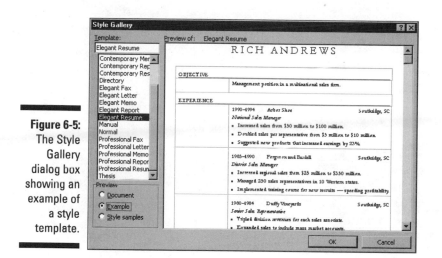

Choosing a style

Styles define the overall appearance of the text in your document. To help you organize and choose different styles, Word provides *style templates,* (such as Elegant Fax) which contain one or more pre-defined styles that you can use to format your text. For example, one style might make your text appear bold, big, and centered at the top of the page while another style pushes your text to the right margin and displays a gray background behind it, and so on.

Word provides two ways to choose a style:

- ✔ Through the Style list box on the Formatting toolbar
- ✔ Through the Style dialog box

Using the Style list box

To choose a style through the Style list box on the Formatting toolbar:

1. **Click in the paragraph text that you want to format with a particular style.**

   If you haven't typed any text yet, Word applies the style to whatever text you type in Step 4.

2. **Click the Style list box on the Formatting toolbar to choose a style.**

   A list of different styles appears, as shown in Figure 6-6. (Depending on how your toolbars look, you may have to click the double downward-pointing arrows on the Formatting toolbar to display the Style list box.)

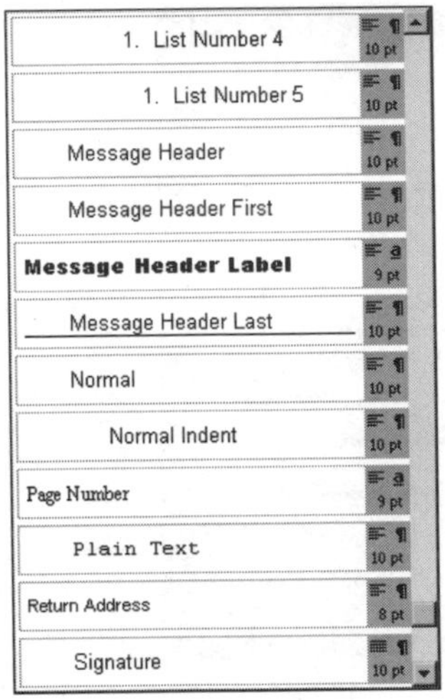

Figure 6-6:
Pick a
style from
the Style
list box.

3. **Click the style that you want to use.**

4. **Type your text and watch Word format it before your eyes. (Or Word formats your text right away, if you moved the cursor to an existing block of text in Step 1.)**

Using the Style dialog box

Because Microsoft likes to give you several different ways to accomplish the same task (thereby increasing the chance for you to get confused even more), you can try another way of choosing a style for your text. You may like using the Style dialog box because you get a preview of what your text will look like before you choose a particular style.

To choose a style using the Style dialog box:

1. **Click in the paragraph text that you want to format with a particular style.**

   If you haven't typed any text yet, Word applies the style to whatever text you type in Step 4.

2. **Choose Format➪Style.**

   A Style dialog box appears, as shown in Figure 6-7.

3. **Click the style that you want to use.**

4. **Click Apply.**

5. **Type your text and watch Word format it before your eyes. (Or Word formats your text right away, if you moved the cursor to an existing block of text in Step 1.)**

   Figure 6-8 shows a typical document that uses different styles.

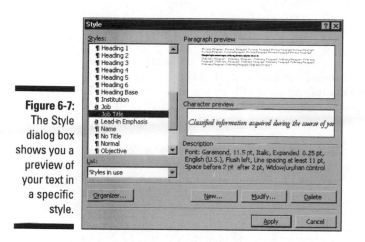

Figure 6-7:
The Style
dialog box
shows you a
preview of
your text in
a specific
style.

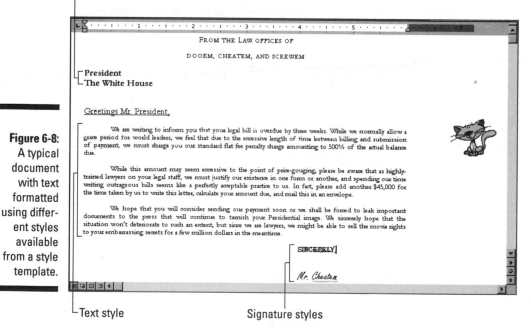

Heading style

Text style   Signature styles

Figure 6-8:
A typical
document
with text
formatted
using differ-
ent styles
available
from a style
template.

Making Lists

Some people like making lists of things so they know what they're supposed to do, what they're supposed to buy, and what they really don't feel like doing but feel guilty enough about that they try to do it anyway. To help accommodate list makers all over the world, Word creates lists quickly and easily.

Word lets you make two types of lists: numbered and bulleted. As their names suggest, a numbered list displays each item with a number in front, while a bulleted list displays a bullet in front of each item, as shown in Figure 6-9.

You can left-align, right-align, center, or justify any of your bulleted or numbered lists. Aren't computers an exciting example of how technology can empower the average user?

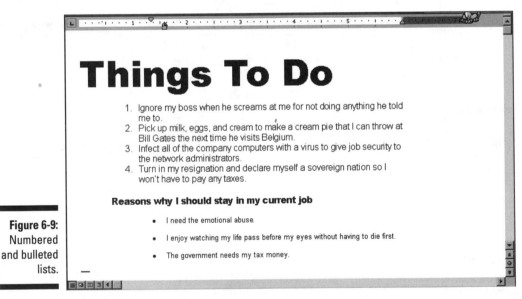

Figure 6-9: Numbered and bulleted lists.

To create a numbered or bulleted list:

1. **Select the text that you want to turn into a list.**

2. **Choose Format⇨Bullets and Numbering.**

   The Bullets and Numbering dialog box appears, as shown in Figure 6-10.

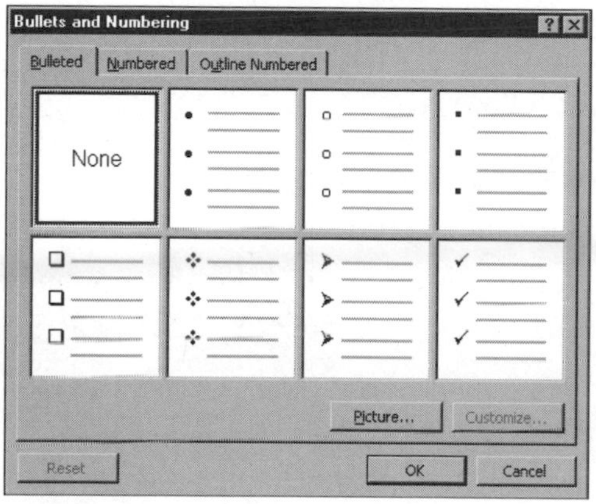

Figure 6-10:
The Bullets
and
Numbering
dialog box.

3. Click the Bulleted tab to create a bulleted list or the Numbered tab to create a numbered list.

You see two rows of boxes that show the various numbering or bullet styles.

4. Click inside the box that shows the type of bullets or numbering that you want to use; then click OK.

Word automatically converts your selected text into a list.

If you choose a numbering or bullet option without first selecting text, Word automatically formats whatever you type next into the type of list you chose.

If you don't care about the style of bullets or numbering that Word uses, just click the Numbering or Bullets button on the Formatting toolbar and then start typing your text. Word applies its default numbering (using numbers such as 1 and 2) or bullet style (displaying a simple black dot) to your text as you type.

Aligning Text with Tables

Tables let you organize information in rows and columns, which can be useful for displaying information in an easy-to-read format. With a table you can organize essential text so people can find and read it easily, rather than trying to find important information buried inside a paragraph.

Before you get started with tables, you need to know some things about rows and columns, including the following:

✔ A *row* displays information horizontally.

✔ A *column* displays information vertically.

✔ A *cell* is a single box formed by the intersection of a row and a column.

Making a table

You may be happy to know that Word provides three different ways to make a table in your documents:

✔ Draw the table in your document with the mouse

✔ Define the size of a table by typing in the exact number of rows and columns

✔ Define the size of a table with the mouse and pull-down menus

Drawing a table with the mouse

If you want to create tables right away, you can draw the table's approximate size using the mouse. You can modify its height and width later. To create a table using the mouse:

1. **Choose Table⇨Draw Table.**

   A Tables and Borders window appears, and the mouse pointer turns into a pencil icon.

2. **Move the mouse where you want the table to appear.**

3. **Hold down the left mouse button and drag the mouse to draw the table as shown in Figure 6-11.**

Figure 6-11:
Drawing
a table.

4. **Release the left mouse button.**

   Word displays your table as a solid line. Notice the mouse pointer appears as a pencil icon.

5. **Drag the mouse inside the table where you want to draw a row or column. You can draw a dotted line vertically, horizontally, or diagonally to define your cells.**

   Word draws a dotted line, as shown in Figure 6-12. Repeat this step as many times as necessary.

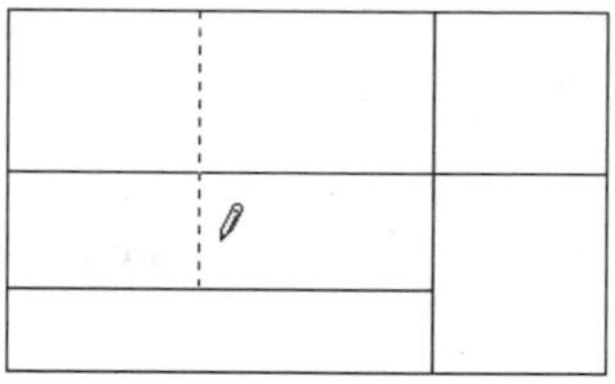

Figure 6-12: Drawing rows and columns in a table.

6. **Press Esc when you're done drawing your rows and columns.**

   The mouse cursor changes from a pencil icon back to an I-shaped icon. At this point you can click inside a cell and type text in your newly created table.

7. **Click the close box of the Tables and Borders window to make it go away.**

Defining a table from the Table menu

If you want to create tables the slower way, which gives you more control over your table's appearance, use the Word drop-down menus:

1. **Choose Table➪Insert➪Table.**

   The Insert Table dialog box appears, as shown in Figure 6-13.

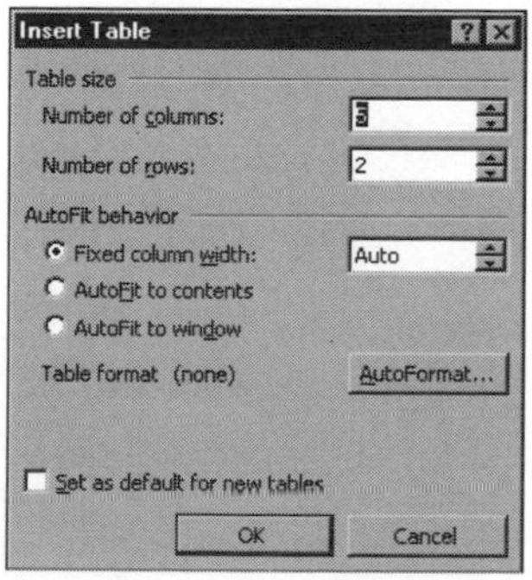

Figure 6-13: The Insert Table dialog box.

2. **In the Number of Columns box, type the number of columns you want.**

3. **In the Number of Rows box, type the number of rows you want.**

4. **In the AutoFit Behavior menu, click one of the following option buttons:**

    • **Fixed Column Width:** You can choose Auto to force Word to make column widths the size of the longest item stored in the entire table, or you can define a specific value, such as 0.5 inches.

    • **AutoFit to Contents:** Adjusts column widths depending on the longest item in each column.

    • **AutoFit to Window:** Adjusts the table based on the size of the window used to display the table.

5. **Click AutoFormat.**

    The Table AutoFormat dialog box appears, as shown in Figure 6-14.

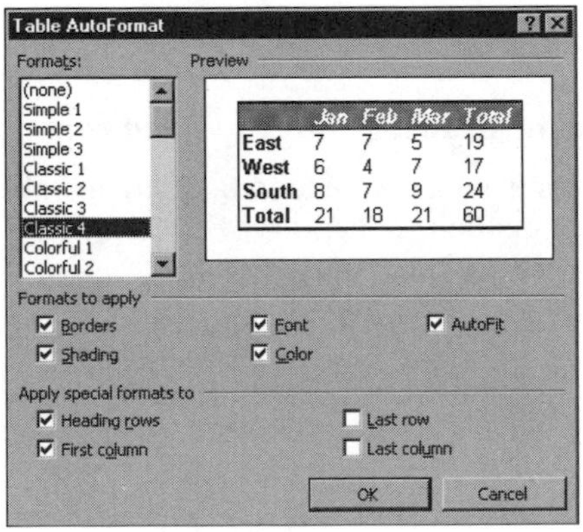

Figure 6-14:
The Table
AutoFormat
dialog box.

6. **Click one of the table formats (such as Classic 3 or Simple 1) in the Formats list and try out the various formatting options available in the dialog box.**

    The Preview window shows a sample of the selected table format. When you click any check boxes in the Formats to Apply group and the Apply Special Formats To group, the Preview window shows how these options affect the selected table format's appearance.

7. **After you select your table format preference and any optional formatting options, click OK.**

    The Insert Table dialog box appears again (refer to Figure 6-13).

8. **Click OK.**

Making a table from the Insert Table button

In the name of freedom and confusion, you can also make a table by clicking the Insert Table button on the Standard toolbar. This method works faster but doesn't give you as many options for defining how you want your table to look.

To create a table by clicking the Insert Table button:

1. **Click the Insert Table button on the Standard toolbar.**

   A table appears underneath the button, as shown in Figure 6-15.

2. **With the mouse pointer on the top-left square of the table, drag the mouse down and to the right to select the number of rows and columns you want your table to have.**

3. **Release the left mouse button.**

   Word draws a table in your document.

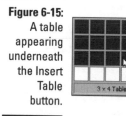

Figure 6-15:
A table appearing underneath the Insert Table button.

3 x 4 Table

Changing the size of your tables

In case you made your table too large or too small, you can always resize the whole thing by following these steps:

1. **Choose View⇨Print Layout or click the Print Layout View button in the bottom left-hand corner of the screen.**

2. **Move the mouse pointer over the table you want to resize.**

   The moment you move the mouse pointer inside the table, Word displays the Move handle (on the upper left-hand corner) and the Resize handle (in the bottom right-hand corner) of the table as shown in Figure 6-16.

Figure 6-16:
The Move
and Resize
handles
magically
appear
when you're
in the Print
Layout view
and move
the mouse
pointer over
a table.

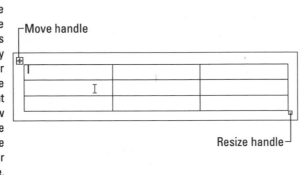

3. **Move the mouse pointer over the Resize handle.**

   The mouse pointer turns into a two-way pointing diagonal arrow.

4. **Hold down the left mouse button and drag the mouse.**

   Word draws a dotted line to show you the size of your table.

5. **Release the left mouse button when you finish resizing the table.**

Moving a table

You may want to move your table in a document. To do this:

1. **Choose View⇨Print Layout or click the Print Layout View button in the bottom left-hand corner of the screen.**

2. **Move the mouse pointer over the table you want to move.**

   The moment you move the mouse pointer inside the table, Word displays the Move handle (on the upper left-hand corner) and the Resize Handle (in the bottom right-hand corner) of the table (refer to Figure 6-16).

3. **Move the mouse pointer over the Move handle.**

   The mouse pointer turns into a four-way pointing arrow.

4. **Hold down the left mouse button and drag the mouse.**

   Word draws a dotted line to show you the location of your table.

5. **Release the left mouse button when the dotted line is where you want to move the table.**

Entering and editing table data

A blank table is pretty useless, so you may want to add data inside the tables you create. To enter and edit data, just click the desired cell and use the regular keyboard keys to type or edit. You can also use the following methods to move around within the table:

- Press the Tab key to move the cursor to the next cell to the right in the same row.
- Press Shift+Tab to move backward (to the left) in the row.
- Use the ↑ and ↓ keys to move from row to row.

Deleting tables

Word gives you two ways to delete a table:

- Delete the entire table, including the contents of the table.
- Delete just the contents of the table (leave the blank cells and formatting intact).

To delete only the contents of the table but not the table itself:

1. **Click the mouse anywhere inside the table.**
2. **Choose Table⇨Select⇨Table.**

   Word highlights your chosen table.
3. **Press Delete.**

To delete the contents of the table and the table itself:

1. **Click the mouse anywhere inside the table.**
2. **Choose Table⇨Delete⇨Table.**

   Word deletes your chosen table.

Converting a table into text

Rather than completely obliterating a table, Word gives you the option of getting rid of a table but keeping the text inside.

To convert a table into text:

1. **Click the mouse anywhere inside the table that you want to delete.**

2. **Choose Table➪Convert➪Table to Text.**

   The Convert Table to Text dialog box appears as shown in Figure 6-17.

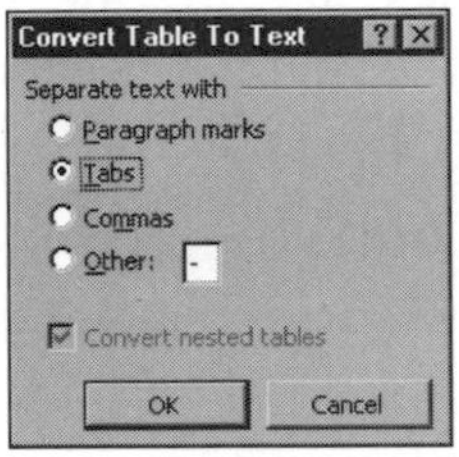

Figure 6-17:
The Convert
Table to Text
dialog box.

3. **Choose how you want Word to separate text (by Paragraphs, Tabs, Commas, or Other) and click OK.**

   Your table disappears but leaves its text behind.

Turning text into a table

If you have a bunch of text, you can have Word convert it into a table. To convert text into a table:

1. **Highlight the text that you want to turn into a table.**

2. **Choose Table➪Convert➪Text to Table.**

   The Convert Text to Table dialog box appears as shown in Figure 6-18.

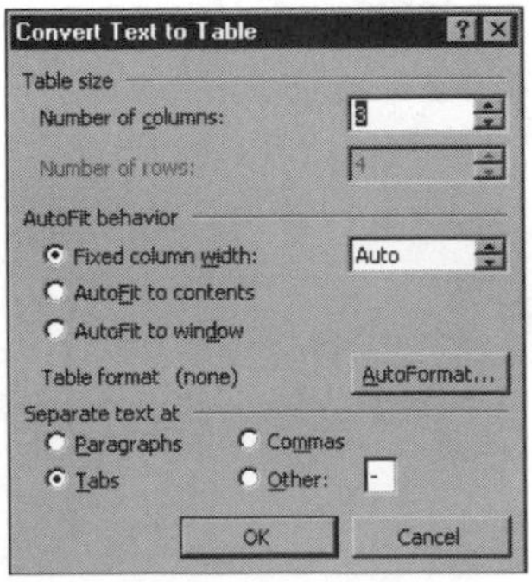

Figure 6-18:
The Convert
Text to Table
dialog box.

3. **In the AutoFit Behavior menu, click one of the following option buttons:**

   - **Fixed Column Width:** You can choose Auto to force Word to make column widths the size of the longest item stored in the entire table, or you can define a specific value yourself, such as 0.5 inches.

   - **AutoFit to Contents:** Adjusts column widths depending on the longest item in each column.

   - **AutoFit to Window:** Adjusts the table based on the size of the window used to display the table.

4. **Click AutoFormat.**

   The Table AutoFormat dialog box appears (refer to Figure 6-14).

5. **Click one of the table formats (such as Classic 3 or Simple 1) in the Formats list and try out the various formatting options available in the dialog box.**

   The Preview window shows a sample of the selected table format. When you click any check boxes in the Formats to Apply group and the Apply Special Formats To group, the Preview window shows how these options affect the selected table format's appearance.

6. **After you select your table format preference and any optional formatting options, click OK.**

   The Convert Text to Table dialog box appears again (refer to Figure 6-18).

7. **Click the option button to tell Word how to separate text (by Paragraphs, Tabs, Commas, or Other) and click OK.**

   Word converts your chosen text into a table.

Adding or deleting rows, columns, and cells, oh my!

After you create a table, you may want to make it bigger or smaller by adding or deleting rows and columns. To delete a row or column:

1. **Put the cursor in the row or column that you want to delete.**

   You can either use the keyboard cursor keys or click the table.

2. **Choose Table⇨Select⇨Column (or Row).**

   Word highlights your chosen row or column.

3. **Choose Table⇨Delete⇨Columns (or Rows).**

To delete a single cell (which may make your table look funny):

1. **Put the cursor in the cell that you want to delete.**

   You can either use the keyboard cursor keys or click in the cell.

2. **Choose Table⇨Delete⇨Cells.**

   A Delete Cells dialog box appears.

3. **Click an option button (such as Shift Cells Left) and click OK.**

To add a row or column:

1. **Put the cursor in any row or column.**

2. **Choose Table⇨Insert ⇨Columns to the Left (or Columns to the Right or Rows Above or Rows Below).**

To add a single cell:

1. **Put the cursor in the table where you want to add a cell.**

2. **Choose Table⇨Insert⇨Cells.**

   An Insert Cells dialog box appears.

3. **Click an option button (such as Shift Cells Right) and click OK.**

Changing the dimensions of a table's columns and rows

Normally, Word displays all columns with the same width and all rows with the same height. However, if you want some rows or columns to be a different size, Word gives you two options for changing them:

- ✔ Use the mouse to visually change the height or width of rows and columns
- ✔ Define exact dimensions for the height or width of rows and columns

Visually changing the height of a row

To change the row height of a table visually:

1. **Choose View⇨Print Layout or click the Print Layout View button in the bottom left-hand corner of the screen.**

   Word displays a vertical ruler on the left side of the screen and a horizontal ruler at the top of the screen.

2. **Place the mouse cursor over one of the Adjust Table Row (gray) markers on the vertical ruler, as shown in Figure 6-19.**

3. **Hold down the left mouse button and drag the mouse up or down.**

   Word displays a dotted line to show you what the height of your chosen row will be when you release the mouse button.

4. **Release the left mouse button when you're happy with the height of your row.**

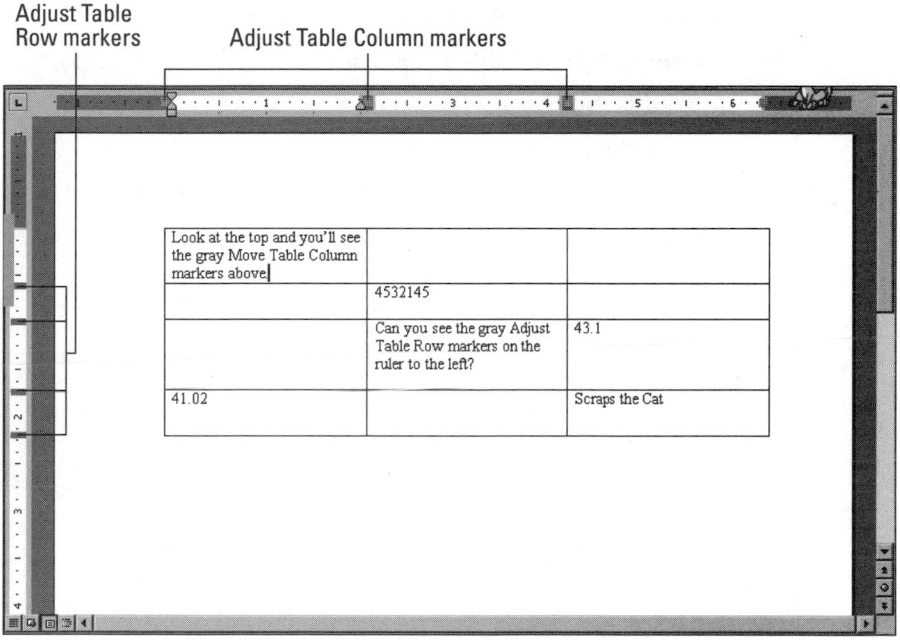

Adjust Table
Row markers   Adjust Table Column markers

Look at the top and you'll see the gray Move Table Column markers above		
	4532145	
	Can you see the gray Adjust Table Row markers on the ruler to the left?	43.1
41.02		Scraps the Cat

Figure 6-19:
Use the
vertical
ruler (on
the left) to
adjust the
height of
a row.

Visually changing the width of a column

To change the column width of a table visually:

1. **Choose View⇨Print Layout or click the Print Layout View button in the bottom left-hand corner of the screen.**

   Word displays a vertical ruler on the left side of the screen and a horizontal ruler at the top of the screen.

2. **Move the mouse cursor over one of the Move Table Column markers (square gray markers) in the horizontal ruler (refer to Figure 6-19).**

   When the mouse cursor appears directly over a Move Table Column marker, the cursor turns into a two-headed arrow.

3. **Hold down the left mouse button and drag the mouse right or left.**

   Word displays a dotted line to show you what the width of your chosen column will be after you release the mouse button.

4. **Release the left mouse button when you're happy with the width of your column.**

Defining exact dimensions for the height of a row

To tell Word to use exact dimensions for the height of a row:

1. **Click in the row that you want to adjust.**

2. **Choose Table⇨Table Properties.**

   A Table Properties dialog box appears.

3. **Click the Row tab.**

   The Row tab appears in the Table Properties dialog box.

4. **Click in the Specify Height box and click the up or down arrows to choose a height (such as 0.74 inches).**

5. **Click in the Row Height Is box and choose At least or Exactly.**

   If you choose the At Least option for the Row Height, your rows will never be smaller than the dimensions you specify, but may be larger, depending on the amount of text you type in it. If you want rows to remain a fixed height, choose the Exactly option instead.

6. **Click OK.**

Defining exact dimensions for the width of a column

To give exact dimensions to define a column width:

1. **Click in the column that you want to adjust.**

2. **Choose Table⇨Table Properties.**

   A Table Properties dialog box appears.

3. **Click the Column tab.**

   The Column tab appears in the Table Properties dialog box.

4. **Click in the Preferred Width box and click the up or down arrows to choose a width (such as 2.15 inches).**

5. **Click in the Measure In box and choose Inches or Percent.**

   If you choose to measure your column width in inches, you can specify an exact size for your columns. If you don't care to be that specific but just want your columns to look okay no matter whether you resize the table, choose the Percent option instead.

6. **Click OK.**

Chapter 7

Creating Fancy Newsletters and Web Pages

*Y*ou can use Word 2000 to write letters, reports, or threatening notes to people you don't like. With a little bit of creativity and a lot of patience, you can also use Word to format and publish those letters, reports, and notes. By using Word's limited desktop publishing features, you can make simple newsletters, brochures, and flyers without using a separate desktop publishing program (like Microsoft Publisher).

In addition, all the Microsoft Office 2000 programs, including Word, have the ability to save any document (an Excel worksheet, a PowerPoint presentation, an Access database, and so on) as a HyperText Markup Language (HTML) file, suitable for displaying on the World Wide Web. Although using a dedicated Web page editing program (such as Microsoft FrontPage) may offer more flexibility, using Word to create or edit Web pages can be much faster and easier, especially if you already know how to use Word.

Playing with Footers and Headers

Headers and footers are chunks of text that appear at the tops and bottoms of your pages. *Headers* appear at the top of the page (think of where your head appears in relation to your body), while *footers* appear at the bottom (think of where your feet appear).

Both headers and footers can appear on each page of a document and contain information, such as the publication title, the section or chapter title, the page number, and/or the author's name. If you look at the odd-numbered pages in this book, you can see that the chapter number, chapter title, and page number appear at the top of the page as a header. Headers and footers are useful for displaying identical or nearly identical text on two or more pages, such as document titles or page references (such as Page 4 of 89). Although you can type this same text over and over again on each page, letting Word do the work for you is much easier.

You have two ways to view a document's headers and footers:

- Choose View⇨Header and Footer
- Choose View⇨Print Layout (or click the Print Layout View button on the bottom left-hand corner of the screen)

If you switch to Print Layout View, you can see how your headers and footers will look on each page but you won't be able to edit them.

Adding headers and footers

To add a header or footer:

1. **Choose View⇨Header and Footer.**

   Word displays the Header and Footer toolbar along with a Header (or Footer) text box where you can type a header (or footer), as shown in Figure 7-1.

2. **Type your header (or footer) text in the Header (or Footer) text box and/or click a toolbar button to have Word insert the page number, number of pages, date, or time.**

   If you want to have one piece of information appear on the left end of the header, one in the center, and one on the right end, press Tab between them.

Header text box   Show Previous┐ ┌Show Next

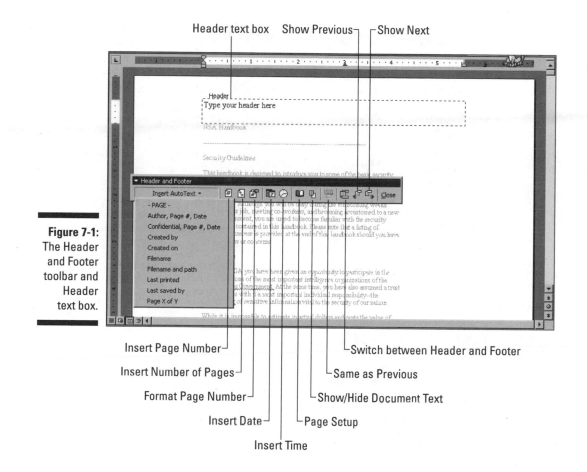

Figure 7-1:
The Header
and Footer
toolbar and
Header
text box.

Insert Page Number┘
Insert Number of Pages┘
Format Page Number┘
Insert Date┘
Insert Time

└Switch between Header and Footer
└Same as Previous
└Show/Hide Document Text
└Page Setup

If you click the Insert Page Number, Insert Number of Pages, Insert Date, or Insert Time buttons to insert the page number, date, or time in your header, Word automatically updates this information from page to page (for the page number information) or each time you open the document (for the date and time information).

You can also click Insert AutoText on the toolbar to have Word insert commonly used text for headers and footers, such as Page X of Y.

3. **Click the Switch Between Header and Footer button.**

Word displays the Footer text box.

4. **Type your text in the Footer text box and/or click a toolbar button.**

Refer to Step 2 for directions.

5. **Click Close on the Header and Footer toolbar to dismiss the toolbar.**

Modifying page numbering

When you tell Word to include page numbers in your headers or footers, Word starts numbering from page one and displays Arabic numbers like 1, 3, and 49. If you want to number your pages differently (such as numbering them as i, ii, iii, or a, b, c), or to tell Word to make the first page number 97, you have to use the Page Number Format button on the Header and Footer toolbar. To use the Page Number Format button:

1. **Choose View➪Header and Footer.**

2. **Highlight the page numbers in your header or footer.**

   The page number appears shaded gray.

3. **Click the Format Page Number button on the Header and Footer toolbar.**

   The Page Number Format dialog box appears, as shown in Figure 7-2.

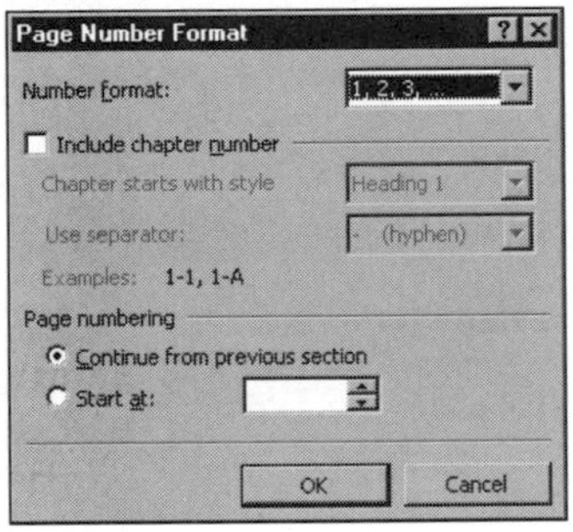

Figure 7-2:
You can change the way Word displays page numbers with the Page Number Format dialog box.

4. **Click in the Number Format list box and choose a page numbering style (such as 1, 2, 3 or i, ii, iii).**

5. **In the Page Numbering group, click one of the following option buttons:**

   • **Continue from Previous Section:** numbers pages sequentially

   • **Start At:** lets you define the starting page number other than 1

6. **Click OK.**

Setting Up Multicolumn Documents

To create a newsletter or brochure, you may need to display text in two or more columns to give it a professional look. Word lets you divide your documents into multiple columns.

Note: If you use more than four columns on a single page, none of the columns can display much text.

Making columns the fast way

To create multiple columns quickly:

1. **Choose Edit⇨Select All or press Ctrl+A.**
2. **Click the Columns button on the Standard toolbar.**

   The Column menu appears, as shown in Figure 7-3.

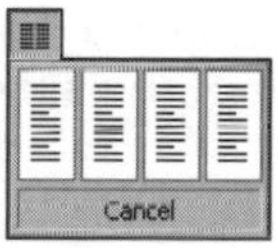

Figure 7-3:
The Column
menu
appears
below the
Column
button.

3. **Highlight the number of columns you want by dragging the mouse to the right.**

   Word immediately converts your document into a multicolumn document.

Making custom columns

To create customized columns:

1. **Choose Edit⇨Select All or press Ctrl+A.**
2. **Choose Format⇨Columns.**

   The Columns dialog box appears, as shown in Figure 7-4.

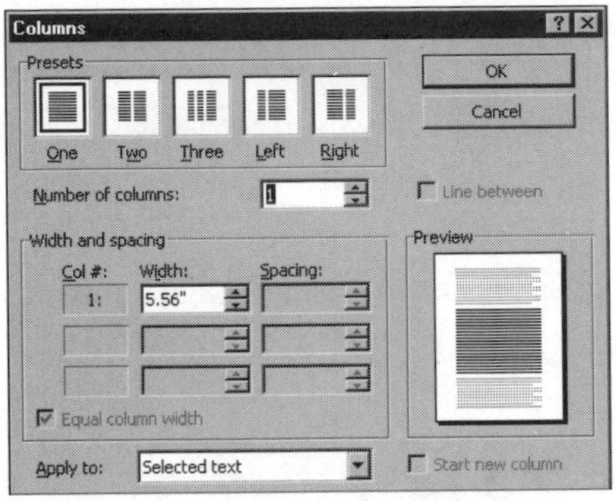

Figure 7-4:
Creating
multiple
columns
with the
Columns
dialog box.

3. **You can either click one of the column types shown in the Presets group or type a number of columns in the Number of Columns box.**

4. **Click (or clear) the Equal Column Width check box.**

   If the Equal Column Width check box is clear, you can define the width of each column individually.

5. **Click the Width box in the Width and Spacing group and click the up or down arrow to specify the exact dimension of each column width.**

6. **Click the Spacing box in the Width and Spacing group and click the up or down arrow to specify the exact dimension of the spacing between each column.**

7. **Click OK.**

   Word displays your document in multiple columns, customized to your specifications.

Putting Your Words in a Text Box

Normally, when you type in Word, the text flows from top to bottom (or if you're using columns, from one column to another). Although this setup can be convenient in most cases, sometimes you may want to use a text box instead.

Text boxes act like little containers that hold text. The advantage of text boxes is that you can move text boxes anywhere on a page — even beyond the text area (although the text in the box won't print then). You can also lock text boxes to specific locations on a page, or they can be locked to paragraphs so that they float in your document.

Many newspapers and magazines display something called a *pull-quote*, which is a little text box that displays an interesting sentence or two to entice you to read the rest of the page, such as "Alien creatures take over the White House!"

Creating a text box

To create a text box in a document:

1. **Choose Insert⇨Text Box.**

   The mouse cursor turns into a crosshair, and Word automatically switches to the Print Layout View whether you like it or not.

2. **Place the crosshair cursor on the spot in your document where you want to insert the text box; hold down the left mouse button and drag the mouse diagonally down from left to right to draw a rectangle of the desired size.**

3. **Release the left mouse button.**

   The Text Box window appears along with the text box itself (defined by a gray border), as shown in Figure 7-5.

4. **Type in the text that you want to appear in the text box.**

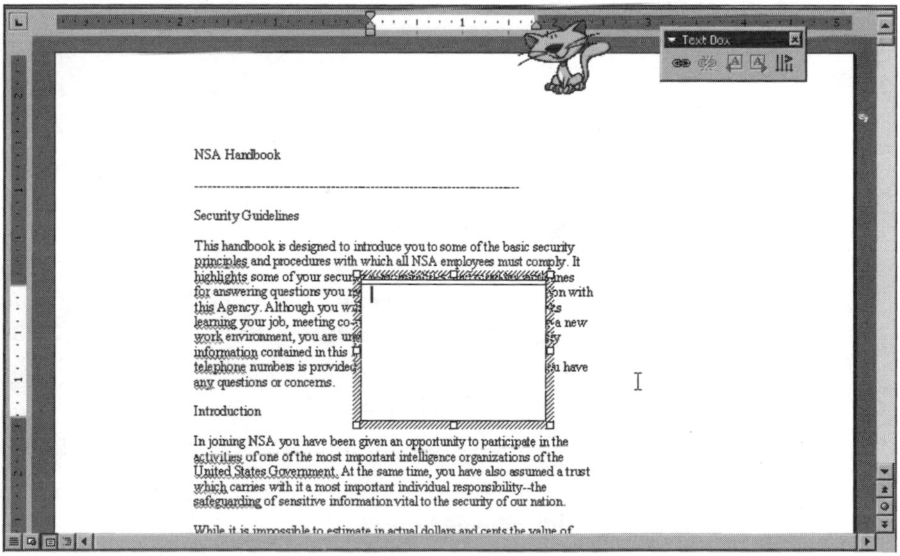

Figure 7-5: A text box plopped in the middle of a perfectly good document.

5. **Click anywhere outside the text box.**

The gray borders of the text box disappear, although you may need to turn on word wrapping (explained in the section "Wrapping words around a text box" later in this chapter).

Moving a text box

After you place a text box in a document, you can move it around your document. To move a text box:

1. **Click inside the text box that you want to move.**

The text box displays a gray border around the text.

2. **Place the mouse cursor over the gray border of the text box.**

The mouse cursor turns into a four-headed arrow. Make sure you don't click a text box *handle* (those little squares on corners and four sides of text boxes). If you move the mouse cursor over a handle, the mouse cursor turns into a double-headed arrow.

3. **Hold down the left mouse button, drag the mouse to where you want the text box to be, and release the left mouse button.**

You may have to turn on word wrapping around your text box if you haven't done so already. See the section "Wrapping words around a text box" later in this chapter.

Resizing a text box

After drawing a text box in a document, you can make it bigger, smaller, longer, or taller. To resize a text box:

1. **Click inside the text box you want to resize.**

2. **Place the mouse cursor directly over a text box handle (one of the squares that appears at the corners and in the middle of the sides of the text box).**

The mouse cursor turns into a double-headed arrow.

3. **Hold down the left mouse button and drag the mouse to resize the text box.**

4. **Release the left mouse button.**

You may have to turn on the word wrapping feature if you haven't done so already. See the next section for details.

Wrapping words around a text box

When you place a text box in a document, it covers up any text underneath. So the final step in putting a text box in a document is to define how words *wrap,* or fit, around it. To define word wrapping around a text box:

1. **Click inside the text box that you want words to wrap around.**

2. **Choose Format⇨Text Box.**

   The Format Text Box dialog box appears.

3. **Click the Layout tab.**

   The Layout tab appears, as shown in Figure 7-6.

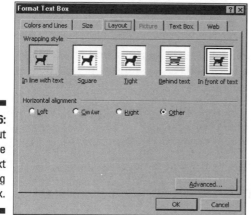

Figure 7-6:
The Layout
tab in the
Format Text
Box dialog
box.

4. **Click a picture in the Wrapping Style group, such as In Line with Text, Square, Tight, Behind Text, or In Front of Text.**

   If you choose Behind Text or In Front of Text, Word won't wrap text around your text box.

5. **Click the Advanced button if you chose Square, Top and Bottom, or In Line with Text.**

6. **Click the Text Wrapping tab.**

   The Advanced Layout dialog box appears, as shown in Figure 7-7.

7. **Click an option button in the Wrap Text group, such as Both Sides, Left Only, Right Only, or Largest Only.**

8. **Click the Top, Bottom, Left, or Right box and type the desired values to define the exact distance between the text box and the text wrapped around it.**

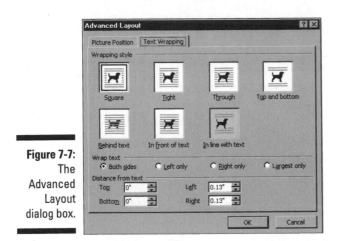

Figure 7-7:
The
Advanced
Layout
dialog box.

9. **Click OK twice.**

The Format Text Box dialog box disappears, and any text hidden underneath your text box magically wraps around your text box instead.

Deleting a text box

If you don't want a text box after all, you can delete it by following these steps:

1. **Click inside the text box you want to delete.**

Gray borders appear around the text box.

2. **Click the gray border of the text box that you want to delete.**

3. **Press Delete.**

Adding Pictures to a Document

Not only can you add text boxes to your documents, but you can add graphics as well. Word gives you the choice of using one of the following six commands when you choose Insert⇨Picture to insert graphics into a document:

✔ **Clip Art:** Lets you insert any picture from the Microsoft Office clip art gallery

✔ **From File:** Adds a picture stored in a graphic file created by another program, such as PC-Paintbrush or CorelDRAW!

✔ **AutoShapes:** Lets you choose from many shapes, such as an oval, rectangle, or star

✔ **WordArt:** Lets you type text that appears in different colors and shapes

✔ **New Drawing:** Lets you create your own drawings consisting of geometric shapes, lines, or WordArt

✔ **From Scanner or Camera:** Lets you add digital photographs

✔ **Chart:** Lets you add a business graph, such as a pie, line, or bar chart

Putting clip art into your document

Clip art consists of pictures that Microsoft paid some artist to draw for you. That way you don't have to torture yourself into learning to draw.

To add clip art to a document:

1. **Choose Insert⇨Picture⇨Clip Art.**

   An Insert ClipArt dialog box appears, as shown in Figure 7-8.

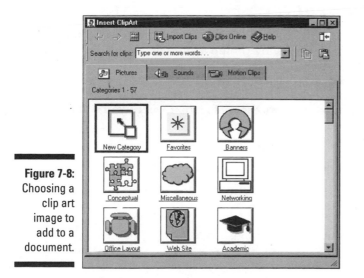

Figure 7-8:
Choosing a clip art image to add to a document.

2. **Click a category (such as Cartoons or Flags).**

3. **Click the clip art you want to use.**

   A pop-up list of icons appears as shown in Figure 7-9.

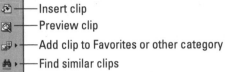

Figure 7-9:
The pop-up
list of icons.

Insert clip
Preview clip
Add clip to Favorites or other category
Find similar clips

4. **Click the Insert Clip icon.**

   Word inserts your chosen clip art in your document.

5. **Click the Close box to make the Insert ClipArt dialog box go away.**

If you click the Preview Clip icon in Step 4 before clicking the Insert Clip icon, you can see a bigger view of your chosen clip art so you can see if you really want to use it or not. The Add Clip to Favorites or Other Category icon lets you store frequently used clip art images. The Find Similar Clips icon helps you locate related clip art images.

Putting existing graphic files into a document

If you've already drawn, copied, bought, or created a graphic file (such as with a digital camera), you can shove it into a Word document.

To add an existing graphic file to a document:

1. **Move the cursor to the approximate location where you want to insert the graphic image.**

2. **Choose Insert➪Picture➪From File.**

   An Insert Picture dialog box appears.

3. **Click the folder containing the graphic file you want to add.**

4. **Click the file you want to use.**

   Word displays your chosen graphic image.

5. **Click Insert.**

Putting an AutoShape into a document

AutoShapes are geometric objects, such as arrows, hearts, and moons that Word has already drawn for you. To add an AutoShape to a document:

1. **Move the cursor to the approximate location where you want to insert the graphic image.**

2. **Choose Insert⇨Picture⇨AutoShapes.**

   An AutoShapes toolbar appears as shown in Figure 7-10.

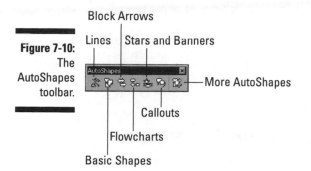

Block Arrows

Lines   Stars and Banners

Figure 7-10:
The
AutoShapes
toolbar.

— More AutoShapes

Callouts

Flowcharts

Basic Shapes

3. **Click the type of AutoShape you want to add (such as Block Arrows or Lines).**

   A pull-down menu of different shapes appears.

4. **Click the AutoShape image you want to use.**

   The mouse turns into a crosshair.

5. **Move the mouse to where you want to draw your AutoShape, hold down the left mouse button, and drag the mouse.**

   Your chosen image appears in your document.

6. **Click the Close box to make the AutoShapes toolbar go away.**

Using WordArt in a document

WordArt is a fancy way to make your text look pretty by combining colors, shapes, and fonts in a unique appearance. To add WordArt to a document:

1. **Move the cursor to the approximate location where you want to insert the graphic image.**

2. **Choose Insert⇨Picture⇨WordArt.**

   A WordArt Gallery dialog box appears.

3. **Click the type of WordArt that you want to add and click OK.**

   An Edit WordArt Text dialog box appears, as shown in Figure 7-11.

4. **Type the text you want to display and click OK.**

Figure 7-11:
The Edit
WordArt
Text dialog
box.

Wrapping words around a picture

A picture in your document may cover up any text underneath. Unless hiding your words is the effect you're looking for, you should make sure that nearby text wraps around your pictures.

To wrap text around a picture:

1. **Click the picture that you want words to wrap around.**
2. **Click the right mouse button.**

   A pop-up menu appears.
3. **Choose Format.**

   The Format dialog box appears.
4. **Click the Layout tab.**
5. **Click a picture in the Wrapping Style group, such as Square or Tight.**
6. **Click an option in the Horizontal Layout group, such as Left or Right.**
7. **Click OK.**

If you click the Advanced button after Step 6, you can define the exact distance that separates text from the border of your picture.

Moving a picture in a document

Because Word doesn't always display your pictures in the exact location you want them, you may have to move the picture to where you want it. To move a picture:

1. **Click the picture that you want to move.**

   Handles appear around your chosen picture.

2. **Hold down the left mouse button.**

3. **Drag the mouse and release the left mouse button when the picture appears where you want it.**

If you need to create documents that require many pictures and columns of text, you should probably use Microsoft Publisher to create your documents rather than Word. See Part VII for more info on using Publisher.

Making Web Pages with Word

Creating your own Web pages within Word is no more difficult than creating an ordinary document within Word. (If you have trouble creating documents in Word, see Chapters 4 through 6 for more information.) Just type, format, and rearrange your text as if you were writing an ordinary business report, summary, or letter of resignation. With a few clicks of the mouse, Word transforms your regular Word document into a mighty Web page that millions can admire over the Internet.

If you have questions about using the Internet, pick up a copy of *Internet For Dummies,* 6th Edition, by John Levine, Carol Baroudi, and Margaret Levine Young, published by IDG Books Worldwide, Inc.

Why create a Web page?

What's all the excitement about creating a Web page with Word? As interest in the Internet increases, more and more people are rushing to get their own Web pages up — either for business, school, or fun. Word lets you create a Web page in a hurry without the hassle of learning clunky HyperText Markup Language (HTML) code.

Why put a page on the World Wide Web in the first place? Many companies post their advertisements as Web pages so they can reach a global audience. Individuals often post Web pages to voice their opinions, offer interesting information that they think others may like (such as recipes or trivia information about favorite rock groups), or advertise their own businesses or services.

By creating and posting a Web page, you can be a part of the rapidly growing global community of people who stare at their computer screens for long periods of time, withholding their own bodily functions just so they can read even more information from all over the world.

Creating a Web page

After you create the Word document (or open an existing Word document) that you want to publish on the Web, you can use Word to turn your document into a Web page. To turn any Word document into a Web page:

1. Open the Word document that you want to convert into a Web page.

In case you forget how to open a Word document, check out Chapter 4.

2. Choose File⇨Save as Web Page.

If you create a Word document from scratch, you may want to first save it as a Word document before saving it as a Web page. That way, if you want to share a copy of your Web page with others, you can either give them the Word document version or the Web page version if they don't have Word.

The Save As dialog box appears.

3. Type a name for your file in the File Name box.

It's a good idea to save your Web page under a different name than your Word document. That way you won't get confused when trying to open either the Word document or the Web page.

4. Click Save.

The Web Page Wizard can help you create great looking Web pages quickly. To use the Web Page Wizard:

1. Choose File⇨New.

The New dialog box appears.

2. Click the Web Pages tab.

3. Click the Web Page Wizard icon.

4. Click OK.

The Web Page Wizard dialog box appears, as shown in Figure 7-12.

5. Click Next.

The wizard dialog box asks for a Web site title and a location to store your Web pages.

6. Type a title for your Web site and a folder (such as C:\My Documents) to store your Web pages. Then click Next.

The wizard dialog box now asks for a navigation style to use.

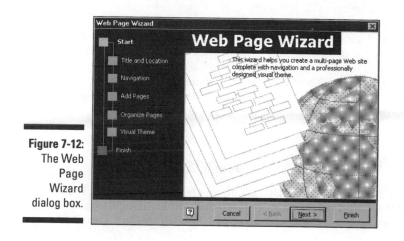

Figure 7-12:
The Web
Page
Wizard
dialog box.

7. **Click a Navigation Style (such as Vertical or Horizontal Frame) and then click Next.**

   The wizard dialog box now asks if you want to add new pages to your Web site.

8. **Add any new pages to your Web pages and click Next.**

   The wizard dialog box asks for you to organize your navigation links on your Web pages.

9. **Rearrange your Web pages the way you want and then click Next.**

   The wizard dialog box gives you the option of defining a visual theme for your Web site.

10. **Click the Add a Visual Theme or No Visual Theme option button.**

    If you click the Add a Visual Theme option button, you can click the Browse Themes button to pick a theme to use.

11. **Click Next.**

12. **Click Finish.**

If you spend a lot of time browsing the World Wide Web, you may find some fascinating Web pages that use all sorts of special effects, like scrolling text, frames, and blinking messages. To see the code behind these fancy effects, choose View⇨Source (in Internet Explorer) or View⇨Page Source (in Netscape Navigator).

After you create your Web pages, you still need to post them to a Web server before they appear on the World Wide Web. Depending on your Internet account, this process can be as easy as copying your Web pages to a Web server computer in the next room, or as cumbersome as uploading your Web pages to a Web server located on a computer in another city, country, or continent. Check with the service you use to access the Internet about getting your pages up on the Web.

Navigating your Web pages

The buttons on the *Web toolbar* help you move around in your own Web pages and on the Web itself. To display the Web toolbar, just choose View➪Toolbars➪Web. The Web toolbar appears, as shown in Figure 7-13.

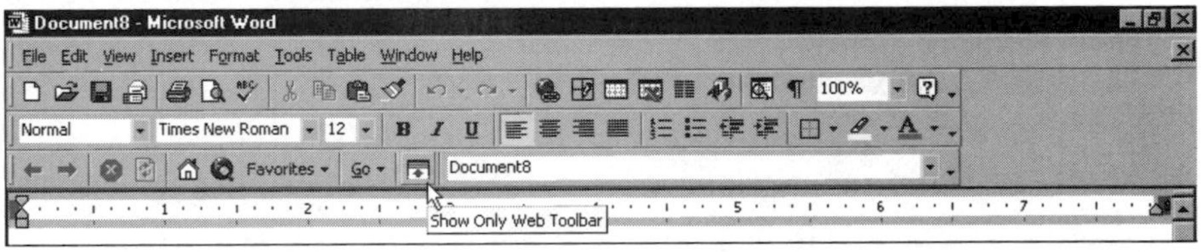

Figure 7-13:
The Web toolbar helps you navigate Web pages.

To make more room to see your document, click the Show Only Web Toolbar button, which makes every toolbar except the Web toolbar disappear. With the Web toolbar, you can click the Back and Forward buttons to navigate your own Web pages or to test external links to other Web sites, such as www.dummies.com.

Making changes to your Web page

After you save your Word document as a Web page, you may want to alter the page in some way — by adding a link or changing the format of some text. To modify a Web page after you save it to your hard disk:

1. **Choose File➪Open.**

   The Open dialog box appears.

2. **Click the Files of Type list box and choose Web Pages.**

3. **Click the Web page that you want to view; then click Open.**

   Word displays your Web page.

4. **Edit your Web page just like you edit a Word document.**

5. **Choose File⇨Save or press Ctrl+S to save your Web page.**

If you plan to dig into the guts of your Web page, choose View⇨HTML Source, to see the actual HTML code that defines how your Web page appears.

Grabbing attention with scrolling text

The number of Web sites appearing on the Web multiplies faster than rabbits on aphrodisiacs. Even if your Web site contains private information for contacting all the stars on *Baywatch,* people won't get far enough into the site to find that information unless the site first attracts their attention.

To grab a reader's attention, turn some of your headlines into *scrolling text,* which simply slides text from one side of the screen to the other. To add scrolling text:

1. **Choose View⇨Toolbars⇨Web Tools.**

   The Web Tools toolbar appears, as shown in Figure 7-14.

Figure 7-14:
The Web
Tools
toolbar.

Scrolling Text icon

2. **Click the Scrolling Text icon on the Web Tools toolbar.**

   The Scrolling Text dialog box appears, as shown in Figure 7-15.

3. **In the Type the Scrolling Text Here box, type the text that you want to scroll.**

   Try to make scrolling text no longer than half the width of the screen. Otherwise, it can be difficult to read.

4. **Click the Behavior list box and choose one of the following:**

   • **Scroll:** Moves text across the screen and, when the text reaches one edge of the screen, displays the text on the opposite side of the screen.

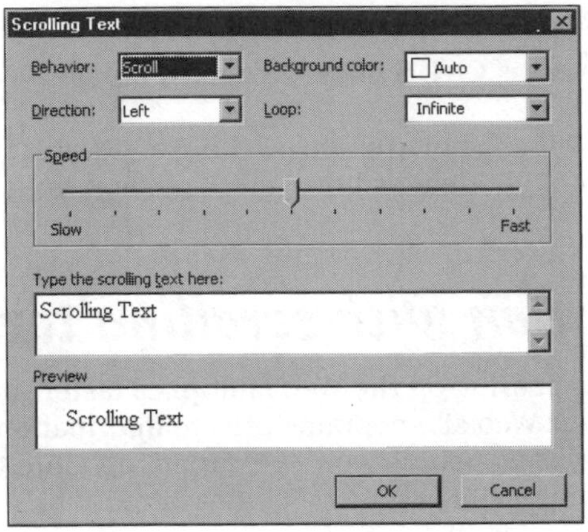

Figure 7-15:
The
Scrolling
Text dialog
box.

- **Slide:** Text moves across the screen and stops when it reaches the opposite side of the screen.

- **Alternate:** Bounces text from left to right, and right to left — from one side of the screen to the other.

5. **Click the <u>D</u>irection list box and choose Left (moves scrolling text from right to left) or Right (moves scrolling text from left to right) to define the direction for the text to move in.**

6. **Click the Background Color list box and choose a background color for your text.**

   To make your text easy to read, make sure that the background color isn't too similar to the color of your text. (White text against a white background can be pretty hard to read.)

7. **Click the <u>L</u>oop list box and choose 1, 2, 3, 4, 5, or Infinite. (The <u>L</u>oop list box appears dimmed if you choose Slide in Step 4.)**

   If you choose a number, the text moves only that number of times across the screen.

8. **Click the <u>S</u>peed slider bar to adjust the scrolling speed from slow to fast.**

9. **Click OK.**

Adding horizontal lines

To make your Web pages easier to read, you may want to add horizontal lines to separate paragraphs.

To add a horizontal rule to your Web page:

1. **Click where you want to add the horizontal rule on the Web page.**
2. **Choose Format⟹Borders and Shading.**
3. **Choose the Horizontal Line button.**

   The Horizontal Line dialog box appears.
4. **Click the type of horizontal line you want to use; then click OK.**

After you draw a line, you can move or resize it later. To resize a line, click the line so handles appear around it, and then drag the handle. To move a line, click the line, and then drag the line to its new location.

Adding pretty pictures to your Web pages

Web pages can get pretty boring if they contain nothing but text. Many Web pages include pictures (hopefully not always X-rated) to spice up their appearance.

The two most common types of pictures that you can add to a Web page are known as *GIF* and *JPG* files (don't worry about the meaning of these file acronyms; they're really not that important). You can find these files offered on other Web sites, sold in clip art packages, or you can make your own GIF or JPEG files by drawing them or capturing them from a scanner or digital camera. One popular clip art package is Corel Web Gallery, which contains several thousand graphic files that you can use in any of your Web pages.

Regardless of where you get your pictures, if they're GIF or JPG files and you save them to your hard disk, you can add them to your Web page by following the steps outlined in the "Adding Pictures to a Document" section earlier in this chapter. Just be careful that you only use GIF or JPG files that you've created or that are in the public domain to avoid getting sued. After all, you don't want to make lawyers any richer than they deserve, do you?

Adding and Removing Hyperlinks

A Word document or Web page can display not only text and graphics but also *hyperlinks*. A hyperlink can appear on a Web page either as a graphic image or as highlighted text. The moment you (or someone else) click the hyperlink, your screen shows a different part of the same Web page or an entirely new Web page altogether.

Word lets you create two types of hyperlinks: internal and external.

Creating an internal link within a Web page

An *internal link* simply lets the reader jump to another part of your Web page, such as from the top of the Web page to a paragraph at the bottom of the Web page. To create an internal link, you have to create a bookmark that tells the link where to go. To create an internal link:

1. **Highlight the destination text or picture where you want users to end up after they click the link.**

   For example, if you want a link to jump to the bottom of your Web page, select the text (as little as a single letter or word) at the bottom of your Web page.

2. **Choose Insert⇨Bookmark.**

   The Bookmark dialog box appears.

3. **Type a name for your bookmark and then click Add.**

4. **Select the text or graphic that you want to turn into an internal hyperlink.**

   If you want users to be able to click a headline to jump to a different part of your Web page, select the headline.

5. **Choose Insert⇨Hyperlink or press Ctrl+K.**

   The Insert Hyperlink dialog box appears, as shown in Figure 7-16.

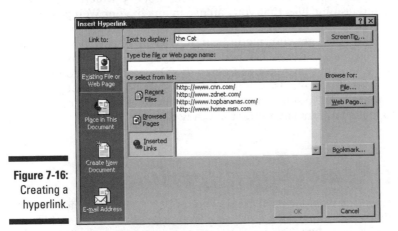

Figure 7-16:
Creating a
hyperlink.

6. **Click the Bookmark button.**

   The Select Place in Document dialog box appears.

7. **Click the bookmark name that you want to link to (the bookmark you named in Step 3); then click OK.**

8. **Click OK to get rid of the Insert Hyperlink dialog box.**

Creating an external link

An *external link* points to another Web page that may be located on any computer on the Internet.

External links are totally out of your control. The computer containing the Web page that your external hyperlinks point to could crash or shut down entirely, leaving your external link pointing to a suddenly nonexistent Web page. Whenever you use external links, check often to make sure that the link still points to a valid Web page.

To create an external link:

1. **Select the text that you want to turn into an external hyperlink.**

   Make sure that the text clearly tells the reader what it's linked to. As another alternative, put plenty of descriptive text around the external hyperlink so users can tell where the hyperlink may take them.

2. **Choose Insert⇨Hyperlink or press Ctrl+K.**

   The Insert Hyperlink dialog box appears (refer to Figure 7-16).

3. **Type the URL (address) of the Web site that you want to link to in the Type the File or Web Page Name box.**

   For example, type **www.dummies.com** to link your Web page to the Dummies Press Web page.

4. **Click OK.**

If you have an Internet account, you can click the Web Page button to load your browser and actually see the Web pages you want your hyperlink to reach.

Removing links

After creating an internal or external link, you may later decide to remove the link — for example, if you redesign your Web page or realize that you linked to the wrong Web page. To remove a link:

1. **Select the text designated as a hyperlink.**

2. **Choose Insert⇨Hyperlink or press Ctrl+K.**

   The Insert Hyperlink dialog box appears (refer to Figure 7-16).

3. **Click the Remove Link button.**

Part III
Playing the Numbers Game with Excel 2000

In this part . . .

Throw away your adding machine, pocket calculator, and reams of green ledger paper. You won't need any such antiquated tools with Microsoft Excel 2000 on your computer (unless, of course, the power goes out due to the Y2K millennium bug). With Excel 2000, you can create budgets, track inventories, calculate future profits (or losses), and create bar, line, and pie charts so you can see what your numbers are really trying to tell you.

Think of Excel 2000 as your own personal calculating machine that lets you create something as simple as a home budget or something as wonderfully complex as an annual profit and loss statement for a Fortune 500 corporation.

By tracking numbers, amounts, lengths, measurements, or dollars with Excel 2000, you can quickly predict future trends and likely results. Type in your annual salary along with any business expenses you may have, and you can calculate how much income tax your government plans to steal from you. Or play "What if?" games with your numbers and ask questions such as "Which sales region sells the most products," "How much can I avoid paying in taxes if my income increases by 50 percent," and "If my company increases sales, how much of an annual bonus can I give myself while letting my employees starve on minimum wages?"

So if you want to get started crunching numbers, this is the part of the book that shows you how to use Excel 2000 effectively.

Chapter 8

The Basics of Spreadsheets: Numbers, Labels, and Formatting

• •

In This Chapter

▶ Finding out what the heck a spreadsheet is

▶ Typing stuff in a worksheet

▶ Moving around a worksheet

▶ Formatting a worksheet

▶ Sending a worksheet to the printer

• •

*S*preadsheets (such as Microsoft Excel 2000) can help you track budgets, inventories, or embezzlements on your own personal computer. If you need to store formulas and plug in different numbers on a regular basis, you could use a pencil and a calculator. But besides the problems of punching in the wrong numbers, you have the added nuisance of recalculating every formula all by yourself.

Because Microsoft Office 2000 comes with Excel, you may as well get your money's worth and use a spreadsheet to help you calculate numbers instead. To use a spreadsheet, just type in numbers, create formulas, and then add labels to help you understand what specific numbers represent. After you do that, you may want to format your numbers and labels to make them look pretty.

What Is a Spreadsheet, Anyway?

In the old days, accountants wrote long columns of numbers on sheets of green ledger paper divided by lines to make entering and organizing information in neat rows and columns easy. Essentially, a computer spreadsheet is just the electronic equivalent of green ledger paper. Instead of seeing rows and columns on a piece of paper, you see rows and columns on your computer screen.

Many people use the terms *spreadsheet* and *worksheet* interchangeably. When people talk about a *spreadsheet,* they may be talking about their program (such as Excel or Lotus 1-2-3) or the actual data that they typed into their spreadsheet program. When people talk about a *worksheet,* they mean actual data that they typed into their spreadsheet program. Now isn't that clear?

A spreadsheet consists of the following items, as shown in Figure 8-1:

- ✔ **A worksheet divided into rows and columns.** A *worksheet* acts like a page where you can type numbers and labels. Each worksheet contains up to 256 vertical *columns* and 65,535 horizontal *rows.* Columns are identified by letters (A, B, C, and so on). Rows are numbered (1, 2, 3, and so on).

Name Box   Formula   Formula Bar

Figure 8-1:
The parts
of a typical
Excel
worksheet.

Worksheet   Labels   Numbers   Cell

The evolution of the spreadsheet

Back in 1979, two business students, Dan Bricklin and Bob Frankston, decided that performing calculations with paper, pencil, and adding machines was a complete waste of time. Instead of griping about the tedious work like other graduate students, they decided to do something about it and wrote the world's first spreadsheet program for their Apple II computer.

They called this program VisiCalc, which stands for Visible Calculator. The idea behind VisiCalc (and every spreadsheet since then) was that all you had to do was type in numbers, define how to calculate new results based on those numbers, and let the spreadsheet do the hard work of calculating multiple formulas. All you do is the easy work of typing in the numbers.

Despite the dominance of VisiCalc as the first spreadsheet in the world, VisiCalc has long since died and been forgotten. When people migrated from Apple II computers to IBM PCs and started using Lotus 1-2-3, this change knocked VisiCalc out, and Lotus 1-2-3 became the world's best-selling spreadsheet. When the world migrated from MS-DOS to Windows, Microsoft had the only Windows spreadsheet available at the time, so everyone switched from Lotus 1-2-3 to Excel.

So if the world switches to yet another operating system (possibly Linux), look for even mighty Microsoft Excel to become a footnote in history. But until then, Excel remains the current reigning champ in the spreadsheet world-market.

- ✔ **Cells.** A *cell* is the intersection of a row and a column. When you type data into a worksheet, you have to type it in a cell. Cells are identified by their column letters followed by their row numbers. For example, the cell at the intersection of column G and row 12 is called cell G12.

- ✔ **Numbers.** *Numbers* can represent amounts, lengths, or quantities, such as $50.54, 309, or 0.094.

- ✔ **Labels.** *Labels* identify what your spreadsheet numbers mean, in case you forget. Typical labels are "May," "Western Sales Region," and "Total Amount We Lost Through Fred's Stupidity."

- ✔ **Formulas.** *Formulas* let you calculate new results based on the numbers you type in. Formulas are as simple as adding two numbers together or as complicated as calculating third-order differential equations that nobody really cares about. (Chapter 9 provides more information about creating formulas.)

Spreadsheets may mimic boring paper ledgers, but they also offer additional forecasting and budgeting capabilities. These capabilities let you ask what-if questions such as: "What would happen if the cost of oil went up 10 percent?" "What would happen if our sales plummeted 90 percent?" "What would happen if I gave myself a million-dollar raise despite the fact that sales have plummeted 90 percent?"

Excel also lets you organize multiple worksheets in a collection called a *workbook*. Each workbook can hold several thousand individual worksheets (the limit depends on your computer's memory and your willingness to keep creating additional worksheets). For more information about using workbooks, see Chapter 11.

Putting Stuff in a Worksheet

Before you can type any information into Excel, you have to start the program. In case you forget how to load Excel, refer to Chapter 1 to refresh your memory.

After you start Excel, an empty worksheet appears on the screen. Because an empty worksheet is useless by itself, you need to type data into the worksheet's cells. The three types of data that you can type into a cell are numbers, labels, and formulas.

Entering information in a cell

To type data into a cell:

1. **Click in the cell where you want to type data.**

   Excel highlights your cell with a dark border around the edges. The highlighted cell is called the *active cell* and is the Excel way of telling you, "If you start typing something now, this is the cell where I'm going to put it."

2. **Start typing a number (such as** 8.3**), label (such as** My Loot**), or formula (such as** =A1+F4-G3**).**

   As you type, Excel displays what you're typing in your chosen cell and in the Formula Bar (refer to Figure 8-1).

3. **Do any one of the following actions to make your typed data appear in your chosen cell:**

   • Press Enter.

   • Click the Enter (green check mark) button, next to the Formula Bar.

   • Press an arrow key to select a different cell.

   • Click a different cell to select it.

If you suddenly decide that you don't want your data to appear in the cell before you perform Step 3, press Esc or click the Cancel (red X) button, next to the Formula Bar. If you already typed data in a cell and want to reverse your action, press Ctrl+Z.

If you need to type the names of months or days in adjacent cells, Excel has a handy shortcut that can save you a lot of typing. To use this shortcut:

1. **Click a cell and type a month or day, such as** March **(or Mar.) or** Tuesday **(or Tue.).**

   The Fill handle — a black box — appears at the bottom-right corner of the cell that you just typed in.

2. **Place the mouse cursor directly over the Fill handle so that the cursor turns into a black crosshair.**

3. **Hold down the left mouse button and drag the mouse to the right or down.**

   As you move the mouse, Excel displays the month or day in each cell that you highlight, as shown in Figure 8-2.

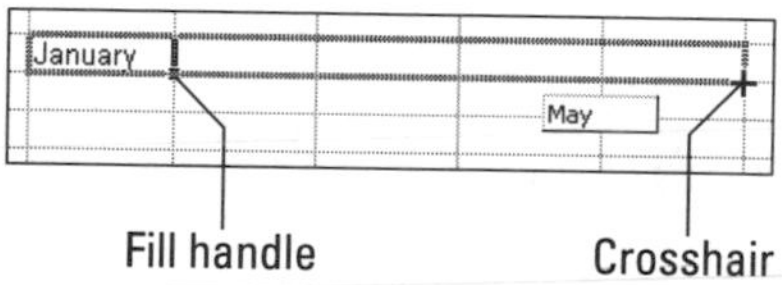

Figure 8-2:
Filling a row
or column of
cells with
labels the
easy way.

| January | | | | May | |

Fill handle   Crosshair

4. **Release the left mouse button.**

   Excel automatically types the months or days in the range of cells that you selected.

Deleting and editing the contents of a cell

Sometimes you may need to edit what you typed in a cell, because you made a mistake or you just want to express your creative urges by typing something else in the cell. Or you may just want to get that data out of there altogether.

To edit or delete data in a cell:

1. **Click or use the arrow keys to select the cell containing the data that you want to edit or delete.**

2. **Press F2, click in the Formula Bar, or double-click the cell containing the data that you want to edit.**

3. **Press Backspace to delete characters to the left of the insertion point or press Delete to erase characters to the right of the insertion point.**

4. **Type any new data.**

5. **To make your typed data appear in your chosen cell, press Enter, click the Enter button (the green check mark next to the Formula Bar) or select a different cell.**

Navigating a Worksheet

A single worksheet can contain up to 256 columns and 65,536 rows. Obviously, your tiny computer screen can't display such a large worksheet all at once, so you can see only part of a worksheet at any given time, much like viewing the ocean through a porthole.

If you create a huge worksheet, you need a way to navigate through the whole thing. Fortunately, Excel provides several different ways to use the mouse or the keyboard to jump around a worksheet.

Using the mouse to jump around a worksheet

To jump around a worksheet with the mouse, you have two choices:

- Click the vertical and horizontal scroll bars.
- Use the wheel on your mouse.

To jump around a document by using the vertical or horizontal scroll bar, you have these choices:

- Click the ↑ and ↓ or ← and → keys to scroll up and down one row or right and left one column at a time.
- Drag the scroll box in the scroll bar in the desired direction to jump to an approximate location in your document.
- Click the vertical scroll bar above or below the scroll box to page up or down one screen-length at a time.
- Click the horizontal scroll bar to the right or left of the scroll box to page right or left one screen-width at a time.

Using the keyboard to jump around a document

For those who hate the mouse or just prefer using the keyboard, here are the different ways to jump around your document by pressing keys:

- Press the ↓ key to move one row down in your worksheet.
- Press the ↑ to move one row up in your worksheet.
- Press the → to move one column to the right in your worksheet.
- Press the ← to move one column to the left in your worksheet.
- Hold down the Ctrl key and press ↓, ↑, →, or ← to jump up/down or right/left one adjacent row or column of data at a time.
- Press the PgDn key (or Page Down on some keyboards) to jump down the worksheet one screen-length at a time.
- Press the PgUp key (or Page Up on some keyboards) to jump up the worksheet one screen-length at a time.
- Hold down the Ctrl key and press the Home key to jump to the A1 cell in your worksheet, which appears in the upper-left-hand corner of every worksheet.
- Hold down the Ctrl key and press the End key to jump to the last cell in your worksheet.
- Press the End key and then press ↓, ↑, →, or ← to jump to the end/beginning or top/bottom of data in the current row or column.

You can open any Excel worksheet (even a blank one will do) and practice using all the different methods of navigating around a worksheet. Then you can memorize the commands you find most useful and forget about the rest.

Using the Go To command

When you want to jump to a specific cell in your worksheet, the Go To command is a lot faster than either the mouse or the keyboard.

To use the Go To command:

1. **Choose Edit⇨Go To or press Ctrl+G.**

   The Go To dialog box appears.

2. **Type a cell reference (such as A4 or C21) or click a cell reference or cell name displayed in the Go To list box.**

3. **Click OK.**

Each time you use the Go To command, Excel remembers the last cell references you typed in. If you have any named cells or cell ranges (see the next section "Naming cells and ranges"), Excel automatically displays these cell names in the Go To dialog box.

Naming cells and ranges

If you don't like referring to cells as E4 or H31, you can assign more meaningful names to a single cell or range of cells. Assigning names can make finding portions of a worksheet much easier. For example, finding your budget's 1999 income cell is a lot easier if it's called "income99" instead of F22.

To assign a name to a cell or range of cells:

1. **Click the cell that you want to name, or select the range of cells that you want to name by dragging (holding down the left mouse button while moving the mouse) over the cells.**

   The cell is highlighted as the active cell. (Or the range is highlighted, and the first cell in the range becomes the active cell.) The active cell's address appears in the Name Box.

2. **Click in the Name Box.**

   Excel highlights the cell address.

3. **Type the name that you want to assign to the cell or cell range.**

4. **Press Enter.**

   The name that you assigned appears in the Name Box.

Names must start with a letter, must be one word, and cannot contain more than 255 characters. "MyIncome" is a valid cell name, but "My Income for 1999" is not, because of the spaces between the words. Rather than use a space, use underscores such as "My_Income_for_1999."

Jumping to a named cell or cell range

After you name a cell or cell range, you can jump to it by following these steps:

1. **Click the downward-pointing arrow to the right of the Name Box.**

   Excel displays a list of all named cells or cell ranges in the current workbook.

2. **Click the cell name that you want to jump to.**

   Excel highlights the cell or range of cells represented by the name you chose.

Deleting a named cell or cell range

You may later decide that you don't need a name to represent a particular cell or cell range. To delete a cell name:

1. **Choose Insert⇨Name⇨Define.**

   The Define Name dialog box appears.

2. **Click the cell name that you want to delete and click Delete.**

   Repeat this step for each cell name that you want to delete.

3. **Click OK.**

Deleting a cell name doesn't delete the contents of any cells in the worksheet.

Using the Excel Toolbars

Like all of the Microsoft Office 2000 programs, Excel provides several ways to choose a command. You can press a keystroke combination, use pull-down menus, or click an icon displayed on a toolbar.

The two most common toolbars are the Standard toolbar and the Formatting toolbar. (Excel actually offers over a dozen different toolbars, but the Standard and Formatting toolbars are the main ones you use.) These two toolbars automatically appear when you first install and start Excel. You can hide them later to make your screen look less cluttered, if you want.

Unlike previous versions, Excel 2000 automatically modifies its toolbars to display the icons that you use most often. So if your toolbar keeps looking different each time you use it, it's because Excel is trying to display the icons representing your most commonly used commands. If you want to modify the way Excel displays its menus, see Chapter 3.

Exploring the Standard toolbar

The Standard toolbar offers access to the program's most frequently used commands, arranged from left to right in roughly the order of their frequency of use, as shown in Figure 8-3.

Figure 8-3:
The pretty
icons on the
Standard
toolbar.

The Standard toolbar features the following commands:

- ✔ **New:** Creates a new worksheet.
- ✔ **Open:** Opens an existing worksheet.
- ✔ **Save:** Saves your current worksheet.
- ✔ **E-mail:** Sends the current worksheet as e-mail.
- ✔ **Print:** Prints your current worksheet.
- ✔ **Print Preview:** Shows you what your worksheet will look like when printed on your printer.
- ✔ **Spelling:** Checks the spelling of your labels in a worksheet.
- ✔ **Cut:** Moves the currently selected text to the Clipboard, the invisible Windows storage area.
- ✔ **Copy:** Copies the currently selected text to the Clipboard.
- ✔ **Paste:** Places in the current worksheet whatever text is currently on the Clipboard.
- ✔ **Format Painter:** Copies the formatting of the currently selected text so that you can apply that formatting to any text you select next.
- ✔ **Undo:** Reverses the action of your last command.
- ✔ **Redo:** The opposite of Undo — restores what the Undo command last did.
- ✔ **Insert Hyperlink:** Creates a link to a Web page.
- ✔ **AutoSum:** Adds up a column of numbers.
- ✔ **Paste Function:** Adds a built-in mathematical function to a cell.
- ✔ **Sort Ascending:** Rearranges a column of data from lowest (top) to highest (bottom).
- ✔ **Sort Descending:** Rearranges a column of data from highest (top) to lowest (bottom).
- ✔ **Chart Wizard:** Displays a wizard for helping you create a chart based on your data.
- ✔ **Drawing:** Displays the Drawing toolbar so you can add lines, shapes, or arrows.

✔ **Zoom:** Adjusts the magnification of your document.

✔ **Microsoft Excel Help:** Displays (or hides) the Office Assistant that you can click to get more help using Excel.

✔ **More Buttons:** Displays or hides buttons on the Standard toolbar.

To quickly find out what each button on the Standard toolbar does, move the mouse pointer over a button and then wait a second or two until the *ScreenTip* — a brief explanation of the button — appears.

Using the Formatting toolbar to change the way worksheets look

The Formatting toolbar contains commands to make your text look pretty with different fonts, type sizes, and typefaces (such as bold, italics, and underline), as shown in Figure 8-4.

Figure 8-4:
The
Formatting
toolbar.

| Arial | ▾ | 10 | ▾ | **B** | *I* | U | ≡ ≡ ≡ 國 | $ % , | ⁺⁰⁰ ⁰⁰ | 걸 걸 | ⧠ ▾ 🖉 ▾ A ▾ |

The buttons on the Formatting toolbar appear in the following order, from left to right:

✔ **Font:** Controls the *font* — the look of the letters — of the currently selected text.

✔ **Font Size:** Controls the size of the currently selected text.

✔ **Bold:** Makes selected text **bold.**

✔ **Italic:** Makes selected text *italic.*

✔ **Underline:** <u>Underlines</u> selected text.

✔ **Align Left:** Makes the lines of the selected text line up on the left (with an uneven right margin).

✔ **Center:** Centers selected text between the left and right margins.

✔ **Align Right:** Makes the lines of the selected text line up on the right (with an uneven left margin).

- **Merge and Center:** Centers data in a single cell or centers data between two or more cells.
- **Currency Style:** Displays numbers with a currency sign.
- **Percent Style:** Displays numbers with a percentage sign.
- **Comma Style:** Displays large numbers with a comma.
- **Increase Decimal:** Increases the number of visible decimal places.
- **Decrease Decimal:** Decreases the number of visible decimal places.
- **Decrease Indent:** Decreases the indentation within a cell.
- **Increase Indent:** Increases the indentation within a cell.
- **Borders:** Displays borders around a cell or range of cells.
- **Fill Color:** Displays selected text against a different color background.
- **Font Color:** Displays selected text in a different color.
- **More Buttons:** Displays or hides buttons on the Formatting toolbar.

To use any of the commands on the Formatting toolbar, select the text that you want to format, and then click the appropriate button or the downward-pointing arrow of the list box on the Formatting toolbar.

Excel offers more toolbars than just the Standard and Formatting toolbars, but these two toolbars contain the most common commands you need. In case you get curious and want to see all the Excel toolbars, choose View⇨Toolbars and a menu appears, listing all the toolbars available with names like Drawing, PivotTable, and Web.

Making Your Worksheet Pretty with Formatting

Rows and columns of endless numbers and labels can look pretty dull. Because a plain, boring worksheet can be as hard to understand as a tax form, Excel gives you the option of *formatting* your cells.

By formatting different parts of your worksheet, you can turn a lifeless worksheet into a powerful persuasion tool that can convince your boss to approve your budget proposals — and give him the impression that you gave it more thought than you really did.

Excel offers an almost unlimited variety of formatting options. You can change fonts, borders, number styles, and alignment to make your worksheets look pretty.

Using AutoFormat

If you aren't a designer but want fancy formatting without a lot of effort on your part, use the Excel AutoFormat feature. *AutoFormat* can automatically format a range of cells for you, according to one of many formatting styles.

To use AutoFormat:

1. **Highlight two or more adjacent cells that you want to format.**

2. **Choose Format⇨AutoFormat.**

   The AutoFormat dialog box appears, as shown in Figure 8-5.

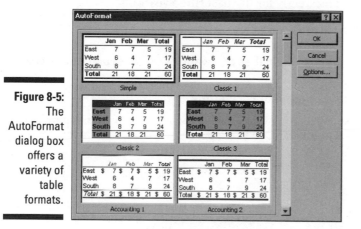

Figure 8-5:
The
AutoFormat
dialog box
offers a
variety of
table
formats.

3. **Click a format that you want to use.**

4. **Click OK.**

   Excel automatically formats the range of cells that you selected in Step 1.

If you want to restrict the types of formatting that AutoFormat can apply, click the Options button in the AutoFormat dialog box. Deselect the Formats that apply options you don't want AutoFormat to use. For example, if you don't want Excel to change fonts, remove the check from the Font check box by clicking it.

Conditional formatting

To help make your data easier to read, Excel can use *conditional formatting.* Conditional formatting means that if the contents of a cell meet a certain condition (such as being greater than 8,100 or less than 340), Excel displays the cell contents with pre-defined formatting. Excel can format the cell contents in many ways, such as in bright red, dark green, italics, or any other type of formatting that you want to use.

Conditional formatting can help you track the value of certain numbers such as profits, losses, sales results, or quantities of illegal substances delivered. For example, you may want to display your profits in a large font and your losses in a much smaller font (so nobody notices that your company has been losing money consistently for the past three years).

To use conditional formatting:

1. **Highlight one or more cells that you want Excel to format under certain conditions.**

2. **Choose Format⇨Conditional Formatting.**

   The Conditional Formatting dialog box appears, as shown in Figure 8-6. The first list box contains "Cell Value Is."

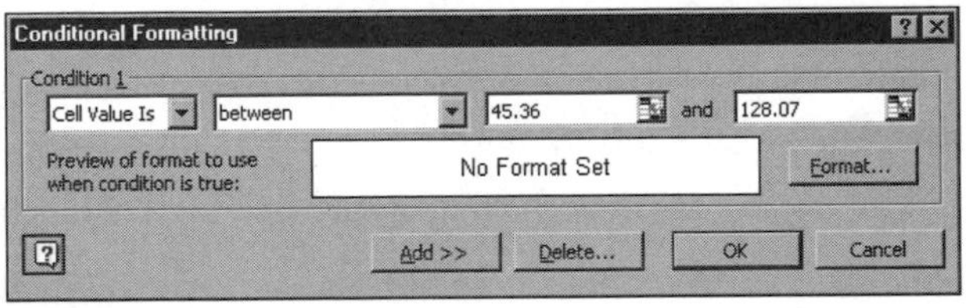

Figure 8-6:
The Conditional Formatting dialog box can define when to format a cell depending on the cell content.

3. **Click in the second list box from the left and choose a criteria to use such as between, not equal to, less than, or greater than.**

4. **Type the value (or values) you want to use in the remaining list boxes.**

5. **Click the Format button.**

   A Format Cells dialog box appears, as shown in Figure 8-7.

6. **Choose the type of formatting you want (font, font size, color, border, pattern, and so on) and click OK.**

   The Conditional Formatting dialog box appears again, showing you a preview of the formatting you chose.

7. **Click OK in the Conditional Formatting dialog box.**

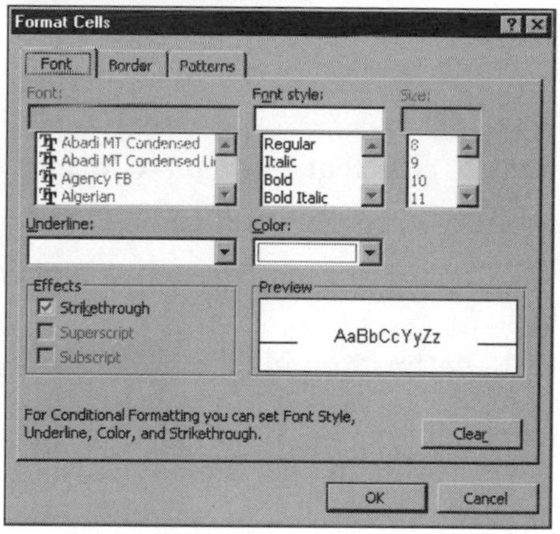

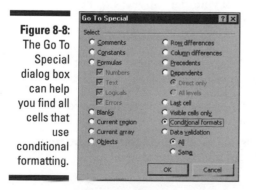

Figure 8-7:
The Format
Cells dialog
box defines
how you
want your
cell to
appear.

A cell that uses conditional formatting looks just like any other cell, which can make it difficult to find if you need to modify the formatting later. To help you find all cells that use conditional formatting:

1. **Choose Edit⇨Go To or press Ctrl+G.**

   The Go To dialog box appears.

2. **Click the Special button.**

   The Go To Special dialog box appears, as shown in Figure 8-8.

Figure 8-8:
The Go To
Special
dialog box
can help
you find all
cells that
use
conditional
formatting.

3. **Click the Conditional Formats option button and then click OK.**

   Excel highlights all cells that use conditional formatting.

Changing fonts in your cells

AutoFormat and conditional formatting are shortcuts for making Excel format cells for you, but you may want to format cells yourself.

To change the font:

1. **Highlight the cell or range of cells that you want to format.**
2. **Click the Font list box on the Formatting toolbar and choose a font.**
3. **Click the Font Size list box on the Formatting toolbar and choose a size (such as 12 or 16).**
4. **Click the Bold, Italic, or Underline button on the Formatting toolbar.**

If the Formatting toolbar isn't visible, you can make it appear by choosing View➪Toolbars➪Formatting.

To quickly bold, italicize, or underline a cell, highlight the cell (or cells) and press Ctrl+B (for bold), Ctrl+I (for italics), or Ctrl+U (for underline).

For more options in formatting one or more cells, highlight the cells you want to format and press Ctrl+1. A Format Cells dialog box appears, giving you more options for formatting your cells.

Adjusting column widths

Unless you specify otherwise, Excel displays all columns in equal widths. However, you may soon find that some of your data appears truncated, scrunched, weird, or otherwise not displayed the way you intended. This problem occurs when your columns are too narrow.

To fix this problem, you can adjust columns to make them wider or narrower. To adjust the column widths quickly:

1. **Place the mouse cursor directly over one of the vertical borders of the column heading that you want to modify.**

   For example, if you want to adjust the width of column B, move the mouse cursor over the border between columns B and C.

2. **Hold down the left mouse button and drag the mouse to the left or right.**

   The mouse cursor appears as a double-headed arrow. Excel also displays a dotted vertical line to show you the approximate width of your column.

3. **Release the left mouse button when the column is the width you want.**

If you double-click the border between column headings, Excel automatically modifies the column on the left to make it just wide enough to display the longest entry in that column.

If you want to get real precise about defining your column widths:

1. **Click in the column you want to modify.**

2. **Choose Format⇨Column⇨Width.**

   A Column Width dialog box appears.

3. **Type a number to specify the column width (such as 14.5) and click OK.**

Adjusting row heights

Excel normally displays all rows in equal heights. However, you may want to make some rows taller or shorter than others.

To change the height of a row quickly:

1. **Place the mouse cursor directly over one of the horizontal borders of the row that you want to modify.**

   The mouse cursor turns into a double-pointing arrow.

2. **Hold down the left mouse button and drag the mouse up or down.**

   Excel displays a dotted vertical line along with a small box that tells you the exact height of the row.

3. **Release the left mouse button when the row is the height you want.**

For people who want to define the row height exactly:

1. **Click in the row you want to modify.**

2. **Choose Format⇨Row⇨Height.**

   A Row Height dialog box appears.

3. **Type a number to specify the column width (such as 12.95) and click OK.**

Making borders around a cell

You may want to highlight a particular cell by using borders, which can appear as dark or double lines around an entire cell or just on the top or bottom of the cell.

To define borders around a cell:

1. **Click in the cell (or highlight a range of cells) where you want to add a border.**

2. **Choose Format⇨Cells, or press Ctrl+1.**

   A Format Cells dialog box appears.

3. **Click the Border tab.**

   The Border tab appears in the Format Cells dialog box, as shown in Figure 8-9.

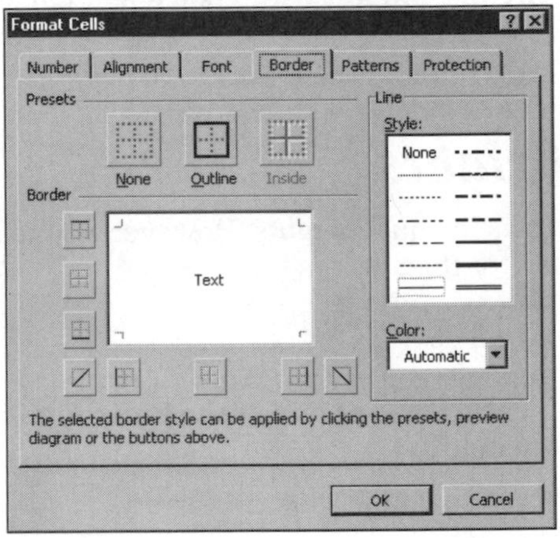

Figure 8-9:
The Border tab in the Format Cells dialog box for displaying borders around a cell.

4. **Click the type of border you want in the Border group (such as a border on the left side of the cell or on the top).**

5. **Click in the Style group to choose a border style (such as dotted lines).**

6. **Click OK.**

For a faster way to create borders around a cell, click in a cell and then click the Borders button on the Formatting toolbar. When a menu of different border styles appears, click the border style you want to use.

Displaying numbers in different ways

Normally, when you type a number in a cell, Excel displays it as a plain, simple number, like 54 or 908.83. This option is okay for most purposes, but sometimes you may want to display numbers as currency (such as $3.90), percentages (such as 83.2%), fractions (such as ½), or as scientific notation (such as 5.09E+05).

To format your numbers:

1. **Select the cells containing the numbers that you want to format.**

2. **Choose Format⇨Cells, or press Ctrl+1.**

   The Format Cells dialog box appears.

3. **Click the Number tab.**

   The Number tab appears in the Format Cells dialog box, as shown in Figure 8-10.

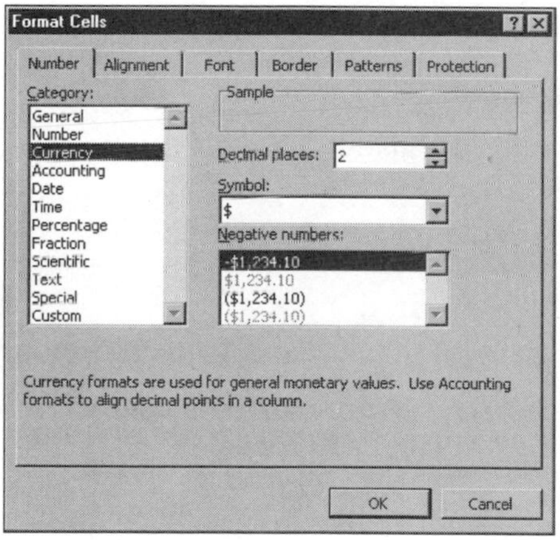

Figure 8-10: The Number tab in the Format Cells dialog box.

4. **Click the Category list box and choose the type of format you want to use to display your numbers, such as Currency, Percentage, or Scientific.**

   Depending on the format style you choose (Currency, Accounting, Date, and so on), you may need to choose additional options to define the exact way to display numbers in your chosen format.

5. **Click OK.**

For a faster way to format numbers, click in a cell and then click the Currency Style, Percent Style, Comma Style, Increase Decimal, or Decrease Decimal button on the Formatting toolbar.

Saving Worksheets for Posterity

Saving your work is important so that you can edit and review it later. Depending on what you want to do, you can save your Excel worksheets as a file or as a Web page.

Saving your worksheets in a file

After you type numbers, labels, or formulas into a worksheet, you probably want to save the worksheet in a file so you won't have to type everything all over again.

To save a workbook, including all its worksheets, follow these steps:

1. **Choose one of the following:**

   • Click the Save button (the picture of a disk) on the Standard toolbar.

   • Press Ctrl+S.

   • Choose File⇨Save.

   If you haven't saved the file before, the Save As dialog box appears.

2. **Click in the File name box and type a name for your Excel workbook, such as Fake Accounting or Bribery Records.**

3. **Click Save.**

Saving your file under a new name

After you create enough worksheets, you may want to create a new worksheet based on the design of an existing worksheet. Rather than create a new worksheet from scratch, you can save your existing worksheet under a different name and then modify that new named file.

To save your file under a different name, follow these steps:

1. **Choose File⇨Save As.**

   The Save As dialog box appears.

2. **Click in the File name box and type a name for your Excel workbook, such as Fake Accounting or Bribery Records.**

3. **Click in the Save as Type list box and choose a file format to use.**

   At this point you can choose some really weird file formats like WK4 (1-2-3) or DBF 3 (dBASE III).

4. **Click Save.**

Excel worksheets are compatible with Excel 97 files, but not with older versions of Excel such as those created by Excel 5.0. If you want to save an Excel worksheet so someone else can edit it using an older version of Excel, choose the Save As command and choose the appropriate version of Excel such as Excel 5.0/95 or Microsoft Excel 4.0 Worksheet in the Save as Type list box of the Save As dialog box.

If for some reason you need to share your Excel files with a spreadsheet that isn't listed in the Save As dialog box, use a universal file format such as SYLK (Symbolic Link), DIF (Data Interchange Format), or CSV (Comma delimited). These file formats may lose some formatting, but they keep your numbers and formulas intact so you can exchange Excel data to another spreadsheet or another computer altogether.

Saving Excel worksheets as Web pages

Excel gives you the additional option of saving documents as Web pages. Chances are good you won't use Excel by itself to create a whole collection of Web pages; but you can create tables or charts in Excel and then turn them into Web pages later.

To convert an Excel worksheet into a Web page:

1. **Choose File⇨Save as Web Page.**

   The Save As dialog box appears.

2. **Click the Change Title button.**

   A Set Page Title dialog box appears.

3. **Type the title that you want to appear at the top of your Web page and click OK.**

4. **Click Save.**

To view your Excel worksheet as a Web page, choose File⇨Web Page Preview.

Printing a Worksheet

After you type numbers, labels, and formulas into a worksheet, you eventually want to print it out so you don't have to make everyone look at your worksheet on your tiny computer screen. Before printing out a worksheet (and possibly wasting precious natural resources such as paper and ink), use the Print Preview feature first.

Using Print Preview to see your worksheet

Excel's Print Preview lets you see how your worksheet looks before you actually print it. That way, you can see things like whether your margins are aligned properly and whether columns or rows fit on a single page.

To use Print Preview:

1. **Choose File⇨Print Preview.**

   Excel displays your worksheet in minuscule print and displays the cursor as a magnifying glass, as shown in Figure 8-11.

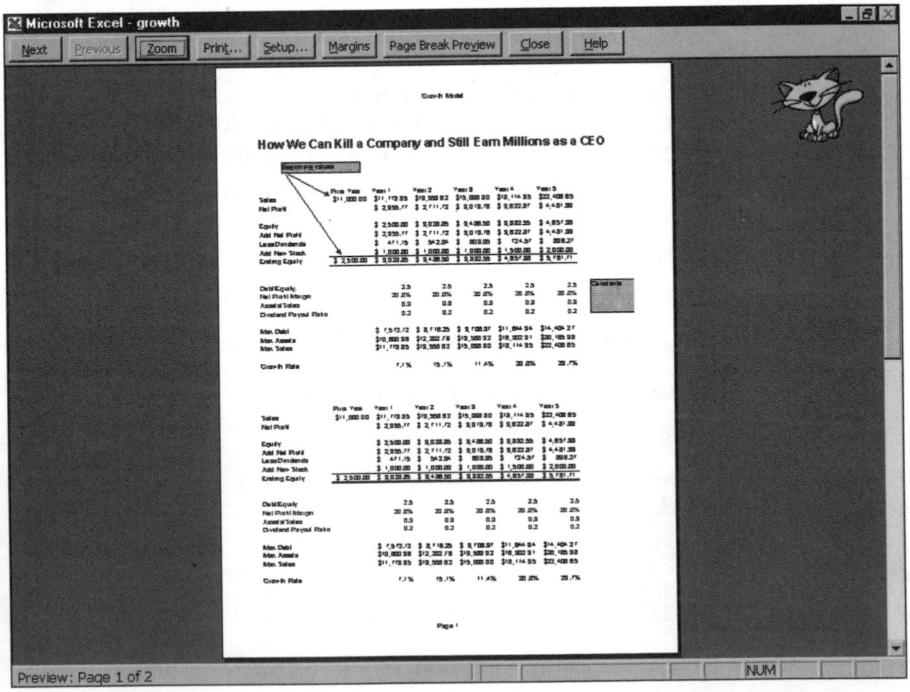

Figure 8-11: A worksheet displayed in Print Preview.

2. **Move the mouse cursor (the magnifying glass) over the document and click to view your document in its full size.**

3. **Click Close to exit Print Preview or Print to start printing right away.**

Printing worksheets

When you decide to print out your worksheet, Excel gives you a variety of ways to do so:

1. **Make sure your printer is turned on, properly connected to your computer, loaded with paper, hasn't been drop-kicked through the third-story window out of frustration, and so on.**

2. **Choose one of the following:**

   • Press Ctrl+P.

   • Choose File⇨Print.

   The Print dialog box appears.

3. **Click in the Name list box and choose the printer to use.**

4. **In the Print range group, click an option button to choose the pages you want to print.**

   You can choose All, or type a page number or range to print in the From and To boxes.

5. **Click in the Number of copies box and type the number of copies you want.**

6. **Click in the Print What list box and choose what you want to print, such as Selection (which prints any cells you've already highlighted), Entire workbook, or Active sheet(s).**

7. **Click OK.**

If you want to print your entire worksheet right away, click the Print button on the Standard toolbar. If you want to specify which pages you want to print and how many copies, choose one of the other methods (Ctrl+P or File⇨Print).

Chapter 9

Having Fun with Formulas and Functions

You could stay up all night, adding rows and columns of numbers together by using paper and a pocket calculator, but you may as well use Microsoft Excel instead (especially because you already paid for it when you bought Microsoft Office 2000). Just tell Excel what you want it to calculate, and feed it one or more numbers; within seconds, Excel spits out the results.

Besides addition, subtraction, division, and multiplication, Excel also lets you create more complicated calculations. This capability comes in handy when you need statistical results, scientific calculations, or financial formulas to compare how much money you're losing in the stock market every month to how much cash you're spending on collectible baseball cards.

Creating Formulas

Excel is like a fancy calculator that lets you calculate any type of a result — as long as you know what you're doing in the first place. To create a formula:

1. **Click the cell where you want to display the results of a calculation.**

2. **Type = (the equal sign) followed by your formula.**

   For example, if you want a formula that multiplies the contents of cell B3 by the contents of cell C3, type **=B3*C3**.

3. Press Enter.

Excel displays the results of your calculation.

To give you an idea of all the different types of formulas that you can create, Table 9-1 shows the most common calculations performed with a formula. The numbers shown in the Example column represent data stored in other cells. For example, in the Addition row, you may actually type **=B3+G12** where B3 contains the number 5 and G12 contains the number 3.4.

Table 9-1	Common Formula Calculations		
Operator	*What It Does*	*Example*	*Result*
+	Addition	=5+3.4	8.4
-	Subtraction	=54.2-2.1	52.1
*	Multiplication	=1.2*4	4.8
/	Division	=25/5	5
%	Percentage	=42%	0.42
^	Exponentiation	=4^3	64
=	Equal	=6=7	False
>	Greater than	=7>2	True
<	Less than	=9<8	False
>=	Greater than or equal to	=45>=3	True
<=	Less than or equal to	=40<=2	False
<>	Not equal to	=5<>7	True
&	Text concatenation	="Bo the" & " Cat"	Bo the Cat

When you create a formula, you can either type numbers in the formula (such as 56.43 + 89/02) or use mysterious things called *cell references* (such as B5 + N12). While you may need to type numbers in a formula occasionally, the real power of Excel comes from using cell references.

Cell references let you take the contents of a specific cell and use those contents as part of your calculation. That way you can create multiple formulas that feed data into several other formulas.

What the heck are references?

In the working world, you give references to employers who want to check up on your background. In the world of Excel, you use references to identify cells containing numbers that you want to use in a formula to calculate a result.

Referencing a single cell

There are two ways you can reference a cell in Excel:

- Use the column and row labels, such as A4 or C7.
- Use your own column and row labels, such as Feb or Sales.

For example, suppose you have numbers stored in cells B5 and B6, as shown in Figure 9-1. In this example, cell B7 contains the formula:

```
=B5+B6
```

Figure 9-1: Using cell references to calculate a result.

	A	B	C	D	E
1		Where Your Tax Dollars Go			
2	*How Governments Spend Your Money*				
3					
4		Balance Sheet			
5	Alcohol and secretaries	$ 487,560			
6	Weapons for killing citizens we can't afford to feed	$ 91,455			
7	Total =	$ 579,015			
8					
9					

When you reference another cell, that cell can contain either data (such as numbers) or a formula (that calculates a result based on data obtained from other cell references).

The cell references in the above formula are B5 and B6, which tells Excel, "Find the number stored in cell B5 and add it to the number stored in B6."

If using cell references like C5 or E8 seems too cryptic to you, you can use your own labels to identify particular cells. For example, Figure 9-2 shows column labels (Jan, Feb, Mar, and Apr) and row labels (Jet fighters, Guns and ammo, Missiles, and Nerve gas).

To make Excel accept labels as part of a formula:

1. **Choose Tools↹Options.**

   The Options dialog box appears.

2. **Click the Calculation tab.**

   The Calculation tab appears in the Options dialog box, as shown in Figure 9-3.

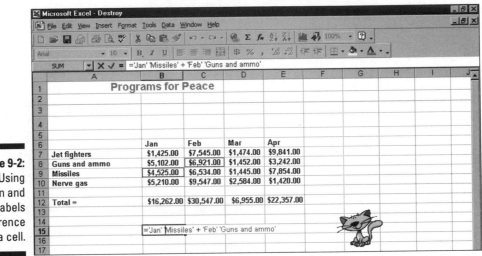

Figure 9-2:
Using
column and
row labels
to reference
a cell.

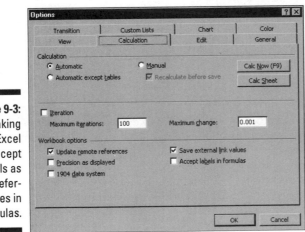

Figure 9-3:
Making
Excel
accept
labels as
cell refer-
ences in
formulas.

3. Click in the Accept Labels in Formulas check box so a check mark appears.

If a check mark already appears, skip to Step 4.

4. Click OK.

After you tell Excel to use labels in formulas, you can create formulas that use labels, such as the following:

```
= Jan Missiles + Mar Missiles
```

This tells Excel, "Take the number stored in the cell found below the 'Jan' column label and to the right of the 'Missiles' row label and add it to the number stored in the cell found below the 'Mar' column label and to the right of the 'Missiles' row label."

For labels that consist of two or more words, you have to surround them with single quotation marks, as follows:

```
= 'Jan' 'Guns and ammo' + 'Mar' 'Nerve gas'
```

If you double-click a cell containing a formula that uses column and row labels, Excel highlights the cell's references (refer to Figure 9-2).

If you delete a column or row label that's used in a formula, your formula won't work anymore.

If you change a column or row label that's used in a formula, Excel automatically changes your formula.

Using cell references in a formula

To create a formula using a cell reference:

1. **Click the cell where you want the results of the formula to appear.**

2. **Type = (the equal sign).**

3. **Choose one of the following methods:**

   - Type the cell reference (such as B4 or the cell label such as 'Jan' 'Jet fighters').

   - Click the cell containing the number that you want to use in your formula (such as B4).

4. **Type an operator, such as + (the plus sign).**

5. **Repeat Steps 3 and 4 as often as necessary to build your formula.**

6. **Press Enter.**

Now if you change the number in a cell that's referenced in another cell's formula (such as B4 in this example), Excel automatically calculates a new result.

TIP

Because the most common calculation is adding numbers together, Excel has a special feature, called *AutoSum,* specifically designed to help you add rows or columns of numbers. Just remember that AutoSum can't add rows or columns of numbers if an empty cell appears in the middle of a row or column of numbers.

To use AutoSum:

1. **Select the range of cells containing the numbers that you want to add together.**

2. **Click the AutoSum button on the Standard toolbar.**

   Excel automatically adds up the selected cells and displays the result at the bottom of the column or to the right of the row that you selected. Figure 9-4 shows AutoSum adding cells C7 through C10.

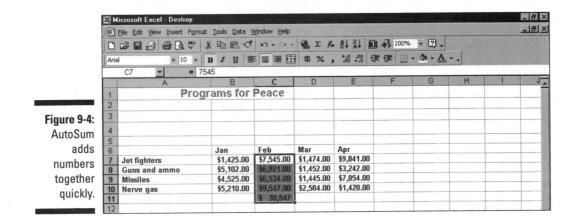

Figure 9-4: AutoSum adds numbers together quickly.

The magic of parentheses

The simplest formulas can use two cell references and one operator, such as =B4*C4. However, you'll likely need to create more-complicated formulas, involving three or more cell references. With so many cell references, you should use parentheses to organize everything.

For example, suppose you want to add together the numbers in cells D3, D4, and D5 and then multiply the total by a number in cell D6. To calculate this result, you may try to use the following formula:

```
=D3+D4+D5*D6
```

Unfortunately, Excel interprets this formula to mean "multiply the number in D5 by the number in D6 and then add this result to the numbers in D3 and D4." The reason has to do with *order of operations* — Excel searches a formula for certain operators (such as *) and calculates those results before calculating the rest of the formula left to right.

Say you have the following values stored in the cells:

D3 $45.95

D4 $199.90

D5 $15.95

D6 7.75%

The formula =D3+D4+D5*D6 calculates the number $247.09, which isn't the result you want at all.

What you really want is to add all the numbers in cells D3, D4, and D5 and then multiply this total by the number in D6. To tell Excel to do this, you have to use parentheses:

```
=(D3+D4+D5)*D6
```

The parentheses tell Excel, "Hey, stupid! First add up all the numbers stored in cells D3, D4, and D5 and then multiply this total by the number stored in D6." Using the same values for D3, D4, D5, and D6 as in the example without parentheses, Excel now calculates $20.29, which is the result you wanted.

If you figure out nothing else from this section or from high school algebra, remember that you must always organize multiple cell references in parentheses to make sure that Excel calculates them in the right order.

Referencing two or more cells

Sometimes you may need to reference two or more cells. A group of multiple cells is called a *range*. The two types of cell ranges are

✔ Contiguous ranges (cells next to each other), such as D3+D4+D5

✔ Noncontiguous ranges (cells that are not next to each other), such as D3+T44+Z89

Specifying a contiguous range

A contiguous range of cells is nothing more than a bunch of cells touching one another, such as cells stacked one over the other or side by side. You can specify contiguous cells by using the colon. For example, typing A2:A5 tells Excel to use the cells A2, A3, A4, and A5.

You can also specify adjacent cells spanning two or more columns or rows. For example, typing D2:E5 tells Excel to use the cells D2, D3, D4, D5 and the cells E2, E3, E4, and E5.

Contiguous ranges are most useful when using Excel's built-in *functions,* such as =SUM(D2:D6), which adds together all the numbers stored in cells D2 through D6. Functions are mathematical formula shortcuts that Excel has already created for you. To use these shortcuts, you just have to choose the right function rather than type a complicated formula. Some other built-in functions that work with contiguous ranges include AVERAGE, MAX, MIN, and COUNT. You can find out more about functions in the "Picking a Function to Use" section later in this chapter.

Suppose you want to use the following formula:

```
=(D3+D4+D5)*D6
```

Cells D3, D4, and D5 are a contiguous range of cells, so you can simplify the formula by just typing the following:

```
=SUM(D3:D5)*D6
```

The D3:D5 reference tells Excel, "Hey, dunderhead! Take all the numbers stored in cells D3 through D5 and sum (add) them all together; then multiply this result by the number in D6."

To specify a contiguous range in a formula:

1. **Click the cell where you want the results of the formula to appear.**

2. **Type = (the equal sign).**

3. **Type the built-in function that you want to apply to your contiguous range, such as SUM or AVERAGE, and then type the left parenthesis, which looks like this: (.**

4. **Click the cell containing the first number that you want to use in your formula (such as cell D3).**

5. **Hold down the left mouse button and drag the mouse to select the entire cell range that you want to include.**

   Excel highlights your selected cell range with a dotted line, as shown in Figure 9-5.

6. **Let go of the mouse button and type the right parenthesis, which looks like this:).**

7. **Type the rest of your formula (if necessary) and press Enter.**

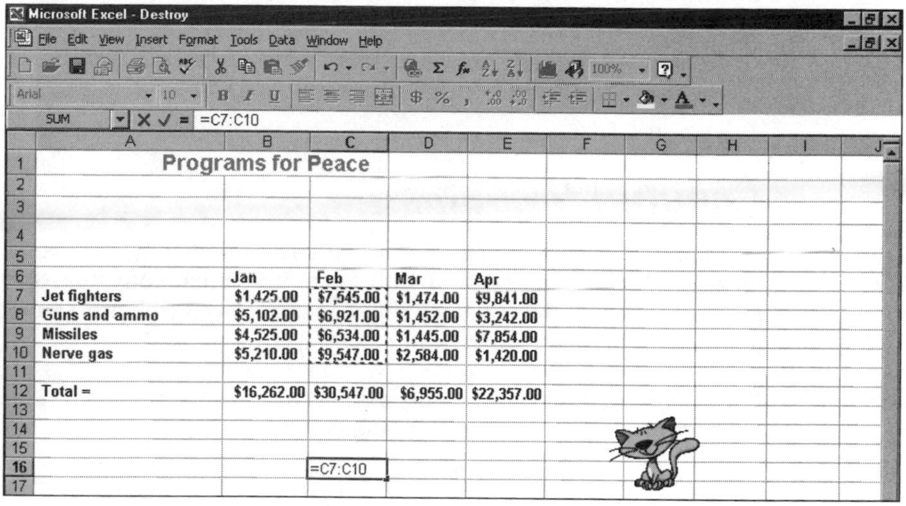

Figure 9-5:
Selecting a
contiguous
range of
cells.

Specifying a noncontiguous range

If you want to include certain numbers in a formula that are stored in cells that are not touching one another, you need to create a noncontiguous range. For example, consider the following formula:

```
=SUM(D3,G5,X7)
```

This formula tells Excel, "Take the number stored in cell D3, add it to the number stored in cell G5, and add the result to the number stored in cell X7."

To specify a noncontiguous range in a formula:

1. **Click the cell where you want the results of the formula to appear.**

2. **Type = (the equal sign).**

3. **Type the built-in function that you want to apply to your noncontiguous range, such as SUM or AVERAGE, and then type the left parenthesis, which looks like this: (.**

4. **Click the cell containing the first number that you want to use in your formula (such as cell D3). (Or just type the cell reference you want to use, such as D3.)**

5. **Type , (a comma).**

6. **Click the cell containing the next number that you want to use in your formula (such as cell D7). (Or just type the cell reference you want to use, such as D7.)**

7. **Repeat Steps 5 and 6 as often as necessary.**

8. **Type a right parenthesis, which looks like this:), and press Enter when you're finished building your formula.**

Copying formulas

Just like high school was a lot easier if you copied someone else's homework, creating formulas in Excel is much easier if you just copy an existing formula. Excel changes the formula cell references automatically for each row or column of numbers.

For example, if you need to add the first five numbers in column A, B, and C together, your formula in cell A6 may look like this:

```
=SUM(A1:A5)
```

When you copy and paste this formula into cells B6 and C6, Excel automatically changes the formula in cell B6 to read:

```
=SUM(B1:B5)
```

and changes the formula in cell C6 to read:

```
=SUM(C1:C5)
```

Copying an existing formula is especially useful when you have rows or columns of numbers that use the exact same type of formula, such as five columns of numbers that all display a total at the bottom, as shown in Figure 9-6.

Figure 9-6:
Copying and
pasting
a formula
can make
calculating
the results
of rows or
columns
easier.

	A	B	C	D	E	F	G	H	I
1			Amount of Bad Food Served in School Cafeterias						
2			(Measured in metric tons)						
3									
4		Mystery Meat	Orange Drink	Hard Noodles	Sticky gravy	Rejected Canned Goods			
5	Jan	4521	8541	41002	1530	9874			
6	Feb	599	4478	4585	24453	2154			
7	Mar	2105	1547	1156	5456	2140			
8	Apr	1475	846	1256	5402	5874			
9	May	2102	153	6845	8616	4445			
10	Jun	4810	66485	2489	2557	81054			
11	Jul	5168	48702	25489	6528	8460			
12	Aug	5439	54858	1891	1463	8468			
13	Sep	1381	14754	17485	31245	5489			
14									
15	Total =	27600							
16									
17									

Microsoft Excel - Oil

File Edit View Insert Format Tools Data Window Help

Arial   10   B I U

C15   =

To copy a formula and paste it for other rows or columns to use:

1. **Type the formula you want to copy.**
2. **Highlight the cell containing the formula you want to copy.**
3. **Press Ctrl+C or click the Copy button on the Standard toolbar.**

   Excel displays a dotted line around the cell that you highlighted in Step 2.
4. **Highlight the cell or range of cells where you want to paste the formula.**
5. **Press Ctrl+V or click the Paste button on the Standard toolbar.**

   Excel displays the results of the formula in your chosen cell or range of cells.

Editing Your Formulas

After you type a formula into a cell, you can always go back and edit it later. This capability comes in handy when you type a formula incorrectly (such as when you forget to use parentheses).

Displaying formulas

Before you can edit a formula, you have to find it. A cell with a formula in it looks exactly like a cell with just a regular number in it. That's because a cell with a formula shows the results of the formula, not the formula itself — so you may have trouble distinguishing between cells containing plain-old-numbers and cells containing formulas.

To display all your formulas in a worksheet, just press Ctrl+`. That odd little mark, which you type while holding down the Ctrl key, appears on the same key as the tilde symbol (~). On some keyboards, this key appears to the left of the 1 key on the top row. On other keyboards, this key appears at the bottom, near the spacebar.

When you press Ctrl+`, Excel displays all your formulas in the worksheet, as shown in Figure 9-7. If you press Ctrl+` a second time, Excel hides your formulas.

	Microsoft Excel - Oil				
	File Edit View Insert Format Tools Data Window Help				
	D18	=			
	A	B	C	D	E
1			Amount of Bad Food		
2				(Measured in metric tons)	
3					
4		Mystery Meat	Orange Drink	Hard Noodles	Sticky gravy
5	Jan	4521	8541	41002	1530
6	Feb	599	4478	4585	24453
7	Mar	2105	1547	1156	5456
8	Apr	1475	846	1256	5402
9	May	2102	153	6845	8616
10	Jun	4810	66485	2489	2557
11	Jul	5168	48702	25489	6528
12	Aug	5439	54858	1891	1463
13	Sep	1381	14754	17485	31245
14					
15	Total =	=SUM(B5:B13)	=SUM(C5:C13)	=SUM(D5:D13)	=SUM(E5:E13)
16					

Figure 9-7:
Displaying
formulas
in a
worksheet.

Wiping out a formula

The quickest way to edit a formula is to wipe it out completely and start all over again. When you want to exercise your destructive urges and delete a formula for good, follow these steps:

1. **Click the cell containing the formula that you want to delete.**

2. **Press Delete or Backspace.**

   Excel wipes out your formula.

These steps work for deleting the contents of any cell. If you delete something by mistake, you can recover it by immediately pressing Ctrl+Z.

Changing a formula

If you just want to edit a formula, by typing a parenthesis or adding another cell reference, you can use the Formula Bar, which is shown in Figure 9-8. Each time you click a cell containing a formula, the Formula Bar displays the formula you're using so you can view the whole thing and edit it.

To edit a formula:

1. **Click the cell containing the formula that you want to edit.**

   Excel dutifully displays that formula on the Formula Bar (see Figure 9-8).

2. **Click in the Formula Bar so that a cursor appears in it.**

Figure 9-8:
Displaying a
formula in
the Formula
Bar.

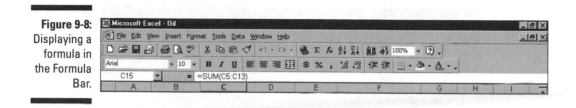

3. **Edit your formula as you please.**

   Press Backspace or Delete to erase part of your formula. Use the → and ← keys to move the cursor around; type any corrections.

4. **Press Enter.**

   Excel calculates a new result for that cell, based on your modified formula.

For a faster way to edit a formula in a cell, double-click that cell and type or edit the formula directly in the cell.

Picking a Function to Use

Quick! Write out the formula to calculate the depreciation of an asset for a specified period, using the fixed-declining-balance method. If you have absolutely no idea what the previous sentence means, you're not alone. However, even if you do know what that sentence means, you may still have no idea how to create a formula to calculate this result.

Rather than forcing you to rack your brains and create cumbersome and complicated formulas on your own, Excel comes with predefined formulas called *functions*.

The main difference between a function and a formula is that a function just asks you what cell references (numbers) to use, while a formula forces you to choose your cell references and tell Excel whether to add, subtract, multiply, or divide. For simple calculations, you can create your own formulas, but for really complicated calculations, you may want to use a built-in function instead.

Just in case you're wondering, you can use functions within any formulas you create. For example, the following formula uses the SUM function but also uses the multiplication operator:

```
=SUM(D4:D5)*D7
```

To help you choose the right function, Excel comes with the Paste Function feature, which guides you step-by-step to choosing a function and filling it with cell references. Relax — you don't have to do it all yourself.

To use the Paste Function feature:

1. **Click the cell where you want to use a function.**

2. **Click the Paste Function button (the button with the cursive f and little x), or choose Insert⇨Function.**

   The Paste Function dialog box appears, as shown in Figure 9-9.

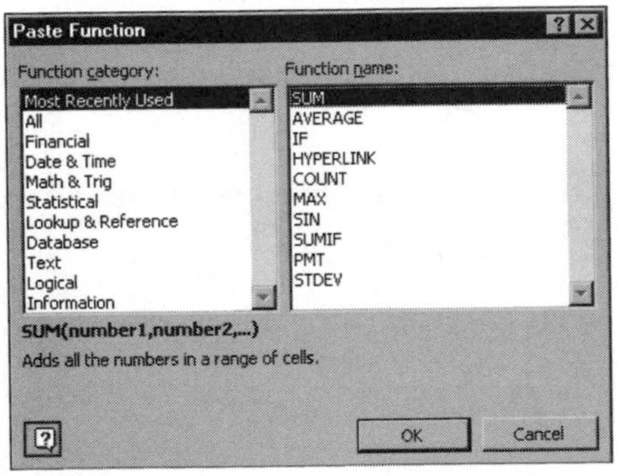

Figure 9-9: The Paste Function dialog box.

3. **In the Function Category list box, click the category that contains the type of function you want to use (Financial, Statistical, and so on).**

4. **In the Function Name list box, click the function that you want to use.**

   Each time you select a function, Excel displays a brief explanation of that function at the bottom of the dialog box.

5. **Click OK.**

   Excel displays a second dialog box, asking for specific cell references, as shown in Figure 9-10. Depending on the function you chose in Step 4, the dialog box that appears after Step 5 may look slightly different.

6. **Click the cells containing the numbers that you want to use (such as cell E3) or type the cell reference yourself.**

   You may have to move the dialog box out of the way to see your worksheet. To move the dialog box, place the mouse pointer over the dialog box title bar, hold down the left mouse button, and drag the mouse.

7. **Click OK.**

   Excel calculates a value based on the function that you chose and the numbers that you told it to use in Step 6.

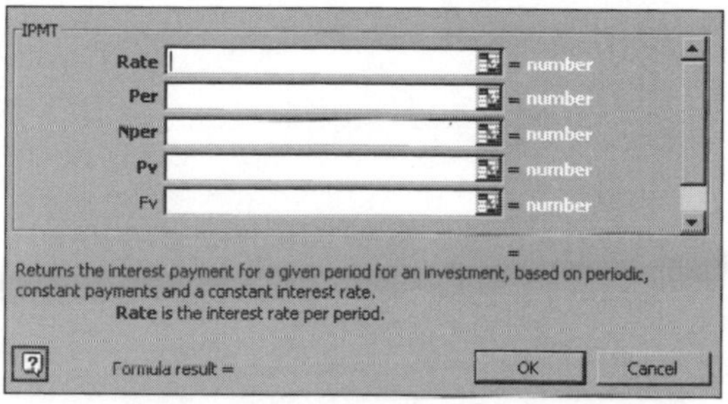

Figure 9-10: A typical dialog box asking for specific cell references to use.

Common Excel functions

Although Excel contains several hundred different functions, you may never use all of them in your lifetime. Here's a short list that you can use as a reference the next time you want to use one of the common functions:

Function Name	What It Does
AVERAGE	Calculates the average value of numbers stored in two or more cells
COUNT	Counts how many cells contain a number instead of text
MAX	Finds the largest number stored in two or more cells
MIN	Finds the smallest number stored in two or more cells
ROUND	Rounds a decimal number to a specified number of digits
SQRT	Returns the square root of a number
SUM	Adds the values stored in two or more cells

Chapter 10

Charting Your Numbers

● ●

In This Chapter

▶ Dissecting the parts of a chart
▶ Using the Chart Wizard
▶ Changing your chart

● ●

A picture may be worth a thousand words, but unless your picture makes sense, the only words it's likely to evoke are four-letter ones.

With Excel you can create long rows and columns containing numbers that nobody understands. So to make your data easier to comprehend, Excel helps you turn those numbers into charts that visually show trends, quantities, or patterns at a glance.

Understanding the Parts of a Chart

Excel can create gorgeous (or ugly) charts that graphically represent the numbers in your worksheets. Of course, to provide maximum flexibility, Excel offers numerous graphing options that may overwhelm you.

But take heart — after you enter your data in a worksheet, creating a chart is just a matter of letting Excel know which information you want to use, what type of chart you want, and where you want to put it. Although you don't need to know much charting lingo to create charts, you should understand a few terms that are confusing at first.

Most charts contain at least one data series. A *data series* is just a set of numbers for a particular category. For example, one data series may be sales results for January, February, and March, and another data series may be the sales of five different products over the same period.

Charts also have an x-axis and a y-axis. The *x-axis* is the horizontal plane (that's left to right), and the *y-axis* is the vertical plane (that's top to bottom).

To help you understand your numbers, a chart may also include a chart title (such as Chart of Our 1999 Losses) and a legend. A *legend* identifies what the different parts of a chart represent, as shown in Figure 10-1.

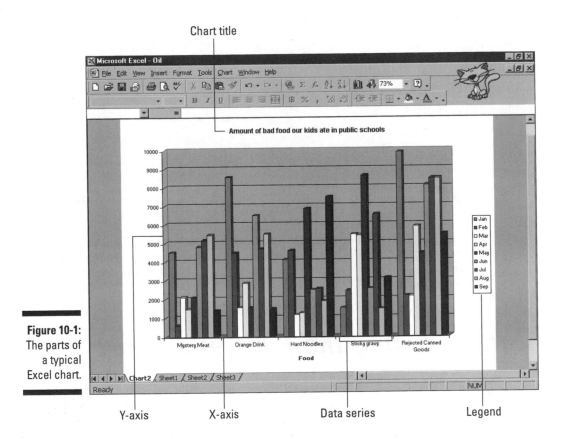

Figure 10-1:
The parts of
a typical
Excel chart.

Some of the more common types of charts include the following, which are shown in Figure 10-2:

- ✔ **Line chart:** A line chart consists of one or more lines where each line represents a single item, such as hot dog buns or transmission failures. You can use a line chart to show trends over time in your data, such as whether sales of different products have been rising (or declining) over a five-year period.

- ✔ **Area chart:** Identical to a line chart except that an area chart provides shading underneath each line to emphasize its values. If you plan to plot more than four items, an area chart can become cluttered and difficult to read.

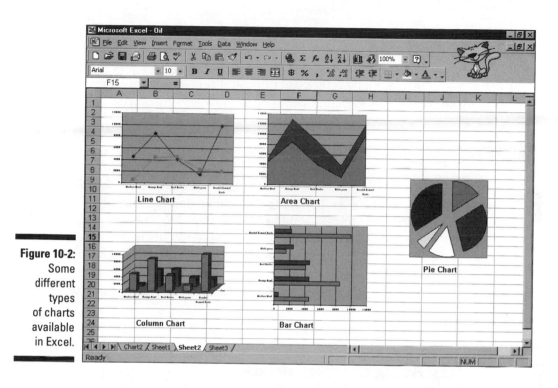

Figure 10-2:
Some
different
types
of charts
available
in Excel.

- **Column chart:** You can compare two or more items over time (such as sales of white bread versus wheat bread over a six-month period). By displaying columns which represent different items side by side, you can see how each product (represented by a column) is selling per month and how each product is selling in relation to other products.

- **Bar chart:** Essentially a column chart tipped on its side, a bar chart displays bars of different lengths from left to right. Bar charts are most useful for comparing two or more items or amounts over time. For example, a bar chart may consist of five different bars where each bar represents a different product and the length of each bar represents profits made from each product.

- **Pie chart:** Compares how separate parts make up a whole, such as determining how much money each sales region contributes (or takes away from) a company's profits each year.

REMEMBER

Many charts are also available in 3-D, which just gives a different look to the chart. Some people find 3-D charts easier to read; others think that 3-D makes the chart look more complicated than it needs to be.

Creating a Chart with the Chart Wizard

To help you create charts (almost) automatically, Excel offers the Chart Wizard, which kindly guides you through the process of creating charts from your data.

Creating Excel charts is easiest when your data is set up in a table format using adjacent rows and columns.

To create a chart with the Chart Wizard:

1. **Select all the cells, including the column and row headings, containing the data that you want to chart.**

   Excel uses column headings for the x-axis title and row headings for the chart legend. (You can always change the headings used in your chart later.)

2. **Click the Chart Wizard button on the Standard toolbar or choose Insert⇨Chart.**

   The Chart Wizard dialog box appears, as shown in Figure 10-3.

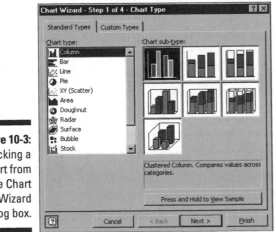

Figure 10-3: Picking a chart from the Chart Wizard dialog box.

3. **In the Chart Type list box, click the type of chart you want (such as Line, Pie, or Stock).**

4. **In the Chart Sub-type group, click the variation of the chart you want.**

5. **Click Next.**

   The second Chart Wizard dialog box appears, showing you what your chart looks like, as shown in Figure 10-4.

Collapse Dialog button ⌐

Figure 10-4:
After you
finish
making your
selections
from the
Chart
Wizard
dialog
boxes, the
Chart
Wizard
shows you
what your
chart looks
like.

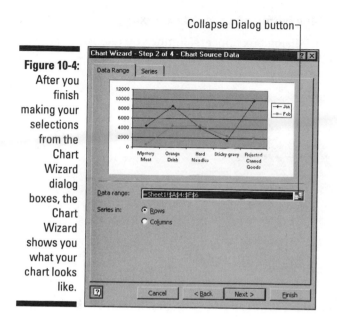

6. **Click either the Rows or Columns option button to change the way Excel uses your data to create a chart.**

   Choosing the Rows option button means that Excel uses your row labels (if any) to appear on the x-axis of your chart. Choosing the Columns option button means that Excel uses your column labels (if any) to appear on the x-axis of your chart.

7. **Click the Collapse Dialog button.**

   The Chart Wizard shrinks to a tiny floating window as shown in Figure 10-5.

Figure 10-5:
The Chart
Wizard as a
tiny floating
window.

Expand Dialog button ⌐

8. **Select the labels and data you want to chart. (You can skip this step if you don't want to change the labels and data you chose in Step 1.)**

   Excel highlights your chosen data with a dotted line.

9. Click the Expand Dialog button and then click Next.

The third Chart Wizard dialog box appears, letting you choose a chart title as well as titles for the x-axis and y-axis (see Figure 10-6).

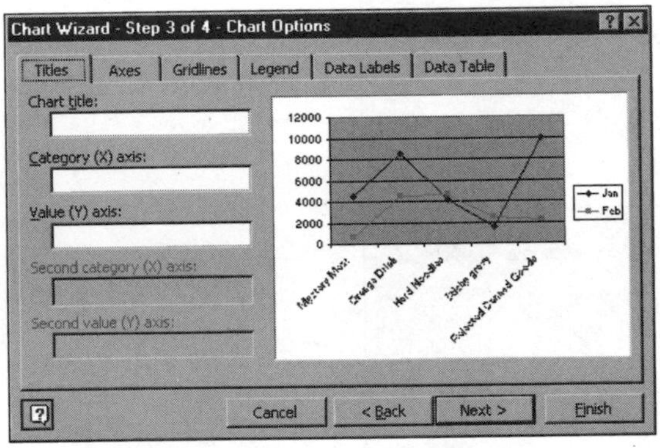

Figure 10-6:
Typing titles in the third Chart Wizard dialog box.

10. Type any titles that you want to add to your chart; then click Next.

The fourth Chart Wizard dialog box appears, as shown in Figure 10-7, asking whether you want to place your chart on the same worksheet as your data or on a separate sheet. Sometimes you may prefer keeping the chart on the same worksheet as the data used to create it. Other times you may want to put the chart on a separate worksheet, especially if the chart is as big as your entire computer screen.

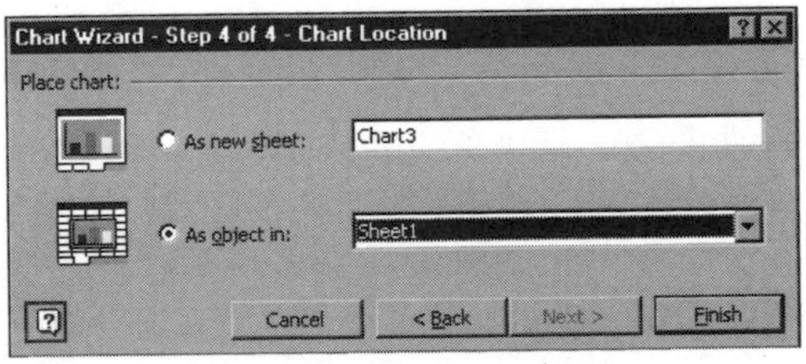

Figure 10-7:
Choosing where to place your chart.

11. Click either the As New Sheet or the As Object In option button and choose the worksheet where you want to place the chart.

12. Click the Finish button.

Excel draws your chart for you and places it on your chosen worksheet.

Editing Your Charts

The Chart Wizard helps you create a chart quickly, but afterward, you may decide to go back and modify your chart a little to make it prettier, move it around, or resize it. Just remember that you can always change any chart you create, so don't be afraid of experimenting and letting your imagination go wild.

Moving, resizing, and deleting an entire chart

Sometimes you may not like where Excel puts your chart. So rather than suffer under the tyrannical rule of Excel, take matters into your own hands and change the chart's position and size yourself.

To move, resize, or delete an entire chart:

1. **Click the chart that you want to move, resize, or delete.**

   After you select a chart, little black rectangles, called *handles,* appear on the corners and the sides of the chart's border.

2. **Choose one of the following:**

   Note: You can only move or resize a chart if you chose the As Object In option button in Step 9 in the section "Creating a Chart with the Chart Wizard."

   • **To move a chart to a new location without changing the size of the chart, click the edge of the chart and drag it.**

   Place the mouse cursor inside the chart (not on one of the handles) and hold down and move the left mouse button so the mouse cursor turns into a four-headed arrow. Drag the mouse and notice how Excel shows you an outline of where your chart will appear if you release the mouse button at that point. When you're satisfied with the location, release the left mouse button.

   • **To change the size of a chart, drag a handle.**

   Place the mouse cursor directly over a handle and hold down the left mouse button so the mouse cursor turns into a two-headed arrow. Drag the mouse and notice how Excel shows you an outline of how your chart looks if you release the mouse button at that point. When you're satisfied with the size, release the left mouse button.

Note: Middle handles change the location of one side of the chart only; corner handles control two sides at once. If you drag the top-middle handle, for example, you can move the top side of the chart to make the chart taller or shorter (the bottom side stays where it is). If you drag the top-right corner handle, you move both the top side and the right side at the same time.

- **To delete a chart, press Delete.**

Editing the parts of a chart

In addition to moving, resizing, or deleting the parts of a chart, you can also modify them as well. For example, if you misspell a chart title, suddenly decide you really want an x-axis title, or don't like the colors in your chart legend, you can change whatever it is you don't like. You can change any part of a chart at any time, so be bold and experiment as much as you want, especially if you're being paid to goof around with Excel.

An Excel chart consists of several objects that you can modify. Most charts include these common parts:

- ✔ **Chart area:** The entire box that contains the plot area plus the legend
- ✔ **Plot area:** The actual chart (pie, bar, line, and so on) and its X- and Y-axis labels
- ✔ **Legend:** A small box that defines what each color represents on the chart
- ✔ **Chart title:** Text that describes the chart's purpose

Changing a chart title

After you create a chart, you may find that you want to modify the chart title. To edit your chart title:

1. **Click the chart title that you want to edit.**

   A gray box appears around your chart title.

2. **Click anywhere inside the chart title so the I-beam cursor appears inside the chart title.**

3. **Type any changes you want to make in your chart title (or delete the title altogether, if you want).**

   You can use the arrow keys, the backspace key, and delete key to edit your title.

Formatting a chart title or legend entry

In addition to (or instead of) changing a chart title, you may just want to change the formatting style used to display a chart title or legend entry. To change the formatting of chart titles or legend entries:

1. **Click the chart title or legend that you want to format.**

   Handles appear around your chosen chart title or legend entry. (If you want to edit a particular legend entry, you have to click twice on that particular legend entry.)

2. **Right-click the chart title or legend entry.**

   A pop-up menu appears.

3. **Click the Format command (such as Format Legend or Format Chart Title).**

   A Format Chart Title or Format Legend Entry dialog box appears.

4. **Choose the font, font style, size, color, and any other formatting options you want to apply to your legend entry.**

5. **Click OK.**

Picking a different type of chart

Some charts look better than others, so if you first pick a chart type (bar, for example) that doesn't visually make your data any easier to understand, try picking a different chart type, such as a pie, line, or scatter chart. To change your chart type:

1. **Right-click the edge of the chart that you want to change.**

   Handles appear around the chart and a pop-up menu appears.

2. **Choose Chart Type.**

   The Chart Type dialog box appears (refer to Figure 10-3).

3. **Click a chart type that you want to use; then click OK.**

Changing the chart type can change the entire look of your chart, possibly messing up its appearance. If the chart looks really messed up after you change its type, press Ctrl+Z right away to undo your last action.

Using the Chart toolbar

If you're going to modify charts often, you may want to display the Chart toolbar, which provides several icons that you can click to view and modify the appearance of your chart.

To display (or hide) the Chart toolbar, choose View⇨Toolbars⇨Chart. The Chart toolbar appears, as shown in Figure 10-8.

The Chart toolbar features the following:

- **Chart Objects:** Allows you to select part of your chart, such as the legend or category axis, without having to click it

- **Format Plot Area:** Allows you to change the colors and borders of your chart plot area (which is the portion of your chart that actually displays columns, lines, bars, pie charts, and so on)

- **Chart Type:** Allows you to quickly choose a different chart type for plotting your data, for example, by switching from a column chart to a pie chart

- **Legend:** Highlights the data on your worksheet that defines the labels displayed in the legend

- **Data Table:** Displays the actual data used to create the chart

- **By Row:** Defines the Y-axis labels using the row labels

- **By Column:** Defines the X-axis labels using column labels

- **Angle Text Downward:** Changes the appearance of X- and Y-axis labels to appear downward

- **Angle Text Upward:** Changes the appearance of X- and Y-axis labels to appear upward

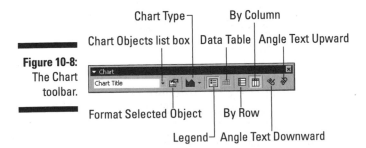

Figure 10-8:
The Chart toolbar.

Chapter 11

Working with Worksheets and Workbooks

• •

• •

*E*very Excel file consists of exactly one workbook. Each workbook contains one or more worksheets to help you organize your data.

For example, you may want to create one worksheet to display data from your company's first-quarter sales results, a second worksheet to display data from second-quarter sales results, a third worksheet to display data from third-quarter sales results, and a fourth worksheet to display data from fourth-quarter sales results.

Each time you need to add new numbers and formulas, you can either put them on an existing worksheet or create a new worksheet and store them there.

Manipulating Your Worksheets

Each time you start Excel, it automatically creates a workbook for you along with three blank worksheets so you can start typing numbers, text, labels, and formulas. Excel displays the name of each worksheet on a tab that appears near the bottom of the screen, as shown in Figure 11-1.

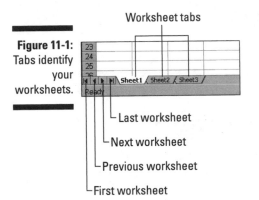

Figure 11-1:
Tabs identify
your
worksheets.

Worksheet tabs

Last worksheet

Next worksheet

Previous worksheet

First worksheet

If you have several worksheets, you may have to click one of the following arrows to display the worksheets that may be temporarily hidden from view:

- ✓ **First worksheet:** Displays the top worksheet (usually the last worksheet you added to the workbook)
- ✓ **Previous worksheet:** Displays the previous worksheet tab
- ✓ **Next worksheet:** Displays the next worksheet tab
- ✓ **Last worksheet:** Displays the bottom worksheet (usually one of the first worksheets in a workbook)

Naming your worksheets

Excel has no imagination whatsoever so it always names worksheets something generic and boring, like Sheet1 or Sheet4. Unless you feel that your information is equally generic and boring, you may want to give your worksheets more descriptive names.

To name your worksheets:

1. **Double-click the tab containing the worksheet name that you want to change; or choose Format➪Sheet➪Rename.**

    Excel highlights the worksheet name on the tab.

2. **Type a new name, preferably one that's descriptive of the worksheet contents (Worthless data from 1999, for example).**

3. **Press Enter.**

Worksheet names can be up to 31 characters long and can include spaces, punctuation, and almost anything else you care to type from your keyboard.

Creating and deleting worksheets

Ideally, each worksheet contains a single set of related data, such as the value of individual stocks in your investment portfolio, or your monthly household budget. To help you organize related data in single, separate worksheets, Excel lets you create additional worksheets whenever you need them.

To add a new worksheet to a workbook, choose Insert⇨Worksheet. Excel inserts a worksheet to the left of the currently displayed worksheet.

If you create too many worksheets, Excel may temporarily hide some of the worksheet tabs from view. To see all the different worksheets stored in your workbook, click one of the arrow buttons (refer to Figure 11-1).

If you no longer need the data that's stored on a particular worksheet, you can delete the entire worksheet along with any data that it contains. (Just make sure that you really, *really* don't need that data.)

If you delete a worksheet, you cannot undo the action, so be absolutely sure that you want to delete it before you even think about following the steps below.

To delete an existing worksheet from a workbook:

1. **Click the tab of the worksheet that you want to delete.**

2. **Choose Edit⇨Delete Sheet.**

   A dialog box appears, asking whether you're sure that you want to delete your chosen worksheet.

3. **Click OK.**

Rearranging worksheets

Each time you create a worksheet, Excel displays your newly created worksheet's tab on the far left (creating the illusion that the new worksheet is on top of the stack of worksheets). If you can live with this setup, fine, but if you'd rather arrange the order of your worksheets yourself:

1. **Click the tab of the worksheet that you want to move and leave the mouse pointer over that tab.**

   The worksheet appears on-screen.

2. **Hold down the left mouse button and drag the tab left or right until the black, downward-pointing arrow that appears points to the location between the worksheet tabs where you want the worksheet to be.**

   The mouse cursor turns into an arrow pointing to a document, and a black, downward-pointing arrow points to where Excel will move your worksheet when you release the mouse button.

3. **Release the left mouse button.**

   Excel moves your chosen worksheet to the location where the black, downward-pointing arrow last appeared.

The order of your worksheets does not affect the data stored on each worksheet. Rearranging the order of your worksheets is for your convenience only.

Modifying Your Worksheets

A worksheet acts like a big, blank piece of paper where you can type stuff. Just as you can format individual cells (see Chapter 8), so can you format entire worksheets to make them look pretty, businesslike, or absolutely intimidating (which is great if you're giving a presentation to people who favor appearance over substance).

Inserting and deleting rows and columns

After you type stuff in a worksheet, you may suddenly discover that you forgot a column or row entry. To make room for the missing entry, Excel can insert a new row or column anywhere in your worksheet at any time.

To insert a row or column in your worksheet, open the worksheet that you want to modify; then follow these steps:

1. **Choose one of the following:**

   • Click anywhere in the row that you want to "push down" to insert a new row. For example, if you want to insert a new row between rows 11 and 12, click any cell in row 12.

- Click anywhere in the column that you want to "push to the right" to insert a new column. For example, if you want to insert a new column between columns C and D, click any cell in column D.

2. **Choose Insert⇨Rows or Insert⇨Columns.**

   Excel squeezes your new row or column in your worksheet and automatically renumbers the rows or columns.

To delete a row or column:

1. **Click the row or column that you want to delete.**

2. **Choose Edit⇨Delete.**

   The Delete dialog box appears.

3. **Click the Entire Row or Entire Column option button and then click OK.**

   Excel deletes your chosen row or column and automatically renumbers the remaining rows or columns in the worksheet.

Linking worksheets with formulas

Despite all the fancy new features of Excel, the program's primary purpose is still to let you type numbers and create formulas that calculate new results. Because Excel provides multiple worksheets, you can put first-quarter sales results on one worksheet, second-quarter sales results on a second worksheet, third-quarter sales results on a third worksheet, and fourth-quarter sales results on a fourth worksheet. Now if you want to find your annual sales results, all you have to do is *link* the totals from each of the four separate worksheets to a fifth worksheet.

To create a formula that appears on one worksheet but uses data stored on a second (or third, or fourth, or whichever) worksheet:

1. **Click the cell where you want the formula to appear.**

2. **Type = (the equal sign).**

3. **Click the worksheet tab containing the data that you want to use in your formula.**

4. **Click the cell containing the data that you want to use.**

   Excel automatically types the cell reference in the Formula Bar, such as `'1999 worthless data'!B13` (where '1999 worthless data' is the name of the worksheet and B13 is the cell on that worksheet that contains the data you want to use).

Normally, when you want to use data stored in a cell, you just have to use the cell name, such as B12. However, if you want to tell Excel to use data stored on a different worksheet, you must first specify the worksheet name in single quotes, followed by an exclamation mark, followed by the actual cell name. For example, consider the following cell reference:

```
'First quarter sales results'!C45
```

This tells Excel, "Look for a worksheet named 'First quarter sales results' and then use the data stored in cell C45 on that worksheet." (If your worksheet name is one word, such as Sheet1, you don't have to surround it with single quotes if you don't want to.)

5. **Click the Formula Bar and type an operator, such as + (the plus sign).**

6. **Repeat Steps 3 through 5 as often as necessary to complete the formula.**

7. **Press Enter.**

Preparing to Print Your Work

Before rushing right out and printing every worksheet (and most likely wasting paper in the process), take a few moments to adjust the way your worksheets will look before you print them. That way, your worksheets can look as beautiful as they appear on your computer screen.

If you just want to start printing right away, see Chapter 8.

Squeezing or expanding your worksheets

Nothing is more frustrating than creating a spreadsheet where everything fits on one page except for one line that prints on a second page. Rather than print your spreadsheet on two pages where the second page is mostly blank, you can tell Excel to squeeze all your work on a single page. Or you can tell it to expand the spreadsheet so that more of the data falls on the second page.

To shrink or expand your spreadsheet:

1. **Choose File⇨Print Preview.**

   Excel displays your worksheet exactly how it will appear in print, so you can decide whether you need to squeeze or expand it.

2. **Click the Setup button.**

   The Page Setup dialog box appears, as shown in Figure 11-2.

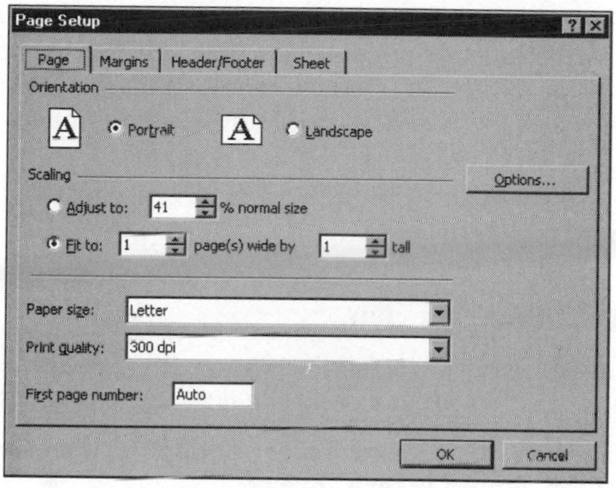

Figure 11-2:
The Page
Setup
dialog box.

3. **Click the Page tab.**

4. **Choose one of the following:**

   - **Click the Adjust To option button and click the % Normal Size list box to change the size of your worksheet.**

     To shrink your worksheet, choose a percentage less than 100, such as 90. To expand your worksheet, choose a percentage larger than 100, such as 120.

   - **Click the Fit To option button.**

     If the data on your worksheet doesn't fit within the side margins of one page, you can cram all the data on one page anyway by typing **1** in the Page(s) Wide list box. If the data on your worksheet doesn't fit within the top and bottom margins of one page, you can cram all the data on one page by typing **1** in the Tall list box.

5. **Click OK.**

   Excel displays your newly scaled worksheet.

6. **Click the Close button in the Print Preview window when you're happy with the appearance of your worksheet.**

Breaking worksheets into separate pages

When you want to print a worksheet, you may worry about how the worksheet will appear on a printed page. Normally, Excel fills an entire page with your worksheet data and then starts printing your data on a second page.

Excel can automatically take care of separating your worksheet into different pages, but you may want to specify page breaks yourself. Say you don't want your worksheet data to print on a single page. You can divide it so half the data prints on one page and half the data prints on a second page.

Creating a page break

To place a page break in a worksheet:

1. **Choose View⇨Page Break Preview.**

   Excel shows your worksheet. Dotted lines show the page breaks due to your paper size. Solid lines are for page breaks that you've inserted.

2. **Click in the cell where you want to insert both a vertical and horizontal page break; then choose Insert⇨Break.**

   Excel draws both a vertical and horizontal page break to the left and top of the cell that you chose in Step 2.

3. **Choose View⇨Normal.**

Deleting a page break

If you don't like the page breaks you added, you can eliminate them entirely by following these steps:

1. **Choose View⇨Page Break Preview.**

   Excel shows your worksheet with all your page breaks.

2. **Move the mouse pointer over the solid blue page break line that you want to delete.**

   The mouse pointer turns into a double-pointing arrow.

3. **Hold down the left mouse button and drag the mouse to the top or left side of your worksheet.**

4. **Release the left mouse button.**

   Excel shows you how your worksheet will print.

5. **Choose View⇨Normal.**

Changing the paper size and orientation

Sometimes a worksheet won't fit into the confines of a typical piece of paper. When that happens, you can tell Excel to print your worksheets on legal-size paper or sideways so the whole worksheet fits on a single page.

Changing the page orientation

The two types of page orientation are portrait and landscape. *Portrait orientation* means that the page is taller than it is wide, which is how painters usually orient the canvas when painting someone's portrait. *Landscape* means that the page is wider than it is tall.

Use landscape orientation when you want to print your worksheets sideways on a sheet of paper — nine times out of ten, your worksheets are wider than they are tall.

To change the page orientation of your worksheet:

1. **Choose File⇨Print Preview.**

2. **Click the Setup button.**

   The Page Setup dialog box appears.

3. **Click the Page tab. (Refer to Figure 11-2.)**

4. **Click the Portrait or Landscape option button.**

5. **Click OK.**

Choosing the size of your paper

Many people use paper that measures 8½-x-11 inches. Of course, if you want to cram more of your worksheet on a single page, you can stuff your printer with a larger size of paper. Right after you load your printer with a different size of paper, you also have to tell Excel the size of your new paper so it prints your worksheets correctly.

To tell Excel the size of the paper to print on:

1. **Choose File⇨Print Preview.**

2. **Click the Setup button.**

   The Page Setup dialog box appears.

3. **Click the Page tab.**

4. **Click the Paper Size list box and choose a paper size (such as Letter or A4).**

5. **Click OK.**

6. **Click Close.**

Printing gridlines

The whole purpose of displaying gridlines and headings is to help you place your labels, numbers, and formulas. Normally, when you print a worksheet, you don't want your gridlines and row or column headings to appear because they can be as distracting as wires holding up a puppet show. But sometimes you do want the gridlines and headings to show so you can see exactly what each cell contains.

To make Excel print gridlines and headings:

1. **Choose File➪Print Preview.**

2. **Click the Setup button.**

   The Page Setup dialog box appears.

3. **Click the Sheet tab.**

   The Sheet tab of the Page Setup dialog box appears, as shown in Figure 11-3.

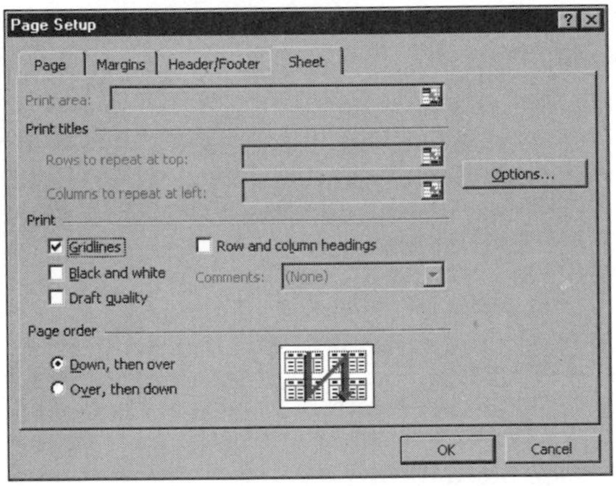

Figure 11-3:
The Sheet tab of the Page Setup dialog box.

4. **Click the Gridlines and/or the Row and Column Headings check boxes. If a check appears in the box, the specified item will print.**

5. **Click OK.**

   Excel shows you how your worksheet will print with (or without) gridlines.

6. **Click Close.**

Adding headers and footers

If you have a worksheet that spans several pages, you may want to create headers and footers that include the page number or a title. To add a header or footer to a worksheet:

1. **Choose File⇨Page Setup.**

   A Page Setup dialog box appears.

2. **Click the Header/Footer tab.**

   The Header/Footer tab appears in the Page Setup dialog box, as shown in Figure 11-4.

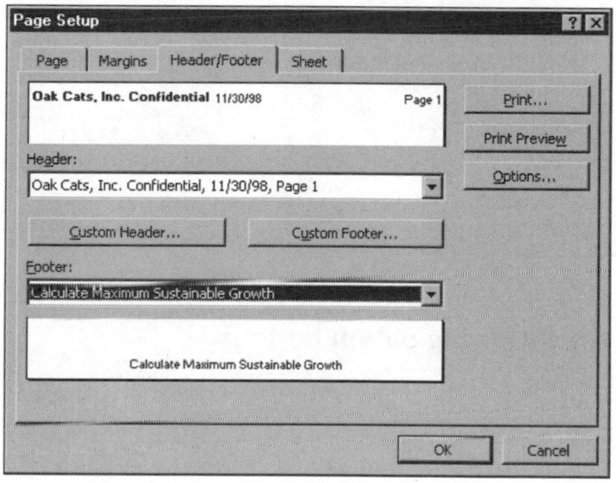

Figure 11-4:
Defining headers and footers for an Excel worksheet.

3. **Click the Custom Header or Custom Footer button and type your header or footer.**

4. **Click OK twice.**

Printing workbooks and worksheets

When you finally decide to print your Excel data, you have three choices to print:

- The entire workbook (every single worksheet in the workbook)
- One worksheet
- A range of cells stored on one worksheet

To print your data:

1. **Highlight the cells that you want to print out. (You can skip this step if you want to print an entire workbook or one worksheet.)**

2. **Choose File⇨Print or press Ctrl+P.**

    The Print dialog box appears, as shown in Figure 11-5.

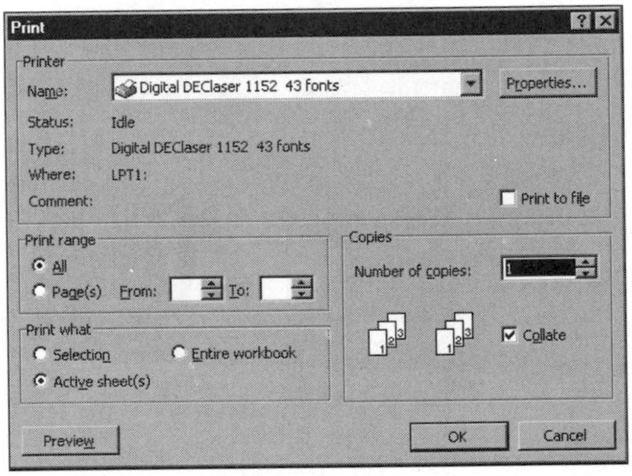

Figure 11-5:
The Print
dialog box.

3. **Click in one of the following option buttons:**

    • Entire Workbook

    • Active Sheet(s)

    • Selection

4. **Click the Preview button if you want to see a preview of your worksheets; otherwise skip this step.**

    Excel shows you what it plans on printing in case you decide to print. To exit Print Preview, click Close and then return to Step 2.

5. **Click in the Number of Copies box and type a number. (If you want to print five copies, type 5.)**

6. **Make sure that your printer is turned on, the cable is connected properly, and the printer has paper; then click OK.**

Part IV
Making Presentations with PowerPoint 2000

The 5th Wave — By Rich Tennant

"AND TO COMPLETE OUR MULTIMEDIA PRESENTATION,..."

In this part . . .

The fear of public speaking is the number one fear of most people — with the fear of death running a distant second. To help you overcome public speaking and presentation fears, Microsoft PowerPoint 2000 can help you organize and design a presentation that can keep others so amused that they won't even bother looking at you.

When you use PowerPoint 2000 to create a presentation, you won't ever need to rely on mere words, pointless hand gestures, or crudely drawn diagrams scribbled on a white board. With PowerPoint 2000, you can give flawless presentations that people will remember.

The next time you need to dazzle an audience (with facts or fabricated lies that look like facts) flip through this part of the book and see how PowerPoint 2000 can help you create dazzling slide show presentations and handouts that can clarify (or distort) topics for your audience's benefit.

Chapter 12

Creating Slide Show Presentations

*T*he number one fear of many people is speaking in public. (The number two fear is wasting time sitting through a boring presentation.) Giving a speech can be terrifying, but displaying a presentation along with your speech can provide an important crutch — visuals. *Visuals* can take the form of handouts, 35mm slides, black-and-white or color overhead transparencies, or computer images displayed on a monitor or projected on a screen.

Visuals can help structure your presentation so you don't have to memorize everything yourself. Instead, you can display pretty charts and talk about each one without having the entire audience staring at you all the time.

To help you create presentation slide shows on your computer, Microsoft Office 2000 includes a presentation program called PowerPoint 2000. By using PowerPoint, you can show presentations on your computer or print them out as nifty handouts.

PowerPoint can help you make visually interesting presentations, but all the special visual effects in the world can't save a worthless presentation. Before rushing to create a PowerPoint slide show presentation, take some time to decide what's important to your audience and what you want to accomplish with your presentation (sell a product, explain why dumping oil into the ocean is harmless to the environment, raise support to sell weapons to unstable Third World countries just for the money, and so on).

Creating a Presentation

When you want to create a PowerPoint presentation, you have four choices:

- ✔ Create the presentation from scratch, which can be tedious and time-consuming as well as boring and mind-deadening.

- ✔ Ask a coworker to do all the work for you so you can take all the credit (not always practical).

- ✔ Use the PowerPoint AutoContent Wizard to guide you through the steps of creating a presentation.

- ✔ Use one of the PowerPoint presentation templates so all you have to do is type in your own information.

Although you can create a presentation from scratch, letting PowerPoint create most of a presentation for you is so much easier. If you create a presentation with the AutoContent Wizard or use a template, you can always modify the presentation later if you feel extra-creative.

Presenting the AutoContent Wizard

To help you create a presentation that demands attention, PowerPoint offers the *AutoContent Wizard,* which lets you put together a presentation almost without thinking — which is the way most people prefer to work anyway. The AutoContent Wizard can create a presentation in minutes, so all you have to do is go back and type in your own text.

To use the AutoContent Wizard:

1. **Choose File⇨New.**

   The New Presentation dialog box appears.

2. **Click the General tab.**

3. **Click the AutoContent Wizard icon and then click OK.**

   An AutoContent Wizard dialog box appears.

4. **Click Next.**

   Another AutoContent Wizard dialog box appears, asking for the type of presentation you want to give (such as Communicating Bad News or Recommending a Strategy).

5. **Click the desired type of presentation (such as Brainstorming Session or Communicating Bad News) and then click Next.**

   Another AutoContent Wizard dialog box appears, asking how you want to use your presentation.

6. **Click an option button (such as On-screen Presentation or Web Presentation) and then click Next.**

   Yet another AutoContent Wizard dialog box appears, asking you to name your presentation and give your name. Whatever you type appears on the first slide of your presentation.

7. **Type your title, name, and any additional information in the appropriate text boxes and then click Next.**

   The final AutoContent Wizard dialog box appears, letting you know that you're finished answering questions.

8. **Click Finish.**

   PowerPoint displays your first slide along with an outline for your entire presentation, as shown in Figure 12-1.

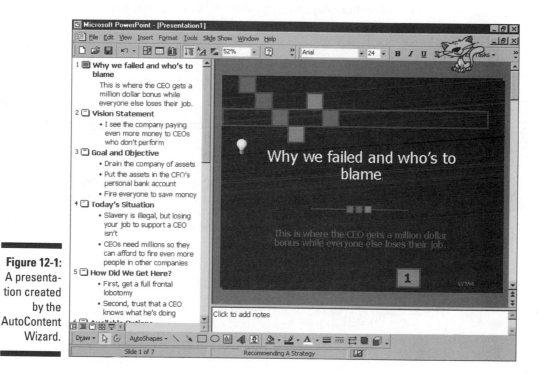

Figure 12-1: A presentation created by the AutoContent Wizard.

Filling in the blanks with a PowerPoint template

As an alternative to using the AutoContent Wizard, you can pick a pre-designed PowerPoint *template* and just type in your text. By creating a presentation based on a template, you can make a presentation quickly without much effort, thought, or time.

The main difference between the AutoContent Wizard and PowerPoint templates is that the AutoContent Wizard guides you through the creation of your presentation. A PowerPoint template simply contains a pre-designed style and layout for your slide that you can modify (just as long as you know what you're doing).

To create a presentation with a PowerPoint template:

1. **Choose File➪New.**

   The New Presentation dialog box appears.

2. **Click the Presentations tab.**

3. **Click the template (such as Business Plan or Company Meeting) that best describes the kind of presentation you want; then click OK.**

   PowerPoint displays the first slide of the template, ready for you to edit and customize for your own needs.

Learning PowerPoint's Toolbars

PowerPoint provides two toolbars that contain the most commonly used commands. These two toolbars, the Standard toolbar and Formatting toolbar, automatically appear when you first install and start PowerPoint. You can hide them later or move them around the screen if you want.

Unlike previous versions, PowerPoint 2000 automatically modifies its toolbars to display the icons you use most often. So if your toolbar looks different each time you use it, it's because PowerPoint is trying to display the icons representing your most commonly used commands.

Exploring the Standard toolbar

The *Standard toolbar* offers access to the program's most frequently used commands, arranged from left to right in roughly the order of their frequency of use, as shown in Figure 12-2.

Figure 12-2:
The pretty icons on the Standard toolbar.

The Standard tool bar features the following commands:

- ✓ **New:** Creates a new presentation
- ✓ **Open:** Opens an existing presentation
- ✓ **Save:** Saves your current presentation
- ✓ **E-mail:** Sends the current presentation as an e-mail
- ✓ **Print:** Prints your current presentation
- ✓ **Spelling:** Checks the spelling of your labels in a presentation
- ✓ **Cut:** Moves the currently selected text to the Clipboard, the invisible Windows storage area
- ✓ **Copy:** Copies the currently selected text to the Clipboard
- ✓ **Paste:** Places in the current worksheet whatever text is currently on the Clipboard
- ✓ **Format Painter:** Copies the formatting of the currently selected text so that you can apply that formatting to any text you select next
- ✓ **Undo:** Reverses the action of your last command
- ✓ **Redo:** Opposite of Undo — restores what the Undo command last did
- ✓ **Insert Hyperlink:** Creates a link to a Web page
- ✓ **Tables and Borders:** Displays (or hides) the Tables and Borders toolbar
- ✓ **Insert Table:** Adds a table to a slide
- ✓ **Insert Chart:** Inserts a Microsoft Excel chart
- ✓ **New Slide:** Adds a new slide to your presentation
- ✓ **Expand All:** Displays all slide text in the left pane
- ✓ **Show Formatting:** Shows (or hides) the formatting of slide text in the left pane
- ✓ **Grayscale Preview:** Toggles between showing your slides in color and black-and-white
- ✓ **Zoom:** Adjusts the magnification of your presentation
- ✓ **Microsoft PowerPoint Help:** Displays (or hides) the Office Assistant that you can click to get more help using PowerPoint
- ✓ **More Buttons:** Displays or hides buttons on the Standard toolbar

To quickly find out what each button on the Standard toolbar does, point the mouse over a button and then wait a second or two until the *ScreenTip* — a brief explanation of the button — appears.

Using the Formatting toolbar to change the way presentations look

The *Formatting toolbar* contains commands to make your text look pretty with different fonts, type sizes, and typefaces (such as bold, italics, and underline). The buttons on the Formatting toolbar appear in the following order from left to right, as shown in Figure 12-3.

Figure 12-3:
The
Formatting
toolbar.

The following commands appear left to right on the Formatting tool bar:

- **Font:** Controls the *font* — the look of the letters — of the selected text
- **Font Size:** Controls the size of the selected text
- **Bold:** Makes selected text **bold**
- **Italic:** Makes selected text *italic*
- **Underline:** <u>Underlines</u> selected text
- **Text Shadow:** Displays a shadow on selected text
- **Align Left:** Makes the lines of the selected text line up on the left (with an uneven right margin)
- **Center:** Centers selected text between the left and right margins
- **Align Right:** Makes the lines of the selected text line up on the right (with an uneven left margin)
- **Numbering:** Automatically numbers separate text paragraphs
- **Bullets:** Automatically displays a bullet in front of each paragraph
- **Increase Font Size:** Slightly increases the font size of selected text
- **Decrease Font Size:** Slightly decreases the font size of selected text
- **Promote:** Moves text to the left in the left pane
- **Demote:** Moves text to the right in the left pane
- **Animation Effects:** Displays (or hides) the Animation Effects toolbar
- **Common Tasks:** Pull-down list of the most common PowerPoint commands
- **More Buttons:** Displays or hides buttons on the Formatting toolbar

PowerPoint offers more toolbars than just the Standard and Formatting toolbars, but these two toolbars contain the most common commands that you need.

Understanding the PowerPoint Interface

When you create a presentation, PowerPoint 2000 displays a *Tri-Pane view*, which displays three window panes, as shown in Figure 12-4.

The PowerPoint includes the following:

- **The Presentation Outline pane:** Displays the text of your entire presentation, organized as an outline, for easy viewing and editing.

- **The Slide pane:** Displays the text and graphics of the current slide (explained in more detail in Chapter 13).

- **The Notes pane:** Displays any notes you want to include for each slide.

Collapsed outline heading   Slide pane   Slide title   Slide text

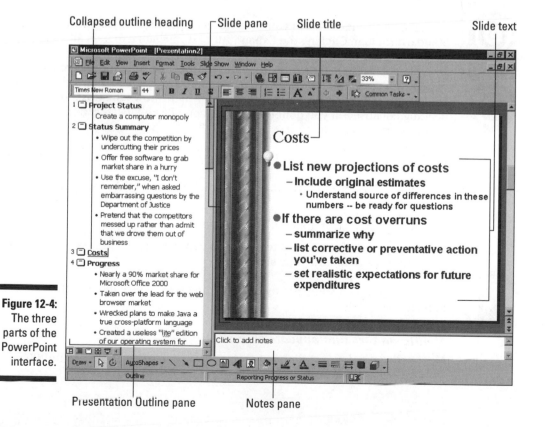

Figure 12-4:
The three parts of the PowerPoint interface.

Presentation Outline pane   Notes pane

Using the Presentation Outline pane

The Presentation Outline window pane displays your slide titles as outline headings and the text on each slide as outline subheadings. With the Presentation Outline pane, you can:

✔ View and edit slide titles

✔ Add, delete, or edit text that appears on each slide

✔ Add, delete, or rearrange your slides

The whole purpose of the Presentation Outline pane is to show you the overall design of your PowerPoint presentation without worrying about the actual appearance or formatting of your presentation.

Viewing and editing your slide titles

The Presentation Outline pane displays all your slide titles as outline headings. If you have many slides in your presentation, you can collapse your outline so it only displays slide titles and not any text that appears on any slides.

To collapse all slide titles in your outline, click the Expand All button on the Standard toolbar. Clicking the Expand All button again expands all slide titles.

To collapse just one slide title, double-click the icon that appears to the left of the outline heading that you want to collapse. PowerPoint underlines collapsed slide titles, as shown in Figure 12-4, which shows the Costs outline heading collapsed. If you double-click the icon of a collapsed slide title, PowerPoint expands it.

To edit a slide title:

1. **In the Presentation Outline pane, click the slide title that you want to edit.**

   An I-beam cursor appears in your chosen slide title.

2. **Type any text you want to add. You can use the Backspace, Delete, or arrow keys to edit your slide title.**

You can also edit a slide title by clicking directly on the slide title that appears on a slide.

Modifying text that appears on a slide

Most slides display text that appears on the slide. Using the Presentation Outline pane, you can add, delete, or modify any text on a slide.

To add text to a slide using the Presentation Outline pane:

1. **Click to the far right of the slide title where you want to add text and then press Enter.**

   PowerPoint displays a new slide icon directly underneath the slide title you chose in Step 1.

2. **Click the Demote button (the right arrow) on the Formatting toolbar.**

   Demoting the slide icon makes any text you type appear on the slide you choose.

3. **Type the text that you want to appear on the slide.**

   As you type your text, PowerPoint magically displays your text on the slide so you can see how it looks.

If a slide already contains text, click to the far right of that text in the Presentation Outline pane, press Enter, then type the text you want to add.

The position of text underneath a slide title defines that text's position on the slide. To move text and rearrange the text that appears on a slide:

1. **In the Presentation Outline pane, move the mouse pointer to the far left of the text (over the bullet to the left of the text) that you want to move.**

   PowerPoint displays the mouse pointer as a four-way pointing arrow.

2. **Hold down the left mouse button and move the mouse.**

   The mouse pointer turns into a double-pointing arrow. A line appears to show you where PowerPoint will move the text when you release the left mouse button.

3. **Release the left mouse button when the line appears where you want to move the text.**

Once you create text, you can always edit it later.

Adding a slide

Each outline heading in the Presentation Outline pane represents one slide. To add a new slide:

1. **Move the mouse pointer to the far left of an outline heading in the Presentation Outline pane and click the mouse.**

   The outline heading that you choose appears after the new slide you want to add.

2. **Press Enter.**

   PowerPoint displays a slide icon directly above the outline heading that you chose in Step 1.

3. **Press the up arrow key to move the cursor to the newly created outline heading.**

   PowerPoint displays a blank slide.

4. **Type an outline heading in the Presentation Outline pane.**

   As you type, PowerPoint automatically displays your outline heading in both the Presentation Outline pane and in the Slide pane.

If you want to add a new slide and choose the slide's layout for displaying text and graphics:

1. **Move the mouse pointer to the far left of an outline heading and click the left mouse button.**

   The outline heading that you choose appears after the new slide you want to add.

2. **Choose Insert⇨New Slide or press Ctrl+M.**

   A New Slide dialog box appears, as shown in Figure 12-5.

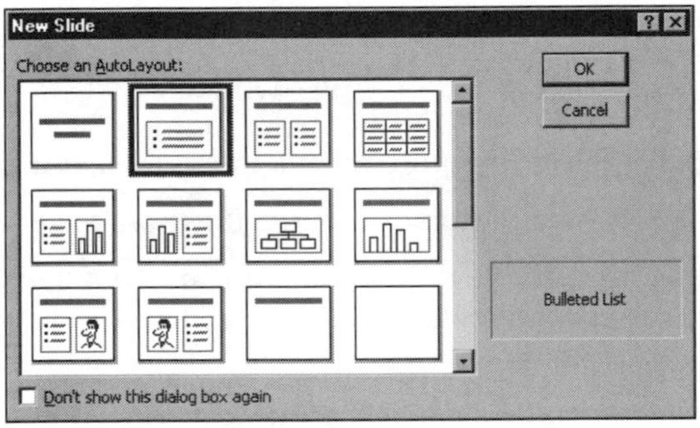

Figure 12-5:
The New Slide dialog box lets you choose the visual appearance of your newly created slide.

3. **Click the slide design that you want to use and click OK.**

4. **Type an outline heading in the Presentation Outline pane.**

   Any text that you type appears in both the Presentation Outline pane and in the Slide pane.

Deleting a slide

Sometimes you may want to delete a slide that you no longer need. To delete a slide:

1. **Move the mouse pointer over the slide icon of the slide in the Presentation Outline pane that you want to delete and click the left mouse button.**

   PowerPoint highlights the outline heading along with any subheadings that appear underneath.

2. **Press Delete.**

   PowerPoint deletes your chosen slide.

If you made a mistake and deleted the wrong slide, press Ctrl+Z to recover the slide you just wiped out.

Rearranging your slides

The Presentation Outline pane is great for showing the order of your slides. If you don't like the order, you can rearrange slides at any time.

If you have a large number of slides, you may want to collapse your outline headings to make it easier to see your actual slide titles. To collapse your outline headings, click the Expand All button on the Standard toolbar.

To rearrange your slides:

1. **In the Presentation Outline pane, move the mouse pointer over the slide icon of the outline heading (slide title) that you want to move and hold down the left mouse button.**

   PowerPoint highlights your outline heading and any subheadings underneath it.

2. **Drag the mouse.**

   PowerPoint displays a horizontal line at the slide's new location and turns the mouse pointer into a double-pointing arrow.

3. **Release the left mouse button when the line is where you want your slide moved.**

You can use the preceding steps above to rearrange subheadings, which means you can move text from one slide to another slide.

Using the Presentation Outline pane to rearrange your slides is fine, but you can't see how all your slides look in relation to one another. If you prefer to rearrange your slides visually:

1. **Choose View⇨Slide Sorter.**

   PowerPoint displays all your slides on the screen at once, as shown in Figure 12-6.

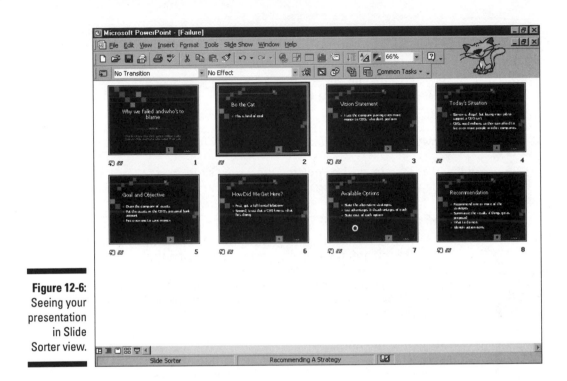

Figure 12-6:
Seeing your
presentation
in Slide
Sorter view.

2. **Place the mouse pointer over the slide that you want to move and hold down the left mouse button.**

   PowerPoint highlights the slide with a black border.

3. **Drag the mouse pointer to where you want to move the slide.**

   PowerPoint displays a vertical line where your slide will move to when you release the left mouse button.

4. **Release the left mouse button when the line is where you want your slide.**

   PowerPoint automatically renumbers your slides to reflect the new arrangement.

5. **Choose View⇨Normal.**

To increase or decrease the number of slides visible in Slide Sorter view with the Zoom command, choose one of the following:

  ✔ Choose View⇨Zoom and then click the option button associated with the percentage that you want to display (such as 66% or 50%).

  ✔ Click the Zoom Control list box on the right end of the Standard toolbar and choose a percentage (such as 100% or 25%).

Converting outline headings into subheadings (and vice versa)

An *outline heading* appears as a slide title and *outline subheadings* appear as text on a slide. Through the wonders of modern technology, PowerPoint lets you turn outline headings into subheadings and subheadings into outline headings.

To turn an outline heading into a subheading: In the Presentation Outline pane, click anywhere inside the outline heading that you want to convert into a subheading and then click the Demote button on the Standard toolbar.

To turn a subheading into an outline heading: In the Presentation Outline pane, click anywhere inside the subheading that you want to convert into an outline heading and then click the Promote button on the Standard toolbar.

Adding notes to a slide

The *Notes pane* lets you type notes to go along with each slide. You can refer to these notes during your presentation or pass them out as handouts so your audience has a handy reference during and after your presentation.

Text that you type on the Notes portion of a slide doesn't appear on the slide itself. Notes are just a way to keep related text together with your slides.

To type a note for a slide:

1. **Click in the Notes pane.**

   PowerPoint displays each slide with a text box at the bottom where you can type notes, refer to Figure 12-4.

2. **Type any text that you want.**

Saving Your Presentations

Unless you enjoy creating everything from scratch over and over again, you should save your work. Depending on what you want to do, you can save your PowerPoint presentations as a file or as a Web page.

Saving your presentation in a file

To save a presentation you can click the Save button (the picture of a disk) on the Standard toolbar, press Ctrl+S, or choose File⇨Save.

If you haven't saved the file before, the Save As dialog box appears, asking you to choose a filename and a directory to store your file in.

Saving your file under a new name

One easy way to create a presentation quickly is to open an existing presentation file, then save the file under a new name. This way, you can just modify an existing presentation rather than create everything all over again.

To save your file under a different name, choose File⇨Save As and type in a new name for the file.

PowerPoint 2000 presentations are compatible with PowerPoint 97 files, but not with older versions of PowerPoint, such as those created by PowerPoint 95 or PowerPoint 4.0. To save a PowerPoint presentation so someone else can edit it using an older version of PowerPoint, choose the Save As command and then choose the appropriate version of PowerPoint, such as PowerPoint 4.0, in the Save as Type list box of the Save As dialog box.

Saving PowerPoint presentations as Web pages

If you create a particularly memorable presentation, you may want to post it on a Web page. To save a presentation as a Web page:

1. **Choose File⇨Save as Web Page.**

   The Save As dialog box appears.

2. **Click the Change Title button.**

   A Set Page Title dialog box appears.

3. **Type the title that you want to appear at the top of your Web page and click OK.**

4. **Click Save.**

To view your PowerPoint presentation as a Web page, choose File⇨ Web Page Preview or load your Web browser (such as Netscape Navigator) and load your newly created Web page to see how it will look when posted on the Internet.

Saving PowerPoint presentations to go

Many people create PowerPoint presentations on their desktop computer where they can fine-tune and modify their presentation. Then they pack up their presentation and store it on a laptop computer that they take to another location.

To make this process easier, PowerPoint includes a special Pack and Go feature that crams all the files you need in one location. That way, you minimize the chances of forgetting an important file 3,000 miles away from your desktop computer.

To use PowerPoint's Pack and Go feature, load the PowerPoint presentation that you want to transfer and follow these steps:

1. **Choose File⇨Pack and Go.**

   The Pack and Go Wizard dialog box appears.

2. **Click Next.**

   The Pack and Go dialog box asks which presentation you want to pack up, as shown in Figure 12-7.

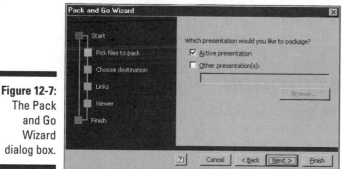

Figure 12-7:
The Pack
and Go
Wizard
dialog box.

3. **Click the Active Presentation check box to choose the presentation that you're currently viewing. Then click Next.**

   The Pack and Go dialog box asks where you want to store your presentation.

4. **Click in the appropriate option button, such as A:\ drive and then click Next.**

   The Pack and Go dialog box asks whether you want to include linked files and fonts. If you chose some really weird fonts, you may want to choose the Embed TrueType Fonts check box. Including linking files and fonts makes your PowerPoint presentation file smaller, but forces you to keep track of several other files that your presentation may require. Embedding creates one fat PowerPoint presentation file, which can be inconvenient for transferring to another computer.

5. Click in the appropriate check boxes and then click Next.

The Pack and Go dialog box asks whether you want to include the PowerPoint viewer if you'll be running the presentation on a computer that doesn't have PowerPoint 2000 installed.

6. Click in the appropriate option button and then click Next.

If you choose to copy your presentation to a floppy disk, get a stack of blank floppy disks ready in case your presentation takes up multiple floppy disks.

7. Click Finish.

After PowerPoint finishes packaging up your presentation, it displays a dialog box informing you that it has finished packing up your presentation.

8. Click OK.

After you package a PowerPoint presentation to another disk (such as a floppy or ZIP disk), your entire presentation appears compressed in a file called `Pngsetup`. You have to run this file before you can see the actual slides that make up your presentation. To run the Pngsetup file, click the Start button on the Windows taskbar, choose Run, click Browse, and search for the folder containing the Pngsetup file. Then click OK in the Run dialog box.

Printing a Presentation

After you get your presentation in the shape that you want it in, you can print out your hard work so that you can create handouts or wallpaper your office with your wonderfully creative presentations. To print a presentation:

1. Choose File⇨Print.

The Print dialog box appears.

2. Click the Print What list box and choose one of the following:

- **Slides:** Prints one slide per page so you can see all the text and graphics on each slide

- **Handouts:** Prints one or more miniature versions of your slides on a page that audience members can take home and study later

- **Notes Pages:** Prints only your notes for each slide, which you can either hand out to your audience or keep for yourself

- **Outline View:** Prints your Presentation Outline so you can see the overall structure of your presentation without graphics getting in the way

You can also limit the print job to specific slide numbers by clicking the Current Slide option button or filling in the Slides text box in the Print Range area with the slide numbers you want to print.

3. **Click OK.**

Chapter 13

Adding Text and Colors to Slides

· ·

In This Chapter

▶ Using text boxes

▶ Picking backgrounds for slides

▶ Adding pictures to slides

· ·

*T*he two main elements of a slide are text boxes and pictures, which can make your slides more visually stimulating and exciting, and keep people awake long enough to listen to your message.

Text boxes contain text (no surprise there), while pictures can contain clip art, files created by other programs, images you store with a digital camera, images created by a scanner, or digitized photographs that you downloaded from the Internet.

PowerPoint displays three panes on the screen at the same time: the Presentation Outline, the Slide pane, and the Notes pane. This chapter focuses mostly on using the Slide pane.

Adding Text to Your Slides

Text can provide the valuable information that you're trying to implant into the brains of your audience. Before you can type text on a slide, you need to create a text box on the slide. PowerPoint gives you four ways to create a text box on a slide:

✔ Create a new slide and PowerPoint automatically creates one or more text boxes.

✔ Create a subheading in the Presentation Outline pane and then type text. PowerPoint automatically creates a text box to hold your text.

✔ Click the Text Box icon on the Drawing toolbar and draw the text box on a slide.

✔ Choose Insert➪Text Box and draw the text box on a slide.

Moving, resizing, and deleting a text box

After you create a text box, you may want to move it to a new location on your slide, resize it to hold more text, or delete it altogether.

To move, resize, or delete a text box:

1. **In the Slide pane, click in the text box that you want to move, resize, or delete.**

   A border with white handles appears around the text box and an I-beam cursor appears in your text, as shown in Figure 13-1.

Figure 13-1:
A text box normally appears invisible until you click the text inside.

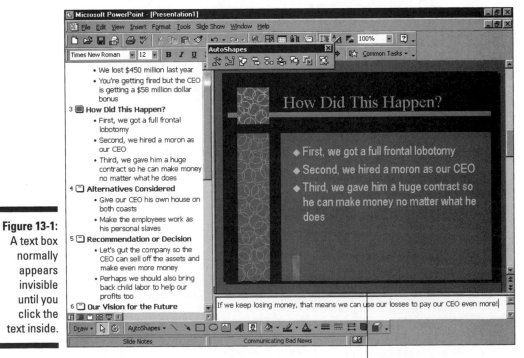

Slide pane

2. **Choose one of the following:**

- **To move the text box:** Place the mouse cursor on the border of the text box so the cursor turns into a four-headed arrow. Hold down the left mouse button, drag the mouse to the location where you want the text box to move, and release the left mouse button.

- **To resize the text box:** Place the mouse cursor over a white handle along the border of the text box so that the cursor turns into a two-headed arrow. Hold down the left mouse button, drag the mouse to resize the text box, and release the left mouse button.

- **To delete the text box:** Click the border of the text box. Press Delete or choose Edit⇨Clear.

 If you accidentally move, resize, or delete a text box, press Ctrl+Z to undo your last action.

Editing text inside a text box

After you create a text box, you can always go back later and modify the text inside the box by changing the font, text style, or the text itself. To edit the text inside a text box:

1. **Click in the text box that you want to edit.**

   A border with white handles appears around the text box and an I-beam cursor appears in your text (refer to Figure 13-1).

2. **Edit your text as you would in any word-processing program.**

To make sure that you don't misspell something crucial in your presentation and then present a glaring error in 48-point type for everyone to see, check your spelling by pressing F7, choosing Tools⇨Spelling, or by clicking the Spelling button on the Standard toolbar.

Changing the Layout and Appearance of Slides

PowerPoint provides several background styles that you can use to enhance the appearance of your slides. As a general rule, the simpler the background, the less obtrusive it will be. Also keep in mind that a background that's too dark or too light can make any text on your slide difficult to read.

The three main parts of a presentation that you can modify are:

- **Colors:** Defines different colors on a slide, such as its background, text, title, and fill color
- **Design template:** Defines the overall appearance of a slide, including the background pattern and text fonts
- **Slide layout :** Defines the placement of text and graphics on a slide

No matter how you change a slide's color, layout, or design template, you can always modify individual parts of a slide on your own, such as moving or adding a text box.

Picking a new color scheme for your slides

Rather than just change the background color of your slides, you might want to change the entire *color scheme* of your slides. To change the color scheme:

1. **Choose Format⇨Slide Color Scheme.**

   The Color Scheme dialog box appears, as shown in Figure 13-2.

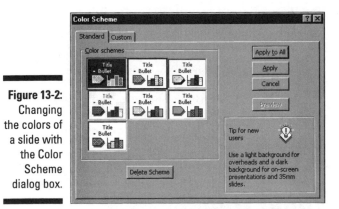

Figure 13-2: Changing the colors of a slide with the Color Scheme dialog box.

2. **Click one of the pre-defined color schemes displayed in the Color Scheme dialog box.**

3. **Click OK.**

If you want to individually define the different colors of your slide:

1. **Choose Format⇨Slide Color Scheme.**

2. **Click the Custom tab.**

   The Color Scheme lists all the colors that you used for the different parts of your slide, such as the background and title text, as shown in Figure 13-3.

3. **Click the part of your slide that you want to change (such as the Background or Title text).**

4. **Click the Change Color button.**

   A Color dialog box appears.

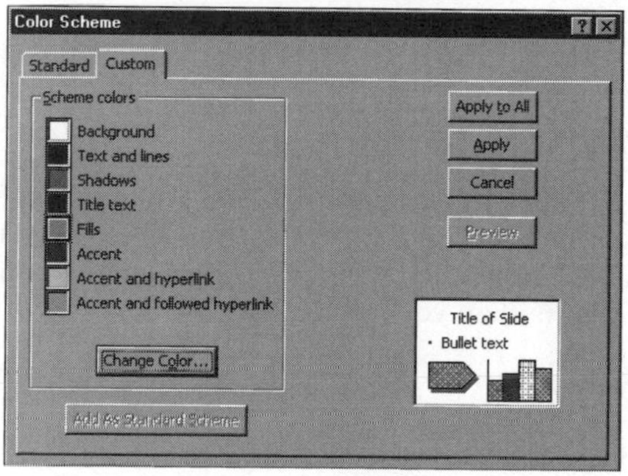

Figure 13-3:
The Color Scheme dialog box shows the exact colors used in every part of your slides.

5. **Click the color that you want and click OK.**

6. **Repeat Steps 3 through 5 until you finish changing all the colors you want. Then click Apply to All to change all the slides in your presentation, or click Apply to change the currently displayed slide.**

Picking a new style template

Changing the colors of a slide can improve the appearance of your slides, but in some cases, this can be like putting make-up on a gargoyle and hoping to make it look more attractive. In both cases, the problem goes much deeper than surface appearances.

To get down to the root of the problem, try changing the style template that you're using for your slides. The *style template* defines the design and layout of your slides, but not the colors.

When you change the style template that you're using for your presentation, it affects every slide in your presentation. When you change colors, you can just change the colors for one slide or all your slides.

To change the style template of a slide:

1. **Choose F̲ormat⇨Apply̲ Design Template.**

   The Apply Design Template dialog box appears.

2. **Click the design template you want (such as Cactus or Factory); then click the Apply button.**

   PowerPoint ruthlessly changes the style for every slide in your entire presentation.

If you don't like a design template, press Ctrl+Z to go back to the previously used design template.

Changing your slide layout

Just to give you more options for modifying the appearance of your slides, PowerPoint lets you pick a new slide layout. A *slide layout* defines the position of text and pictures on a slide. After you choose a slide layout, you can always move text and pictures around on your own.

To pick a new slide layout:

1. **Display the slide you want to modify.**

   Either click the slide icon in the Presentation Outline pane, or use the vertical scroll bar in the Slide pane to display the slide you want to change.

2. **Choose F̲ormat⇨Slide L̲ayout.**

   The Slide Layout dialog box appears, as shown in Figure 13-4.

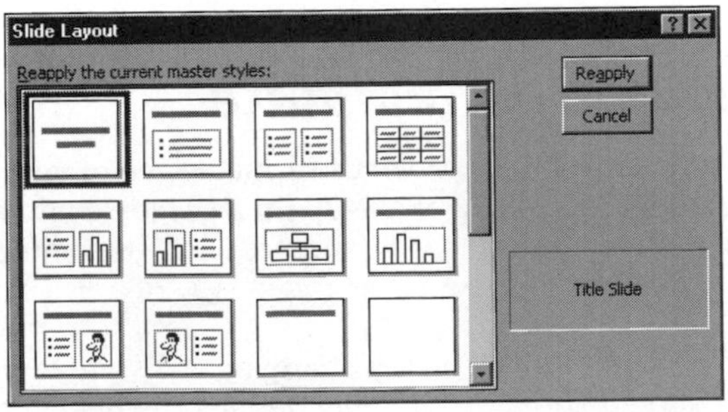

Figure 13-4:
Picking a
new layout
from the
Slide Layout
dialog box.

3. **Click the new layout that you want to use for the current slide in your presentation; then click the Apply button.**

   PowerPoint changes the layout of the currently displayed slide.

4. **Repeat Steps 1 through 3 for each slide that you want to modify.**

Chapter 14

Showing Off Your PowerPoint Presentations

In This Chapter

▶ Making neat transitions
▶ Preparing your presentation for the public
▶ Presenting your slide shows

*A*fter you create a slide show with Microsoft PowerPoint, you want to show it off so that other people can ooh and ahh over it. Because the appearance of your presentation is often more important than substance (which may explain why your boss is getting paid more than you are), Microsoft PowerPoint provides all sorts of ways to spice up your slide show. Some of these ways include Hollywood-style transitions from one slide to another, sound effects to accompany each slide, and scrolling text that makes your slides more entertaining to watch.

Just remember that old saying about too much of a good thing. If you go too far with special effects, you can make your slide show memorable for being obnoxious. Choose your slide show presentation features carefully.

Making Nifty Transitions

Almost everyone has been held captive watching a boring slide show in a classroom, a living room, or a conference room. One slide appears, and everyone yawns. A new slide appears, and everyone yawns again and secretly checks the time.

On the other hand, almost everyone has also been captivated by an informative, inspiring, or just plain interesting slide show that makes the whole audience pay attention and almost regret that the time has passed by so quickly. Of these two options, you want your presentations to be more like the latter.

So to help keep your slide show interesting, PowerPoint lets you create special transitions between your slides. Your slides can dissolve from one into the other on-screen, wipe themselves away from left to right, slide up from the bottom of the screen to cover the previous slide, or split in half to reveal a new slide underneath.

Microsoft PowerPoint lets you create two types of transitions for your slides:

- ✔ **Visual transitions:** Determine how your slide looks when it first appears
- ✔ **Text transitions:** Determine how the text on your slide appears

Creating visual transitions for your slides

A *visual transition* determines how your slide appears, such as sliding across the screen or popping up right away. To create the visual transition for each slide in your presentation:

1. **Display the slide that you want to modify.**

   Either click the slide icon in the Presentation Outline pane, or use the vertical scroll bar in the Slide pane to display the slide that you want to change.

2. **Choose Slide Show⇨Slide Transition.**

   The Slide Transition dialog box appears, as shown in Figure 14-1.

Figure 14-1:
The Slide
Transition
dialog box.

3. **Click the Effect list box and choose an effect — such as Cut, Dissolve, or Wipe Right.**

   PowerPoint shows you the effect in the picture box.

4. **Choose the speed of the transition by clicking the Slow, Medium, or Fast option button.**

   Look at the picture box to see the effect of the chosen speed.

5. **In the Advance area, choose how the current slide advances to the next.**

   Click the On Mouse Click check box if you want to advance this slide by clicking the mouse. Click the Automatically After check box and, in the Seconds box, type the number of seconds for PowerPoint to wait before advancing to the next slide so your PowerPoint presentation can proceed to the next slide automatically.

6. **If you want a sound to play whenever the current slide appears, click the Sound list box and choose a sound.**

   Click the Loop until Next Sound check box if you want your chosen sound to keep playing continuously until the presentation comes to another slide with a different sound assigned to it.

   Use this option sparingly: Having sound playing continuously may eventually annoy your audience.

7. **Click the Apply button to make the current slide use these transition settings. If you want these settings to apply to all the slides in this presentation, click the Apply to All button.**

   Or repeat these steps and choose different settings for each slide, if you want.

Creating your slides text transition

The whole idea behind *text transitions* is to make your slide appear without any text at first or with only a part of its text revealed; then each click of the mouse causes a new chunk of text to slide into view. Such dramatics can keep your audience interested in watching your slides if only to see what unusual and amusing effects you may have created during the time you were supposed to do some actual work.

Text transitions affect an entire text box, whether it contains one word or several paragraphs. If you want different transitions for each word, line, or paragraph, you have to create separate text boxes.

To create a transition for the text on a slide, follow these steps for each slide that you want to add a transition to:

1. **Display the slide that you want to modify.**

   Either click the slide icon in the Presentation Outline pane, or use the vertical scroll bar in the Slide pane to display the slide that you want to change.

2. **Click in a text box on a slide.**

   PowerPoint highlights your chosen text box with a border and handles.

3. **Choose Slide Show⇨Preset Animation.**

   Another menu appears.

4. **Choose a text transition — such as Flying or Drop In.**

5. **Choose Slide Show⇨Animation Preview to see what that transition looks like.**

Creating custom transitions

In case you don't like the text or visual transitions provided with PowerPoint, feel free to create your own. While transitions are less important than the actual content of your presentation, they can be more fun to work on. (This explains why the Microsoft programmers kept adding different animated actions to all the new Office Assistants in Office 2000.)

If you have enough time (or just want to goof around), try creating your own transitions by following these steps:

1. **Display the slide that you want to modify.**

   Either click the slide icon in the Presentation Outline pane, or use the vertical scroll bar in the Slide pane to display the slide that you want to change.

2. **Choose Slide Show⇨Custom Animation.**

   A Custom Animation dialog box appears, as shown in Figure 14-2.

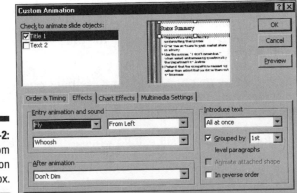

Figure 14-2:
The Custom
Animation
dialog box.

3. **Click the Effects tab.**

4. **Click the Che<u>c</u>k to Animate Slide Objects list box to choose the text boxes on your slide that you want to animate.**

5. **In the <u>E</u>ntry Animation and Sound group, choose a text transition (such as Fly), a direction (such as From Left), and a sound (such as Whoosh).**

6. **Repeat Steps 4 and 5 for each text box that you want to animate.**

7. **In the <u>I</u>ntroduce Text group, click the list box and choose how you want your text to appear (such as All at Once or By Word).**

8. **Click the Order & Timing tab.**

   The Animation Order list box shows which text boxes appear first, second, third, and so on.

9. **Click a text box and click the Up or Down Move arrows to arrange the order your text boxes appear on the slide.**

10. **Click <u>P</u>review to see what your text transitions look like.**

11. **Click OK.**

Preparing Your Presentation for the Public

After your slide show is perfectly organized, complete, and ready to go — you can reveal it to the unsuspecting public. For maximum flexibility, PowerPoint lets you add different elements to your presentation to help you progress through the presentation manually or display it as a self-running presentation for others to view themselves.

Adding buttons

Most presentations display slides one after another in the same boring order. Keeping a single order is fine sometimes, especially if you're giving the presentation, but it can be too confining if others are going to watch your presentation without your supervision.

Instead of forcing someone to view your slides one after another, you can put *buttons* on your slides. Clicking a button can display any slide, whether it's the first, last, next, previous, or sixth slide from the last.

Adding buttons (which PowerPoint calls *hyperlinks*) gives your audience the chance to jump from one slide to another. That way, you (or the people controlling your presentation) have greater freedom and flexibility in delivering your presentation.

Creating a hyperlink to another slide

To create a button or hyperlink on a slide:

1. **Display the slide where you want to add hyperlink buttons.**

   Either click the slide icon in the Presentation Outline pane, or use the vertical scroll bar in the Slide pane to display the slide that you want to change.

2. **Choose Slide Show⇨Action Buttons.**

   A menu of different buttons appears.

3. **Click a button from the menu.**

   The mouse cursor turns into a crosshair.

4. **Place the mouse where you want to draw the button, hold down the left mouse button, drag the mouse to draw your button, and then release the left mouse button.**

   The Action Settings dialog box appears.

5. **Click the Hyperlink To option button, click the list box, and then choose a slide such as Next Slide or Last Slide Viewed.**

6. **Click OK.**

   To test your button, choose View⇨Slide Show.

After you create a hyperlink button, you may want to change what slide the button jumps to when it's clicked. Click the button that you want to change, click the right mouse button, and choose Hyperlink⇨Edit Hyperlink to summon the Action Settings dialog box, where you can choose the new destination slide.

Deleting a hyperlink button

One day you may want to remove a certain hyperlink button from your presentation. You can delete a hyperlink button at any time by following these steps:

1. **Display the slide containing the hyperlink buttons you want to delete.**

   Either click the slide icon in the Presentation Outline pane, or use the vertical scroll bar in the Slide pane to display the slide that you want to change.

2. **Click the hyperlink button that you want to delete.**

   PowerPoint highlights your chosen hyperlink button.

3. **Press Delete or choose Edit⇨Clear.**

Defining how to present your slide show

Many people use PowerPoint to create presentations that they can give to a group of people. However, you can also create self-running presentations that someone else can control. For example, a museum can put a computer in the lobby so visitors can view a PowerPoint presentation that shows them the main attractions they may want to see.

To define how to display your presentation:

1. **Choose Slide Show⇨Set Up Show.**

   The Set Up Show dialog box appears.

2. **Click one of the following option buttons:**

   - **Presented by a Speaker (full screen):** Slides take up the full screen and you can navigate them with a mouse or keyboard.

   - **Browsed by an Individual (window):** Slides appear in a window with PowerPoint's menus and toolbars fully visible. You can navigate slides with a mouse or keyboard.

   - **Browsed at a Kiosk (full screen):** Slides take up the full screen but you can only navigate them with a mouse, so make sure to put hyperlink buttons on your slides for this option to work properly.

3. **Click one or more of the following check boxes:**

   - **Loop Continuous until 'Esc':** Keeps repeating your entire presentation until someone presses the Esc key.

   - **Show without Narration:** Eliminates any narration that you may have recorded using the Slide Show⇨Record Narration command. (The Record Narration feature lets you add your own voice or other sounds through a microphone. To find out more about this feature, look at *PowerPoint 2000 For Windows For Dummies,* by Doug Lowe, IDG Books Worldwide, Inc.)

   - **Show without Animation:** Eliminates all the fancy text and slide transitions you may have painstakingly created.

4. **In the Advance Slides group, click either the Manually or Using Timings If Present option button.**

5. **Click OK.**

If you choose the Browsed at a Kiosk option button in Step 2 and Using Timings If Present option button in Step 3, choose Slide Show⇨Slide Transition and make sure all your slides have the Automatically After check box chosen. Otherwise there is no way to advance through your slide show presentation.

Testing your slide show

Before showing your presentation during that crucial business meeting, you should test your slide show. That way, if you find any mistakes or annoying visual effects, you can edit them out and they won't detract from your presentation.

Besides making sure your text and slide transitions work, make doubly sure that your spelling and grammar is correct. Nothing can make you look dumber than spelling your own company's name wrong.

To test your slide show:

1. **Choose Slide Show⇨View Show, or press F5.**

   PowerPoint displays your first slide.

2. **To see the next slide, press either the right or the down arrow key, or click the left mouse button. To see the previous slide, press either the left or the up arrow key.**

3. **Pat yourself on the back or go back to the drawing board.**

4. **Press Esc to end the slide show.**

Part V

Getting Organized with Outlook 2000

The 5th Wave   By Rich Tennant

WANDA HAD THE DISTINCT FEELING HER HUSBAND'S NEW SOFTWARE PROGRAM WAS ABOUT TO BECOME INTERACTIVE.

In this part . . .

After a few days on the job, most people's desks disappear under a pile of memos, reports, and papers. If you want to actually use your desk as a writing surface rather than a filing cabinet, you may need Microsoft Outlook 2000 to help organize your life.

Microsoft Outlook 2000 can track appointments you'd rather avoid, store names of people you might forget (accidentally or on purpose), and organize e-mail in a single location so you don't have to search all over your hard disk for an important message that could determine the future of your career or your business.

Outlook 2000 can handle all your personal information so you can focus on doing the work that really needs to get done. Who knows? If Outlook makes you productive enough at work, you just may find that you have enough time to relax and take that extended lunch break you've needed for so long.

Chapter 15

Scheduling Your Time

● ●

In This Chapter

▶ Making an appointment

▶ Changing an appointment

▶ Printing your schedule

● ●

*T*o help you keep track of pressing appointments, pending tasks, and important names and addresses, Microsoft Office 2000 includes a personal information organizer called Microsoft Outlook 2000.

Microsoft Outlook acts like an electronic version of a day planner. By tracking your appointments, tasks, and contacts on your computer, you can always be sure to remember your daily, weekly, monthly, and even yearly tasks. Unless, of course, you forget to turn on your computer.

If your computer happens to be attached to a *local area network* (LAN), multiple people can share a single appointment book. That way, all employees can see when others are busy or out of the office, when they have time to come to a meeting, and when they're supposed to meet a deadline.

In this chapter, you see how to use Outlook for scheduling appointments. Chapter 16 explains how to use Outlook for creating to-do lists and tracking important names and phone numbers. Chapter 17 shows you how to use Outlook for organizing your e-mail.

The first time you start Outlook, you'll be forced to wade through the Outlook Startup Wizard, which configures Outlook. If you aren't sure of any of the settings, just use the default settings and keep clicking the Next button until the Startup Wizard goes away.

Making an Appointment

If you're not careful, you can often overload yourself with so many appointments that you never have time to do any work (which may not always be such a bad thing). To avoid scheduling conflicts, use Outlook to schedule your appointments so you can see when you have time available and when you're all tied up doing the things that somebody else thinks you should be doing because they're important.

Making a new appointment

Outlook lets you schedule appointments decades in advance. To make an appointment in Outlook:

1. **Switch to Calendar view by doing one of the following:**

   • Choose View⇨Go To⇨Calendar.

   • Click the Outlook Shortcuts button in the Outlook Bar and then click the Calendar icon.

   The Calendar view appears, as shown in Figure 15-1.

2. **Click the day on which you want to schedule an appointment.**

   Outlook highlights the current day in a box. If you click another day (such as tomorrow or a day three weeks from today), Outlook highlights your newly chosen day in gray but still displays a box around the current day.

3. **Click the time on the Appointment list that you want your appointment to begin, such as 11:00 or 3:00.**

   Outlook highlights your chosen time.

4. **Type short description for your appointment, such as** Lunch with Pam **or** Dinner at Boring Office Banquet.

   Outlook displays your text in the Appointment list and highlights it with a blue border.

5. **Move the mouse pointer over the bottom edge of the border surrounding your appointment.**

   The mouse pointer turns into a double-pointing arrow.

6. **Hold down the left mouse button and drag the mouse down to the time when you hope the appointment will end.**

   Congratulations! You've just stored an appointment in Outlook.

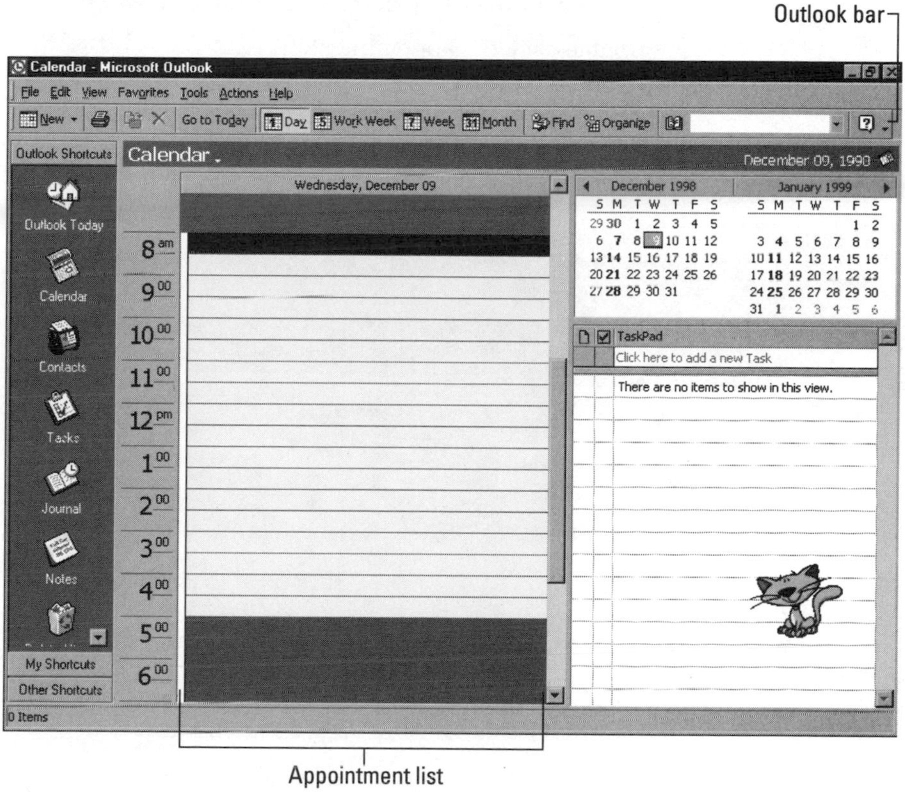

Outlook bar

Figure 15-1:
Viewing the
Outlook
calendar in
the Day
view.

Appointment list

Editing an appointment

After you create an appointment, you may want to edit it to specify the appointment location, the appointment subject, the exact starting and ending times, and whether Outlook should beep a reminder before you risk missing the appointment altogether.

To edit an appointment in Outlook:

1. **Switch to Calendar view by using one of the following techniques:**

   • Choose View⇨Go To⇨Calendar.

   • Click the Outlook Shortcuts button in the Outlook Bar and then click the Calendar icon.

   The Calendar view appears. (Refer to Figure 15-1.)

2. **Click the calendar day that contains the appointment you want to edit.**

3. **Open the appointment by doing one of the following:**

   • Double-click the appointment.

   • Click the appointment and press Ctrl+O.

   • Right-click the appointment and click Open.

   The Appointment dialog box appears, as shown in Figure 15-2.

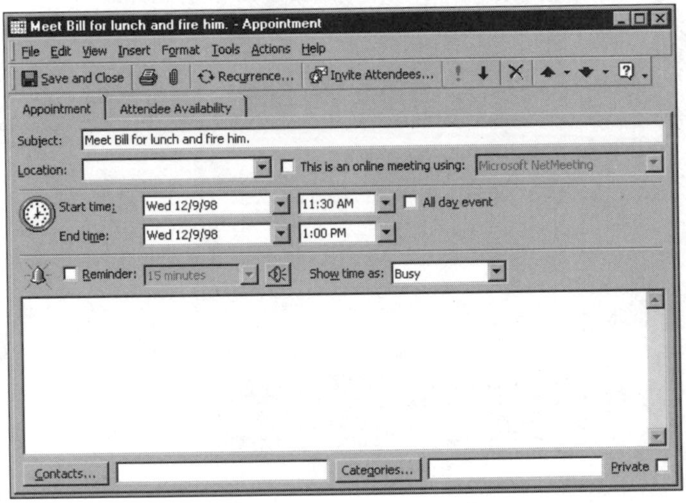

Figure 15-2:
The
Appointment
dialog box.

4. **Click in the Subject text box and type or edit a description of your appointment.**

   For example, type **Turn in my two-week notice and flee my job by running naked through the parking lot.**

5. **Click in the Location text box and type the location of your appointment.**

   If you have typed a location for other appointments, you can click the downward-pointing arrow and click a location you've used before. This can come in handy in case some of your appointments occur in the same locations, such as in a specific meeting room.

6. **Click in the Start Time list boxes to specify the date and time when the appointment begins.**

7. **Click in the End Time list boxes to specify the date and time when the appointment ends.**

8. **If you want Outlook to remind you of your appointment, click the Reminder check box to put a check mark in it.**

   Click the Reminder list box to specify when Outlook should remind you of your appointment (such as 15 minutes or 1 hour beforehand). As long as Outlook is running on your computer (even if it is minimized or hidden by another program), it can remind you of an appointment no matter what other program you may be using at the time.

9. **Click the Sho<u>w</u> Time As list box and choose Free, Tentative, Busy, or Out of Office.**

   If you're on a network, you can give coworkers an idea of whether they can bother you during your appointment. Choosing Out of Office, for example, makes Outlook indicate on your schedule that you're out of the office during the time allotted to this appointment. (If you're not connected to a network, Step 9 is purely for your own benefit in reviewing your schedule.)

10. **Click the <u>S</u>ave and Close button near the top of the dialog box.**

    Outlook displays your appointment on-screen.

Appointments for which you've set the Reminder option show up with alarm bell icons. When the time comes to remind you of an upcoming appointment, Outlook displays the Reminder box, as shown in Figure 15-3. You can have Outlook remind you of the same appointment again by clicking in the Remind Me Again In drop-down list and specifying when you want to be reminded next.

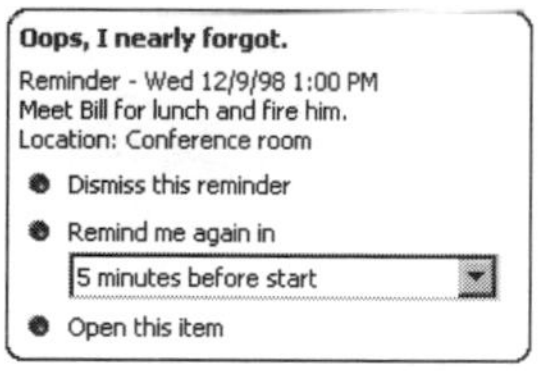

Figure 15-3:
The
Reminder
box pops
up to notify
you of an
upcoming
appointment.

> **Oops, I nearly forgot.**
> Reminder - Wed 12/9/98 1:00 PM
> Meet Bill for lunch and fire him.
> Location: Conference room
> ● Dismiss this reminder
> ● Remind me again in
>   [5 minutes before start] ▼
> ● Open this item

The Reminder feature works only when Outlook is running. If you want to be reminded of appointments, make sure that you don't exit Outlook. (You can minimize the program so it doesn't clutter your screen, though.) If you exit Outlook, the program can't remind you of your upcoming appointments, which essentially defeats the purpose of using Outlook to store your important appointments.

Seeing the big picture of your appointments

To help you organize your life, Outlook provides five different ways to display your appointments:

- ✔ **Day:** Shows a single day, hour by hour (refer to Figure 15-1), so you can see what appointments you may have already missed today.

- ✔ **Outlook Today:** Shows all appointments and tasks scheduled for today. (See Figure 15-4.)

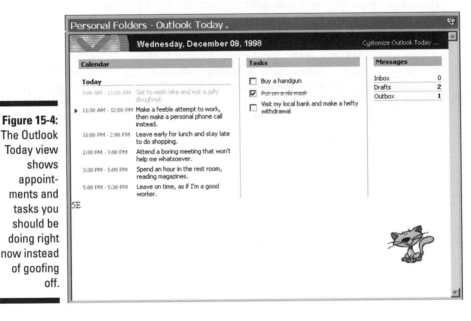

Figure 15-4: The Outlook Today view shows appointments and tasks you should be doing right now instead of goofing off.

- ✔ **Work Week:** Shows all appointments for a single week (see Figure 15-5) except for Sundays and Saturdays.

- ✔ **Week:** Shows all appointments for a single week, including Sundays and Saturdays. (See Figure 15-6.)

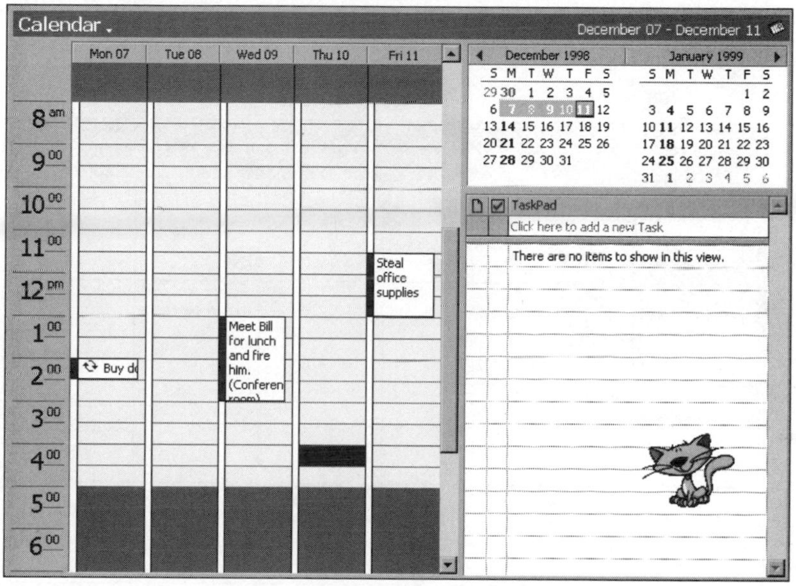

Figure 15-5:
Seeing your appointments in Work Week view.

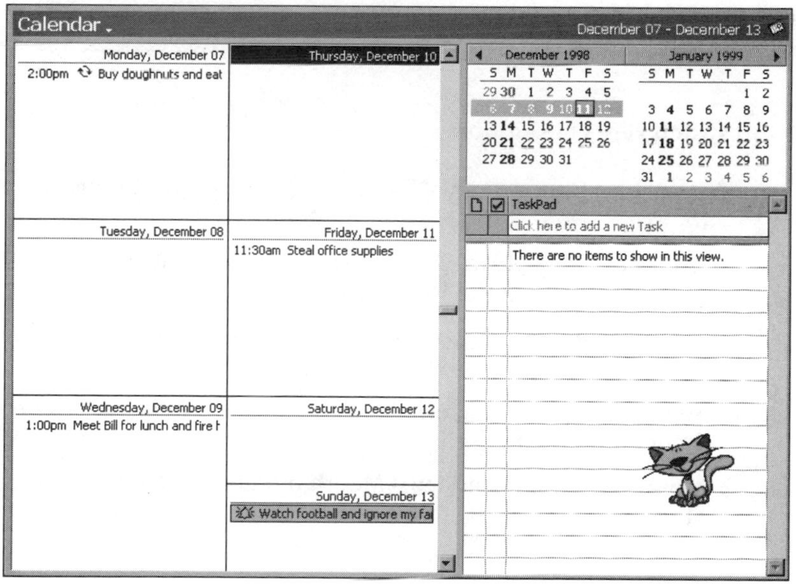

Figure 15-6:
The slightly different look of the Week view.

✔ **Month:** Shows all appointments for a calendar month (see Figure 15-7) so you can check your long-range appointments.

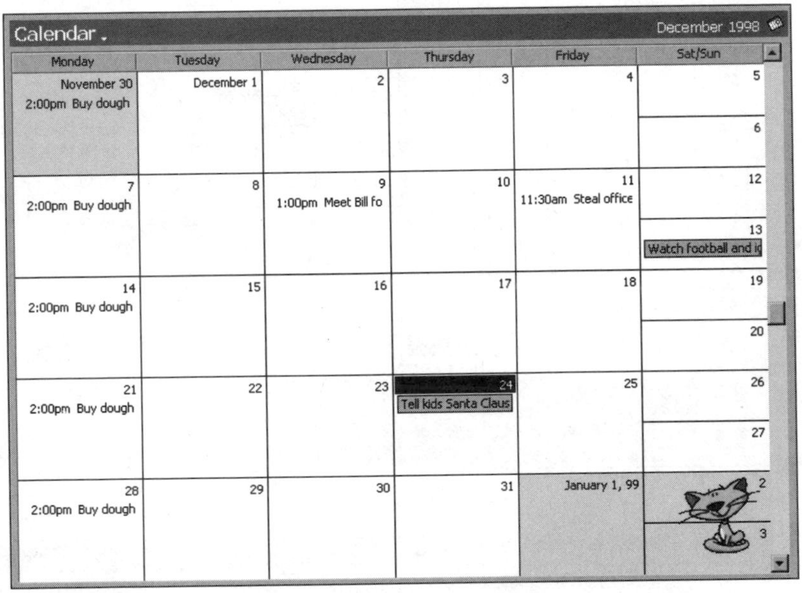

Calendar .					December 1998
Monday	Tuesday	Wednesday	Thursday	Friday	Sat/Sun
November 30 / 2:00pm Buy dough	December 1	2	3	4	5 / 6
7 / 2:00pm Buy dough	8	9 / 1:00pm Meet Bill fo	10	11 / 11:30am Steal office	12 / 13 Watch football and ...
14 / 2:00pm Buy dough	15	16	17	18	19 / 20
21 / 2:00pm Buy dough	22	23	24 Tell kids Santa Claus	25	26 / 27
28 / 2:00pm Buy dough	29	30	31	January 1, 99	2 / 3

Figure 15-7:
Seeing your appointments in Month view.

To switch views in Outlook:

✔ **Day view:** Choose View⇨Day or click the Day button on the Standard toolbar.

✔ **Outlook Today view:** Click the Outlook Shortcuts button in the Outlook Bar and then click the Outlook Today icon.

✔ **Work Week view:** Choose View⇨Work Week or click the Work Week button on the Standard toolbar.

✔ **Week view:** Choose View⇨Week or click the Week button on the Standard toolbar.

✔ **Month view:** Choose View⇨Month or click the Month button on the Standard toolbar.

Changing an appointment

Despite your best efforts at planning, you may need to move or edit your appointments to avoid someone you don't like or to spend more time with someone you do like. To edit an appointment:

1. **Click the appointment that you want to edit.**

2. **Press Ctrl+O or double-click the appointment that you want to modify.**

   The Appointment dialog box appears. (Refer to Figure 15-2.)

3. **Make your changes to the appointment.**

   For example, click the Start Time or End Time list box and type a new time to change the start or end time or date for your appointment.

4. **Click the Save and Close button.**

If you're in Day, Work Week, or Week view, you can also change the time of an appointment by following these steps (you can't change the date for the appointment with this method):

1. **Click the appointment for which you want to change the start or end time.**

   Outlook highlights the appointment.

2. **Move the mouse cursor over the bottom of the appointment (if you want to change the end time) or the top of the appointment (if you want to change the start time) until the cursor turns into a two-headed arrow.**

3. **Hold down the left mouse button and drag the appointment to a new end or start time.**

If you only need to change an appointment's start and end time (but not its duration), move the mouse pointer over the left border of the appointment. The mouse pointer turns into a four-way pointing arrow. Hold down the left mouse button and drag the mouse to move the appointment to a new start and end time. Then release the left mouse button.

If you're in Work Week, Week, or Month view, you can change the date of an appointment by following these steps:

1. **Click the appointment that you want to change.**

   Outlook highlights the entire appointment.

2. **Hold down the left mouse button and drag the mouse until the mouse rests on the new date for the appointment.**

3. **Release the left mouse button.**

Deleting an appointment

After an appointment has passed or when an appointment has been canceled, you can delete it to make room for other appointments. To delete an appointment:

1. **Click the appointment that you want to delete.**

   If you are in the Outlook Today view, Outlook displays the Appointment dialog box. (Refer to Figure 15-2.)

2. **Choose Edit⇨Delete or press Ctrl+D.**

If you delete an appointment by mistake, press Ctrl+Z to recover it again.

If you delete an appointment from within the Outlook Today view, you can never recover it again, so make sure you really want to delete an appointment from within Outlook Today before you do so.

Defining a recurring appointment

You may have an appointment that occurs every day, week, month, or year (such as going to lunch with the boss on the first Monday of the month, running an errand every morning, or leaving work early every Friday afternoon). Instead of entering these *recurring appointments* again and again, you can enter them once and define how often they occur. From that point on, Outlook automatically schedules your recurring appointments unless you specifically tell it otherwise.

Making a recurring appointment

To define a recurring appointment in the Day, Work Week, Week, or Month view:

1. **Choose Actions⇨New Recurring Appointment.**

   The Appointment Recurrence dialog box appears, as shown in Figure 15-8.

2. **In the Appointment Time group, click the Start list box and enter the start time for your recurring appointment by clicking the down-pointing arrow until the right time shows up.**

   You can also type a time, such as **8:13**, in the Start list box.

3. **Click the End list box and enter the end time for your recurring appointment.**

4. **Click the Duration list box and enter the length of your appointment.**

5. **Click one of the following option buttons to specify the frequency of the appointment: Daily, Weekly, Monthly, or Yearly. Or choose a specific day, such as Sunday or Tuesday.**

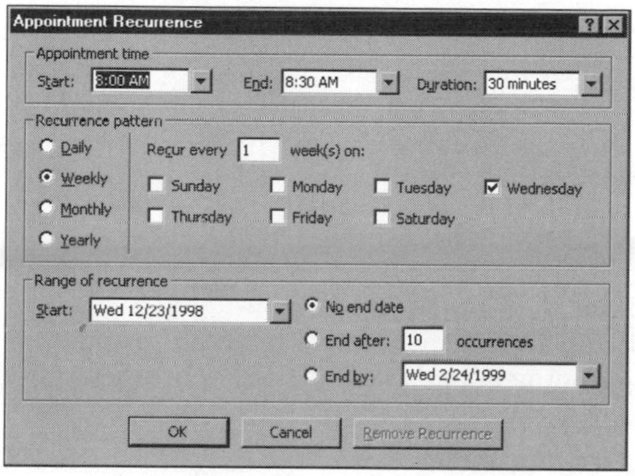

Figure 15-8:
Creating a
recurring
appointment
by using the
Appointment
Recurrence
dialog box.

6. **In the Range of Recurrence area, click the Start list box and click the date when you want your recurring appointment to begin.**

7. **Click one of the option buttons in the Range of Recurrence area to define when you want the recurring appointments to end.**

   You can specify a number of occurrences (End after), an end date (End by), or no ending at all (No end date).

8. **Click OK.**

   The Appointment dialog box appears for you to define your recurring appointment.

9. **Type your appointment in the Subject box (for example, Leave early from work).**

10. **Type the location of your appointment in the Location box.**

11. **Click the Reminder check box if you want Outlook to flash you a reminder message.**

    Click the Reminder list box to specify when Outlook should remind you of your appointment (such as 15 minutes or 1 hour beforehand).

12. **Click the Show Time As list box and choose Free, Tentative, Busy, or Out of Office.**

    See Step 9 in the "Editing an appointment" section for more information about these options.

13. **Click the Save and Close button.**

    Outlook displays your appointment on-screen, as shown in Figure 15-9. You can spot a recurring appointment by the revolving arrows that show up next to the appointment description.

2^{00}

👁️↻↻ Repress the urge to tell my boss what I really think of him

3^{00}

You can turn any existing appointment into a recurring appointment by double-clicking an appointment and clicking the Recurrence button.

Editing a recurring appointment

To edit a recurring appointment from the Day, Work Week, Week, or Month view:

1. **Click the recurring appointment that you want to edit.**

2. **Press Ctrl+O or double-click the appointment.**

   The Open Recurring Item dialog box appears.

3. **Click one of the following option buttons:**

   • **Open This Occurrence:** To edit just this specific appointment (for example, just the instance of the recurring appointment that takes place on October 18)

   • **Open the Series:** To edit the entire series of recurring appointments (for example, the whole series of "leave work early on Friday" appointments)

   Outlook displays the Appointment Recurrence dialog box. (Refer to Figure 15-8.)

4. **Make any changes to your recurring appointment (such as changing the start and end times or the days it occurs) and then click the Save and Close button.**

Printing Your Schedule

Unless you carry a laptop computer around with you all day, you may occasionally need to print your appointment schedule on paper so you can carry it easily and copy it for all your fans and relatives. To print your appointments from the Day, Work Week, Week, or Month view:

1. **Switch to Calendar view by doing one of the following:**

   • Choose View➪Go To➪Calendar.

   • Click the Outlook Shortcuts button in the Outlook Bar and then click the Calendar icon.

   The Calendar view appears. (Refer to Figure 15-1.)

2. **Choose one of the following:**

   • Choose File➪Print.

   • Press Ctrl+P.

   • Click the Print icon on the Standard toolbar.

   The Print dialog box appears, as shown in Figure 15-10. (*Note:* If you click the Print icon on the Standard toolbar, Outlook goes ahead and prints your entire appointment schedule without giving you a chance to go through Steps 3 through 5.)

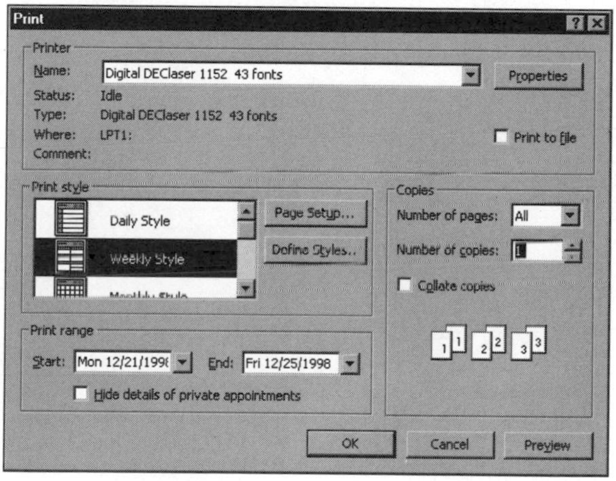

Figure 15-10:
The Print
dialog box.

3. **Click a style in the Print Style box (such as Weekly Style or Monthly Style).**

   This option defines how you want your schedule to print out — as a Daily, Weekly, or Monthly schedule.

4. **Click the Preview button to see what your schedule will look like when it is printed.**

5. **Click the Print button to start printing.**

After Step 4 but before Step 5, you can click the Page Setup button, click the Paper tab, and define how you want your schedule to print in the Size list box. You can print your schedule as a booklet, a Day-Timer page, a Day-Runner page, or a Franklin Day Planner page.

Chapter 16

Setting Tasks and Making Contacts

. . . .

In This Chapter

▶ Storing names and addresses

▶ Organizing names by categories

▶ Creating a to-do list

. . . .

*B*esides letting you make and break appointments, Microsoft Outlook lets you create your own to-do lists (so you don't have to waste money buying special paper labeled "Things to do today") as well as store valuable names, addresses, phone numbers, and other important information about people who may be able to further your career.

For more information about using Outlook 2000's wonderful features, pick up a copy of *Microsoft Outlook 2000 For Dummies,* by Bill Dyszel (IDG Books Worldwide, Inc.).

Organizing Contact Information

Most folks have business cards that they can hand out to people who may be useful to them in the future. People stuck in the Dark Ages store their business card collection in a Rolodex file, but you can progress to the twenty-first century by storing names and addresses in Outlook instead. By using Outlook, you can quickly copy your valuable business contacts and share them with others or just get rid of your cumbersome Rolodex file and put a much more cumbersome computer on your desk instead.

Storing contact information

To store information about a contact in Outlook, start Outlook and then follow these steps:

1. **Switch to Contacts view by using one of the following methods:**

   - Choose View➪Go To➪Contacts.

   - Click the Outlook Shortcuts button in the Outlook Bar and then click the Contacts icon.

   The Contacts view appears, as shown in Figure 16-1.

2. **Choose Actions➪New Contact or press Ctrl+N.**

   The Contact dialog box appears, as shown in Figure 16-2.

3. **Type the name, address, phone number, and any other information you want to store about the contact in the appropriate boxes.**

   If you type a company name, make sure you type it consistently. Don't type it as "IDG Books" one time and just "IDG" another time, or Outlook won't consider them the same company.

   - If you click the Full Name button, a Check Full Name dialog box appears. In it, you can specify a title (such as Dr. or Ms.); first, middle, and last name; and a suffix (such as Jr. or III).

   - If you click the Address button, a Check Address dialog box appears. Here, you can specify a street name, city, state or province, postal code, and country.

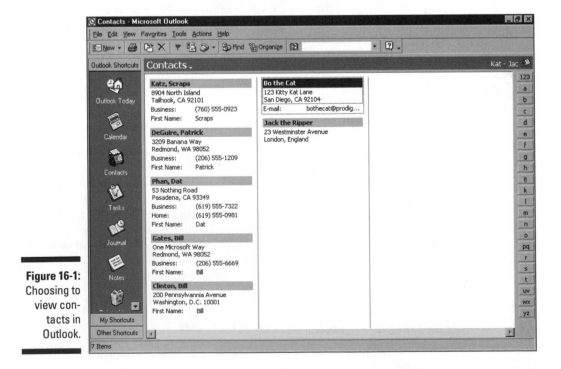

Figure 16-1: Choosing to view contacts in Outlook.

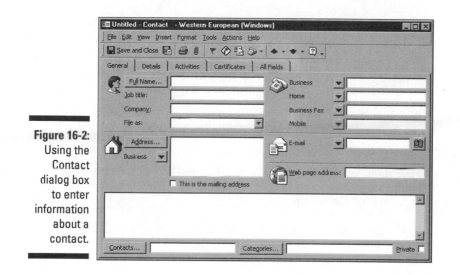

Figure 16-2:
Using the
Contact
dialog box
to enter
information
about a
contact.

- If you click the list box that appears directly below the Address button, you can specify two or more addresses for each person, such as a business address and a home address.

- The This is the Mailing Address check box lets you specify which address to use when sending postal mail.

- The button that looks like an open book that appears to the right of the E-mail list box displays a list of e-mail addresses that you have previously stored for all your contacts.

4. After you finish entering the information, click Save and Close.

You don't have to fill in every single box. For example, you may just want to store someone's name and phone number. In this case, you don't need to type in the address or any other irrelevant information.

Changing your point of view

Storing and displaying names and addresses is necessary and simple. But you could use a Rolodex file to do that. Where the real power of your computer and Outlook comes into play is in sorting and displaying different views of your information to help you find just the information you need. You have seven ways to display your contacts in Outlook:

- ✔ **Address Cards:** Displays names (sorted alphabetically by last name), addresses, phone numbers, and e-mail addresses.

- ✔ **Detailed Address Cards:** Displays every piece of information about a person, such as company name, fax number, and job title.

- **Phone List:** Displays names and phone numbers (including business, home, fax, and mobile phone numbers) in row-and-column format for easy viewing.

- **By Category:** Displays information according to categories such as Business, Hot Contacts, Key Customer, and Suppliers.

- **By Company:** Displays names grouped according to company name. (Useful for finding multiple names belonging to the same company.)

- **By Location:** Displays information by country, city, and state/province.

- **By Follow-Up Flag:** Displays contacts identified with a follow-up flag, which you can add to a contact by pressing Ctrl+Shift+G or by choosing Actions➪Flag for Follow-Up.

To choose a different view to display your contact information, make sure you're in the Contacts view and then follow these steps:

1. **Choose View➪Current View.**

    A pop-up menu appears.

2. **Choose the desired view (such as Detailed Address Cards or Phone List).**

    Outlook displays your contact information in your chosen view.

Sorting your contacts alphabetically

No matter how you decide to display your list of contacts (in Address Cards view or Phone List view), you may still have trouble finding the person you want at any given time. To help you sort through your list of contacts, Outlook can sort your lists alphabetically by last name, first name, or any other criterion you want (such as by company name). To sort your contacts:

1. **Choose View➪Current View➪Customize Current View.**

    A View Summary dialog box appears, as shown in Figure 16-3.

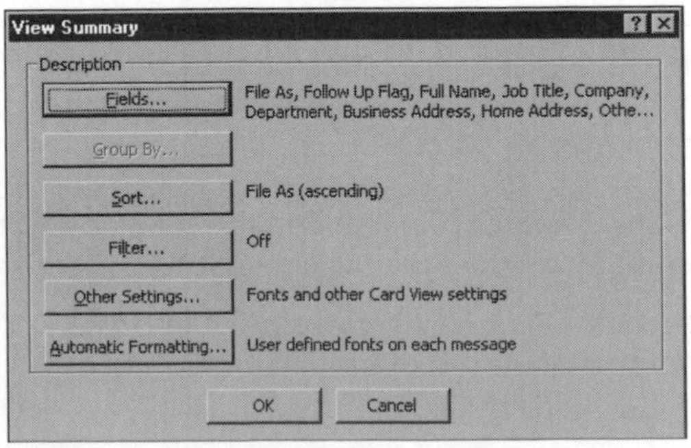

Figure 16-3:
The View
Summary
dialog box.

2. Click the Sort button.

A Sort dialog box appears, as shown in Figure 16-4.

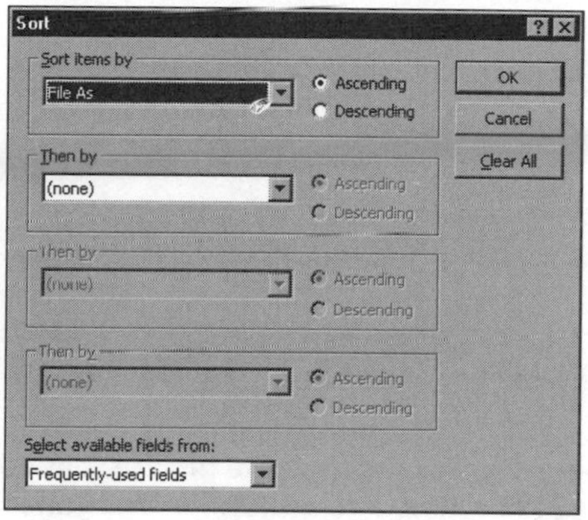

Figure 16-4:
The Sort
dialog
box can
help you
rearrange
your
contacts.

3. Click the Sort Items By list box and choose a category for Outlook to sort by (such as First Name, Home Address, Pager, and so on).

4. Click the Ascending or Descending option button, depending on how you want Outlook to display the contacts after it finds them.

5. If you want to sort by a secondary category, choose it in the first Then By list box and then click the Ascending or Descending option button for that category.

If you sort by last name, for example, and Outlook finds several people with the last name of Doe, this secondary category determines how to sort all the Does.

If you want to specify a third or fourth category for Outlook to sort by, repeat Step 5 for the other Then By list boxes.

6. Click OK twice.

Outlook magically sorts your entire contact list by your chosen criteria.

If you change the Contacts list to Phone List, By Category, By Company, or By Location view, you can quickly sort by clicking the gray column heading. For example, to sort by company name, click the Company gray column heading.

Searching your contacts

Sorting is great when you want to organize your entire contact list, but you often don't care about 99 percent of your contacts; you just want to find the information for one contact. To search for a specific contact, make sure you're in Contacts view and then follow these steps:

1. **Choose Tools➪Find.**

   The Find Items in Contacts window appears, as shown in Figure 16-5.

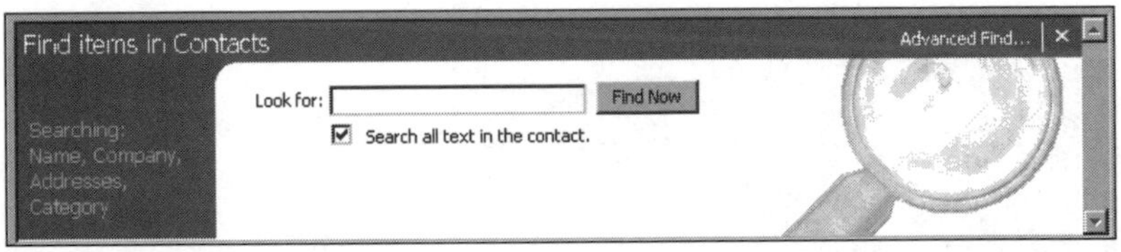

Figure 16-5:
The Find
Items in
Contacts
window.

Find items in Contacts   Advanced Find... | × |

Look for: [   ]   [Find Now]
Searching: ☑ Search all text in the contact.
Name, Company,
Addresses,
Category

2. **In the Look For box, type the phrase (first name, last name, and so on) that you want to find.**

   To make the search faster, type as much of the phrase that you want to find. For example, instead of typing **F** to search for everyone with a first name that begins with F, make it more specific and type as much of the name as possible, such as **FRAN**.

3. **Click Find Now.**

   Outlook displays the contacts that match your search criteria. You can double-click the contact that you want to view.

4. **Click the close box of the Find Items in Contacts window.**

   Outlook displays all of your contacts again when you close the Find Items in Contacts window.

For a more sophisticated way to find specific contacts, choose Tools➪ Advanced Find or press Ctrl+Shift+F. The Advanced Find dialog box appears and gives you more options for searching your list of contacts.

Categorizing your contacts

If you're a busy person (or just a pack rat who can't resist storing every possible name and address that you find), you may find your Outlook contact list so full of names that trying to find any single name can be cumbersome.

To solve this problem, you can organize your contacts into *categories*, such as personal or customer contacts. When you want to see information for just a particular group of contacts, you can tell Outlook to sort your contact list by the appropriate category.

Defining a category for a contact

Before you can ask Outlook to organize your contacts by category, you need to define which contacts belong in the category. To define a category for each contact, make sure you're in the Contacts view and then follow these steps:

1. **Click a contact that you want to categorize.**

2. **Choose Edit⇨Categories.**

   The Categories dialog box appears, as shown in Figure 16-6.

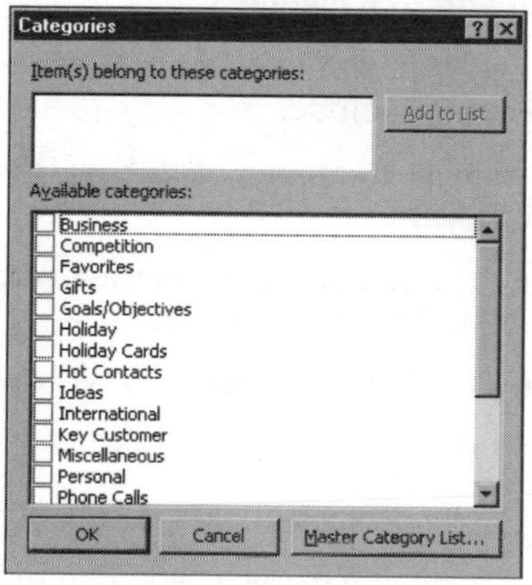

Figure 16-6:
Defining a
category
for your
contacts.

3. **Click the check box for each category that your contact belongs in.**

   Many contacts may logically belong in multiple categories, such as under the Business, Hot Contacts, and Key Customer categories.

4. **Click OK.**

As a faster method for categorizing your contacts, right-click a contact and click Categories from the pop-up menu. Then follow Steps 3 and 4.

In case you want another way to define a category for a contact, or if you want to organize multiple contacts into a category:

1. **Click the Organize button on the toolbar.**

   The Ways to Organize Contacts window appears, as shown in Figure 16-7.

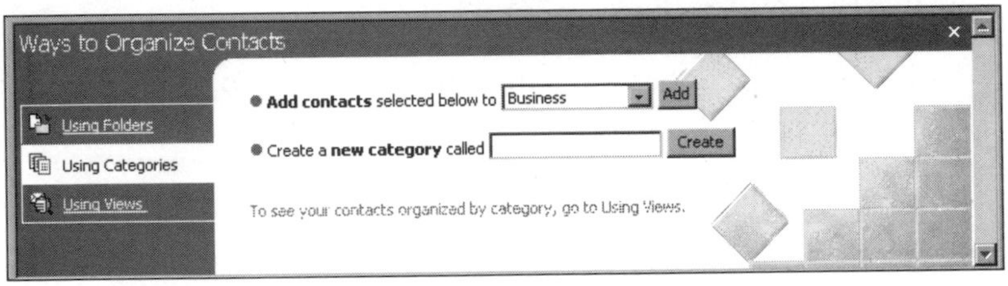

Figure 16-7:
Defining
categories
for contacts
by using the
Organize
button.

2. **Click the contacts you want to add to a category.**

   You can choose multiple contacts by holding down the Ctrl key and clicking on the contacts you want to include.

3. **In the Add Contacts list box, choose a category (such as Business or Hot Contacts) and click the Add button.**

   To create a new category, type the category name in the Create a New Category Called text box and click the Create button.

4. **Click the close box of the Ways to Organize Contacts window.**

Sorting contacts by categories

After you assign your contacts to different categories, Outlook can show you only those contacts within a given category. That way, you can quickly find business-related contacts, personal contacts, or top secret contacts. To view your contacts by category:

1. **Choose View⇨Current View⇨By Category.**

   Outlook displays all the categories you've checked, as shown in Figure 16-8.

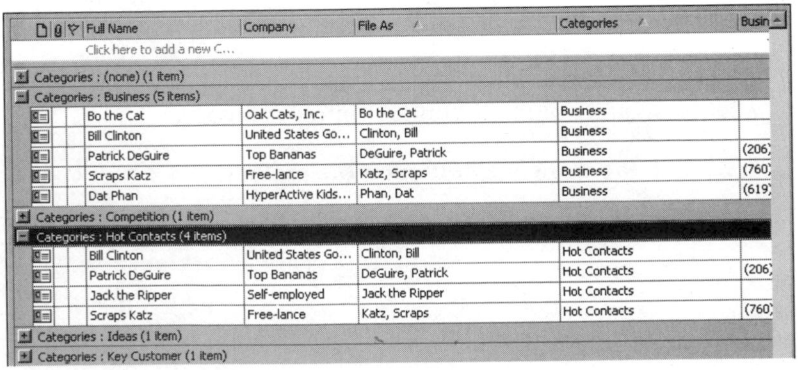

Figure 16-8:
Organizing
your con-
tacts by
categories.

2. **Click the plus sign next to the category that contains the contacts you want to view.**

   For example, if you want to see all Business contacts, click the plus sign next to the Categories: Business heading.

3. **Double-click the contact that you want to view.**

   The Contact window appears, displaying all the information for your chosen contact.

4. **Click Save and Close when you're done viewing or editing the contact.**

Managing Your Tasks

To keep from wasting your days doing trivial tasks and forgetting all your important ones, you can create a daily to-do list in Outlook and check off your tasks as you complete them.

Creating tasks for a to-do list

To create a to-do list:

1. **Switch to Tasks view in one of the following:**

   • Choose View⇨Go To⇨Tasks.

   • Click the Outlook Shortcuts button in the Outlook Bar and then click the Tasks icon.

   The Tasks view appears, as shown in Figure 16-9.

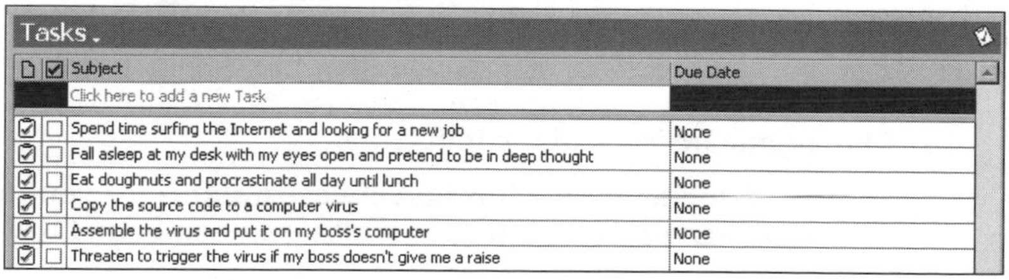

Figure 16-9:
Viewing the
Outlook
Tasks view.

☐ ☑	Subject	Due Date
	Click here to add a new Task	
☑ ☐	Spend time surfing the Internet and looking for a new job	None
☑ ☐	Fall asleep at my desk with my eyes open and pretend to be in deep thought	None
☑ ☐	Eat doughnuts and procrastinate all day until lunch	None
☑ ☐	Copy the source code to a computer virus	None
☑ ☐	Assemble the virus and put it on my boss's computer	None
☑ ☐	Threaten to trigger the virus if my boss doesn't give me a raise	None

2. **Click the Click Here to Add a New Task text box and type a task.**

3. **Click the Due Date box. (Skip Steps 3 through 5 if you don't want to choose a due date.)**

   A downward-pointing arrow appears.

4. Click the downward-pointing arrow.

A calendar appears.

5. Click a due date and press Enter.

Outlook displays your task.

Editing a task

After you create a task, you can edit it later to set a reminder or track how much of the task you've completed. To edit a task:

1. Double-click a task or click the task and press Ctrl+O.

The Task dialog box appears, as shown in Figure 16-10.

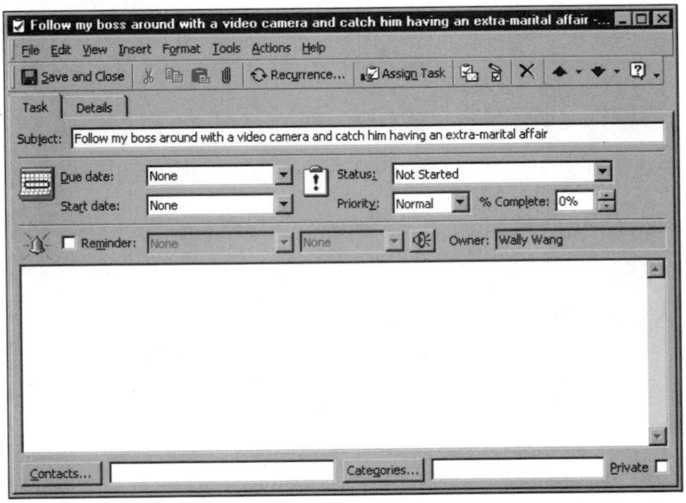

Figure 16-10:
The Task
dialog box
lets you
define
additional
information
for your
task.

2. Choose one or more of the following:

• **Click the Status list box and choose a status for your task, such as In Progress, Completed, or Waiting on Someone Else.**

A task's status lets you see how each task is progressing (or not progressing) and exists for your own benefit to help you manage your time more effectively.

• **Click the Priority list box and choose Low, Normal, or High.**

Categorizing tasks by priority lets you identify the tasks that really need to get done and the tasks that you can safely ignore and hope they go away.

- Click the % Complete list box to specify how much of the task you've already completed.

- Click the Reminder check box and specify a date and time for Outlook to remind you of this particular task.

   If you click the alarm button (it looks like a megaphone), you can specify a unique sound that Outlook plays to remind you of your task.

- Type your task in more detail in the big text box at the bottom of the Task dialog box.

3. Click Save and Close.

You can view your task list and a calendar at the same time if you choose Calendar view and choose Outlook Today, Day, Work Week, or Week view. From any of these views, you can check off completed tasks just by clicking in each task's check box.

Categorizing your tasks

To help you organize your tasks, Outlook can store tasks according to different categories such as Business tasks or Key Customers tasks. To assign a task to a category:

1. **Click the task that you want to assign to a category.**

2. **Choose Edit⇨Categories.**

   The Categories dialog box appears. (Refer to Figure 16-6.)

3. **Click the check box for each category that your contact belongs in.**

   The Contact dialog box appears again.

4. **Click OK.**

Changing the way you view your tasks

Are you always busy but never feel like you get anything worthwhile done? Outlook can help you organize your tasks by displaying your task list in ten different ways. To choose a different view to display your task information:

1. **Switch to Tasks view by using one of the following methods:**

   - Choose View⇨Go To⇨Tasks.

   - Click the Outlook Shortcuts button on the Outlook Bar and then click the Tasks icon.

   The Tasks view appears (refer to Figure 16-9).

2. **Choose View➪Current View.**

    A drop-down list of views appears:

    - **Simple List:** Displays tasks and due dates.

    - **Detailed List:** Displays tasks, status, due dates, percentage completed, and categories.

    - **Active Tasks:** Displays all tasks except those already completed.

    - **Next Seven Days:** Displays all tasks due within the next week. (If you haven't defined a task's due date, you won't see that task by using this view.)

    - **Overdue Tasks:** Displays all tasks that you should have finished by today. (If you haven't defined a task's due date, you won't see that task by using this view.)

    - **By Category:** Displays tasks by category.

    - **Assignment:** Displays tasks assigned to others.

    - **By Person Responsible:** Displays tasks by the name of the person who's supposed to make sure it gets done.

    - **Completed Tasks:** Displays all tasks already completed (a short list for most people); you may want to keep completed tasks around to show others that you're actually doing something important, but otherwise, just deleting a completed task is probably easier.

    - **Task Timeline:** Displays a timeline for a task. (If you haven't defined a task's start and due dates, you won't see that task by using this view.)

3. **Choose the view you desire.**

    Outlook displays your contact list in your chosen view.

Moving a task

Normally, Outlook organizes your tasks in the order that you created them. Because this order isn't always the most efficient way to organize tasks, take some time to move tasks around. To move a task:

1. **Click the task that you want to move.**

2. **Hold down the left mouse button.**

3. **Drag the mouse.**

    Outlook displays a red horizontal line showing you where it will move your task the moment you let go of the left mouse button.

4. **Release the left mouse button when the task appears where you want it.**

Finishing a task

Despite that natural tendency to procrastinate, many people actually do complete the tasks they set for themselves every now and then. To tell Outlook that you've finished a task, click the check box of the task you have actually completed.

Outlook displays a check mark in the check box, dims the task, and draws a line through the task.

When you complete a task, Outlook stores the task so you can show people at a later date all the tasks you've completed by choosing View➪ Current View➪Completed Tasks. To remove a task from Outlook's memory, you have to delete a task, as we explain in the following section.

Deleting a task

After you complete a task (or just decide to ignore it permanently), you may want to delete it from Outlook so it doesn't clutter up your screen:

1. **Double-click the task that you want to delete.**

   A Task dialog box appears.

2. **Choose File➪Delete, press Ctrl+D, or click the Delete icon on the task dialog box toolbar.**

Make sure you really want to delete a task before you complete Step 2 because Outlook doesn't let you undelete any tasks you delete.

Chapter 17

Organizing Your E-Mail

E-mail is a quick and simple way to communicate with people all over the world. Nearly everyone seems to have an e-mail account, and some people even have multiple e-mail accounts. Unfortunately, if you have several e-mail accounts, you may find your e-mail scattered in different places so that you have a hard time seeing who just sent you a message and whom you've sent e-mail to lately.

Outlook can help you not only write, send, and read e-mail, but also funnel all your e-mail from your Internet accounts into one central mailbox. That way, when you want to read, write, or delete e-mail, you can do it all from within a single program.

Setting Up Outlook to Work with E-Mail

When you install Microsoft Office 2000, Outlook digs through your computer and finds out what it needs to know to work with e-mail from an Internet account. However, you may later add or cancel an Internet account, so you need to know how to tell Outlook about these changes to your e-mail.

Defining an e-mail account for Outlook to use requires technical details such as knowing your Internet's POP3 or SMTP information. If you don't have the faintest idea what this might be, call your Internet service provider for help or ask a more knowledgeable friend to help you out.

Connecting to the Internet

You need an Internet account before you can send or retrieve e-mail with Outlook 2000. If you have an America Online account, you will not be able to use Outlook 2000 for reading or sending e-mail.

Outlook 2000 can send and retrieve e-mail in two ways:

- ✔ Through the Internet only
- ✔ Through Microsoft Exchange or Microsoft Mail, in addition to the Internet

You can configure Outlook 2000 for sending and retrieving e-mail by following these steps:

1. **Choose Tools⇨Options.** An Options dialog box appears.

2. **Click the Mail Services (or Mail Delivery) tab and then click the Reconfigure Mail Support button.** An E-mail Service Options dialog box appears, as shown in Figure 17-1.

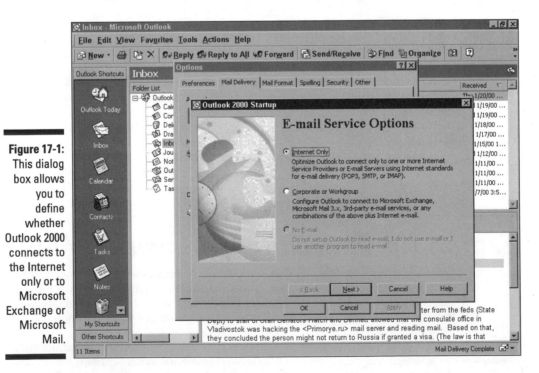

Figure 17-1: This dialog box allows you to define whether Outlook 2000 connects to the Internet only or to Microsoft Exchange or Microsoft Mail.

3. **Click the Internet Only or Corporate or Workgroup radio button and click Next.** A dialog box appears, notifying you of the changes you have defined.

4. **Click Yes to change your Outlook 2000 configuration.**

Using Outlook 2000 with the Internet only option

Before you can use Outlook 2000 to send and retrieve e-mail, you need to connect Outlook 2000 to your e-mail account by following these steps:

1. **Choose Tools⇨Accounts.** An Internet Accounts dialog box appears.

2. **Click the Add button.** A pop-up menu appears, as shown in Figure 17-2.

3. **Click the Mail tab.** An Internet Connection Wizard dialog box appears.

4. **Type your name that you want displayed in the From field of your e-mail messages and click Next.**

5. **Type your e-mail address and click Next.**

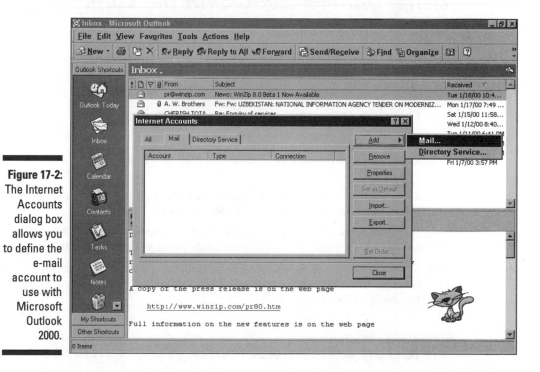

Figure 17-2: The Internet Accounts dialog box allows you to define the e-mail account to use with Microsoft Outlook 2000.

6. **Type your POP3 or IMAP server name (such as pop.prodigy.net) and the SMTP server name (such as smtp.prodigy.net).** You may need to ask your ISP (Internet service provider) for this information. Click Next.

7. **Type your account name and password (optional).** If you do not type your password, you will have to type your password each time you wish to send and retrieve e-mail. Click Next.

8. **Click the radio button that defines how you connect to the Internet, such as through a dial-up account or through a LAN.** Click Next. If you connect to the Internet by using a LAN, you can skip to Step 10.

9. **Click the radio button to use an existing dial-up connection or to create a new dial-up connection.** If you choose to create a new dial-up connection, you will need to type in the phone number for your ISP. Click Next.

10. **Click Finish.**

You can define two or more e-mail accounts for Outlook 2000. That way, you can store and organize e-mail from multiple accounts just by using Outlook 2000.

Using Outlook 2000 with the Corporate or Workgroup option

If you have configured Outlook 2000 to use the Corporate or Workgroup settings, you can connect Outlook 2000 to your e-mail account by following these steps:

1. **Choose Tools⇨Services.** A Services dialog box appears.

2. **Click the Add button.** An Add Service to Profile dialog box appears.

3. **Click Internet E-mail and click OK.** A Mail Account Properties dialog box appears.

4. **Type a name for this account, your own name, your organization, your e-mail address, and your reply e-mail address.**

5. **Click the Servers tab and type the POP3 server name, the SMTP server name, your e-mail account name, and your password.**

6. **Click the Connection tab and click on a radio button to define how to connect to your e-mail account, either through a local area network or the phone line.** Then click OK.

Deleting e-mail accounts from Outlook

If you move to a different company or switch Internet service providers, your old e-mail account may no longer be valid. Rather than keep this obsolete information lodged in Outlook, delete it to keep Outlook from trying to send and retrieve e-mail from a dead e-mail account. To delete an e-mail account from Outlook:

1. **Choose Tools⇔Services.**

    The Services dialog box appears. (Refer to Figure 17-1.)

2. **Click the Internet e-mail account that you want to delete and then click the Remove button.**

    A dialog box appears asking whether you're sure you want to delete your e-mail account.

3. **Click Yes.**

4. **Click OK.**

Storing e-mail addresses in Outlook

The trouble with e-mail addresses is that they look as cryptic as if a cat walked across your keyboard. Typical Internet addresses consist of letters separated by periods and that silly at-sign character (@), as in bothekat@aol.com.

Type one character wrong, and Outlook won't know how to send e-mail to the correct destination. In a desperate effort to make computers less user-hostile, Outlook lets you store names and e-mail addresses in the Address Book. That way, you have to type the e-mail address and get it exactly right just once. After that, you can just choose an address by clicking a name from the Address Book list.

Making your Personal Address Book

Before you can store names and addresses in your Personal Address Book, you have to tell Outlook to make a Personal Address Book for you first.

To make a Personal Address Book:

1. **Choose Tools⇔Services.**

    The Services dialog box appears.

2. **Click Add.**

    The Add Service to Profile dialog box appears.

3. **Click Personal Address Book and then click OK.**

    A Personal Address Book dialog box appears.

4. **Click the Browse button if you want to define a location to store your Personal Address Book.**

5. **Click the First Name or Last Name option button to define how to sort names in your Personal Address Book.**

6. **Click OK three times.**

REMEMBER

Before you can use your Personal Address Book, you have to exit from Outlook and restart it.

Stuffing addresses in your Personal Address Book

After you create a Personal Address Book, you can start storing names and addresses in it. To store a name and e-mail address in Outlook:

1. **Choose Tools⇨Address Book or press Ctrl+Shift+B.**

   The Address Book dialog box appears, as shown in Figure 17-3.

2. **In the Show Name in The list box, choose Personal Address Book.**

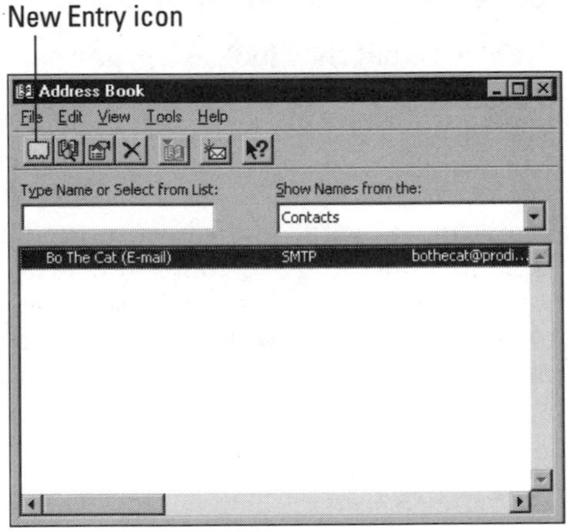

New Entry icon

Figure 17-3:
Storing
e-mail
addresses
in the
Address
Book
dialog box.

3. **Choose File⇨New Entry or click the New Entry icon.**

   The New Entry dialog box appears, as shown in Figure 17-4.

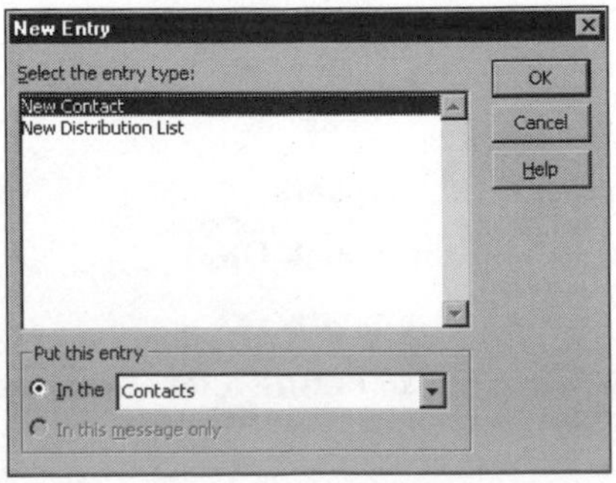

Figure 17-4:
The New
Entry dialog
box.

4. **Click New Contact and then click OK.**

   A Contact dialog box appears, as shown in Figure 17-5.

5. **Type the person's name and e-mail address in the appropriate text boxes. Then click the Save and Close button.**

   Outlook displays your entry in the Address Book.

6. **To make the Address Book window go away, choose File⇨Close or click the close box (the X in the top right corner).**

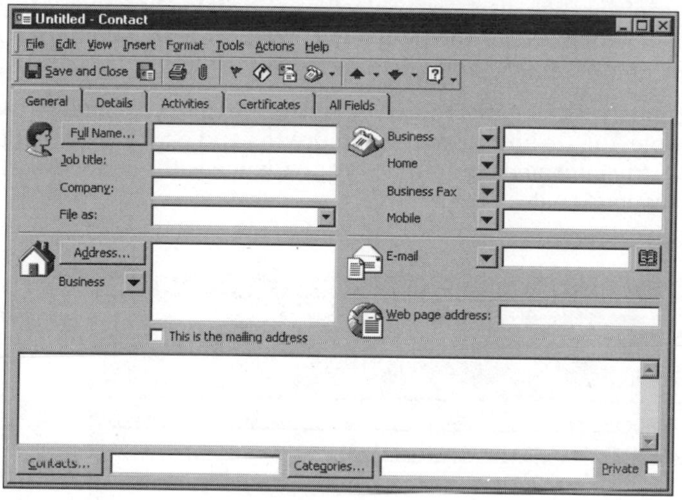

Figure 17-5:
Add an
e-mail
address
in the
Contact
dialog box.

Creating an E-Mail Message

You can write e-mail in Outlook when you're online (connected to the Internet) or when you're offline (not connected to the Internet).

You don't need to connect to the Internet to write e-mail, but you eventually have to connect to the Internet to send your e-mail.

To create an e-mail message:

1. **Switch to the Outlook Today view in one of the following ways:**

   • Choose View⇨Go To⇨Outlook Today.

   • Click the Outlook Today icon in the Outlook bar.

   The Outlook Today view appears.

2. **Choose Actions⇨New Mail Message or press Ctrl+N.**

   The Message dialog box appears, as shown in Figure 17-6.

3. **Type an address to which you want to send your e-mail in the To text box.**

   If you want to send e-mail to an address stored in your Address Book, click the To button and then double-click the name of the recipient. Then click OK. If the recipient isn't in your Address Book, type his or her e-mail address in the To box (for example, `bothekat@aol.com`).

   To send the same e-mail to two or more people, click the To button and then double-click another name.

   To send a "carbon copy" of the e-mail to other people, click the Cc button. Outlook displays a Select Names dialog box that lets you choose e-mail addresses for the people you want to send e-mail to. You can also type another e-mail address directly in the Cc box.

   Although clicking the To and Cc buttons can send e-mail to two or more people, the Cc button is meant more to send e-mail to someone so they can stay informed on your correspondence without necessarily having to respond to it.

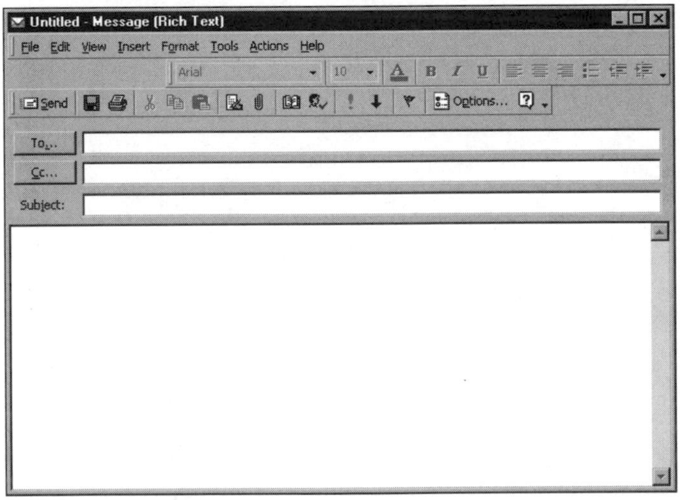

Figure 17-6:
Writing
e-mail in the
Message
dialog box.

4. **In the Subject box, type a subject for your message.**

   For example, type **Secret plans for eliminating gravity from the planet**.

5. **Type your message in the big text box at the bottom of the Message dialog box.**

   Choose Tools⇨Spelling or press F7 to check the spelling in your message.

6. **Click the Send button.**

   Outlook sends your e-mail right away if you're currently connected to the Internet. Otherwise, Outlook stores your message in the Outbox folder.

TIP

If you don't want to send your e-mail right away, skip Step 6 and see the section "Storing e-mail in your Drafts folder," later in the chapter.

Using the Drafts folder

Don't feel that you have to write an e-mail message all at once and send it off right away. You may want to write part of a message, review it later, and then rewrite, add, or modify it before finally sending it off.

When you want to store your e-mail temporarily before finishing it, you can put it in a special folder called the Drafts folder. Like the name implies, the Drafts folder can contain rough drafts of all the e-mail you haven't finished writing but plan to send out eventually.

Storing e-mail in your Drafts folder

To store e-mail in your Drafts folder:

1. **Follow Steps 1 through 5 in the "Creating an E-Mail Message" section in this chapter.**

2. **Choose File⇨Move to Folder or press Ctrl+Shift+V.**

   The Move Item To dialog box appears.

3. **Click the Drafts icon and then click OK.**

   A dialog box appears that lets you know that Outlook has copied your e-mail message to the Drafts folder instead of moving it.

4. **Ignore the frightening tone of this dialog box and click OK.**

5. **Choose File⇨Close.**

   A dialog box appears, asking whether you want to save the current e-mail message.

6. **Click No (because you already saved a copy of the e-mail message in your Drafts folder).**

Editing e-mail in your Drafts folder

After you store e-mail in your Drafts folder, you may need to edit it so you can eventually send it off. To edit e-mail in your Drafts folder:

1. **Choose one of the following ways to switch to the Outlook Today view:**

   • Choose View⇨Go To⇨Outlook Today.

   • Click the Outlook Today icon in the Outlook bar.

   The Outlook Today view appears.

2. **Choose View⇔Go To⇔Drafts or click Drafts under the Messages heading in the Outlook Today view.**

    A list of e-mail drafts appears.

3. **Double-click the e-mail draft that you want to edit.**

    Outlook displays your e-mail draft on the screen.

4. **Edit your e-mail message and click the Send button (or click the Save button and choose File⇔Close to store your e-mail back in the Drafts folder).**

If you want to delete an e-mail draft, click the message you want to delete and then click the Delete button or choose Edit⇔Delete.

Using the Outbox folder

Until you connect to the Internet, Outlook stores any e-mail messages that you have not yet sent in the Outbox folder.

Viewing and editing messages in the Outbox folder

To view all the messages trapped temporarily in your Outbox folder:

1. **Choose one of the following methods to switch to the Outlook Today view:**

    • Choose View⇔Go To⇔Outlook Today.

    • Click the Outlook Today icon in the Outlook bar.

    The Outlook Today view appears.

2. **Choose View⇔Go To⇔Folder or press Ctrl+Y. (As a shortcut, click Outbox under the Messages heading in the Outlook Today view. Then skip to Step 4.)**

    A Go to Folder dialog box appears.

3. **Click the Outbox icon and click OK.**

    Outlook displays a list of e-mail messages that are waiting to be sent.

4. **Double-click the e-mail message you want to view.**

5. **Click the Save button and choose File⇔Close to store your e-mail back in the Outbox folder.**

If you want to delete e-mail stored in your Outbox folder, click the message you want to delete and then click the Delete button or choose Edit⇔Delete.

REMEMBER

To send e-mail stored in your Outbox folder, follow the steps in the following section "Sending e-mail from the Outbox folder."

Sending e-mail from the Outbox folder

Messages stored in the Outbox folder remain there until you decide to send them on their way. To send e-mail from the Outbox folder:

1. **Switch to the Outlook Today view in one of the following ways:**

   - Choose View⇨Go To⇨Outlook Today.
   - Click the Outlook Today icon in the Outlook bar.

   The Outlook Today view appears.

2. **Choose View⇨Go To⇨Folder or press Ctrl+Y. (As a shortcut, click Outbox under the Messages heading in the Outlook Today view. Then skip to Step 4.)**

   A Go To Folder dialog box appears.

3. **Click the Outbox icon and click OK.**

   Outlook displays a list of e-mail messages that are waiting to be sent.

4. **Click the e-mail message you want to send.**

   To choose more than one e-mail message, hold down the Ctrl key and click each message you want to send. To select a continuous range of e-mail messages, click the first message you want to send, hold down the Shift key, and then click the last message you want to send.

5. **Click the Send/Receive button.**

Retrieving and Reading E-Mail

As long as you have an Internet account, you can use Outlook to read and organize your e-mail.

Retrieving e-mail

To retrieve e-mail:

1. **Choose one of the following ways to switch to the Outlook Today view:**

   - Choose View⇨Go To⇨Outlook Today.
   - Click the Outlook Today icon in the Outlook bar.

   The Outlook Today view appears.

2. **Choose Tools⇨Send/Receive.**

   A menu appears, listing all the Internet accounts you've defined for Outlook.

3. **Click the Internet account you want to retrieve mail from.**

   If Outlook finds e-mail for you, it kindly stores your e-mail in the Inbox folder.

If you're already connected to your Internet account, you can retrieve your e-mail by just clicking the Send/Receive button on the toolbar.

Reading an e-mail message

To read an e-mail message:

1. **Choose View⇨Go To⇨Inbox, press Ctrl+Shift+I, or click Inbox under the Messages heading in the Outlook Today view.**

   The Inbox window appears.

2. **Click the e-mail message that you want to read.**

   The contents of your chosen message appear at the bottom of the screen.

3. **Choose File⇨Close or click the close box of the message window.**

4. **After you finish reading the message, click another message.**

   If you want to reply to an e-mail message, skip Step 3 and follow the steps listed in the next section, "Replying to an e-mail message."

Replying to an e-mail message

You often need to reply to someone who has sent you an e-mail message, either out of courtesy or because you want something from them. Replying to e-mail is easy because Outlook automatically knows where to send your reply without making you retype that cryptic e-mail address. To reply to an e-mail message:

1. **Follow Steps 1 and 2 in the previous section, "Reading an e-mail message."**

2. **Choose Actions⇨Reply, press Ctrl+R, or click the Reply button on the toolbar.**

   If you want your reply to go to everyone who received the original message, choose Actions⇨Reply to All or press Ctrl+Shift+R.

   The Message dialog box appears with a copy of the original message in the message window and the recipient's e-mail address (or recipients' e-mail addresses) already typed for you.

3. **Type your reply and then click the Send button.**

Rather than send your reply right away, you can store it in the Drafts or Outbox folder by following the steps in the preceding sections "Using the Drafts folder" and "Using the Outbox folder," in this chapter.

Forwarding e-mail

Rather then reply to an e-mail, you may want to pass an e-mail message on to someone else, which can be an amusing way to distribute jokes while you are at work. Passing along messages is known by a more stuffy, technical term as *forwarding* an e-mail message. To forward an e-mail message:

1. **Follow Steps 1 and 2 in the section, "Reading an e-mail message," earlier in this chapter.**

2. **Choose Actions⇨Forward, press Ctrl+F, or click the Forward button on the toolbar.**

   The Message dialog box appears with the original e-mail message already typed in for you.

3. **Type an address to whom you want to send the e-mail.**

   If you want to send e-mail to an address stored in your Address Book, click the To button and then click the recipient's name. If you want to send the message to someone who isn't in your Address Book, then you have to type the e-mail address in the To box.

5. **Type any additional message that you want to send along with the for-warded message.**

6. **Click the Send button.**

Deleting Old E-Mail

If you don't watch out, you may find your Inbox overflowing with ancient e-mail messages that you no longer need. Rather than waste valuable hard disk space storing useless e-mail messages, take some time periodically to clean out your Inbox.

Besides the Inbox, another folder that may get cluttered is the Sent Items folder, which contains copies of every e-mail message you've sent out. Although you may like to keep a record of these messages for future refer-ence, you will probably want to wipe out at least some of your sent messages at some point.

Deleting e-mail

To delete an e-mail message in your Inbox or Sent Items folder:

1. **Choose <u>V</u>iew⇨<u>G</u>o To⇨<u>I</u>nbox or press Ctrl+Shift+I.**

   Or choose <u>V</u>iew⇨<u>G</u>o To⇨<u>F</u>older, click the Sent Items icon, and then click OK to delete messages in the Sent Items folder.

2. **Click the message that you want to delete.**

   If you want to delete multiple messages, hold down the Ctrl key and click each message you want to delete. If you want to delete a range of messages, hold down the Shift key, click the first message you want to delete, and then click the last message you want to delete.

3. **Choose <u>E</u>dit⇨<u>D</u>elete, press Ctrl+D, or click the Delete button on the toolbar.**

   Outlook deletes your chosen messages.

When you delete messages, Outlook stores them in the Deleted Items folder. That way, you have one last chance of recovering any e-mail that you want to save before you permanently delete the messages — see the next section, "Recovering e-mail from Deleted Items."

Recovering e-mail from Deleted Items

If you delete a message from your Inbox or Sent Items folder and suddenly decide that you need it after all, you can still recover it. All you have to do is get it out of your Deleted Items folder. To recover e-mail from your Deleted Items folder:

1. **Click the Deleted Items icon on the Outlook bar.**

   Or choose <u>V</u>iew⇨<u>G</u>o To⇨<u>F</u>older, click the Deleted Items icon, and then click OK to open the Deleted Items folder.

2. **Click the e-mail message that you want to recover.**

   If you want to recover a number of messages, you can select multiple messages by holding down the Ctrl key and clicking each message.

3. **Choose <u>E</u>dit⇨<u>M</u>ove to Folder or press Ctrl+Shift+V.**

   The Move Items dialog box appears.

4. **Click the Inbox icon and then click OK.**

   The message appears in your Inbox in its original condition. (If you want, you can choose a folder other than Inbox.)

Deleting e-mail for good

Until you delete your e-mail messages from the Deleted Items folder, those messages can be retrieved and read by others. At the very least, your unwanted messages still just sit around and take up space on your hard disk until you get rid of them for good.

After you delete e-mail from the Deleted Items folder, you can never recover the message. So you'd better make sure you mean it.

To delete e-mail from your computer forever:

1. **Click the Deleted Items icon on the Outlook bar.**

   Or choose View➪Go To➪Folder, click the Deleted Items icon, and then click OK.

2. **Click the e-mail message that you want to delete.**

   If you want to delete a number of messages at one time, you can select multiple messages by holding down the Ctrl key and clicking each message.

3. **Choose Edit➪Delete or press Ctrl+D.**

   A dialog box appears, warning you that you are about to permanently delete the e-mail messages.

4. **Click the Yes button.**

   Kiss your chosen e-mail messages good-bye.

If you're in a hurry and want to dump all the e-mail stored in your Deleted Items folder, choose Tools➪Empty "Deleted Items" Folder.

Dealing with Junk E-Mail

Because e-mail doesn't cost anything to send (other than the cost of setting up an Internet account), many businesses (legal or shady) send thousands of e-mail messages to everyone possible in hopes of making a sale. Such random e-mail messages are known as *junk e-mail* or *spam,* which you may not want to waste your time reading.

You can usually recognize junk e-mail because the subject heading appears in all capital letters, such as MAKE MONEY FAST!!!; uses plenty of exclamation marks to attract your attention; or contains a suspicious subject heading designed to entice you to read the e-mail, such as "About your credit card account."

To keep you from wasting time browsing through e-mail that you don't really want, Outlook provides a handy way to automatically route junk e-mail to a separate folder. That way you can either read it later (if you want) or just delete the e-mail without bothering to read it.

Defining junk e-mail

Outlook has no idea how to identify junk e-mail. So to tell Outlook which e-mail addresses to ignore, you have to receive a message you want to define as junk e-mail and then tell Outlook, "See this message? Assume any messages coming from this e-mail address are also junk e-mail."

Many junk e-mailers open and close e-mail accounts rapidly to prevent people from identifying their messages as junk e-mail. If a junk e-mailer sends you messages from different e-mail addresses, Outlook won't be able to identify the e-mail as junk.

To identify and route junk e-mail:

1. **Choose <u>V</u>iew⇨<u>G</u>o To⇨<u>I</u>nbox or press Ctrl+Shift+I.**

2. **Click the messages that you want to define as junk e-mail.**

   You can define any e-mail as junk e-mail, including messages from your boss.

3. **Choose <u>A</u>ctions⇨<u>J</u>unk E-mail⇨Add to <u>J</u>unk Senders list.**

   Outlook adds the e-mail address to its Junk Senders list.

After defining certain mail as junk mail, you need to follow the instructions in the "Moving or highlighting your junk e-mail" section to complete Outlook's training to recognize and act upon future junk e-mail.

Moving or highlighting your junk e-mail

After you tell Outlook what type of e-mail addresses to watch out for, Outlook acts like a well-trained secretary and gives you two choices for what to do with your junk e-mail. Outlook can

✔ Highlight junk e-mail in your Inbox

✔ Move junk e-mail automatically into another folder

If you choose to highlight your junk e-mail in your Inbox, you can still browse through your junk e-mail in case you find something interesting or stupid enough to make fun of later.

If you have Outlook automatically move junk e-mail into another folder, such as the Deleted Items folder, you can always browse through these messages later, too.

To tell Outlook what to do when it finds junk e-mail:

1. **Choose View➪Go To➪Inbox or press Ctrl+Shift+I.**
2. **Choose Tools➪Organize.**

   The Ways to Organize Inbox window appears.
3. **Click the Junk E-mail icon.**
4. **Click the first list box that appears to the right of "Automatically."**

   Choose either "move" or "color."
5. **Click the second list box.**

   Choose either a destination folder (such as Deleted Items) or a color, depending on whether you chose "move" or "color" in Step 4.
6. **Click the Turn On button.**
7. **Click the close box in the Ways to Organize Inbox window.**

Viewing your list of junk e-mail senders

In case you want to view all the e-mail addresses that you told Outlook to consider as senders of junk e-mail, follow these steps:

1. **Choose View➪Go To➪Inbox or press Ctrl+Shift+I.**
2. **Choose Tools➪Organize.**

   The Ways to Organize Inbox window appears.
3. **Click the Junk E-Mail icon.**
4. **Click the Click Here hyperlink at the bottom of the Ways to Organize Inbox window.**

   Outlook shows a different view of the Ways to Organize Inbox window.
5. **Click the Edit Junk Senders hyperlink.**

   An Edit Junk Senders dialog box appears.
6. **Click an address that you want to edit and then click one of the following buttons:**
   - **Add:** Adds a new e-mail address to define as a sender of junk e-mail.
   - **Edit:** Edits a currently stored e-mail address.
   - **Delete:** Deletes a currently stored e-mail address.

7. Click OK.

8. Click the close box in the Ways to Organize Inbox window.

Part VI
Storing Stuff in Access 2000

In this part . . .

*P*ersonal computers provide an excellent tool for storing information in databases. Because databases can be so useful and crucial for many businesses, it's no surprise that the Professional and Premium Editions of Microsoft Office 2000 come with a special database program called Microsoft Access 2000.

For those of you who enjoy deciphering computer terminology, Access 2000 is a *relational database*. For those of you who don't care to decipher computer terminology, the previous sentence means that Access 2000 lets you store stuff in different ways.

This part of the book gets you started storing stuff in Access 2000. By the time you finish reading this part of the book, you'll feel comfortable enough to create databases with Access 2000. After you store information in a database, take that extra step and find out how to create form letters, reports, and mailing labels with the combined power of Access 2000 and Word 2000.

Chapter 18

Stuffing Information into a Database

· ·

In This Chapter

▶ Understanding database basics

▶ Entering your data

▶ Viewing your data

· ·

Despite the power of a personal computer, many people still insist on storing important names, addresses, and phone numbers in Rolodex files, on index cards, or on sheets of paper stuffed into folders. Although sometimes convenient, paper is terrible for retrieving and analyzing information. Just look at a typical file cabinet and ask yourself how much time would be required to find the names and phone numbers of every customer who lives in Missouri and ordered more than $5,000 worth of your products in the past six months.

Instead of relying on memory or slips of paper to organize your information, use Microsoft Access 2000. Access lets you not only store and retrieve information but also sort, manipulate, and analyze that information to spot trends or patterns in your data (so you can tell when your company is losing money and may fire you at any moment). The more you know about your information, the better off you are when dealing with your less knowledgeable, computer-illiterate competitors, coworkers, or supervisors.

If you bought the Standard or Small Business edition of Microsoft Office 2000, you have to buy Access 2000 separately.

For storing names and addresses you may find Outlook much easier and faster than Access. (For more on Outlook 2000, check out Part V.) If you need to store more complicated information such as customer invoices or inventory part numbers, use Access.

Database 101

Although the fancy term *programmable relational database* may sound intimidating (or just plain stupid), Access is nothing more than a fancy filing cabinet that allows you to dump information in and yank it back out again. Before you can dump information into Access, however, you have to tell the program what type of information you want to store. A typical Access database file consists of the following elements:

- ✔ **One or more fields:** A *field* contains one chunk of data, such as a name, fax number, or a telephone number.

- ✔ **One or more records:** A *record* contains two or more related fields, such as a person's name, address, phone number, and employee ID number.

- ✔ **One or more forms:** A *form* acts like an on-screen version of a piece of paper. Forms display one or more records on the screen, such as a person's name, address, and phone number.

- ✔ **One or more database tables:** A database *table* contains one or more records. For example, one database table may contain names and addresses of your customers, and another database table may list all the products stored in your inventory.

- ✔ **A database file:** A database *file* contains one or more tables. A database file is the physical file stored on your hard disk with a name like SALES99.MDB. (If you erase this file, you erase your entire database.) Access always saves its database files with a funny file extension: MDB, which stands for *M*icrosoft *data*base.

You can use Access in two ways. You may use Access to store, view, and delete information, such as the names of your friends, their addresses, their mobile phone numbers, and their birthdays.

A second, more complicated way to use Access is to create custom databases, such as a database for tracking patients in a hospital so you can track the time and date they arrive, the medication they require, what doctors they see, and (most importantly) how much money they owe. Custom databases can actually become miniature programs in themselves, usually designed to fit a specific purpose, such as managing inventory in an electronics company or creating a mailing list program for charities.

Because designing custom databases can get complicated, we don't cover custom databases in this book. If you want more information about creating custom databases, pick up a copy of *Access 2000 For Dummies,* by John Kaufeld, published by IDG Books Worldwide, Inc.

Creating a new database file

Think of a database as a filing cabinet devoted to holding one type of data, such as information related to taxes or business. When you want to create a database, Access gives you two choices.

- ✔ You can create an entire database from scratch, defining the fields (such as name, phone number, part number, birth date, and so on) that describe the type of information you want the database to hold.

- ✔ You can use the Access Database Wizard to guide you through the process of creating a database.

 Most of the time, the Access Database Wizard is the easier way to create a database. Remember, you can always modify a database after you create it with the wizard. Leave starting from scratch to those with too much time on their hands.

To create a new database file by using the Database Wizard:

1. **Start Microsoft Access.**

   The opening Microsoft Access dialog box appears, as shown in Figure 18-1.

Figure 18-1:
When you first start Access, you can create a new Access database or open an existing one.

Microsoft Access
Create a new database using
○ Blank Access database
○ Access database wizards, pages, and projects
⦿ Open an existing file
db2
Northwind Sample Database
Contacts Sample Database
Address Sample Database
Inventory Sample Database
OK   Cancel

2. **Click the Access Database Wizards, Pages, and Projects option button and then click OK.**

   The New dialog box appears, as shown in Figure 18-2.

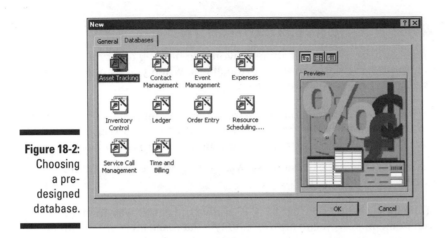

Figure 18-2:
Choosing
a pre-
designed
database.

3. **Click the type of database that you want to use (such as Asset Track-ing, Inventory Control, or Contact Management) and then click OK.**

Depending on which database you choose, Access displays slightly different figures than what you see in this book. The figures in this chapter show what happens when you choose the Contact Management Database Wizard.

The File New Database dialog box appears, as shown in Figure 18-3.

Figure 18-3:
Giving your
database a
name with
the File New
Database
dialog box.

4. **Type a name for your database in the File Name box and click the Create button.**

If you want to store your database in a specific folder, click the Save In list box and choose the folder.

After a few seconds, the Database Wizard dialog box appears, letting you know the type of information that the database will store.

5. Click Next.

Another Database Wizard dialog box appears, listing the tables and fields that it will create. See Figure 18-4.

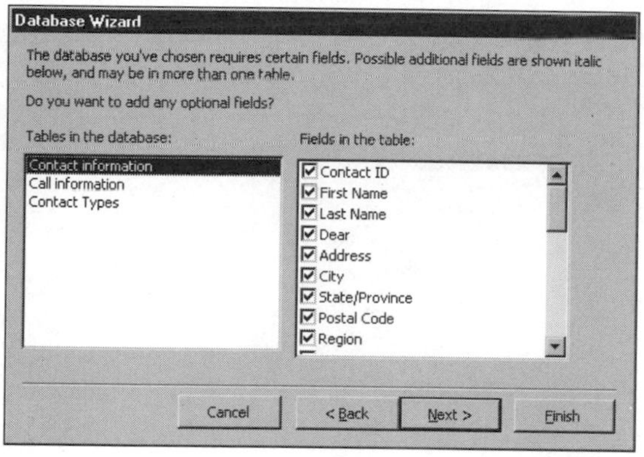

Figure 18-4:
The Database Wizard kindly shows you the tables and fields already defined for your chosen database.

6. Click the check boxes of the additional fields that you want to store in your database (or clear any check boxes to remove any fields that you don't want to include in your database); then click Next.

You may have to repeat Step 6 if your database contains two or more database tables.

Still another Database Wizard dialog box appears, giving you the chance to select a background picture for your database forms, as shown in Figure 18-5.

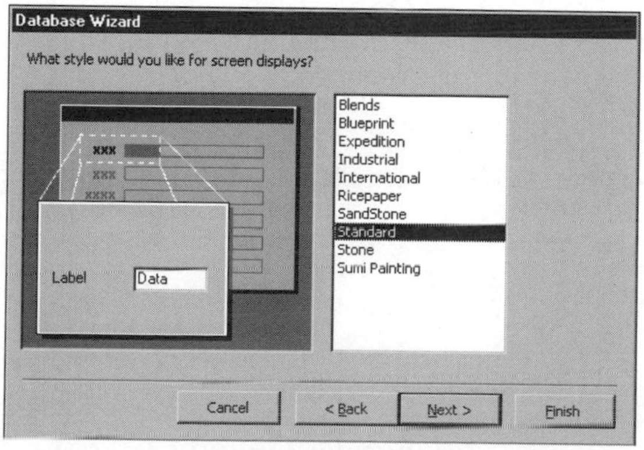

Figure 18-5:
Picking a screen display for your database.

7. **Choose a screen display style (choose Standard if you don't like fancy backgrounds) and click Next.**

   Another Database Wizard dialog box appears, asking what style you want to use for printed reports, as shown in Figure 18-6. A *report* is a printed copy of your database information. Choosing a style simply gives you the freedom to make your report look fancy.

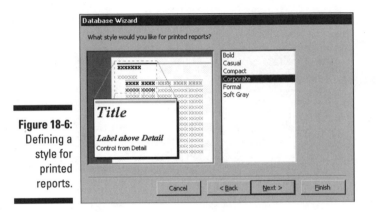

Figure 18-6:
Defining a
style for
printed
reports.

   To help you pick the style best suited to your needs, click several different styles one at a time and check out the left-hand window to see what each style looks like.

8. **Choose a style and then click Next.**

   One more Database Wizard dialog box appears, asking you for the database title. (Access displays the database title on the Switchboard window. The database title is purely cosmetic and doesn't affect the design or organization of your database whatsoever.)

9. **Type a title for your database (such as Valuable names or People I have to deal with) and then click Next.**

   The last Database Wizard dialog box appears, letting you know that it's finished asking you annoying questions.

10. **Click Finish.**

   Access creates your database and displays the Main Switchboard, as shown in Figure 18-7.

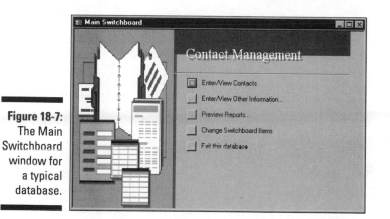

Figure 18-7: The Main Switchboard window for a typical database.

Opening an existing database

To open a database file that you've created — to enter new information, view existing information, or edit or delete information — follow these steps:

1. **Start Microsoft Access.**

   Access opens, displaying a dialog box (refer to Figure 18-1).

2. **Click Open an Existing File option and click the database name that you want to open.**

3. **Click OK.**

If Access is already running and you want to open an existing database:

1. **Choose File➪Open or press Ctrl+O.**

   The Open dialog box appears.

2. **Click the database name that you want to open; then click Open.**

Looking at the parts of your database

When Access creates a database, the database actually consists of two separate windows:

- ✔ The Main Switchboard window
- ✔ The Database window

The Main Switchboard window provides a simple one-click method of using your database so you can view, edit, and print your database information (refer to Figure 18-7).

If you create a database from scratch (without using the Database Wizard) your database doesn't have a Main Switchboard window.

The Database window shows all the separate reports, modules, forms, tables, and macros that make up your entire database, as shown in Figure 18-8.

Figure 18-8:
The
Database
window for
a typical
database.

To switch between the Main Switchboard window and the Database window, choose Window⇨Main Switchboard or Window⇨Database.

The whole purpose of the Main Switchboard window is to hide the ugly details of managing a database. If you really want to get involved with creating, modifying, and programming Access, switch to the Database window. If you just want to use a database and couldn't care less about the fine details, use the Main Switchboard window instead.

What's what in Access 2000

Reports let you print information from a database in a neat, eye-appealing fashion. *Forms* display information from a database in a user-friendly window that resembles a paper form. *Tables* display information (such as names and phone numbers) in rows and column format. *Macros* are shortcuts you can use to make Access easier to use. *Modules* contain commands that let you automate your database so others can use them.

The only reason to know about reports, modules, macros, and so on is if you plan on tinkering with your database. If you're the type who can't resist digging under the hood of your car to see how you can improve things, you may need to know about modules, macros, and so on. If you're just happy to know how to drive a car and couldn't care less how it works, you can safely ignore all this technical stuff.

Using a Database

After Access creates a database, the new database is completely empty (and also completely useless) until you start stuffing your own information into it.

While you type your data, Access saves it to disk. That way if the power goes out or if Windows crashes, your data will (hopefully) still be stored on your hard disk.

Entering data through the Main Switchboard

The easiest way to stuff data into a new or existing database is from the Main Switchboard window. To use the Main Switchboard window to add new data:

1. **Choose <u>W</u>indow⇔Main Switchboard.**

   The Main Switchboard window appears.

2. **Click one of the Enter/View buttons on the Main Switchboard window.**

   For example, if you want to add a new contact in the database displayed in Figure 18-7, click Enter/View Contacts.

   Access displays a form, showing the first record in your database and the fields where you can type information, as shown in Figure 18-9.

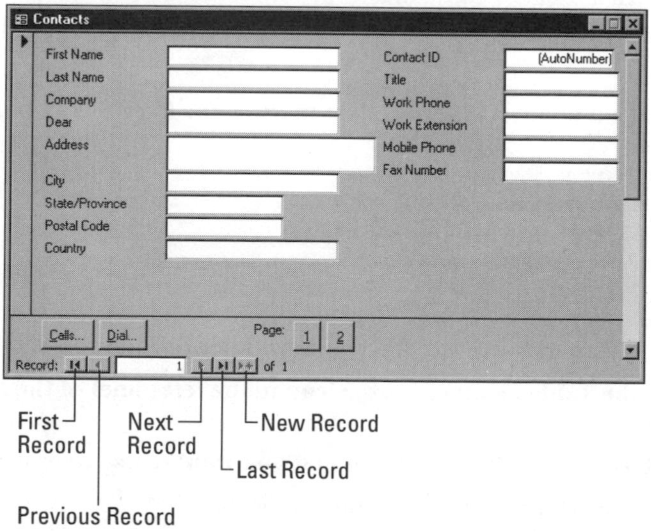

Figure 18-9:
A form showing an empty record in a typical database.

First Record
Previous Record
Next Record
Last Record
New Record

3. **Click the field where you want to add data (such as First Name or Address); then type the data.**

4. **To type data for the next record, choose Insert⇨New Record, click the New Record button that appears on the toolbar, or click the Next Record button on the form.**

   Access displays a blank record.

5. **Repeat Steps 3 and 4 for each new record that you want to add to your database.**

6. **After you enter the data you want, click the close box of the window.**

If you have several records in a database, you can view them by clicking one of the following buttons that appear on the database form:

- ✔ **First Record button:** Displays the first record of the database

- ✔ **Previous Record button:** Displays the record that comes before the one you're currently viewing

- ✔ **Next Record button:** Displays the record that comes after the one you're currently viewing

- ✔ **Last Record button:** Displays the last record of the database

Entering data through a table or form

If you don't use the Main Switchboard, Access gives you two ways to enter data: through a table or through a form. Entering data in a table lets you see multiple records at once. Entering data in a form lets you see one record at a time.

Entering data into a form is equivalent to using the Main Switchboard to enter data.

To enter data in a table or form:

1. **Open an existing database.**

2. **Choose Window⇨Database.**

   Access displays the Database window (refer to Figure 18-8).

3. **Click the Tables icon or Forms icon in the left panel of the Database window.**

4. **Double-click the table or form that you want to use to enter data.**

   Access displays your chosen table or form.

5. **Type your data in the appropriate fields.**

   To move from one field to another, use the mouse, press Tab, or press Shift+Tab.

6. **When you finish, click the close box of the Table or Form window.**

Deleting data

Eventually, you may want to delete individual field data or even entire records. For example, you may have a record in your database containing information about someone that you never want to speak to again, such as a former spouse or roommate. Rather than have that person's name and address constantly haunt you by their existence in your database, you can delete that record and (figuratively) eliminate that person's name from the face of the earth — or at least the face of your computer.

Access provides two ways to delete data:

✔ Just delete the information stored in a field (useful for editing a single field, such as the address of someone who has moved).

✔ Delete all the information stored in an entire record (useful for wiping out all traces of a single record, which can be handy to completely obliterate all information about a person who no longer works for your company).

Deleting data in a field

To delete data stored in a field:

1. **Follow the steps in the "Entering data through the Main Switchboard" section or "Entering data through a table or form" section until you find the record containing data that you want to delete.**

2. **Click the field that contains the data that you want to delete.**

3. **Choose one of the following methods to delete the data:**

   • Press Delete or Backspace to delete one character at a time.

   • Drag the mouse to select the data; then press Delete or Backspace to delete the entire selected data.

Deleting an entire record

Deleting a single field or two can be useful for editing your records. But if you want to wipe out an entire record altogether, follow these steps:

1. **Follow the steps in the "Entering data through the Main Switchboard" section or "Entering data through a table or form" section until you find the record containing data that you want to delete.**

2. **Choose Edit⇨Delete Record or click the Delete Record button on the toolbar.**

   A dialog box appears, warning that if you continue, your deleted record will be lost for good.

3. **Click the Yes button (but only if you're sure that you want to delete your chosen record forever).**

Make sure that you really want to delete the entire record — you won't be able to retrieve your deleted data afterwards.

Modifying the Structure of a Database

The Database Wizard can create a database for you automatically, but you may want to create a database from scratch, or modify a database created by the Database Wizard. The two most common parts of a database that you may need to add, delete, or modify are tables and forms.

Tables display data in row and column format, much like a spreadsheet. *Forms* display data like a paper form on the screen.

Adding a table

To add a table to an existing Access database file:

1. **Open an existing database.**

2. **Choose Window⇨Database.**

   Access displays the Database window (refer to Figure 18-8).

3. **Click the Tables icon in the left panel of the Database window.**

4. **Double-click the Create Table by Using Wizard icon.**

   The Table Wizard dialog box appears as shown in Figure 18-10.

5. **Click the Business or Personal option button.**

   Access displays a list of common fields for Business or Personal databases.

6. **Click the Sample Tables list box and choose the table that most closely matches the table you want to create (such as Contacts or Mailing List).**

7. **Click the Sample Fields list box and click the field that most closely matches the field you want to create (such as LastName or City).**

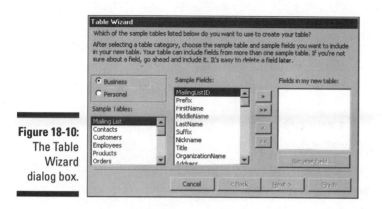

Figure 18-10:
The Table
Wizard
dialog box.

8. **Click the right arrow → button.**

   Access displays your chosen field in the Fields in My New Table list box.
   If you click the Rename Field button, you can (guess what?) rename a
   field.

9. **Repeat Steps 7 and 8 for each field you want to add.**

10. **Click Next.**

    Another Table Wizard dialog box appears.

11. **Type a name for your table and click Next.**

    Still another Table Wizard dialog box appears, asking you whether your
    new table contains records related to other tables stored in your data-
    base. Multiple tables can share the same fields, such as a Customer ID or
    a Company Name field.

12. **Click Next.**

    A final Table Wizard dialog box appears, asking whether you want to
    modify the design of your table or start entering data right away.

13. **Click one of the options and click Finish.**

If you click the Enter Data into the Table Using a Form Option the Wizard
Creates for Me option button, Access creates a plain-looking form where you
can start typing in data.

Deleting a table

You may want to delete a table if you don't need to save the information
stored inside of it.

Deleting a table wipes out any information, such as names and addresses, stored in that table. So make sure you really want to delete a table and all the data in it.

To delete a table:

1. **Open an existing database.**
2. **Choose <u>W</u>indow⇨Database.**

   Access displays the Database window (refer to Figure 18-8).

3. **Click the Tables icon in the left panel of the Database window.**
4. **Click the table that you want to delete.**
5. **Choose <u>E</u>dit⇨<u>D</u>elete, press Delete, or click the Delete icon in the toolbar.**

   A dialog box appears, asking if you really want to delete your chosen table.

6. **Click <u>Y</u>es.**

Press Ctrl+Z if you suddenly decide you don't want to delete your table after all.

Modifying a table

After you create a table, you may want to modify the table (not the data stored inside the table). For example, you may have forgotten to create a field to store a person's employee ID, so you have to create a new field in a table to hold that information. Likewise, you may suddenly decide that you don't want to store people's phone numbers any more, so you can delete that field.

Adding a new field to a table

To add a field to a table:

1. **Open an existing database.**
2. **Choose <u>W</u>indow⇨Database.**

   Access displays the Database window (refer to Figure 18-8).

3. **Click the Tables icon in the left panel of the Database window.**
4. **Click the table where you want to add a new field.**
5. **Click the <u>D</u>esign icon in the Database toolbar.**

   A Table window appears as shown in Figure 18-11.

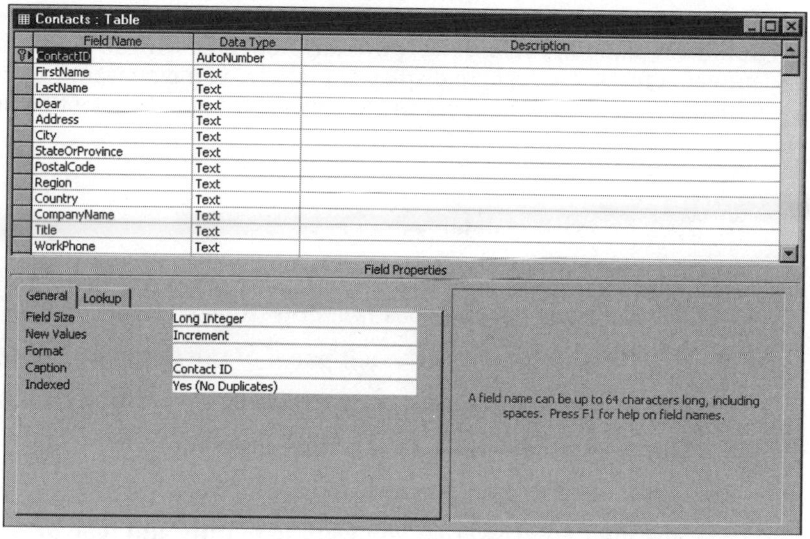

Figure 18-11:
A typical
table
window
where you
can edit or
add a field.

6. **Click the row where you want to insert your new field.**

Access doesn't care where you insert your new field. The location of a field is for your convenience, such as listing the First Name and Last Name fields next to each other.

7. **Choose Insert➪Rows, or click the Insert Rows icon on the toolbar.**

Access inserts a blank row in your table.

8. **Type your field name under the Field Name column.**

9. **Click the Data Type column.**

A downward-pointing arrow appears in the Data Type cell, and a Field Properties pane appears at the bottom of the screen.

10. **Click the downward-pointing arrow in the Data Type column and choose the type of data you want to store, such as Text or Date/Time.**

Depending on the data type you choose, you can modify the field properties by defining the maximum length or acceptable values the field can accept.

11. **Click the close box of the Table window.**

A dialog box appears, asking if you want to save the changes to your table.

12. **Click Yes.**

Modifying a field in a table

After you create a table, define various fields (such as Name, Phone, or Employee Nickname), and type actual data (such as Bob, 555-1234, or

LoserBoss), you may suddenly realize that a particular field needs modification. For example, you may have initially defined a field so small that data appears cut off. Or if a field displays numbers, you may want to modify the appearance of those numbers as currency instead of in scientific notation.

To modify a field in a table:

1. **Open an existing database.**

2. **Choose Window⇨Database.**

   Access displays the Database window (refer to Figure 18-8).

3. **Click the Tables icon in the left panel of the Database window.**

4. **Click the table where you want to modify an existing field.**

5. **Click the Design icon in the Database toolbar.**

   A Table window appears (refer to Figure 18-11).

6. **Click the field (row) that you want to modify and type or edit the field name.**

7. **Click the Data Type column.**

8. **Click the downward-pointing arrow in the Data Type column and choose the type of data you want to store, such as Text or Date/Time.**

   Depending on the data type you choose, you can modify the field properties by defining the maximum length or acceptable values the field can accept.

9. **Click the close box of the Table window.**

   A dialog box appears, asking if you want to save the changes to your table.

10. **Click Yes.**

Deleting a field from a table

To delete a field from a table:

1. **Open an existing database.**

2. **Choose Window⇨Database.**

   Access displays the Database window (refer to Figure 18-8).

3. **Click the Tables icon in the left panel of the Database window.**

4. **Click the table where you want to delete an existing field.**

5. **Click the Design icon in the Database toolbar.**

   A Table window appears (refer to Figure 18-11).

6. **Click the gray box to the left of the field (row) that you want to delete.**

   Access highlights the entire row.

7. **Choose Edit⇨Delete Rows, or press Delete.**

   If the field contains data, a dialog box appears, asking whether you really want to delete the field and any data that may be stored in that field. If the field is empty, no dialog box appears, and you can skip to Step 9.

8. **Click Yes.**

9. **Click the close box of the Table window.**

   A dialog box appears, asking if you want to save the changes that you made to your table.

10. **Click Yes.**

Adding a form

A form mimics a paper form by providing an organized way to view and enter data. Because a form can display your data in different ways, you may later find that all your current forms display too much (or too little) data for certain uses. For example, you may need one form to display the names and medical insurance numbers of people, and a completely different form to display those same people's names, addresses, phone numbers, and contact information.

With multiple forms, you can customize the viewing and adding of data to your Access database for a variety of specific tasks. To add a new form to your database file:

1. **Open an existing database.**

2. **Choose Window⇨Database.**

   Access displays the Database window (refer to Figure 18-8).

3. **Click the Forms icon in the left panel of the Database window.**

4. **Double-click Create Form by Using Wizard icon.**

   A Form Wizard dialog box appears as shown in Figure 18-12.

5. **Click the Tables/Queries list box and choose a table containing the data you want to display on your form.**

6. **Click the Available Fields list box and choose the field you want to add to your form.**

7. **Click the right arrow → button to add fields to the Selected Fields list.**

8. **Repeat Steps 6 and 7 for each field you want to display on your form.**

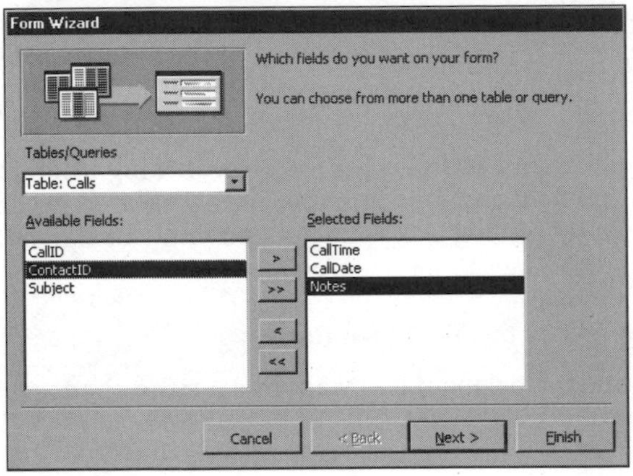

Figure 18-12:
The Form
Wizard
dialog box
for design-
ing a new
form.

9. **Click Next.**

   Another Form Wizard dialog box asks you to choose a layout for your form.

10. **Click one of the options (such as Tabular or Justified) and click Next.**

    Yet another Form Wizard dialog box asks you to choose a style for your form.

11. **Click a form style such as Blueprint or Sandstone and click Next.**

    A final Form Wizard dialog box asks for a title for your form.

12. **Type a name for your form and click Finish.**

    Access displays your form as shown in Figure 18-13.

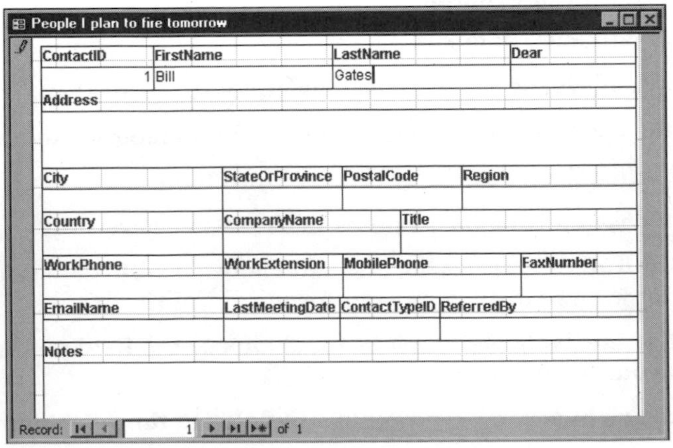

Figure 18-13:
Access can
create
a form for
you auto-
matically.

Deleting a form

If you delete a form, you can't recover it again. So, make sure you really want to delete the form before you do.

When you delete a form, you do not delete any data that the form displays. (If you want to delete the actual data stored in Access, you have to delete the table containing that data. Refer to the earlier section "Deleting data.")

In case you no longer need a particular form, you can get rid of it by following these steps:

1. **Open an existing database.**

2. **Choose <u>W</u>indow⇨Database.**

   Access displays the Database window (refer to Figure 18-8).

3. **Click the Forms icon in the left panel of the Database window.**

4. **Click the form that you want to delete.**

5. **Choose <u>E</u>dit⇨<u>D</u>elete, press Delete, or click the Delete icon in the toolbar.**

   A dialog box appears, asking if you really want to delete your chosen table.

6. **Click <u>Y</u>es.**

Modifying a form

Forms just display data on the screen, making it easy for people to view or type in new information. The two most common items you will need to modify on a form will be labels and text boxes.

Labels are purely decorative but are often used to describe what type of information appears in a text box, such as a name or phone number. *Text boxes* provide a blank box where actual data appears.

There are many ways to modify a form, but the most common way is to add or delete a new field that appears on a form. For more information on the different ways to modify a form, pick up a copy of *Access 2000 For Dummies,* by John Kaufeld, published by IDG Books Worldwide, Inc.

Adding a new field to a form

If you want to add a new field, you need to add a text box (to hold the actual data) and a label (to describe the type of information that appears in the text box). To add a text box (field) to a form:

1. **Open an existing database.**

2. **Choose <u>W</u>indow⇨Database.**

   Access displays the Database window (refer to Figure 18-8).

3. **Click the Forms icon in the left panel of the Database window.**

4. **Click the form that you want to modify.**

5. **Click <u>D</u>esign.**

   Access displays your form along with a form toolbox as shown in Figure 18-14.

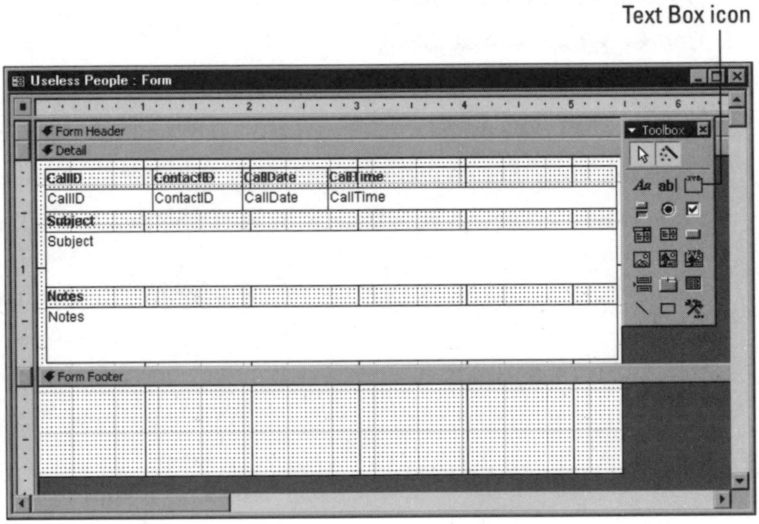

Text Box icon

Figure 18-14: To modify a form, you can use a form toolbox.

6. **Click the Text Box icon in the form toolbox.**

   The mouse cursor changes into a crosshair with a text box icon attached to it.

7. **Move the mouse to the spot on the form where you want to draw your text box.**

8. **Hold down the left mouse button and drag the mouse to draw the text box.**

9. **Release the left mouse button when the text box is the size you want it.**

   Access draws the text box along with a label.

10. **Double-click the frame of text box.**

    A Text Box properties dialog box appears as shown in Figure 18-15.

Figure 18-15:
In the Text
Box proper-
ties dialog
box you
specify the
type of data
to display.

Text Box: Text16	[X]

Format | Data | Event | Other | All

Name Text16
Control Source . . . .
Format . . . .
Decimal Places . . . . Auto
Input Mask . . . .
Default Value . . . .
Validation Rule . . . .
Validation Text . . . .
Status Bar Text . . . .
Enter Key Behavior . . . . . . Default
Allow AutoCorrect . . . . Yes
Visible . . . . Yes
Display When . . . . Always

11. **Click the Control Source box.**

   A downward-pointing arrow appears.

12. **Click the downward-pointing arrow.**

   A list of fields stored in your database appears.

13. **Click a data source, such as FirstName or Address.**

   The data source you choose tells Access what type of data to display in your newly created text box.

14. **Click the close box of the Text Box properties dialog box.**

15. **Double-click the field label.**

   A Label properties dialog box appears.

16. **Click the Caption box and type a caption for your new field (such as Employee ID or Marital Status).**

   Whatever you type in the Caption box appears on your form.

17. **Click the close box of the Label properties dialog box.**

18. **Click the close box of the Form window.**

   A dialog box appears, asking if you want to save changes to your form.

19. **Click Yes.**

After creating a new field, you may have to resize the field or its caption to make the entire text visible.

Modifying a field on a form

After you create a field, you may need to resize or move the field so it looks nice and pretty on your form. To resize a field:

1. **Open an existing database.**

2. **Choose Window⇨Database.**

   Access displays the Database window (refer to Figure 18-8).

3. **Click the Forms icon in the left panel of the Database window.**

4. **Click the form that you want to modify.**

5. **Click Design.**

   Access displays your form along with a form toolbox.

6. **Click the field or its accompanying caption.**

   Access highlights the field or caption with black handles around its border.

7. **Move the mouse over a handle so the mouse cursor turns into a double-pointing arrow.**

8. **Hold down the left mouse button and drag the mouse to resize the field or caption.**

9. **Release the left mouse button when the field or caption is the size you want it.**

10. **Click the close box of the Form window.**

    A dialog box appears, asking if you want to save changes to your form.

11. **Click Yes.**

To move a field, follow these steps:

1. **Open an existing database.**

2. **Choose Window⇨Database.**

   Access displays the Database window (refer to Figure 18-8).

3. **Click the Forms icon in the left panel of the Database window.**

4. **Click the form that you want to modify.**

5. **Click Design.**

   Access displays your form along with a form toolbox.

6. **Click the field or its accompanying caption.**

   Access highlights the field or caption with black handles around its border. Notice that the biggest handle is in the upper left-hand corner.

7. **Move the mouse over the big handle in the upper left-hand corner, hold down the left mouse button, and drag the mouse.**

   Access shows you the outline of your field or caption as you move it.

8. **Release the left mouse button when the field or caption is in the location you want.**

9. **Click the close box of the Form window.**

   A dialog box appears, asking if you want to save changes to your form.

10. **Click Yes.**

Deleting a field from a form

To add a field to a table, follow these steps:

1. **Open an existing database.**

2. **Choose Window⇨Database.**

   Access displays the Database window (refer to Figure 18-8).

3. **Click the Forms icon in the left panel of the Database window.**

4. **Click the form that you want to modify.**

5. **Click Design.**

   Access displays your form along with a form toolbox.

6. **Click the field or its accompanying caption.**

   Access highlights the field or caption with black handles around its border.

7. **Press Delete.**

8. **Click the close box of the Form window.**

   A dialog box appears, asking if you want to save changes to your form.

9. **Click Yes.**

Saving Your Database

Access gives you three different ways to save your database:

- ✔ As an Access 2000 database file (recommended for most cases)

- ✔ As a foreign database file (good for sharing data stored in an Access database with people who use other database programs like Paradox or dBASE)

- ✔ As a Web page

As you edit, delete, and add new data, Access automatically saves the data you type into your database file. However, if you add or delete fields or tables in your database, you must save the design of your database file. In other words, you don't have to worry about saving changes to the data itself; you need to save only those changes that you make to the database design (fields and tables).

To save changes to your database file:

- ✔ Choose File➪Save.
- ✔ Press Ctrl+S.
- ✔ Click the Save button on the Standard toolbar.

Saving your database in a different file format

Despite Microsoft's best efforts to dominate the world without raising the ire of anti-trust legislators, not everyone uses Access to store their data. In the old days, many people used a slow, cumbersome program called dBASE. Some people eventually graduated to a faster, cumbersome program called Paradox while others defected to rival, cumbersome programs with odd names like Approach or FoxPro.

So if you have to share your data with people who still refuse to use Access, you have to convert your Access data into a file format that other programs (such as Paradox or FoxPro) can read.

Many people actually use their spreadsheets to store data, so Access can also save its databases as a Lotus 1-2-3 or Excel spreadsheet.

Almost every database program in the world can read dBASE III files because that used to be the database standard at one time. So if you want to share your files with other database programs such as FileMaker, FoxPro, or Approach, save your files to dBASE III format.

To convert an Access database table into a different file format:

1. **Open an existing database.**

2. **Choose Window➪Database.**

   The Database window appears.

3. **Click Tables in the left panel of the Database window.**

   Access displays a list of tables in your database.

4. **Click a database table.**

5. **Choose File➪Export.**

   The Export Table To dialog box appears.

6. **Type a name for your file in the File Name text box.**

7. **Click the Save as Type list box and choose a file format to use such as dBASE III or Paradox 5.**

8. **Click Save.**

Saving your database as a Web page

Since the Internet has spread worldwide, many people are eagerly translating all sorts of information into Web pages for everyone to see. In case you have loads of information in an Access database that you feel other people may enjoy looking at, you can convert your Access databases into Web pages too. To convert an Access database object into a Web page:

1. **Open an existing database.**

2. **Choose Window⇨Database.**

   The Database window appears.

3. **Click Tables or Forms in the left panel of the Database window.**

   Access displays a list of tables or forms in your database (refer to Figure 18-8).

4. **Click a database table or form that you want to convert into a Web page.**

3. **Choose File⇨Export.**

   The Export dialog box appears.

4. **Type a name for your Web page in the File Name text box.**

5. **Click the Save as Type list box and choose HTML Documents. (This is Access's silly name for a Web page.)**

6. **Click Save.**

   An HTML Output Options dialog box appears.

7. **Click OK.**

   Access converts your table or form into a Web page.

Chapter 19

Searching, Sorting, and Making Queries

*I*f you just want to stuff data in a database, a computer database offers no advantage over a paper database (such as a filing cabinet), except that copying (and losing) data is easier with a computer database.

The real power of a computer database comes from your ability to search, sort, and retrieve information from the database. Want to know which products are selling the fastest (and which ones deserve to be dropped quietly like a lead anchor)? Access can tell you at the touch of a button. Need to know which of your salespeople are generating the most commissions (and business expenses)? Access can give you this information pronto, too.

The main difference between a computer database and a paper database is that a computer database can perform tasks — such as searching, sorting, and retrieving information — that would be too tedious, boring, or frustrating to do with a paper database. Knowledge may be power, but until you use the power of a computer database, your information may be trapped out of reach.

Searching a Database

Typical paper databases — such as filing cabinets, Rolodex files, and paper folders — are designed for storing and retrieving information alphabetically. By contrast, Access can find and retrieve information any way you want: by area code, by zip code, alphabetically by last name or first name, by state, by date. . . .You get the idea.

Access provides two ways to search a database:

- ✔ You can search for a specific record.
- ✔ You can find one or more records by using a filter.

Access also provides a third way to search a database using something called *queries,* which you can find out about in the "Querying a Database" section later in this chapter.

Finding a specific record

To find a specific record in a database file, you need to know part of the information you want. Because Access can't read your mind, you have to give it clues, such as "Find the name of the person whose fax number is 555-1904" or "Find the phone number of Bill Gates."

When you want to find a specific record, you need to know at least one bit of data about that record. If you want to find a specific phone number, for example, you have to know the first or last name of the person you want to call, the company name, or the street address where he or she lives or works.

The more specific the data that you already know, the faster Access can find the record you want. Asking Access to find the phone number of someone who lives in California takes more time than asking Access to find the phone number of someone whose last name is Bangladore and lives in California. You may have stored the names of several hundred people who live in California, but how many people in your database would have the last name Bangladore?

To find a specific record in a database:

1. **Open the form that displays the information you want to search.**

   For example, if you want to find a person's phone number, open any form that displays phone numbers. You can open a form by clicking one of the Enter/View buttons on the Main Switchboard window, or by choosing Window⇨Database, clicking the Forms icon, and double-clicking the form that you want to display.

2. **Choose Edit⇨Find or press Ctrl+F.**

   The Find and Replace dialog box appears, as shown in Figure 19-1. If the table is completely empty, Access scolds you with a dialog box to let you know you can't use the Find command.

3. **In the Find What text box, type the data that you want to find (such as Jefferson).**

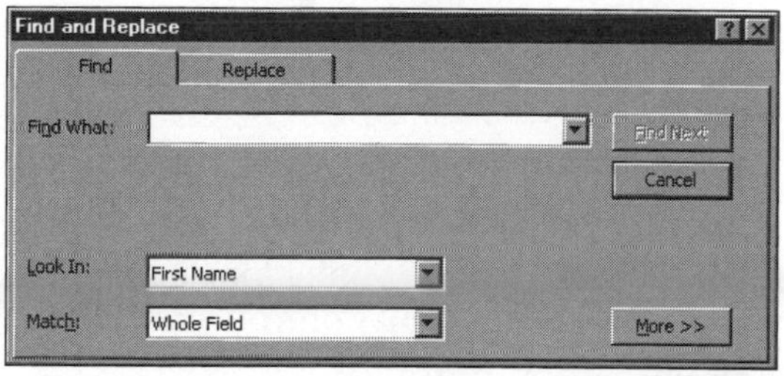

Figure 19-1:
Searching
for a record
by using the
Find and
Replace
dialog box.

4. **Click the Look In list box and choose the field that you want to search (such as First Name or Phone Number).**

5. **Click the Match list box and choose Any Part of Field, Whole Field, or Start of Field.**

   • **Any Part of Field:** The text can appear anywhere in the field (a search for Ann would find both MaryAnne and AnnMarie).

   • **Whole Field:** The text must appear by itself, not as part of another word (a search for Ann would find records containing just Ann by itself; it would not find MaryAnne or AnnMarie).

   • **Start of Field:** The text appears at the beginning of the field (a search for Ann would find AnnMarie and Ann but not MaryAnne).

6. **Click More.**

7. **Click the Search list box and choose Up, Down, or All.**

8. **Click one or more of the following check boxes:**

   • **Match Case:** Tells Access to find only those records that exactly match the capitalization of what you typed in the Find What box. Choosing this option means that if you search for *AnN*, Access finds records containing *AnN* but not records containing *Ann, ann,* or *aNN*.

   • **Search Fields as Formatted:** Tells Access to search for data exactly as it appears. For example, Access can display dates or times in different formats (such as 10/14/97 or 14-Oct-97). If Access displays your data as 10/14/97 and you click this check box, you can search for October dates in your database by typing 10, but not Oct.

9. **Click the Find Next button.**

   Access highlights the first record that contains your chosen data. You may have to move the Find and Replace dialog box so you can see the record that Access finds.

10. **Click Close to close the Find and Replace dialog box. (Or click Find Next if you want to see the next record that contains your chosen data.)**

    Access shows you the record it found in Step 9 or searches for the next matching record.

Finding one or more records by using a filter

When you use the Find command, Access displays the first record that contains the information you want. When you use a *filter*, Access displays only those records that contain the information you're looking for. That way, you can concentrate on viewing only the information you want to see without the rest of your database getting in your way.

Think of the difference between the Find command and a filter in this way: Suppose you want to find a matching pair of socks. The Find command forces you to look through an entire pile of laundry just to find a pair of purple and green argyle socks. A filter separates all argyle socks from the rest of your laundry regardless of color.

When you want to use a filter, you can use the Filter dialog box, which allows you to specify several options:

- ✔ **Field:** Tells Access which fields you want to search. You can choose one or more fields.

- ✔ **Sort:** Tells Access to sort records in alphabetical order (ascending), to sort records in reverse alphabetical order (descending), or not to bother sorting at all (not sorted). We describe sorting records later in the section imaginatively titled "Sorting a Database."

- ✔ **Criteria:** Tells Access to look for specific criteria, such as "Find all the addresses of people who own homes in Oregon or California," or "Find all the addresses of people who own homes in both Oregon and California."

Sorting a database just reorganizes your data, but you can still see all the data stuffed in your database. Filtering by criteria only displays records that match a specific criteria, which means some data may be hidden from view.

Filtering with a form

Forms can display one entire record on the screen. To find one or more records by using a filter:

1. **Open the form containing the information you want to search.**

2. **Choose Records➪Filter➪Filter by Form, or click the Filter By Form button on the Standard toolbar.**

   A Filter by Form dialog box appears, which looks strangely similar to the form you opened in Step 1. Figure 19-2 shows a typical Filter by Form dialog box.

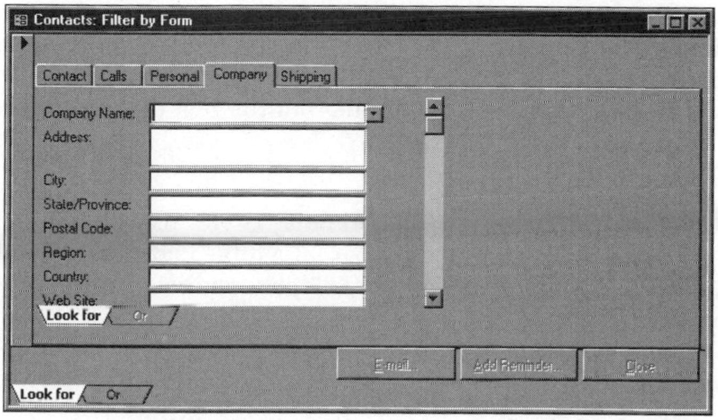

Figure 19-2:
Creating a
filter by
using the
Filter by
Form dialog
box.

3. **Click the field that you want to use as your filter.**

   For example, if you want to find all the people who live in Illinois, click the State/Province field.

   A downward-pointing arrow appears to the right of the field that you click.

4. **Click the downward-pointing arrow.**

   A list appears, containing all the data (such as all the states stored in your database) available in that particular database field.

5. **From this pull-down list, click the data that you want to find (such as IL to find Illinois).**

6. **Repeat Steps 3 through 5 for each field that you want to use for your filter.**

   The more filters you use, the narrower the search — which means that you end up with fewer records to wade through in finding the ones you really want, or you end up filtering out and not seeing records that you actually want to include. Be selective when creating filters.

7. **Choose Filter⇨Apply Filter/Sort.**

   Access displays only those records matching your search criteria. Just to remind you that you're looking at a filtered version of your database, Access politely displays the word (Filtered) on the form.

8. **When you're ready to see your whole database again (and not just the results of the search), choose Records⇨Remove Filter/Sort, or click the Remove Filter button on the Standard toolbar.**

   Choosing this command displays all the information in your database once more.

After using a filter, make sure that you remove the filter by using the Remove Filter/Sort command; otherwise, Access displays only those records matching your last search, and you may think that the rest of your data is gone.

Filtering with a table

Rather than use a filter with a form, you may prefer using a filter with a table. The main advantage of using a filter is that a table can display multiple records at once, while a form can only display one record. To find one or more records by using a filter:

1. **Open the table containing the information you want to search.**

2. **Click the field that you want to use as your filter.**

   For example, if you want to find all people with the last name of Doe, click the Last Name field.

3. **Choose <u>R</u>ecords⇨<u>F</u>ilter⇨<u>F</u>ilter by Selection, or click the Filter By Form button on the Standard toolbar.**

   Access immediately displays only those records that meet your criteria.

4. **When you're ready to see your whole database again (and not just the results of the search), choose <u>R</u>ecords⇨<u>R</u>emove Filter/Sort, or click the Remove Filter button on the Standard toolbar.**

Sorting a Database

To sort a database, you have to tell Access which field you want to sort by and how you want to sort it (in ascending or descending order).

For example, you can sort your database alphabetically by last name, country, or city. Unlike searching, which shows only part of your database, sorting simply shows your entire database from a different point of view.

When you sort a database, you can always restore the original order by choosing <u>R</u>ecords⇨<u>R</u>emove Filter/Sort.

To sort a database:

1. **Open the form or table containing the information you want to search.**

2. **Click the field that you want to sort by.**

   If you want to sort by last names, for example, click the field that contains last names.

3. **Choose Records⇨Sort⇨Sort Ascending (or Descending), or click the Sort Ascending or Sort Descending buttons on the Standard toolbar.**

   The Sort Ascending option sorts from A to Z (or 0 to 9). Sort descending sorts in reverse, from Z to A (or 9 to 0).

   Access obediently sorts your records.

4. **When you're ready to restore the original order to your database, choose Records⇨Remove Filter/Sort.**

Because a table can display multiple records at once, you may find sorting a database through a table easier to see.

Querying a Database

Storing information in a database is okay, but the real fun comes when you use the data that you entered. After all, storing all the names and addresses of your customers is a waste if you don't use the information to help you make more money (which is what business is really all about).

To help you use your stored information effectively, Access provides different ways to analyze your data. When you store information on Rolodex cards, address books, or on paper forms, the information is static. When you store data in Access, the data can be molded, shaped, and manipulated like Silly Putty.

Asking questions with queries

A *query* is a fancy term for a question that you ask Access. After you store information in a database, you can use queries to get the information back out again — and in different forms. A query can be as simple as finding the names and phone numbers of everyone who lives in Arkansas, or it can be as sophisticated as making Access retrieve the names and quantities of all the products sold between November 2 and December 29.

The whole secret to creating effective queries is by knowing what you want and telling Access how to find it.

What's the difference between a query and the Find command?

Both queries and the Find command tell Access to retrieve and display certain data from your database. The main difference between the two is that you can save queries as part of your database file so that you can use them over and over again without defining what you want to look for each time. When you use the Find command, you always have to define what you want to look at each time you use it.

Another big difference is that the Find command only finds one record at a time and doesn't let you specify multiple search criteria.

Use the Find command when you need to search through one or more fields only once. Use queries when you need to search through one or more fields on a regular basis.

Creating a query

When you create a query, you must specify the *search criteria,* the type of data that you want Access to find.

Queries can get fairly complicated, such as asking Access to find the names of all the people in your database who earn less than $75,000 a year, live in either Seattle or Detroit, have owned their own houses for over six years, work in sales jobs, own personal computers, and subscribe to more than three but fewer than six magazines a year.

Just remember that the quality of your answers depends heavily on the quality of your queries (questions). If you create a poorly designed query, Access probably won't find all the data you really need and may overlook important information that can impact your business or your job.

To create a query:

1. **Choose Window⇨Database.**

   The Database window appears.

2. **Click the Queries icon in the left panel.**

3. **Double-click Create Query by Using Wizard icon.**

   The Simple Query Wizard dialog box appears, as shown in Figure 19-3.

4. **Click the downward-pointing arrow to the right of the Tables/Queries list box and click the table that you want to search.**

   Remember: A database table simply contains related information, such as names, addresses, and phone numbers of students. When you choose a database table, you're telling Access to search only within one particular table, not to search the entire database file (which may consist of one or more tables).

5. **Click the Available Fields list box and click a field that you want to display in the query result.**

For example, if you want to display the FirstName and PhoneNumber fields, click one of them (and then come back after Step 6 to click the other one).

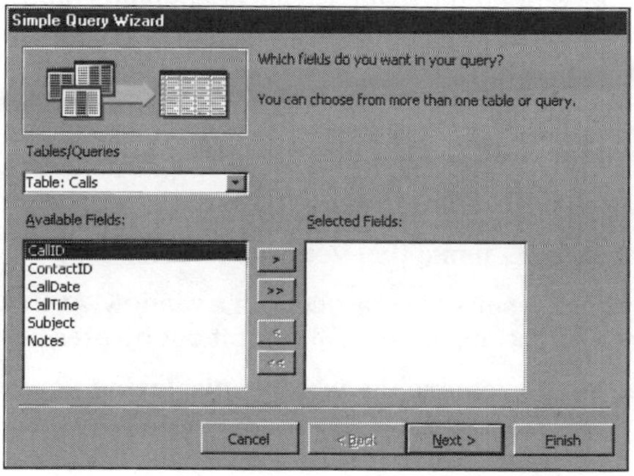

Figure 19-3:
Creating a
query with
the Simple
Query
Wizard
dialog box.

6. **Click the right arrow button that appears between the two big boxes.**

   Access displays your field in the Selected Fields box. Repeat Steps 5 and 6 for each field that you want to use in your query.

7. **Click Next.**

   Access asks what title you want to give your query.

8. **Type a name for your query in the What Title Do You Want for Your Query? text box.**

   Give your query a descriptive name, such as "Tracks low-selling products" or "List of employees I plan to fire."

9. **Click Finish.**

   Access displays the result of your query in a Select Query window. Any time you need to use this query, just double-click the query name in the Database window.

10. **Click the close box of the Select Query window to make it go away.**

Using a query

After you create and save a query, you can use that query as many times as you want, no matter how much you add, delete, or modify the records in your database. Because some queries can be fairly complicated ("Find all the people in North Dakota who owe over $10,000 on their credit cards, own farms, and have sold their crops in the past 30 days"), saving and reusing queries saves you time, which is the whole purpose of computers in the first place.

Queries are most useful if you need to reuse the same query on a regular basis.

To use an existing query, open the database file containing your query and then follow these steps:

1. **Choose <u>W</u>indow⇨Database.**

2. **Click the Queries icon in the left panel.**

   A list of your available queries appears.

3. **Double-click the query name that you want to use.**

   Access displays the results of your query in a window. At this point, you can view your information, or you can print it out by pressing Ctrl+P.

4. **Click the close box to remove the window displaying your query result.**

Deleting a query

Eventually, a query may no longer serve its purpose, as you add, delete, and modify the data in your database. To keep your Database window from overflowing with queries, delete the ones you don't need.

Deleting a query doesn't delete data. When you delete a query, you're just deleting the criteria that you used to search your database with that query.

To delete a query:

1. **Choose <u>W</u>indow⇨Database.**

2. **Click the Queries icon in the left panel.**

   A list of your available queries appears.

3. **Click the query that you want to delete.**

4. **Choose <u>E</u>dit⇨<u>D</u>elete or press Delete.**

   A dialog box appears, asking whether you really want to delete your chosen query.

5. **Click <u>Y</u>es.**

   Your query disappears from the Database window.

If you suddenly realize that you deleted a query by mistake, don't cringe in horror. Immediately choose <u>E</u>dit⇨<u>U</u>ndo Delete or press Ctrl+Z. Access undoes your last command and restores your query to its original state.

Chapter 20

Reporting Your Access 2000 Data

. . . .

. . . .

*A*ccess can store globs of useful (or useless) information within the silicon brains of your computer. However, you may want to print your data once in a while so other people don't have to crowd around your computer screen to see your information.

Fortunately, you can print any data stored in an Access database file. But rather than just print a random jumble of names, addresses, and phone numbers (or whatever data you have in the database), you can design *reports* so that other people can actually understand your data.

For example, you may use Access to keep track of all your customers. At the touch of a button (and with a little help from this chapter), you can create a report that prints out a list of your top ten customers. Touch another button, and Access can spit out a list of your top ten products. A report is simply a way for Access to print out and organize information so you can make sense of it.

Making a Report

A report can selectively display data and make it look so pretty that people forget that your data doesn't make any sense. To make a report from your database:

1. **Choose <u>Window</u>⇨Database.**

   The Database window appears.

2. **Click the Reports icon in the left panel.**

3. **Double-click the Create Report by Using Wizard icon.**

   The Report Wizard dialog box appears, as shown in Figure 20-1.

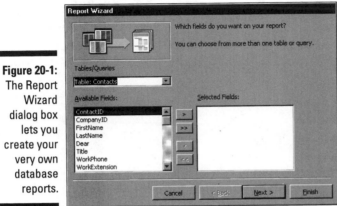

Figure 20-1:
The Report
Wizard
dialog box
lets you
create your
very own
database
reports.

4. **Click the Tables/Queries list box to select a database table to use.**

   For example, if you want to print a report that shows the results of each salesperson in your company, look for the database name that contains this type of information, such as Sales People or Sales Results.

5. **Click the Available Fields list box and choose the fields that you want to print on your report.**

   The Available Fields list box lists all the fields used in the table or query that you select in the Tables/Queries list box. Be selective in choosing which fields to appear on the report — not every field has to appear on a report.

6. **Click the right arrow button, between the Available Fields and Selected Fields boxes.**

   Access displays the chosen field in the Selected Fields box. Repeat Steps 5 and 6 for each field that you want to use in your report.

7. **Click Next.**

   Another Report Wizard dialog box, shown in Figure 20-2, appears and asks whether you want any grouping levels. A *grouping level* tells Access to organize your printed data according to a specific field. For example, if you want to organize the data in your report by state or province, choose the StateOrProvince field for your grouping level. With this grouping level, your report may group all the people in Alabama, Michigan, and Texas in separate parts of your report, letting you find someone in a specific state more easily.

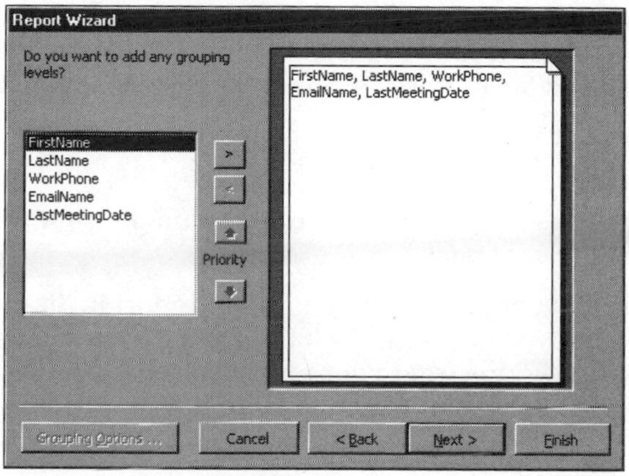

Figure 20-2:
A report
before using
grouped
levels.

8. **If you want to group the information, click the field that you want to group by, and then click the > button.**

Access shows you what your report will look like if you group a level. Grouping levels can help you organize your report by a specific field, such as date or last name. That way you can flip through the report and only see records based on a certain date or name.

9. **Click Next.**

Another Report Wizard dialog box, shown in Figure 20-3, appears and asks what sort order you want for detail records. This is Access's confusing way of asking how you want it to sort the data on your report.

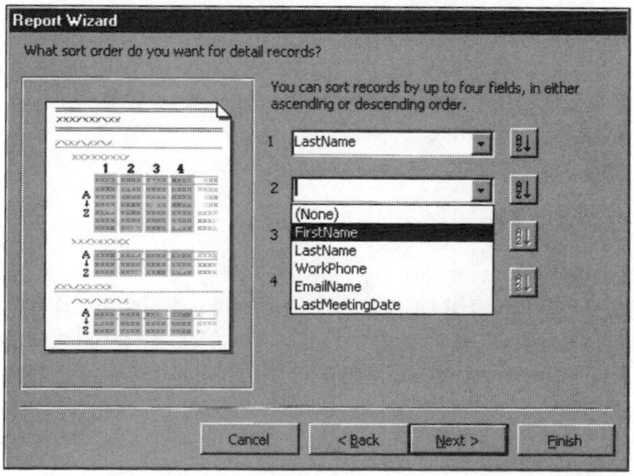

Figure 20-3:
Sorting your
records by
fields in
ascending
or descend-
ing order.

For example, if you defined a grouping level in Step 8, Access can alphabetically sort names within each grouping level by first or last name.

10. **Click the downward-pointing arrow of the 1 list box and choose a field that you want to sort by (if any). If you want to sort by more than one field, choose fields in the 2, 3, and 4 list boxes. Then click Next.**

    Still another Report Wizard dialog box appears and asks, `How would you like to lay out your report?`

11. **Click an option under Layout and an option under Orientation to specify the design of your report.**

    The different layout options simply print your report in different ways, depending on what you like best. Each time you click a layout option, Access politely shows you what your report will look like, in the left portion of the Report Wizard dialog box.

12. **Click Next.**

    Another Report Wizard dialog box appears, asking for a style to use. The style you choose simply defines the fonts used to print out your report. Each time you click a style, Access shows you an example of what your chosen style looks like, in the left portion of the Report Wizard dialog box.

13. **Click a style in the list box and then click Next.**

    Another Report Wizard dialog box appears, asking, `What title do you want for your report?`

14. **Type a title for your report and then click Finish.**

    Your report title should be something descriptive, such as "Profits made in March" or "How much money we lost because of Bob's stupid mistake."

    Access displays your report on-screen.

15. **Choose File⇨Close (or click the close box of the report window).**

    Access displays the Database window again and automatically saves your report in the Reports section of the Database window. The next time you need to use that report, just double-click the report name.

Using a Report

After you create and save a report, you can add or delete as much data as you want. Then when you want to print that data out, use the report that you already designed.

To use an existing report, open the database file containing your report and then follow these steps:

1. **Choose Window⇨Database.**

2. **Click the Reports icon in the left panel.**

    A list of your available reports appears.

3. **Double-click the report name that you want to use.**

   Access displays your chosen report in a window. At this point, you can print it out by choosing File⇨Print, or pressing Ctrl+P.

4. **Click the close box (the X in the upper-right corner) to remove the window displaying your report.**

Deleting a Report

As you add, delete, and modify the data in your database, you may find that a particular report no longer serves its purpose because you no longer need the information it prints out or because you changed the design of your database. To keep your database window from overflowing with useless reports, delete the ones you don't need.

Deleting a report does not delete data. When you delete a report, you're just deleting the way you told Access to print your data.

After you delete a report, you can't retrieve it again, so make sure that you really don't need it anymore before you decide to delete it. To delete a report:

1. **Choose Window⇨Database.**

2. **Click the Reports icon of the Database window.**

   A list of your available reports appears.

3. **Click the report that you want to delete.**

4. **Choose Edit⇨Delete, press the Delete key, or click the Delete icon in the Database window toolbar.**

   A dialog box appears, asking whether you really want to delete your chosen report.

5. **Click Yes.**

   Your report disappears from the Database window.

Giving Your Access Reports a Face-lift

Rather than use Access's rather feeble report-generating abilities, you can combine Access with Word to create better-looking reports. This can combine the professional report-making capabilities of Access with the wonderful writing, formatting, and publishing features available in Word. Of course, you can't work with your Access data in Word until you copy your work from Access into Word.

To use Word to make your Access data look better:

1. **Choose Window⇨Database.**

2. **Click the Tables icon of the Database window.**

3. **Double-click the database table containing the data that you want to copy into Word.**

4. **Choose Tools⇨Office Links⇨Publish It with MS Word.**

   Word displays your chosen Access database table in a Word document as a series of rows and columns.

5. **Make any changes you want to your Access data, or type additional text around the Access data.**

   For example, you can change the font and size of the type. (For more information about using Word 2000, see Part II of this book.)

When you work with an Access database table in a Word document, Microsoft Office 2000 simply copies the data from Access and pastes it into Word. So any changes you make to your data in Word won't affect the data stored in Access and vice versa.

Chapter 21

Getting Paperwork Done with Access 2000 and Word

In This Chapter

▶ Creating form letters and envelopes

▶ Printing addresses on mailing labels and envelopes

Most people dump names, addresses, and phone numbers into databases — and then never do anything with them afterwards. To keep you from turning Access into the electronic equivalent of a storage room, Microsoft Office 2000 lets you combine Access with Word to share data and do something useful like printing out form letters or mailing labels.

Just tell Access which names and addresses you want to use, and Access can print one or more names and addresses on mailing labels or directly on the envelopes. By using Access to store and print names and addresses, you can selectively print names and addresses that meet a certain criteria. For example, you could print the name and address of everyone who ordered a product from you in the past six months, everyone that lives in Wisconsin, or everyone who owes you money and lives in Alaska. With all these neat features, Access can help you create and send form letters and "personalized" mail to complete strangers all over the planet.

Making Form Letters and Envelopes

You're probably familiar with form letters — like the Publisher's Clearing House Sweepstakes letter telling you that you may have just won $10 million. With the power of Access and Word, you, too, can create gorgeous form letters to falsely inflate the hopes of millions of people who trust your company's name.

Any time you need to write custom letters that contain different but pre-dictable data, you can save time by writing a form letter in Word. After you create the form letters, Access can stuff data into the form letter to give it that all-important illusion that you actually created the letter individually.

Making a personalized form letter

The steps to creating a form letter are simple. First you type the text for your form letter (leaving blanks for each person's name and other information you want Access to add later). Then you merge the letter's text with your data-base information to create your "personalized" letters. Finally, you can print these letters.

Before following these steps, make sure you have already created and saved information in an Access database.

1. **Open Microsoft Word.**

   A blank document appears.

2. **Choose Tools⇨Mail Merge.**

   The Mail Merge Helper dialog box appears, as shown in Figure 21-1.

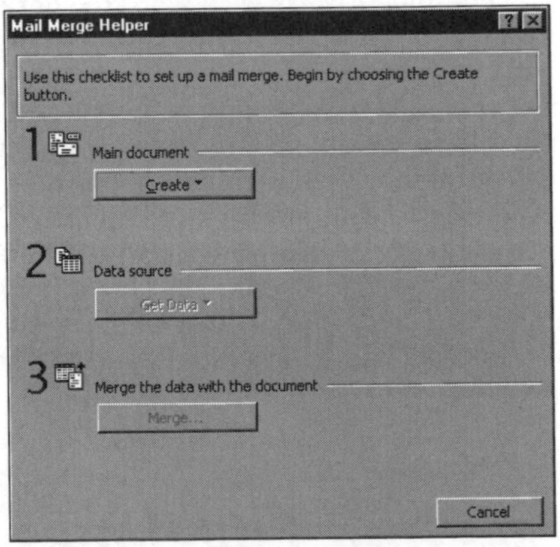

Mail Merge Helper	? X

Use this checklist to set up a mail merge. Begin by choosing the Create button.

1 ▣ Main document

   [Create ▾]

2 ▣ Data source

   [Get Data ▾]

3 ▣ Merge the data with the document

   [Merge...]

   [Cancel]

Figure 21-1: The Mail Merge Helper doing its magic.

3. **Click the Create button and then choose Form Letters.**

   A dialog box appears, asking whether you want to use the active window or create a new main document.

4. **Click Active Window.**

5. **Click the Get Data button and then choose Open Data Source.**

   An Open Data Source dialog box appears. If you click the Files of Type list box and choose MS Access Databases, the dialog box only displays Access databases.

6. **Click a database file to use and click Open.**

   A Microsoft Access dialog box appears, asking which table to use in your chosen database file, as shown in Figure 21-2.

7. **Click the table you want to use and then click OK.**

   If you want to print only a portion of the data stored in your Access database, click the Queries tab and click the query you want to use. (This assumes that you already created a query that finds only the data you want to print.)

   A dialog box appears, notifying you that you need to add merge fields in your document.

8. **Click the Edit Main Document button.**

9. **Type your form letter and click the Insert Merge Field button on the Mail Merge toolbar every time you want data (such as a person's first name or address) to appear in the letter.**

   A field can appear as many times in the letter as you want, and you don't have to use every field in the database. Word displays your database fields in brackets, as shown in Figure 21-3.

   Note: In real life, Word doesn't highlight your merge fields.

10. **After you finish typing and editing the form letter, choose Tools⇨Mail Merge to bring up the Mail Merge Helper dialog box.**

11. **Click Merge in the Mail Merge Helper dialog box.**

    The Merge dialog box appears, as shown in Figure 21-4. If you only want to print names and addresses from certain records, click the From option button and specify the range of records to use, such as record 21 to record 65.

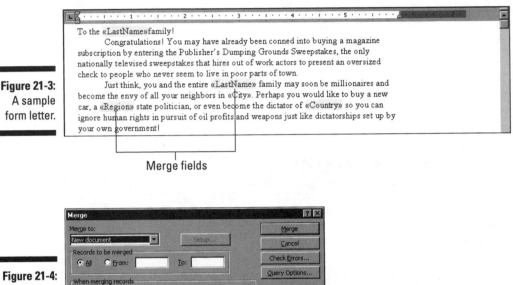

Figure 21-3:
A sample
form letter.

Merge fields

Figure 21-4:
The Merge
dialog box.

12. Click <u>M</u>erge in the Merge dialog box.

Word displays your form letters with actual data inserted, as shown in Figure 21-5.

Note: In normal use, Word doesn't highlight your database information in a form letter.

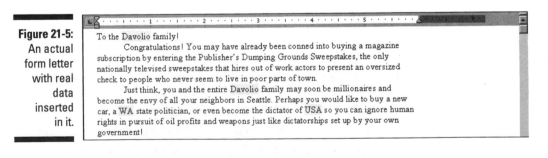

Figure 21-5:
An actual
form letter
with real
data
inserted
in it.

If you're not happy with your form letter for any reason, choose <u>F</u>ile⇔<u>C</u>lose and click No to avoid saving the form letters. Word displays your form letter again without any data in it. At this point you can edit the form letter and return to Step 9.

13. **To print your form letters, choose File⇨Print or press Ctrl+P. If you want to save your form letter for future use, choose File⇨Save or press Ctrl+S.**

    If you choose to save your form letter, you have to type a filename for your form letter, such as Sweepstakes Suckers.

If you save the Word form letter document containing the merge fields, you can print form letters in the future no matter how many changes you make to the Access database you used in the form letter. Just make sure that you don't change the field names in your Access database.

After printing form letters, you don't need to save the Word document unless you plan to use the form letter in the future.

Printing addresses directly on envelopes

Word can yank names and addresses out of an Access database and print them directly on an envelope.

To print an address directly on an envelope, do the following:

1. **Open Microsoft Word (a blank document appears).**

2. **Choose Tools⇨Mail Merge.**

    The Mail Merge Helper dialog box appears (refer to Figure 21-1).

3. **Click the Create button and then choose Envelopes.**

    A dialog box appears, asking if you want to use the active window or create a new main document.

4. **Click Active Window.**

5. **Click the Get Data button and then choose Open Data Source.**

    An Open Data Source dialog box appears. If you click the Files of Type list box and choose MS Access Databases, the dialog box only displays Access databases.

6. **Click a database file to use and then click Open.**

    A Microsoft Access dialog box appears, asking which table to use in your chosen database file (refer to Figure 21-2).

7. **Click the table you want to use and then click OK.**

    Word tells you that it needs to set up your document.

8. **Click Setup Main Document and an Envelope Options dialog box appears.**

9. **Click the Envelope Size list box and then choose an envelope size.**

10. **Click the Printing Options tab and the Printing Options tab appears in the Envelope Options dialog box (see Figure 21-6).**

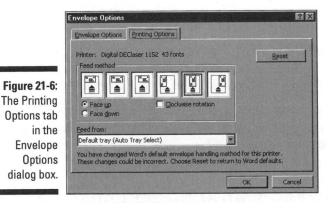

11. **Choose a feed method for your envelopes.**

12. **Click the Feed From list box and then choose how you're going to feed the envelopes into the printer (such as Manual Feed, Default tray, and so on).**

13. **Click OK; the Envelope address dialog box appears.**

14. **Click Insert Merge Field and then choose the field you want to add.**

    You may have to insert a space between each field that you add, such as a space between the FirstName and LastName fields.

15. **Repeat Step 14 for each field you want to add.**

16. **Click OK; the Mail Merge Helper dialog box appears.**

17. **Click Merge (refer to Figure 21-4 to see the Merge dialog box).**

    If you only want to print names and addresses from certain records, click the From option button and specify the range of records to use, such as record 3 to record 89.

18. **Click Merge.**

    Word displays the first record's contents on the screen.

19. **Choose File⇨Close and then choose No so you don't save the document.**

    Word displays the envelope with the merge fields, as shown in Figure 21-7.

20. **Type your return address in the upper-left corner.**

    To avoid typing your return address every time you print an envelope, load Word and choose Tools⇨Options. When the Options dialog box appears, click the User Information tab and type your return address in the Mailing address text box.

21. **Choose Tools⇨Mail Merge to bring up the Mail Merge Helper dialog box.**

22. **Click Merge; the Merge dialog box appears.**

23. **Click Merge and Word displays your envelopes.**

24. **Choose File⇨Print, or press Ctrl+P.**

    Depending on the number of envelopes you're printing, you could be standing at your printer for a long time, feeding envelopes one at a time.

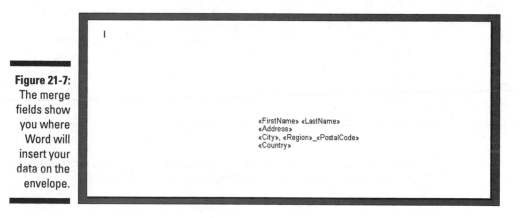

Figure 21-7:
The merge fields show you where Word will insert your data on the envelope.

«FirstName» «LastName»
«Address»
«City», «Region» «PostalCode»
«Country»

If you save the Word document containing the merge fields, you can print addresses on envelopes no matter how many changes you make to the Access database containing those names and addresses.

After printing envelopes, you don't need to save the Word document unless you plan to print similar envelopes in the future.

Making Mailing Labels

Mailing labels are those little stickers that you paste on envelopes so you don't have to type an address directly on each envelope yourself. If you periodically do mass mailings to the same people, you can save time by letting Word and Access print mailing labels for you.

Using mailing labels versus printing addresses on envelopes

Access can print addresses directly on an envelope or on a mailing label that you can paste on an envelope. So when should you print directly on an envelope and when should you use a mailing label? Good question. Unfortunately, no simple answer exists.

If you decide to print an address directly on an envelope, you may have to stand by your printer and feed envelopes in one at a time. Not only does this make you feel like you're wasting your time, but it can be tedious as well, especially if you need to print addresses on hundreds of envelopes.

Mailing labels are much easier to use, and you can paste them on different size envelopes, packages, or boxes. But if you need to print only one or two addresses, it's probably easier just to print the address directly on an envelope instead.

Mailing labels also have another problem. The moment people receive a letter with the address pasted on a mailing label, it immediately signals to them that it's a dreaded form letter, which means people are more likely to throw it out without bothering to open and read it.

So if you need to print lots of addresses, don't mind making your envelopes look like junk mail, or need to print addresses to paste on different-size envelopes or packages, use mailing labels. If you need to print only a few addresses and want to avoid making your envelopes look like junk mail, print the addresses directly on the envelope instead.

By storing names and addresses in an Access database, you can print mailing labels any time you want. To make mailing labels do the following:

1. **Start Microsoft Word and a blank document appears.**

2. **Choose Tools⇨Mail Merge to bring up the Mail Merge Helper dialog box (refer to Figure 21-1).**

3. **Click the Create button and then choose Mailing Labels.**

   A dialog box appears, asking whether you want to use the active window or create a new main document.

4. **Click Active Window.**

5. **Click Get Data and then choose Open Data Source.**

   An Open Data Source dialog box appears. If you click the Files of Type list box and choose MS Access Databases, the dialog box only displays Access databases.

6. **Click a database file to use and then click Open.**

   A Microsoft Access dialog box appears, asking which table to use in your chosen database file (refer to Figure 21-2).

7. **Click the table you want to use and then click OK.**

   Word tells you that it needs to set up your document.

8. **Click Setup Main Document.**

   A Label Options dialog box appears as shown in Figure 21-8.

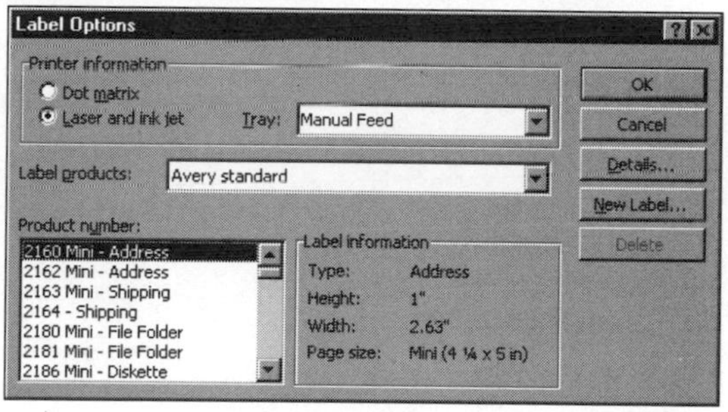

Figure 21-8:
The Label
Options
dialog box
lets you
define the
size of your
mailing
labels.

Label Options

Printer information
- Dot matrix
- Laser and ink jet   Tray: Manual Feed

Label products: Avery standard

Product number:
- 2160 Mini - Address
- 2162 Mini - Address
- 2163 Mini - Shipping
- 2164 - Shipping
- 2180 Mini - File Folder
- 2181 Mini - File Folder
- 2186 Mini - Diskette

Label information
- Type: Address
- Height: 1"
- Width: 2.63"
- Page size: Mini (4 ¼ x 5 in)

OK
Cancel
Details...
New Label...
Delete

9. **Click the Label Products list box and then choose a label type (such as Avery standard).**

10. **Click the Product Number list box and then choose the specific mailing label type you want to use.**

11. **Click OK, which brings up the Create Labels dialog box.**

12. **Click Insert Merge Field and then choose the field you want to add.**

    You may have to insert a space between each field that you add, such as a space between the FirstName and LastName fields.

13. **Repeat Step 12 for each field you want to add.**

14. **Click OK; the Mail Merge Helper dialog box appears.**

15. **Click Merge, which reveals the Merge dialog box (refer to Figure 21-4).**

    If you only want to print names and addresses from certain records, click the From option button and specify the range of records to use, such as record 2 to record 8.

16. **Click Merge and Word displays your mailing labels.**

17. **Choose File⇨Print, or press Ctrl+P (after making sure that you have mailing labels in your printer, of course).**

After you print your mailing labels, you don't have to save the Word document. If you choose File⇨Close and then click No, Word shows you the mailing labels with the merge fields displayed. If you want to print mailing labels in the future, save this file.

Part VII

Designing Pages with Publisher 2000

The 5th Wave   By Rich Tennant

LARRY MAKES HIS LAST BIG BUSINESS DECISION.

In this part . . .

*B*oth small and large businesses often need to create brochures, flyers, newsletters, and Web pages as quickly as possible so they can go back to their real business, which is to make as much money in the shortest amount of time possible.

To help make creating your own publications simple, fast, and actually enjoyable, every edition of Microsoft Office 2000 (except for the Standard edition) comes with Microsoft Publisher 2000, a handy little desktop publishing program.

Because designing and laying out pages isn't something that most people intuitively know how to do, Publisher 2000 provides plenty of help in the form of *wizards,* which can walk you through creating everything from postcards and award certificates to calendars and menus. If a word processor is too primitive for your task, turn to Publisher 2000 and start cranking out all the different types of publications you need without losing your mind or wasting a lot of time in the process.

Chapter 22

Designing a Page

● ●

In This Chapter

▶ Meeting Microsoft Publisher

▶ Creating a publication

▶ Opening a file

▶ Saving your work

▶ Previewing and printing your work

● ●

*M*icrosoft Publisher 2000 is a desktop publishing program that lets you create resumes, newsletters, brochures, greeting cards, Web pages, signs, and even paper airplanes quickly and easily. Unlike a word processor that helps you create and edit text, Microsoft Publisher helps you design the layout of a page with text and graphics.

The main idea behind desktop publishing is to arrange various objects on a page. The most common objects are text boxes (which contain text), picture boxes (which contain photos or other graphic images), and decorative objects (such as lines or borders). By arranging objects artistically on a page, you can design a pretty page (or a pretty horrible-looking page) in no time.

Microsoft Publisher won't let you open more than one file at a time.

Microsoft only includes Microsoft Publisher 2000 in the Premium and Professional versions of Office 2000, so if you have a different version, you have to buy Microsoft Publisher 2000 on your own.

Creating a New Publication with a Wizard

Microsoft Publisher calls a file a *publication*. Publisher gives you two ways to create a publication: from scratch (the hard way) or through a wizard (the easy way).

Microsoft Publisher contains over 2000 different publication templates to choose from to help you create anything from business forms and postcards to gift certificates and newsletters. With so many publication templates to choose from, modifying an existing template may be easier than designing a publication from scratch.

To create a new publication by using a wizard:

1. **Start Microsoft Publisher. (If Microsoft Publisher is already running, choose File⇨Create New Publication.)**

   A Microsoft Publisher Catalog dialog box appears, as shown in Figure 22-1.

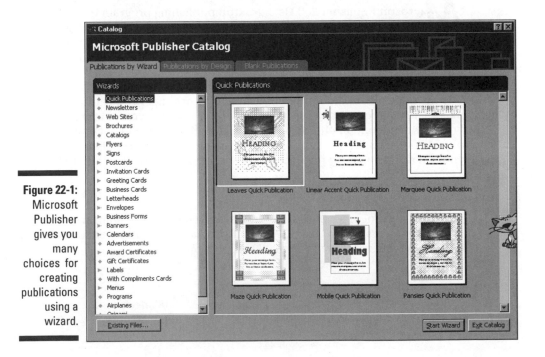

Figure 22-1: Microsoft Publisher gives you many choices for creating publications using a wizard.

2. **Select a wizard, such as Business Cards or Calendars, and Microsoft Publisher displays variations for the publication you choose.**

3. **Click the type of publication you want and then click the Start Wizard button.**

   Depending on the type of wizard you choose, Publisher displays a variety of dialog boxes to help define the exact style of your publication and the type of information (such as addresses or fax numbers) to display in your publication.

   A wizard appears in the left side of the screen, as shown in Figure 22-2.

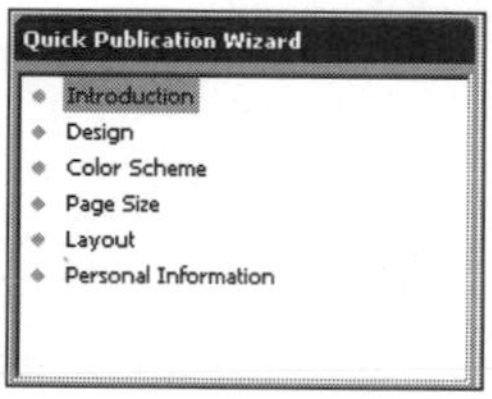

Figure 22-2:
Your publication's wizard appears on-screen, ready to help you complete the design of your publication.

Quick Publication Wizard

- Introduction
- Design
- Color Scheme
- Page Size
- Layout
- Personal Information

4. **Click the Next button in the wizard to modify the design of your publication (or click Finish).**

5. **Click the Hide Wizard button in the bottom left-hand corner of the screen to make the wizard dialog box go away. (If you want the wizard to return, click the Show Wizard button in the bottom left-hand corner of the screen.)**

You can always edit any publication you create with a wizard.

Viewing Your Publication

After you open or create a publication, Microsoft Publisher provides different ways to look at your publication. By providing so many options for viewing your publication, Microsoft Publisher lets you see what you're doing and how your publication will ultimately look when printed or displayed as a Web site.

Changing screen magnification

Most publications you create, such as newsletters or flyers, will likely be larger than your computer screen. And editing can be difficult when you only see part of your publication at any given time.

One solution is to change the screen magnification of your publication, either shrinking it so you can see more of it on the screen, or enlarging it so you can edit your text and pictures in finer detail.

To change your screen's magnification:

1. **Choose <u>V</u>iew⇨<u>Z</u>oom.**

   A pop-up menu appears, as shown in Figure 22-3.

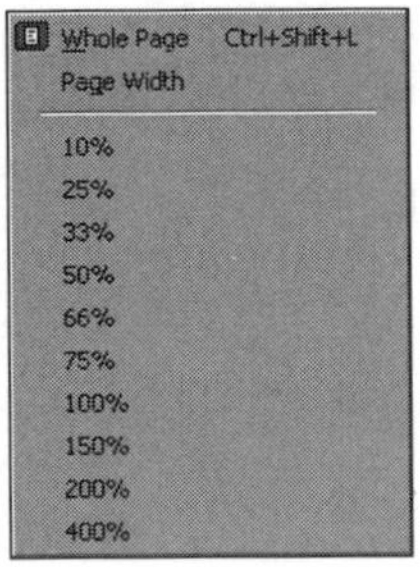

Figure 22-3:
The Zoom
pop-up
menu for
choosing a
specific
screen mag-
nification.

Whole Page	Ctrl+Shift+L
Page Width	
10%	
25%	
33%	
50%	
66%	
75%	
100%	
150%	
200%	
400%	

2. **Choose one of the following:**

   • **<u>W</u>hole Page:** Squeezes the whole page on the screen

   • **Page Width:** Displays the entire width of your page as wide as your computer screen allows

   • **A specific percentage value:** Such as 200% or 66%

You can also specify a percent magnification by clicking the Zoom list box displayed on the Standard toolbar. For a quick way to toggle the magnification of your publication from large to small (or vice versa), press the F9 key.

Showing spaces and paragraph marks

Sometimes the text in your publication may show strange word or paragraph spacing. If this happens, you can reveal (or hide) space and paragraph marks so you can see whether you typed two spaces between words (or none at all) or pressed the Enter key twice after a paragraph.

To see spaces and paragraph marks:

1. **Choose one of the following:**

   - Click the Show Special Characters button on the Standard toolbar.
   - Choose View⇨Show Special Characters.
   - Press Ctrl+Shift+Y.

   Publisher displays the spaces, paragraph marks, and any hidden text in your publication.

2. **Click the Show/Hide Special Characters button again to hide spaces and paragraph marks.**

Seeing two pages at once

If you're creating a newsletter or other long publication that consists of three or more pages, you can display two pages side by side.

Note: You can only display even/odd pages side by side, such as pages 2 and 3 or pages 4 and 5.

To view two pages side by side, do the following:

1. **Choose View⇨Two-Page Spread.**

   A check mark appears on the menu; Publisher displays two pages.

2. **Choose View⇨Two-Page Spread again to return to a single-page display.**

Deciphering the Publisher Toolbars

Like other Microsoft Office 2000 programs, Publisher includes toolbar buttons that represent the commands you most likely need. The two most common toolbars are the Standard toolbar and Formatting toolbar.

Publisher 2000 automatically modifies its toolbars to display the buttons you use most often. So don't be surprised if your toolbar looks slightly different each time you use the program.

Exploring the Standard toolbar

The Standard toolbar offers access to the program's most frequently used commands, arranged from left to right in roughly the order of their frequency of use, as shown in Table 22-1:

Table 22-1	The Microsoft Publisher Standard Toolbar
Button	**What It Does**
	Creates a new publication
	Opens an existing publication
	Saves your current publication
	Prints your current publication (**Note:** When you click the Print button on the Standard toolbar, Publisher immediately starts printing your entire publication, bypassing the Print dialog box)
	Moves the currently selected text to the Clipboard, the invisible Windows storage area
	Copies the currently selected text to the Clipboard
	Places in the current document whatever text is currently on the Clipboard
	Copies the formatting of the currently selected text so that you can apply that formatting to any text you select next
	Reverses the action of your last command
	The opposite of Undo — restores what the Undo command last did
	Displays the currently selected object "on top" of any overlapping objects
	Displays the currently selected object "behind" any overlapping objects
	Rotates the currently selected object
	Shows or hides space and paragraph marks within text
244%	Adjusts the magnification of your publication
−	Decreases the magnification of your publication
+	Increases the magnification of your publication
	Displays (or hides) the Office Assistant that you can click to get more help using Publisher 2000

To find the command that each button on the Standard toolbar represents, point the mouse over a button and wait a second or two until the *ToolTip* — a brief explanation of the button — appears.

Changing appearances with the Formatting toolbar

The Formatting toolbar contains buttons to make your text look pretty with different fonts, type sizes, and typefaces (such as bold, italics, and under-line). Table 22-2 explains the buttons as they appear on the Formatting toolbar.

The Formatting toolbar may not be visible until you click a text box. If you still can't see the Formatting toolbar, choose View⇨Toolbars and make sure that a check mark appears in front of Formatting. Keep in mind, too, that the Formatting toolbar often displays different buttons depending on whether you're editing text, WordArt, a table, or a picture.

Table 22-2	The Microsoft Publisher Formatting Toolbar
Button	**What It Does**
Normal	Controls the *style* — preset specifications for font, font size, paragraph spacing, and so on — of selected text (or whatever paragraph the cursor is currently in)
6.4	Controls the size of selected text
Arial	Controls the *font* — the look of the letters — of selected text
B	Makes selected text **bold**
I	Makes selected text *italic*
U	Underlines selected text
≣	Makes the lines of the selected text line up on the left (with an uneven right margin)
≣	Centers selected text between the left and right margins
≣	Makes the lines of the selected text line up on the right (with an uneven left margin)

(continued)

Table 22-2 *(continued)*

Button	What It Does
	Displays selected text with the left and right margins perfectly straight; unlike centering, justifying stretches full lines to extend to the margins
	Adds (or removes) numbers from selected paragraphs
	Adds (or removes) bullets from selected paragraphs
	Moves selected paragraph to the previous tab stop
	Moves selected paragraph to the next tab stop
	Shrinks the font size of selected text
	Expands the font size of selected text
	Defines the background color of a text box
	Defines the color of a border around a text box (if a border exists)
	Displays selected text in a different color
	Defines a border around a text box
	Defines the margins around a text box
	Rotates a text box 90 degrees to the left
	Rotates a text box 90 degrees to the right

To use any of the commands on the Formatting toolbar, just select the text that you want to format, and then click the appropriate button or the downward-pointing arrow of the list box on the Formatting toolbar.

Navigating Your Way Around a Publication

Because your publication may consist of two or more pages, you may want to edit page 1, then jump immediately to page 37, then back to page 14, and so on. To jump to different pages quickly, Publisher provides several different methods.

Unlike a word processor where you can scroll up or down to view the pages in your document, scrolling up, down, right, or left doesn't display the other pages of a publication.

Using the page navigation control

In the bottom left-hand corner of the screen, Publisher displays icons representing all the pages in your publication. (The icon of the currently displayed page is highlighted.) This collection of icons is known as the page navigation control, as shown in Figure 22-4.

To jump to a specific page, just click the page number icon that you want. For example, to view page 2, click the page icon numbered 2.

Figure 22-4:
The page navigation control lets you jump to a specific page by clicking the mouse.

Using the Go To command

For those who don't like the page navigation control, you can jump to specific pages with the Go To command.

To use the Go To command:

1. **Choose View➪Go To Page or press Ctrl+G.**

   The Go To Page dialog box appears.

2. **Type a page number, press Enter, and the publication jumps to the page that you select.**

Saving Your Stuff

After you create a minor publication masterpiece in Publisher, you probably want to save it so you can use it again in the future.

If you're saving a publication for the first time, Publisher displays a Save As dialog box so you can choose a name. Ideally, you should make your filename as descriptive as possible, such as Ransom Note or Newsletter of Illegal Congressional Activities, so that it jars your memory about the contents of the publication when you haven't looked at the file for a while. The longest a filename can be is 255 characters. Filenames cannot include the forward slash (/), backslash (\), greater-than sign (>), less-than sign (<), asterisk (*), period (.), question mark (?), quotation mark ("), pipe symbol (|), colon (:), or semicolon (;).

Using Publisher's file saver reminder

For people terrified of losing data (a completely justifiable fear, given Windows 95/98/NT's penchant for crashing), you may want to use Publisher's file saving reminder.

This feature simply displays a dialog box periodically to remind you to take that all-important step to save your publication by pressing Ctrl+S. To turn on and specify the amount of time before Publisher reminds you to save your file:

1. **Choose Tools➪Options and the Options dialog box appears.**

2. **Click the User Assistance tab in the Options dialog box.**

3. **Click the Remind to Save Publication check box.**

   If a check mark appears, the reminder feature is turned on. If a check mark doesn't appear, the reminder feature is turned off.

4. **Click the Minutes between Reminders box and type the number of minutes you want Publisher to wait before reminding you to save your publication.**

5. **Click OK.**

Packing your publication to take to another computer

If you want to copy a publication from one computer to another, be careful. Your publication may use fonts and graphics that are not available on the other computer, which means your publication may look funny or be completely unreadable.

To avoid this problem, keep the following thoughts in mind:

✔ Never copy a publication using the ordinary copy command

✔ Always use Publisher's special Pack and Go Wizard

The Pack and Go Wizard embeds all graphics and fonts in a special file that ends with a .PUZ extension. After you copy this special PUZ file to another computer, you have to unpack the file to store the fonts and graphics on the other computer.

If you have a large publication, the Pack and Go Wizard can even split the publication into several smaller files. That way you can copy the smaller, separate files onto multiple floppy disks.

To run the Pack and Go command, do the following:

1. **Choose File⇨Pack and Go⇨Take to Another Computer.**

   The Pack and Go Wizard dialog box pops up. If you haven't saved any changes to your publication, a dialog box pops up, telling you to save your publication now.

2. **Click Next.**

   The Pack and Go Wizard dialog box asks where you want to save your files, as shown in Figure 22-5.

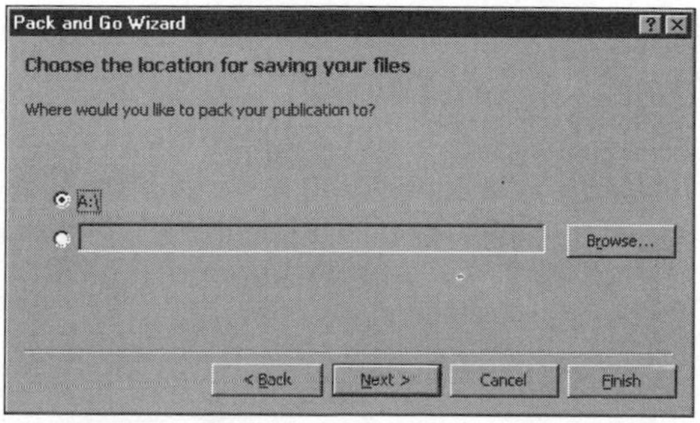

Figure 22-5:
You can pack a publication to a floppy disk or any other directory on your hard disk.

Pack and Go Wizard	? X

Choose the location for saving your files

Where would you like to pack your publication to?

⊙ A:\

○ [   ] Browse...

| < Back | Next > | Cancel | Finish |

3. **Click the A:\ option button, or click Browse and choose a different drive and directory.**

4. **Click Next.**

   The Pack and Go Wizard dialog box asks what you want to include, as shown in Figure 22-6.

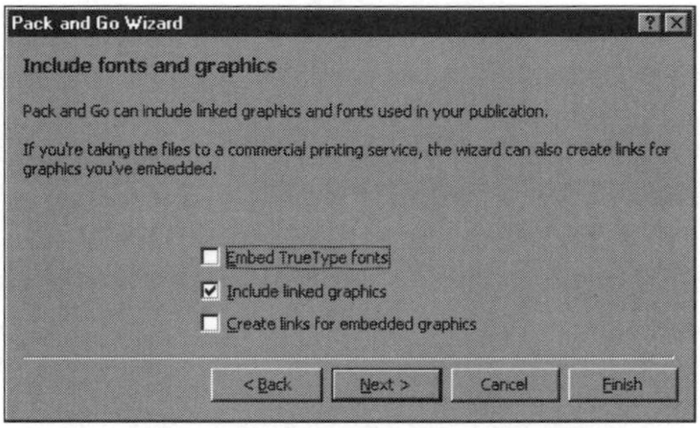

Figure 22-6:
You can include graphics and fonts in a packed publication file.

> **Pack and Go Wizard**   ? ✕
>
> **Include fonts and graphics**
>
> Pack and Go can include linked graphics and fonts used in your publication.
>
> If you're taking the files to a commercial printing service, the wizard can also create links for graphics you've embedded.
>
> ☐ Embed TrueType fonts
> ☑ Include linked graphics
> ☐ Create links for embedded graphics
>
> < Back   Next >   Cancel   Finish

5. **Click the check boxes of all the options you want (such as embedding TrueType fonts) and then click Next.**

   The Embed TrueType Fonts check box buries your publication's fonts as part of your publication file. That way your publication will still look the same on another computer that may not have the fonts that you used to create your publication. If you linked graphics, such as an Excel chart, to your publication, the Include Linked Graphics check box makes sure that the packed version of your publication includes these graphic files as well. If you've added graphics that may change, such as an Excel chart, the Create Links for Embedded Graphics check box insures that your publication will automatically update its graphics any time you modify the graphic in another program, such as Excel. The Pack and Go Wizard dialog box tells you it's ready to start packing your publication.

6. **Click Finish.**

   The Pack and Go Wizard dialog box reminds you to run the UNPACK.EXE file after you copy your packed (.PUZ) publication to another computer.

7. **Click OK.**

   You can now copy the packed publication (.PUZ) files along with the UNPACK.EXE file to another computer.

No matter what the original name of your publication, Publisher stores the packed version of the publication with a really strange name such as PACKED01.PUZ.

To unpack a packed (.PUZ) publication:

1. **Run the Windows Explorer and click the folder where you copied the packed publication and the** UNPACK.EXE **file.**

2. **Double-click the unpack icon.**

   A Microsoft Publisher Unpack Files dialog box appears, as shown in Figure 22-7.

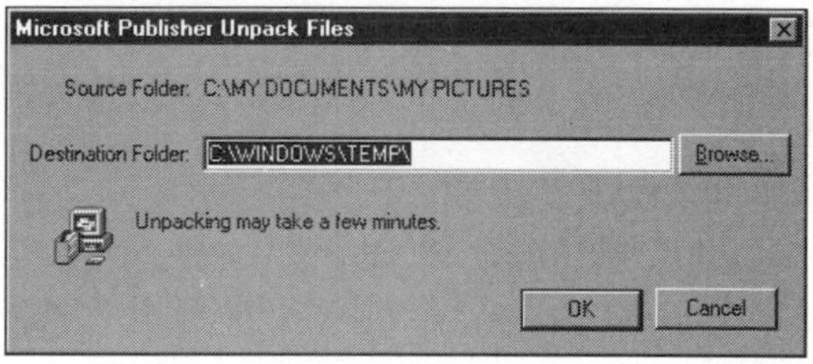

Figure 22-7: The unpack program lets you specify a location to unpack a publication.

Microsoft Publisher Unpack Files	✕
Source Folder: C:\MY DOCUMENTS\MY PICTURES	
Destination Folder: C:\WINDOWS\TEMP\	Browse...
Unpacking may take a few minutes.	
	OK Cancel

3. **Type a directory in the Destination Folder text box, or click B̲rowse and choose a different drive and directory.**

4. **Click OK.**

   A dialog box warns that you may be copying files into a directory that contains files with the same name as your packed publication.

5. **Make sure that the destination folder you chose in Step 3 doesn't contain any identically named files, and then click Y̲es to make the warning dialog box go away.**

   A dialog box appears to inform you that your publication is successfully unpacked.

6. **Click OK.**

After you unpack a publication, you can delete the UNPACK.EXE file to save a little bit of space on your hard disk.

Saving your publication in a different file format

Because not everyone owns a copy of Publisher 2000, you may find that you have to save a publication in a different file format. For example, you may have to save your publication so someone using WordPerfect or Microsoft Word can use it. Although you risk losing formatting when you save your publication in a different file format, it sure beats typing the whole thing all over again in another program.

The following bulleted list shows some of the different file formats that you can use:

- ✓ **Publisher 98 Files:** Compatible with the previous version of Publisher, called Microsoft Publisher 98.

- ✓ **PostScript:** Useful when transferring a file to another desktop publishing program, such as PageMaker or QuarkXPress.

- ✓ **Plain Text:** Useful for transferring to any word processor in the world, but doesn't retain any formatting or graphics.

- ✓ **Rich Text Format:** Many programs can import this file format, often dubbed RTF files. This preserves formatting but won't save any graphics in your publication.

- ✓ **Works 4.0 for Windows:** Saves a publication for the word processor in Microsoft Works 4.0, but loses graphics.

- ✓ **Word:** Saves a publication for various versions of Microsoft Word, but loses graphics.

- ✓ **WordPerfect:** Saves a publication for various versions of WordPerfect, but loses graphics.

To save a publication in another file format:

1. **Choose File➪Save As.**

   The Save As dialog box appears.

2. **Type a name for your publication in the File Name text box.**

3. **Click the Save as Type list box.**

   A list of various file formats appears.

4. **Click the file format you want to use (such as WordPerfect 5.1 for DOS).**

5. **Click Save.**

Chapter 23

Modifying Text and Graphics

● ●

In This Chapter

▶ Creating objects

▶ Playing with text frames

▶ Formatting text

▶ Wrapping text around graphics

▶ Adding and deleting pages

● ●

*T*he two essential elements of a Microsoft Publisher publication are text and pictures, which appear inside boxes (also known as *frames*). You can move and resize text and pictures frames, and layer or overlap them much as children may arrange newspaper clippings on a piece of cardboard. By arranging your various text and picture frames on a page, you can design the layout for each page of your publication.

Creating Text

Before you can type any text on a page, you must first draw a text frame. Publisher gives you two types of text frames:

> ✔ **Text frames:** Displays text that you can format yourself.
>
> ✔ **WordArt frames:** Displays text in a fancy, artistic appearance.

With a text frame, you can individually format characters or words. With WordArt, all the text must look the same. However, WordArt enables you to create more artistic text appearances than an ordinary text frame.

Drawing a text or WordArt frame

To create a text or WordArt frame:

1. **Click the Text Frame or WordArt Frame tool in the Objects toolbar, as shown in Figure 23-1.**

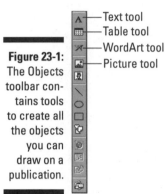

——Text tool
——Table tool
——WordArt tool
——Picture tool

Figure 23-1:
The Objects
toolbar con-
tains tools
to create all
the objects
you can
draw on a
publication.

2. **Move the mouse pointer where you want to draw your text or WordArt frame — the mouse pointer turns into a crosshair.**

3. **Hold down the left mouse button and drag the mouse to draw your text or WordArt frame.**

4. **Release the left mouse button when the frame is the way you want it to look.**

   Publisher draws your text or WordArt frame on the page. If you drew a text frame, a cursor appears inside the text frame. If you drew a WordArt frame, an Enter Your Text Here dialog box appears, as shown in Figure 23-2.

Figure 23-2:
The Enter
Your Text
Here dialog
box lets you
type text
inside a
WordArt
frame.

5. **Type your text. (If you're typing text in a WordArt frame, click the close box of the Enter Your Text Here dialog box when you finish typing.)**

Editing a text frame

A text frame acts like a miniature word processor that lets you delete, format, and type text inside of it.

To edit text inside a text frame:

1. **Click anywhere inside the text frame containing the text that you want to edit.**

2. **Choose one of the following:**

   - Press Backspace, which deletes the character to the left of the cursor.

   - Press Delete, which deletes the character to the right of the cursor.

   - Highlight one or more characters and choose a font, font size, type-style, alignment, or color from the Formatting toolbar. (See Chapter 22 for explanations on all the buttons on the Formatting toolbar.)

Rather than type text in a text frame, you can also insert text from a word-processor document by choosing Insert⇨Text File.

Spell checking and hyphenating text inside a text frame

Publisher includes a spell checker to make sure you don't print flyers advertising your misspellings rather than your business. Publisher also includes an option to turn off hyphenation, so the text on your publications doesn't look broken up and disjointed.

To spell check text inside a text frame, click anywhere inside the text frame that you want to check and press F7 or choose Tools⇨Spelling⇨Check Spelling.

To turn off hyphenation of text inside a text frame, click anywhere inside the text frame that you want to modify and choose Tools⇨Language⇨Hyphenation, or press Ctrl+Shift+H. In the Hyphenation dialog box that appears, click the Automatically Hyphenate the Story check box so that a check mark doesn't appear and then click OK.

Linking text frames

Text frames can only appear in the shape of a rectangle. Unfortunately, sometimes you may need to display text in the top left-hand corner of a page and the rest of that text in the bottom right-hand corner of a page. Because one text frame can't display text in these two locations, you have to use two or more text frames linked together.

Linked text frames let you display text between two or more text frames. If you type too much text in one text frame, the text automatically "spills over" into the next linked text frame much like seawater spilled over the watertight bulkheads in the Titanic. Figure 23-3 shows what text looks like when connected by two text frames.

Figure 23-3:
Linked text
frames
allow text
from one
frame to
"spill over"
into another
text frame.

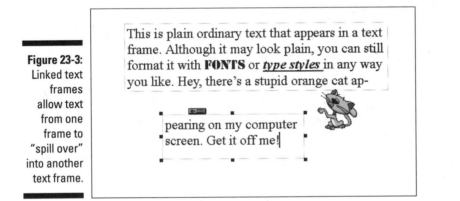

To link one text frame to another text frame:

1. **Click anywhere inside the first text frame.**

2. **Choose Tools⇨Connect Text Frames, or click the Connect Text Frames button on the Standard toolbar.**

   A cursor appears as a pitcher icon.

3. **Click inside the text frame that you want to connect to the text frame you chose in Step 1.**

   Any text that cannot fit in the first text frame automatically appears in the text frame you just chose.

Text from one frame can't "spill over" into two different frames. However, you can link one text frame to another one in a series.

To disconnect a text frame from another text frame, click anywhere inside the first text frame and then click the Disconnect Text Frames button on the Standard toolbar.

Editing a WordArt frame

Unlike a text frame, WordArt gives you a greater variety of ways to format your text with the drawback that you cannot selectively format individual words or characters.

To edit text in a WordArt frame:

1. **Right-click the WordArt Frame that you want to edit.**

2. **Choose Change Object⇨Microsoft WordArt⇨Open from the pop-up menu.**

   A WordArt dialog box appears.

3. **Click the Enter Your Text Here text box and edit your text.**

4. **Click the Choose a Shape list box.**

   A list of different text shapes appears, as shown in Figure 23-4.

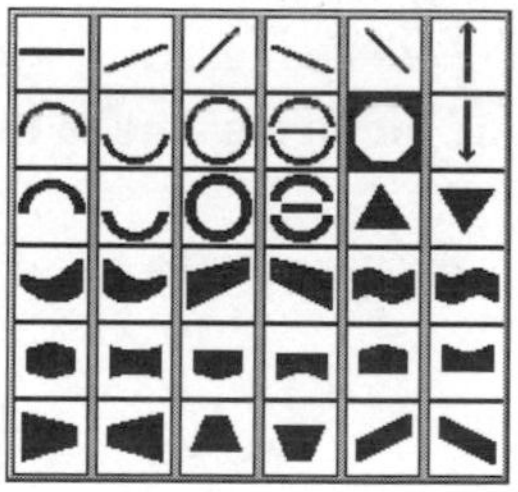

Figure 23-4:
WordArt
can make
text appear
in weird
shapes.

5. **Click the Font, Size, Alignment, or Color list boxes and choose the effects you want.**

6. **Click any of the buttons in the Fill, Effects, or Stretch toolbars.**

   • **Fill:** Adjusts the shadow appearance, patterns, or thickness of text.

   • **Effects:** Modifies the typestyle of text such as bold and italics.

   • **Stretch:** Stretches, rotates, shrinks, and adjusts the spacing of the text.

7. **Click OK.**

If you just want to edit (but not format) text in a WordArt frame, double-click the WordArt frame. An Enter Your Text Here dialog box appears, and you can type or edit your text.

Putting Pictures on a Page

Besides text, the second most important element on a page is graphics, which can be digitized photographs, drawings someone created using a program like PaintShop Pro, Microsoft Paint, Microsoft PhotoDraw, or clip art that Microsoft thoughtfully provides for you.

Putting picture frames on a page

All pictures must appear inside a Picture Frame. To create a picture frame:

1. **Click the Picture Frame tool in the Objects toolbar (refer to Figure 23-1).**

2. **Move the mouse pointer where you want to draw your picture frame.**

   The mouse pointer turns into a crosshair.

3. **Hold down the left mouse button and drag the mouse to draw your picture frame.**

4. **Release the left mouse button when your picture frame is the way you want it.**

   Publisher draws your picture frame on the page. At this point, the picture frame is empty.

Adding graphics inside a picture frame

After you create a picture frame on a page, you can finally display a graphic image inside that picture frame. You can add a graphic file or clip art to a picture frame.

Using a graphic file

Graphic files can be digitized photographs or drawings that someone created using a graphics program, such as cartoons.

To add a graphic file to a picture frame:

1. **Right-click the picture frame.**

2. **Choose Change Picture⇨Picture⇨From File from the pop-up menu.**

An Insert Picture dialog box appears as shown in Figure 23-5. You may have to search through different drives and directories to find the graphic file you want.

Figure 23-5:
The Insert
Picture
dialog box
can show
you a pre-
view of
each picture
file before
you add it to
your picture
frame.

3. **Click the graphic file you want and click Insert.**

   Publisher displays your chosen graphic file in your picture frame.

Using clip art

Because most people can't draw and don't have a collection of digitized photographs they can use, Microsoft kindly includes a bunch of clip art images that you can use instead. Clip art contains common types of images that you may find useful for your newsletters and flyers.

To add a graphic file to a picture frame:

1. **Right-click the picture frame.**

2. **Choose Change Picture⇨Picture⇨Clip Art from the pop-up menu.**

   An Insert Clip Art dialog box appears, as shown in Figure 23-6.

3. **Click the clip art category you want, such as Animals or Office Layout.**

   Publisher displays a variety of different clip art images in the category you choose.

4. **Click the clip art image that you want to use.**

   A pop-up menu appears.

5. **Click the Insert Clip Art button on the toolbar.**

   Publisher displays your chosen clip art in your picture frame.

6. **Click the close box of the Insert Clip Art dialog box to make it disappear.**

Insert Clip Art
Import Clips
Clips Online
Help
Search for clips:
Type one or more words. . .
Pictures
Sounds
Motion Clips
Categories 1 - 57
New Category
Favorites
Banners
Conceptual
Miscellaneous
Networking
Office Layout
Web Site

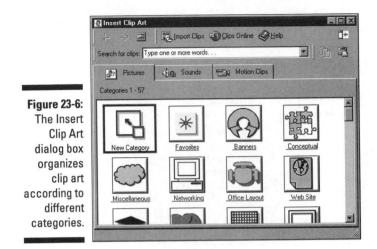

Figure 23-6: The Insert Clip Art dialog box organizes clip art according to different categories.

Wrapping text around a picture frame

You can put a picture frame directly over or partially overlapping a text frame. When a picture frame covers up part of a text frame, Publisher gives you two choices in wrapping the text around the picture frame:

- Wrap text around the rectangular boundaries of the picture frame.
- Wrap text around the actual picture inside the picture frame, ignoring the rectangular boundary of the picture frame, as shown in Figure 23-7.

What you see here is an evil cartoon bird that's
eyeing the orange cat Office Assistant as if pre-
pared to make the
cat its next meal.
Hopefully the bird
will eat up all the
Office Assistants
along with all
the programmers
who worked on
this buggy
Microsoft Of-
fice program
and got paid
millions
while the rest of
us suffer at its
mercy.

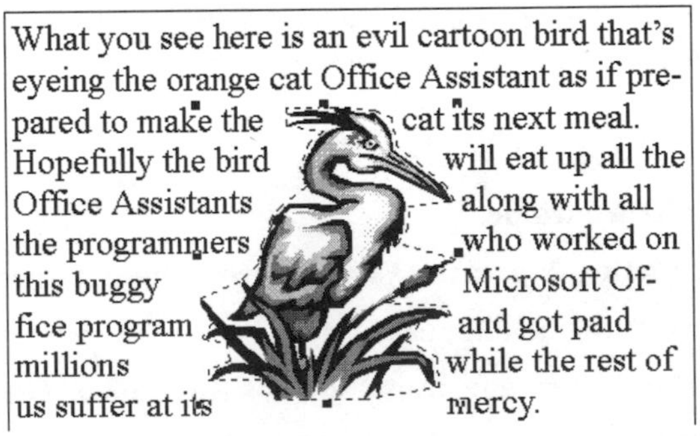

Figure 23-7: Wrapping text around the curved boundaries of the picture itself.

To change the way text wraps around a picture frame:

1. **Right-click the picture frame.**

2. **Choose Change Frame⇨Picture Frame Properties from the pop-up menu.**

    A Picture Frame Properties dialog box appears, as shown in Figure 23-8.

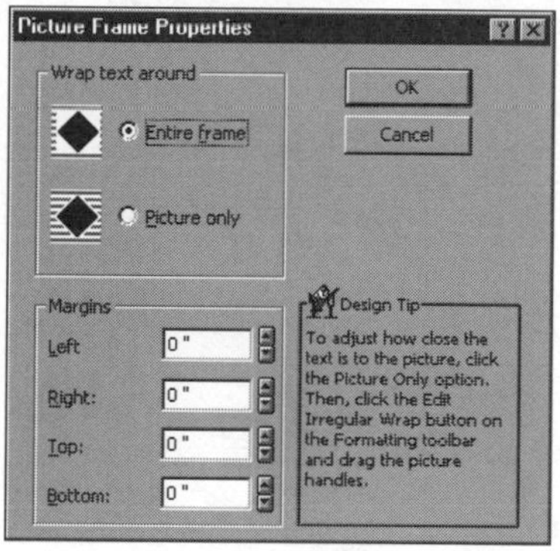

Figure 23-8:
The Picture
Frame
Properties
dialog box
lets you
choose how
to wrap text
around a
picture
frame.

3. **Click either the Entire Frame or Picture Only option button and then Click OK.**

    If you click the Entire Frame option button, you can also specify margins around the picture frame to define how close you want text to appear next to the picture frame.

Manipulating Frames

After you create a text or picture frame, you can always move, resize, copy, or delete it. You can even overlap frames if you wish, which can create unique visual effects or just look plain ugly.

Moving a frame

You can move a frame at any time, so feel free to experiment with different positions for your frames. To move a frame:

1. **Click the frame you want to move.**

    Black squares, called *selection handles,* appear around the frame.

2. Move the mouse pointer over the edge of the frame.

   The mouse pointer turns into a four-way pointing arrow and a truck icon with the word Move on it.

3. Hold down the left mouse button and drag the mouse to move the frame to a new location.

   To move frames a small distance at a time, hold down the Alt key and press one of the arrow keys, such as Alt+→.

4. Release the left mouse button when you're happy with the frame's new location.

If you don't like the new location of the frame, press Ctrl+Z to make it go back where it came from.

Resizing a frame

Sometimes you may want to enlarge or shrink a frame:

1. Click the frame you want to resize.

   Black squares (selection handles) appear around the frame.

2. Move the mouse pointer over a handle on the edge of the frame.

   The mouse pointer turns into a two-way pointing arrow with the word Resize underneath it. (If you move the mouse pointer over a corner handle, you can enlarge or shrink two sides of the frame at once.)

3. Hold down the left mouse button and drag the mouse to resize the frame.

4. Release the left mouse button when you're happy with the new size of the frame.

If you don't like the new size of the frame, press Ctrl+Z.

Aligning frames

Sometimes, you may have multiple text or picture frames that you want to arrange so the top or left sides appear aligned with one another. Aligning text and picture frames gives your publication an organized and neat appearance. To align frames:

1. Hold down the Ctrl key and click all the frames you want to align.

   Gray handles appear around all your selected frames.

2. **Choose Arrange➪Align Objects.**

    The Align Objects dialog box appears, as shown in Figure 23-9.

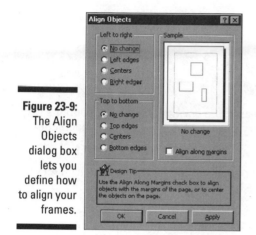

Figure 23-9:
The Align Objects dialog box lets you define how to align your frames.

3. **Click an option button in the Left to Right group and another option button in the Top to Bottom group.**

    Publisher shows you how your objects will align in the Sample box.

4. **Click OK.**

Manipulating overlapping frames

If you move or draw one frame over another, one frame may cover up information displayed by the other frame in much the same way that a sheet of paper dropped on top of a newspaper can obscure the newspaper's headlines.

A frame that's completely visible is considered to be "in front" while a frame that's buried underneath another frame is considered to be "in back."

To rearrange frames:

1. **Click the frame you want to rearrange.**

    Black handles appear around your selected frame.

2. **Choose Arrange and then choose one of the following:**

    • **Bring to Front:** Moves your selected frame "in front" of any overlapping frames so the entire frame is visible.

    • **Send to Back:** Moves your selected frame "in back" of any overlapping frames so the frame may be partially blocked by any overlapping frames.

- **Bring Forward:** Moves your selected frame "in front" of the first frame that overlaps it.

- **Send Backward:** Moves your selected frame "in back" of the first frame that it overlaps.

Making the same frame appear on every page

Publisher divides each page into two parts: the *background,* which contains text and picture frames that appear on every page, and the *foreground,* which contains text and picture frames that only appear on the currently displayed page.

Think of the background as a sheet of paper and the foreground as a sheet of transparent film that lays on top of the background.

To move a frame to the background:

1. **Click the text or picture frame that you want to appear on every page.**

   Black handles appear around your frame.

2. **Choose Arrange⇨Send to Background.**

   A dialog box appears, informing you that your chosen frame is now in the background of every page in your publication.

3. **Click OK.**

To edit frames in the background:

1. **Choose View⇨Go to Background, or press Ctrl+M.**

   Publisher displays all the frames on the background.

2. **Edit any frames you want.**

3. **Choose View⇨Go to Foreground, or press Ctrl+M.**

You may not always want to display background frames on every page. To turn off the background frames for a page, choose View⇨Ignore Background.

In case you want to move a frame from the background to the foreground:

1. **Choose View⇨Go to Background, or press Ctrl+M.**

   Publisher displays all the frames on the background.

2. **Click the text or picture frame that you want to move to the foreground.**

   Black handles appear around your frame.

3. **Choose Arrange⇨Send to Foreground.**

   A dialog box appears, informing you that your chosen frame is now in the background of every page in your publication.

4. **Click OK.**

5. **Choose View⇨Go to Foreground, or press Ctrl+M.**

   Publisher displays your publication with the frames removed from the background.

Adding (and Deleting) Pages

You probably need to add and delete pages in your publication once in a while. To add a page:

1. **Choose Insert⇨Page, or press Ctrl+Shift+N.**

   An Insert Page dialog box appears.

2. **Type the number of pages you want to add in the Number of New Pages text box.**

3. **Click either the Before or After Current Page option button.**

4. **Click one of the following option buttons:**

   - **Insert Blank Pages:** Adds completely blank pages

   - **Create One Text Frame on Each Page:** Automatically draws one text frame on every blank page you're adding

   - **Duplicate All Objects on Page:** Copies another page in your publication

5. **Click OK.**

   Publisher displays your newly created page.

To delete a page:

1. **Choose View⇨Go to Page, or press Ctrl+G.**

   A Go To Page dialog box appears.

2. **Type the number of the page you want to delete. (If you want to delete page 4, type 4.)**

3. **Click OK.**

   Publisher displays your chosen page.

4. **Choose Edit⇨Delete Page.**

   A dialog box appears, asking whether you really want to delete this page.

5. **Click OK.**

If you accidentally delete a page, press Ctrl+Z right away to recover it.

Part VIII

Creating Web Pages and Editing Photos

The 5th Wave   By Rich Tennant

"For further thoughts on that subject, I'm going to download Leviticus and go through the menu to Job, chapter 2, verse 6, file 'J.' It reads..."

In this part . . .

*1*f you're lucky enough to have the Premium or Developer edition of Microsoft Office 2000, you'll find two bonus programs included with your purchase called FrontPage 2000 and PhotoDraw 2000.

FrontPage 2000 is actually one of the most popular Web page designing programs in the world. Because practically everyone is creating a Web page these days for personal or business use, you may as well create your own Web pages too.

Creating Web pages with FrontPage 2000 is simple and fast, so you can focus on typing and editing the actual Web page content without worrying about the underlying details that make the Web page actually appear on the Internet.

After you master the basic details of FrontPage 2000, you may need to use PhotoDraw 2000 to touch up, create, or edit any graphics for your Web pages including logos, digitized photographs, or cartoons to make your Web site friendly to any viewers.

By combining FrontPage 2000 and PhotoDraw 2000, you no longer have an excuse for not creating Web pages that look as sharp and professional as the best Web sites in the world. So fire up FrontPage 2000 and PhotoDraw 2000 and start creating your next Web site today!

Chapter 24

Designing a Web Page with FrontPage

Microsoft FrontPage 2000 is a program designed to create and edit Web pages. Although you can create Web pages using Microsoft Publisher, Word, Excel, PowerPoint, and Access, only FrontPage gives you complete control over every aspect of your Web page layout from creating frames to editing the actual HTML code that makes up your Web page.

If you want to create Web pages quickly, use Word, Publisher, or any other Microsoft Office 2000 program. But if you want more control over the finer details of creating and designing a Web page, use FrontPage.

Unlike other Microsoft Office 2000 programs, those silly cartoon Office Assistants don't appear in Microsoft FrontPage, so you may cheer or moan depending on how you feel towards the Office Assistants. Also, keep in mind that FrontPage 2000 is only available in the Premium and Professional versions of Office 2000.

Only the Premium and Developer editions of Microsoft Office 2000 contain FrontPage 2000. If you have a different edition of Office 2000, you need to buy FrontPage separately.

Creating New Web Pages

With FrontPage, you can create a single Web page or you can create a new Web site (which consists of two or more Web pages).

To create one new Web page:

1. **Choose File⇨New⇨Page.**

   A New dialog box appears, listing available Web page designs you can use.

2. **Click a Web page design that you want to use and then click OK.**

   FrontPage displays your Web page on-screen. Now you just have to do the hard work and type in new text and add new graphics.

To create one new Web site:

1. **Choose File⇨New⇨Web.**

   A New dialog box appears, listing available Web site layouts you can use.

2. **Click the Specify the Location of the New Web text box and type the directory where you want to store your new Web site.**

   It's a good idea to store your Web site in a *directory* (also known as a folder) of its own to keep other files from getting mixed up with your Web site pages.

3. **Click the Web site design you want to use; then click OK and FrontPage displays your Web site on-screen.**

Viewing Your Web Pages

FrontPage provides six different ways to view your Web pages so that you can edit individual Web pages, understand the hyperlinks connecting your Web pages, or view the sizes of your Web pages.

FrontPage displays the six different views in the Views Bar, which appears on the left side of the screen, as shown in Figure 24-1.

To hide or display the Views Bar, choose View⇨Views Bar.

- ✔ **Page:** Displays an individual Web page that you can view and edit. *Note:* If you open a single Web page, you can only use the Page view.

- ✔ **Folders:** Lists all the Web page files, graphic files, and folders used by your Web site.

✔ **Reports:** Provides a detailed list of the types of files in your Web site, how many of each particular file you have (such as the number of graphic files used by your Web site), and the total size of each file.

✔ **Navigation:** Graphically displays how the Web pages of your Web site are linked together.

✔ **Hyperlinks:** Displays the individual hyperlinks for a single Web page or graphic image.

✔ **Tasks:** Lists tasks to remind you or others what needs to be modified next.

Figure 24-1:
The Page
view shows
a single
Web page.

This book only provides a basic introduction to using the Page, Folders, and Hyperlinks views. For more detailed instruction on the Reports, Navigation, and Tasks views, get a copy of *FrontPage 2000 For Dummies* by Asha Dornfest (IDG Books Worldwide, Inc.).

Understanding the FrontPage Toolbars

FrontPage includes toolbar buttons that represent the commands Microsoft thinks you may use most often. The two most common toolbars are the Standard and Formatting toolbars.

Exploring the Standard toolbar

The Standard toolbar offers access to the program's most frequently used commands, arranged from left to right in roughly the order of their frequency of use, as shown in Figure 24-2.

Figure 24-2:
The Standard toolbar in Microsoft FrontPage.

The Standard toolbar features the following commands:

- ✔ **New Page:** Creates a new Web page or Web site (containing multiple Web pages)
- ✔ **Open:** Opens an existing Web page or site
- ✔ **Save:** Saves your current Web page
- ✔ **Publish Web:** Stores your Web pages in a specific folder for eventual posting on a Web server
- ✔ **Folder List:** Displays a list of folders and their contents to the right of the Views Bar
- ✔ **Print:** Prints your Web pages
- ✔ **Preview in Browser:** Displays your Web pages in your browser so you can see what the Web pages will look like when viewed from the Internet
- ✔ **Spelling:** Checks the spelling on your Web pages
- ✔ **Cut:** Moves the currently selected text to the Clipboard, the invisible Windows storage area
- ✔ **Copy:** Copies the currently selected text to the Clipboard
- ✔ **Paste:** Places in the current document whatever text or image that is currently on the Clipboard
- ✔ **Format Painter:** Copies the formatting of the currently selected text so that you can apply that formatting to any text you select next
- ✔ **Undo:** Reverses the action of your last command
- ✔ **Redo:** The opposite of Undo — restores what the Undo command last did

✓ **Insert Component:** Inserts an advanced Web page feature, such as a hit counter, an Office Spreadsheet, or a banner

✓ **Insert Table:** Draws a table

✓ **Insert Picture From File:** Displays a graphic file on a Web page

✓ **Hyperlink:** Creates a hyperlink to another Web site or Web page

✓ **Refresh:** Redraws your currently displayed Web page

✓ **Stop:** Stops FrontPage from continuing with an action that may be taking too long

✓ **Show All:** Hides or displays space and paragraph marks

✓ **Microsoft FrontPage Help:** Displays a help dialog box

Changing appearances with the Formatting toolbar

The Formatting toolbar contains commands to make your text look pretty with different fonts, type sizes, and typefaces (such as bold, italics, and underline). Figure 24-3 shows the Formatting toolbar.

The Formatting toolbar may not be visible until you click in a text box.

Figure 24-3:
The
Formatting
toolbar.

The buttons on the Formatting toolbar appear in the following order, from left to right:

✓ **Style:** Controls the *style* — preset specifications for font, font size, paragraph spacing, and so on — of the currently selected text (or whatever paragraph the cursor is currently in)

✓ **Font:** Controls the *font* — the look of the letters — of the currently selected text

✓ **Font Size:** Controls the size of the currently selected text

✓ **Bold:** Makes selected text **bold**

✓ **Italic:** Makes selected text *italic*

- ✔ **Underline:** <u>Underlines</u> selected text
- ✔ **Align Left:** Makes the lines of the selected text line up on the left (with an uneven right margin)
- ✔ **Center:** Centers selected text between the left and right margins
- ✔ **Align Right:** Makes the lines of the selected text line up on the right (with an uneven left margin)
- ✔ **Numbering:** Adds (or removes) numbers from selected paragraphs
- ✔ **Bullets:** Adds (or removes) bullets from selected paragraphs
- ✔ **Decrease Indent:** Moves selected paragraph to the previous tab stop
- ✔ **Increase Indent:** Moves selected paragraph to the next tab stop
- ✔ **Highlight Color:** Defines the background color of a text
- ✔ **Font Color:** Defines the color of text

To use any of the commands on the Formatting toolbar, select the text to format, and then click the appropriate button or the downward-pointing arrow of the list box on the Formatting toolbar.

Playing with Text on a Web Page

Typing text onto a Web page is similar to typing text in a word processor. You just click where you want the text to appear. FrontPage then displays a cursor to show you where your text will appear when you start typing.

Depending on any other parts of your Web page, such as graphics, the cursor may appear on the far left side of your Web page or somewhere else altogether. You may have to use the space bar or the Tab key to move the cursor where you want your text to appear.

To format text:

1. **Highlight the text that you want to modify.**

2. **Choose Format⇨Font and a Font dialog box appears.**

3. **Choose the formatting that you want (font, underlining, font size, color, and so on) and then click OK.**

   If you click the Apply button, you can see the changes to your text without exiting the Font dialog box.

Adding color and borders to text

To emphasize text, you can put a border around text or change the background and foreground colors.

To add a border around text:

1. **Click the text that you want to surround with a border.**

2. **Choose Format⇨Borders and Shading.**

   A Borders and Shading dialog box appears.

3. **Click Box for a border surrounding your text. (If you just want a border on the top, bottom, or sides of your text, click Custom and click the top, bottom, left, or right border buttons in the Preview group.)**

4. **Click the Style list and choose a style, such as dotted or ridge.**

5. **Click the downward pointing arrow in the Color list box and choose a color.**

6. **Click OK.**

Borders can highlight text, but you may want to include color as well, just to make sure that people don't miss your text. FrontPage gives you the choice of changing the background and foreground color, so you can display shocking hot pink text against a neon green background (and probably hurt the eyes of anyone who looks at it too).

To color your text:

1. **Click the text that you want to color.**

2. **Choose Format⇨Borders and Shading.**

   A Borders and Shading dialog box appears.

3. **Click the Shading tab.**

   The Shading tab appears.

4. **Click the downward pointing arrow next to the Background Color list box and choose a color for your background.**

5. **Click the downward pointing arrow next to the Foreground Color list box and choose a color for your text.**

6. **Click OK.**

Using text styles

Rather than force you to format text yourself, FrontPage can do it for you by using text styles. Text styles usually have odd names such as Heading 1, Normal, and Heading 4. (Just click in the Style list box in the Formatting toolbar to see what types of styles may be available for your Web page.)

To use a text style:

1. **Click the text that you want to format by using a text style.**

2. **Click the downward pointing arrow next to the Style list box and choose a text style, such as Normal or Heading 3.**

   FrontPage automatically formats your text according to your chosen text style.

As an alternative, click the downward pointing arrow next to the Style list box first, choose a text style, and then start typing. Whatever you type automatically appears in your chosen text style.

You cannot apply more than one text style to a paragraph. The end of a paragraph occurs whenever you press Enter or Return. To see paragraph marks that show the end of your paragraphs, click the Show All button on the Standard toolbar (it looks like a paragraph mark).

Adding dynamic HTML effects

In the old days, Web pages looked pretty boring with text and graphics passively appearing on-screen. To spice up Web pages and make them look fancier, programmers created something called *dynamic HTML,* which can make your text respond to the user by sliding across the screen or changing colors when the user clicks it.

Dynamic HTML effects may not work with all types and versions of browsers. For example, Internet Explorer 3.0 can't display dynamic HTML effects but version 4.0 and greater of Internet Explorer can display dynamic HTML effects. Because not everyone uses the latest version of a browser, be aware that not everyone will be able to see dynamic HTML effects on your Web page.

Despite the drawbacks, dynamic HTML effects can make your Web pages more animated and interesting to look at. (Of course, if you don't have any interesting information on your Web site, no one will have a reason to look at your Web site for very long no matter how many special dynamic HTML effects you may use.)

To add dynamic HTML effects:

1. **Click the text that you want to format by using dynamic HTML effects.**

2. **Choose Format⇨Dynamic HTML Effects.**

   The DHTML Effects toolbar appears, as shown in Figure 24-4.

Figure 24-4:
The DHTML
Effects
toolbar lets
you define
what your
text will do.

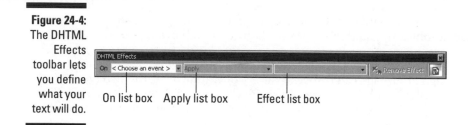

On list box   Apply list box   Effect list box

3. **Click the downward pointing arrow next to the On list box.**

   A list of events appears including Click, Double click, Mouse over, and Page load.

4. **Choose an event (such as Click or Mouse over).**

5. **Click the downward pointing arrow next to the Apply list box.**

   A list of options appears in the Apply list box.

6. **Choose the option you want from the Apply list box.**

   Depending on the event you chose in Step 4, the available options in Step 5 may vary. You may also need to click in the second Apply list box to specify additional options.

7. **Click the close box of the DHTML toolbar to make it go away.**

8. **Choose File⇨Preview in Browser.**

   FrontPage loads your browser and shows you how the DHTML effects will behave. If you haven't saved your Web page yet, a dialog box reminds you to do so.

9. **Choose File⇨Close to get rid of the browser and return back to FrontPage.**

Putting Pretty Pictures on a Web Page

Besides text to provide useful information for others to read, the second most important element for a Web page is graphics. Graphics can be decorative, such as a picture of your company's logo, or actual buttons that link to another Web page.

Because graphics can make a difference between a Web page that looks inviting to read and one that looks just plain revolting, take some time to add graphics to your Web pages so they don't embarrass you with their appearance.

 Although FrontPage can display a variety of graphic files, the two types of graphic files that Web pages can use are GIF and JPEG files. (JPEG files often have the .JPG file extension.) If you want to use a graphic file that's stored in a different file format, such as PCX or BMP, you have to get a special program to convert that file into either a GIF or JPEG format before you can use it in your Web page.

Adding pictures to a Web page

FrontPage can get graphic images from two sources: clip art or from a file stored on your computer. Clip art consists of pre-drawn cartoons that Microsoft forced some starving artist to draw for you to use.

Because clip art can't always offer the exact image you want, many people resort to creating their own images by using a painting or drawing program (which is useful if you're good at drawing). People who can't draw have to resort to getting an image through a scanner, a digital camera, or off the Internet.

To add a clip art image to a Web page:

1. **Click the Web page near the approximate location where you want the clip art image to appear.**

2. **Choose Insert⇨Picture⇨Clip Art and the Clip Art Gallery dialog box appears.**

3. **Click the category of the images you want to examine, such as the Web Site or Office category, and a variety of different clip art images appears.**

4. **Click the graphic image you want to use.**

   A pop-up menu appears, listing four different icons.

5. **Click the top icon (Insert clip).**

    FrontPage displays the clip art image that you choose on the Web page. You may have to move or resize the image to make it fit on the Web page.

To display a graphic file on a Web page:

1. **Click the Web page near the approximate location where you want the graphic file image to appear.**

2. **Choose Insert⇔Picture⇔From File.**

    The Picture dialog box appears. (If you're editing a single Web page, a Select File dialog box appears on top of the Picture dialog box.)

3. **Click the graphic file that you want to use and then click OK.**

    FrontPage displays the image you choose on the Web page. You may have to move or resize the image to make it fit on the Web page.

Displaying a background image

To add a little color to your Web pages, you can choose to display a background image. A background image is nothing more than a single graphic file displayed on your Web pages. Because a single graphic file is rarely large enough to fill an entire page, FrontPage *tiles* your chosen graphic file, where the single image of your graphic file is repeated over and over again.

For best results, a background graphic image should not intrude upon any text or graphics on your Web pages.

To display a background image for your Web page:

1. **Choose Format⇔Background.**

    The Page Properties dialog box appears.

2. **Click the Background Picture check box so a check mark appears.**

3. **Click Browse.**

    A Select Background Picture dialog box appears.

4. **Click the graphic file that you want to use and click OK twice.**

    FrontPage displays your Web page with your chosen image in the background.

Using themes

As a shortcut to choosing a background image and using text styles, FrontPage provides themes. A *theme* contains pre-defined background images, text, and graphic styles for creating different types of Web pages. By using a theme, you're essentially copying the design of an existing Web page. Then you just have to modify the Web page for your own particular use.

To define a theme for your Web page:

1. **Choose Format⇨Theme.**

    The Themes dialog box appears, as shown in Figure 24-5.

2. **Click an option button to choose the theme for All Pages or Selected Page(s).**

3. **Click the theme that you want to use, such as Citrus Punch or Romanesque.**

    FrontPage shows what your chosen theme looks like so that you can approve it or change your mind right now.

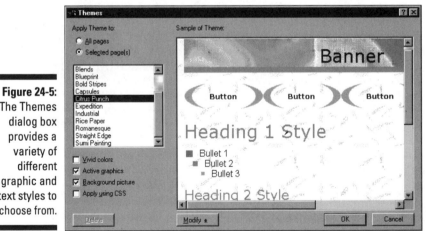

Figure 24-5: The Themes dialog box provides a variety of different graphic and text styles to choose from.

4. **Click OK.**

    FrontPage uses your chosen theme for your Web page. If you've already formatted any text by using a text style, such as Heading 1, it may now look different depending on the theme you chose.

Connecting Everything with Hyperlinks

The final step to making your Web pages useful, interesting, and ready for cyberspace is adding hyperlinks. Both text and graphics can be hyperlinks. A *hyperlink* simply points to another Web page or Web site when the viewer clicks it.

To create hyperlinks:

1. **Click the graphic image (or highlight the text) that you want to turn into a hyperlink.**

2. **Choose Insert⇨Hyperlink, press Ctrl+K, or click the Hyperlink button on the Standard toolbar.**

   A Create Hyperlink dialog box appears, as shown in Figure 24-6.

3. **Click the Web page that you want the hyperlink to display, or type the Web site address (such as** http://www.dummies.com**) in the URL text box.**

4. **Click OK.**

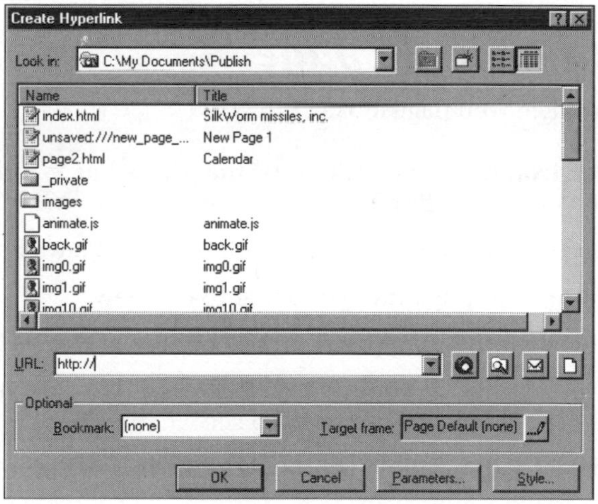

Figure 24-6:
The Create Hyperlink dialog box can create hyperlinks to another Web page or Web site.

To edit or remove a hyperlink:

1. **Click the graphic or text hyperlink that you want to change.**

2. **Choose Insert⇨Hyperlink, press Ctrl+K, or click the Hyperlink button on the Standard toolbar to bring up the Edit Hyperlink dialog box (refer to Figure 24-6).**

3. **Edit the text that appears in the <u>U</u>RL text box. (Or delete the text that appears in the text box to remove the hyperlink.)**

   The URL text box displays the address of another Web site or the name of a Web page.

4. **Click OK.**

Previewing Your Web Pages

After creating, editing, and modifying your Web pages, you may find minor mistakes when you view the pages on the Internet. If so, you have to modify your Web pages and then post them back to the Internet again, which can be time-consuming, annoying, and boring. However, FrontPage provides two handy ways to preview your pages before going through the trouble of posting your Web pages on the Internet.

While previewing your Web pages, if you click a hyperlink that points towards another Web site, such as www.dummies.com, FrontPage tries to load your browser and connect to the Internet.

Previewing a single page

To find out how a single Web page looks:

1. **Click the Page icon in the Views Bar. (If the Views Bar is hidden, choose <u>V</u>iew⇨<u>V</u>iews Bar first.)**

   FrontPage displays the Folder List to the right of the Views Bar.

2. **Double-click the Web page that you want to preview.**

3. **Click the Preview tab that appears on the bottom of the Web page.**

   FrontPage shows you what your chosen Web page will look like over the Internet. You can also click hyperlinks to see whether they work.

4. **Click the Normal tab to return back to editing your Web page.**

Previewing your Web site in a browser

The trouble with previewing your Web pages within FrontPage is that you can't tell how your Web pages may look within an actual browser. As an alternative, FrontPage can load any browser from your hard disk and let you view your Web pages within your chosen browser. By using this method, you can see how your Web pages may look in different versions of Netscape Navigator or Internet Explorer.

To preview your Web pages in a browser:

1. **Choose File➪Preview in Browser to bring up a Preview in Browser dialog box.**

2. **Click the browser that you want to use.**

3. **Click the option button of the screen resolution that you want to use, such as 800 x 600.**

4. **Click Preview.**

   Your chosen browser appears and displays your Web pages. You can also click the hyperlinks to make sure that they work.

5. **Click File➪Close; FrontPage reappears, and your browser goes away.**

For a fast way to preview your Web pages, click the Preview in Browser button on the Standard toolbar in Step 1. Preview displays your Web pages in your default browser right away.

Seeing HTML code

HTML code contains a lot of cryptic symbols that actually define how your Web pages will look on the Internet. FrontPage shields you from the complexities of editing HTML code, but if you're really curious, you can view and edit the HTML code of your Web pages.

Make sure that you know what you're doing if you decide to edit HTML code or you could really mess up your Web pages. For more info on HTML, check out *HTML For Dummies,* 3rd Edition by Ed Tittle and Stephen N. James (IDG Books Worldwide, Inc.).

To view the HTML code of your Web pages:

1. **Click the Page icon in the Views Bar. (If the Views Bar is hidden, choose View➪Views Bar first.)**

   FrontPage displays the Folder List to the right of the Views Bar.

2. **Double-click the Web page that you want to preview.**

   FrontPage displays your chosen Web page.

3. **Click the HTML tab at the bottom of the Web page.**

   FrontPage displays the cryptic HTML code that makes up your Web page, as shown in Figure 24-7.

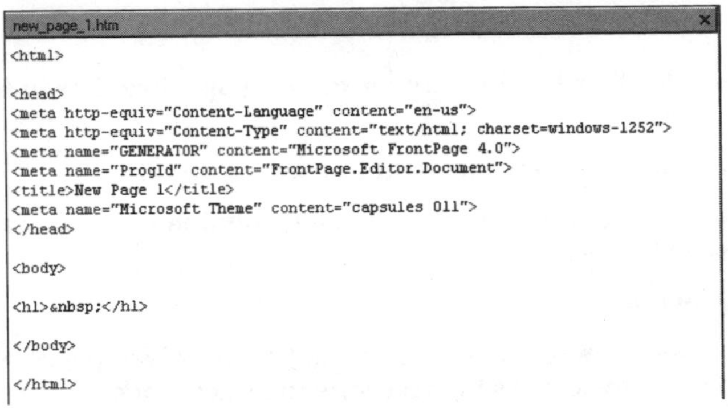

Figure 24-7:
FrontPage
can show
you all the
gory details
of HTML
code, if you
wish.

```
new_page_1.htm                                                          ×
<html>

<head>
<meta http-equiv="Content-Language" content="en-us">
<meta http-equiv="Content-Type" content="text/html; charset=windows-1252">
<meta name="GENERATOR" content="Microsoft FrontPage 4.0">
<meta name="ProgId" content="FrontPage.Editor.Document">
<title>New Page 1</title>
<meta name="Microsoft Theme" content="capsules 011">
</head>

<body>

<h1> </h1>

</body>

</html>
```

4. **Click the Normal tab at the bottom of the Web page to return to an HTML-free view of your Web page.**

Chapter 25

Organizing Your Pages with Tables, Frames, and Lines

. . . .

In This Chapter

▶ Putting text in a table

▶ Constructing a frame

▶ Using framed pages

▶ Adding horizontal lines

. . . .

You only need to add text and graphics to a Web page to make it functional, but why stop there? To help you organize your information,
FrontPage enables you to use tables and frames.

Tables can organize text and graphics in neat rows and columns. Frames can
divide a Web page into two or more parts, which enables you to create Web
pages that are easier for users to navigate while making your Web site look
advanced and up-to-date.

Organizing Text into Tables

While you can type text anywhere on a Web page, it can be cumbersome at
times. Sometimes the text appears exactly where you want it, and other times
you have to keep hitting the space or Tab key to align your text properly.

Rather than torture yourself in this manner, you can use a table to organize
your text. A table displays rows and columns, much like a spreadsheet, where
you can type text. Because each chunk of text appears in its own row and
column (called a *cell*), a table makes it easy to organize your text.

Drawing a table

To give you as many options as possible, FrontPage provides four different ways to draw a table so that you can choose the method you like best (or get confused by all three methods and not be able to use any of them). To draw a table:

1. **Click where you want the table to appear on your Web page.**

2. **Click the Insert Table button on the Standard toolbar.**

   A drop-down menu appears, displaying blank cells.

3. **Hold down the left mouse button and drag the mouse across the drop-down menu to highlight the number of rows and columns you want.**

4. **Release the left mouse button.**

   FrontPage draws your table.

To try another method of drawing a table that gives you more flexibility:

1. **Click where you want the table to appear on your Web page.**

2. **Choose Table➪Draw Table.**

   The mouse pointer turns into a pencil icon.

3. **Move the mouse pointer where you want to draw the table.**

4. **Hold down the left mouse button and drag the mouse to draw the table on the Web page.**

   As you move the mouse, FrontPage displays a dotted outline of your table.

5. **Release the left mouse button.**

   FrontPage draws a table consisting of a single cell.

6. **Move the mouse inside the table, hold down the left mouse button, and drag the mouse.**

   Drawing a line divides the table into smaller cells. Repeat this process as often as necessary to draw the number of cells you need.

7. **Press Esc.**

If you already have a lot of text typed on a page but want to organize it into a table, don't bother creating a new table and typing the text into that table. Instead, FrontPage can convert text into a table automatically. To convert text into a table:

1. **Highlight the text that you want to display in a table.**

2. **Choose Table➪Convert➪Text to Table.**

   A Convert Text to Table dialog box appears.

3. **Click an option button, such as Paragraphs or Commas and then click OK.**

   FrontPage displays your highlighted text in a table.

Adding (and deleting) rows and columns

After you draw your table, you may need to add or delete rows and columns. To add a row or column:

1. **Click the row or column of the table where you want to add another row or column.**

2. **Choose Table➪Insert➪Rows or Columns.**

   An Insert Rows or Columns dialog box appears.

3. **Click the Rows or Columns option button.**

4. **Click the Number Of text box and then type how many rows or columns you want to add.**

5. **In the Location group, click an option button to specify where to insert the new row or column (such as Right of Selection or Above Selection).**

6. **Click OK.**

   FrontPage politely inserts your rows or columns in the table.

Eventually you may decide you have too many rows or columns. So if you want to delete a row or column:

1. **Click the row or column of the table that you want to delete.**

2. **Choose Table➪Select➪Row (or Column).**

   FrontPage highlights your chosen row or column.

3. **Choose Table➪Delete Cells.**

   FrontPage wipes out your chosen row or column.

Changing the size of a table

Most likely FrontPage won't draw a table exactly the size you want. Fortunately, you can resize a table easily by following these steps:

1. **Move the mouse pointer over a table border (either the outside edges or the inside borders).**

   The mouse pointer turns into a double-pointing arrow.

2. **Hold down the left mouse button and drag the mouse.**

   FrontPage displays a dotted line to show you the new location of your table border.

3. **Release the left mouse button.**

Deleting a table

Tables can be handy, but after you draw one, you may decide that you don't need it after all. To completely obliterate a table and its contents:

1. **Click the table you want to delete.**

2. **Choose Table➪Select➪Table.**

   FrontPage highlights the entire table.

3. **Press Delete.**

Framing Your Web Pages

In the old days, Web sites only displayed a single Web page on the entire screen. Unfortunately, this view confused many people because whenever they clicked a hyperlink, the entire page disappeared and a new Web page took its place.

So to provide a sense of continuity among all the Web pages in a Web site, programmers invented frames. *Frames* divide your Web page into two or more parts, where each part can display entirely different Web pages. Because frames often provide their own vertical scroll bar, users can scroll up or down within each frame without affecting the contents of the other frames.

The most common use for frames is for one frame to display a list of hyperlink buttons, and another frame to display the actual contents of a Web page, as shown in Figure 25-1.

Older versions of Netscape Navigator and Internet Explorer cannot display frames. In order to make sure your Web pages can be viewed by everyone (including people who use obscure Web browsers such as Mosaic or Lynx), either avoid frames or create two versions of your Web pages: a framed version and a non-framed version.

Figure 25-1:
Frames
divide a
Web page
into multiple
windows
that can
display
different
Web page
data.

New Page 2 - Microsoft Internet Explorer - [Working Offline]

File Edit View Favorites Tools Help

Back Forward Stop Refresh Home Search Favorites History Mail Print Edit Discuss Links

Welcome to the Computer Virus Center of the Universe!!!

Home
Virii
Hacker Tools
Trojan Horses
Packet Sniffers
Password Cracker
Encryption
Disassemblers

Computer viruses that you can use to bug people you don't like.

Virus Name	File Size	Description
PyroVirus.ZIP	112 Kb	Heats up your computer monitor and blows it up.
AT&Tack.ZIP	259 Kb	Dials out the victim's modem, enabling you access to their computer.
Melt.ZIP	87 Kb	Melts any floppy disks in the disk drive.
Keyboard.ZIP	90 Kb	Alters the keyboard keys at random.
Scream.ZIP	109 Kb	Emits a screaming pitch through the speaker.
AWOL.ZIP	309 Kb	Installs a useless online service on your hard disk that takes forever to

Framed area   Framed area

Creating a framed Web page

To create a framed Web page:

1. **Choose File⇨New⇨Page.**

   A New dialog box appears.

2. **Click the Frames Pages tab.**

   The Preview area on the Frames Pages tab displays a variety of framed page styles that you can choose from.

3. **Click the framed page design that you want to use and then click OK.**

   FrontPage creates an empty framed page, as shown in Figure 25-2.

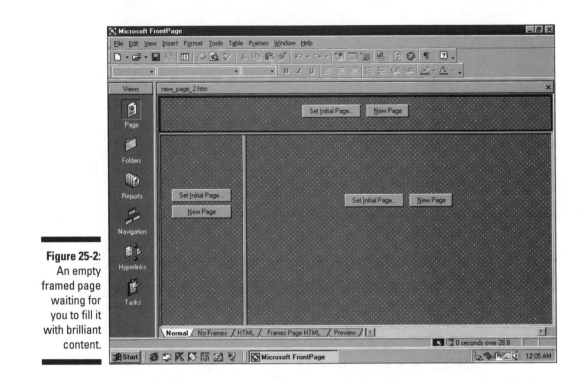

Figure 25-2:
An empty
framed page
waiting for
you to fill it
with brilliant
content.

Filling in a framed Web page

After you create an empty framed Web page, the next step is to fill the frame with information. You can either fill a frame with brand new information (which you have to type or insert on your own), or you can define a frame to display an existing Web page. To place brand new information into a frame:

1. **Click the New Page button inside the frame that you want to use.**

   FrontPage displays an empty frame.

2. **Start typing text or inserting graphics. (See Chapter 24 for more information on adding text and graphics to a Web page.)**

Rather than create new information inside a frame, you can tell FrontPage to display an existing Web page inside your frame instead. To define a Web page to appear in a frame:

1. **Click the Set Initial Page button inside the frame that you want to use.**

   A Select File dialog box appears.

2. **Click the Web page that you want to use inside your frame and then click OK.**

   FrontPage displays the Web page inside your frame.

Changing a framed Web page's properties

After you create a framed page, you can modify it at any time. The simplest way to modify a frame is to change the properties of the frame, which enables you to modify the following:

- The frame's name
- The initial Web page that you want the frame to display
- The frame size
- The frame margins
- Whether the frame can be resizable when viewed inside a browser
- Frame borders
- The frame spacing
- Whether the frame displays scroll bars or not

To modify the properties of a frame:

1. **Click the frame you want to modify. (Make sure you click the Normal tab at the bottom of your Web pages first.)**

2. **Choose Frames⇨Frame Properties.**

   A Frame Properties dialog box appears, as shown in Figure 25-3.

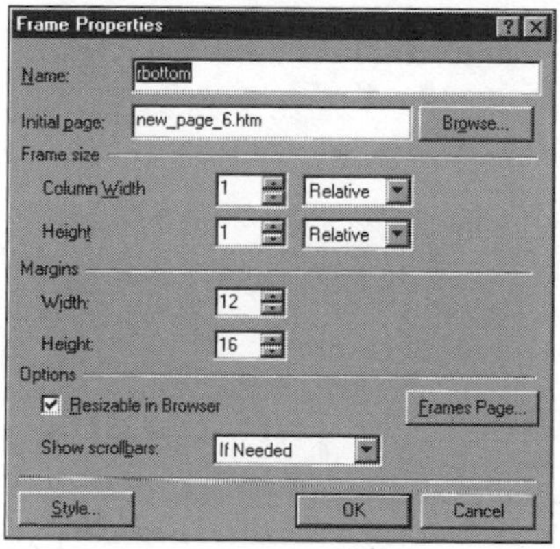

Figure 25-3:
The Frame Properties dialog box.

3. **Click the Name text box and type a new name for your frame if you want.**

4. **Click Initial Page text box and type the Web page that you want the frame to display. (If you click Browse, you can click the Web page that you want to display without having to type a thing.)**

5. In the Frame Size group, click the <u>W</u>idth or Heig<u>h</u>t boxes and type a new frame width or height.

6. In the Margins group, click the W<u>i</u>dth or Height boxes and type a new margin width or height.

7. Click the Show Scrol<u>l</u>bars list box and choose an option, such as If Needed or Always.

8. Make sure a check mark appears in the <u>R</u>esizable in Browser check box. (Or clear the check box if you don't want the frames to be resizable when viewed in a browser.)

9. Click the <u>F</u>rames Page button.

   A Page Properties dialog box appears.

10. Make sure a check mark appears in the Show <u>B</u>orders check box. (Or clear the check box if you don't want the frames to display borders.)

11. Click the Frame Spacing box and type a number to define the width of your frame borders.

12. Click OK.

Deleting a frame

Although you can keep splitting frames like amoebas multiplying, FrontPage also enables you to delete frames in case you have more than you need. To delete a frame:

1. Click the frame you want to delete. (Make sure you click the Normal tab at the bottom of your Web pages first.)

2. Choose F<u>r</u>ames⇨<u>D</u>elete Frame.

   FrontPage wipes out your chosen frame. If you have any unsaved data in your frame, FrontPage politely asks whether you want to save it before deleting the frame.

Viewing your frame as a full screen

Because frames divide your Web page in smaller pieces, you may find that editing a frame can be difficult in such a small space. Fortunately, the clever programmers at Microsoft have already anticipated this problem and solved it by enabling you to view a single frame as a single Web page. That way, you can edit it in a full screen and when you finish, you can see how it looks as a frame. To view a frame as a full screen:

1. **Click the frame that you want to view. (Make sure you click the Normal tab at the bottom of your Web pages first.)**

2. **Choose Frames⇨Open Page in New Window.**

   FrontPage displays your frame as a window all by itself.

3. **Edit your Web page until your heart's content, and then choose File⇨Close, or press Ctrl+F4 to return back to the frame view of your Web page.**

Using Horizontal Lines

As a final method for organizing information on your Web pages, consider using horizontal lines. A horizontal line simply breaks up your Web page so viewers aren't overwhelmed with globs of text or pictures.

If you want really colorful horizontal lines, you are better off inserting a clip art image of a horizontal line, such as a line displaying dripping blood or a line consisting of little Christmas trees. You can find a few FrontPage clip art horizontal lines by choosing Insert⇨Picture⇨Clip Art. When the Clip Art Gallery dialog box appears, click one of the following categories:

✔ Borders & Frames

✔ Dividers & Decorations

✔ Web Dividers

Creating a horizontal line

To add a horizontal line to a Web page:

1. **Click the Web page where you want the line to appear.**

2. **Choose Insert⇨Horizontal Line.**

   FrontPage displays a plain, boring horizontal line across your Web page.

Moving a horizontal line

After you create a horizontal line, you may want to move it to a new location. To move a horizontal line:

1. **Click the horizontal line that you want to move.**

   FrontPage highlights your chosen horizontal line.

2. **Move the mouse pointer over the line, hold down the left mouse button, and drag the mouse.**

   FrontPage displays a cursor where the horizontal line appears when you release the left mouse button.

3. **Release the left mouse button when you're happy with the line's new location.**

Deleting a horizontal line

In case you get tired of looking at a horizontal line, you can delete it by following these steps:

1. **Click the horizontal line that you want to delete.**

   FrontPage highlights your chosen horizontal line.

2. **Press Delete.**

Chapter 26

Editing Images with PhotoDraw

· ·

In This Chapter

▶ Figuring out what the heck Microsoft PhotoDraw 2000 is

▶ Creating a picture

▶ Opening a graphic file

▶ Deciphering PhotoDraw toolbars

▶ Saving your work

▶ Previewing and printing your work

· ·

*P*hotoDraw 2000 is the latest addition to the Microsoft Office 2000 family of products that is soon to become a market leader no matter what its competitors try to do. The main purpose of PhotoDraw is to edit graphic images — those you draw or copy, download from the Internet, scan in with a scanner, or capture by using a digital camera.

Any images that you modify with PhotoDraw can be used to add fancy graphics to any Office 2000 programs such as Word, PowerPoint, Publisher, or FrontPage, so that you can create visually interesting reports, newsletters, or Web sites. If you have no desire to edit, let alone create graphic images, you can safely ignore PhotoDraw or even uninstall it to free up extra space on your hard drive.

PhotoDraw only comes with the Premium and Developer editions of Microsoft Office 2000, so if you don't have either of these versions, you don't have PhotoDraw on your hard disk either.

Creating New PhotoDraw Images

In case you're the artistic type or don't mind the idea of fooling around with graphics even though you may not have the slightest drawing ability, PhotoDraw gives you four ways to create a new graphic image:

- When you first run PhotoDraw, a dialog box pops up, asking what you want to do. Click in the Blank Picture option button and click OK. When a New dialog box appears, click the Picture or Labels tab, click the type of graphic image that you want to create (such as CD Label or Postcard) and click OK.
- Choose File⇨New. When a New dialog box appears, click the Picture or Labels tab, click the type of graphic image that you want to create (such as CD Label or Postcard) and click OK.
- Click the New button on the Standard toolbar.
- Press Ctrl+N.

When you click the New button or press Ctrl+N, PhotoDraw automatically creates a blank screen for you.

Opening a Previously Saved File

Rather than create a new picture, you're more likely to spend time viewing and editing existing pictures. To open a previously saved or created picture, PhotoDraw gives you six choices:

- Press Ctrl+O.
- Click the Open button on the Standard toolbar.
- Choose File⇨Open.
- Choose one of the last four files you saved, which appear at the bottom of the File menu.
- Choose File⇨Visual Open.
- Press Ctrl+Shift+O.

If you choose the last two methods, PhotoDraw displays a Visual Open dialog box that displays all the available pictures that you can choose from, as shown in Figure 26-1.

To increase the number of files displayed at the bottom of the File menu, choose Tools⇨Options and then click the General tab on the Options dialog box that appears. Next to the Recently Used File list check box, type the number of files that you want PhotoDraw to display on its File menu.

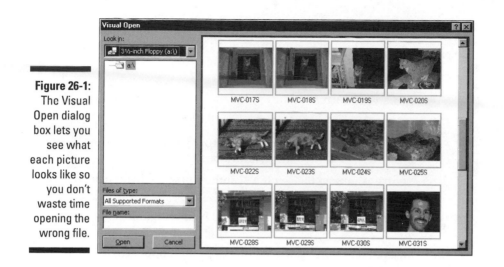

Figure 26-1:
The Visual
Open dialog
box lets you
see what
each picture
looks like so
you don't
waste time
opening the
wrong file.

Figuring Out PhotoDraw Tools

PhotoDraw provides toolbars so you don't have to type weird keystroke combinations or dig through multiple layers of pull-down menus. The two most common toolbars are the Standard toolbar and the Visual Menu.

Exploring the Standard toolbar

The Standard toolbar offers access to the program's most frequently used commands, arranged from left to right in roughly the order of their frequency of use, as shown in Figure 26-2.

Figure 26-2:
The
Standard
toolbar
provides
common
commands
at the click
of a button.

The Standard tool box features the following commands:

- ✔ **New:** Creates a new, blank picture

- ✔ **Open:** Opens an existing picture

- ✔ **Save:** Saves your current picture

- ✔ **Print:** Prints your current picture

- ✔ **Print Preview:** Shows you what your picture will look like when printed on your printer (as long as the printer doesn't jam)

- ✔ **Scan Picture:** Yanks an image off a scanner (provided you have one connected to your computer)

- ✔ **Digital Camera:** Takes an image captured from a digital camera (if you have one)

- ✔ **Cut:** Moves the currently selected object to the Clipboard, the invisible Windows storage area

- ✔ **Copy:** Copies the currently selected object to the Clipboard

- ✔ **Paste:** Places in the current picture or whatever object that is currently on the Clipboard

- ✔ **Replace:** Replaces an object with another object, using the same attributes (such as size or angle of rotation) as the replaced object

- ✔ **Undo:** Reverses the action of your last command

- ✔ **Redo:** Opposite of Undo — restores what the Undo command last did

- ✔ **Select:** Allows you to select an object

- ✔ **Order:** Allows you to arrange objects on top or behind each other

- ✔ **Custom Rotate:** Rotates an object

- ✔ **Line:** Draws a straight line

- ✔ **Curve:** Draws a curved line

- ✔ **Arrow:** Draws an arrow

- ✔ **Rectangle:** Draws a rectangle

- ✔ **Ellipse:** Draws an ellipse

- ✔ **AutoShapes:** Draws an object such as a flowchart symbol or a heart

- ✔ **Insert Text:** Inserts text on the picture

- ✔ **Zoom:** Enlarges or shrinks the picture on the screen

- ✔ **Pan and Zoom:** Enlarges or shrinks a select portion of your picture

- ✔ **Help Contents and Index:** Displays the PhotoDraw help window

To quickly find out what each button on the Standard toolbar does, point the mouse over a button and then wait a second or two until the ToolTip — a brief explanation of the button — appears.

Looking good with the Visual Menu

The Visual Menu allows you to add or manipulate text and graphics in your picture to create special effects, such as creating shadows behind images or adding texture to an image. When you click a button on the Visual Menu, a drop-down list of options appears, enabling you to select a specific command. Figure 26-3 shows the Visual Menu.

Figure 26-3:
The Visual Menu provides a helpful list of commands for manipulating graphics.

The buttons on the Visual Menu appear in the following order from left to right:

- ✔ **Text:** Creates or modifies text
- ✔ **Cut Crop:** Selects or erases select portions of your graphic image
- ✔ **Templates:** Displays graphic images that you can add to your picture
- ✔ **Draw Paint:** Allows you to draw or paint images or shapes
- ✔ **Fill:** Allows you to fill in an image with a pattern or texture
- ✔ **Outline:** Modifies the outer edges of a graphic object
- ✔ **Color:** Modifies the color of an object
- ✔ **Touch Up:** Adjusts a small portion of an image
- ✔ **Effects:** Creates special effects such as blurring an image or displaying a shadow behind an image

To use any of the commands on the Visual Menu, select the object that you want to modify, click the appropriate button on the Visual Menu, and click a command.

Even though your Visual Menu resembles a tool bar, it actually displays drop-down menus, like a menu bar.

Typing Text and Making It Pretty

Text is anything you can type on the keyboard such as letters, numbers, or oddball symbols like ^, &, #, and @.

When you type text in PhotoDraw, your text is considered to be a graphic object that can be manipulated. That means editing your text in PhotoDraw is slightly different than editing text in a word processor such as Word. You'll figure out how to edit text in the section "Editing your text" that follows.

Creating text

When you want to create text, you can't start typing. Instead, follow these steps:

1. **Click the Insert Text button on the Standard toolbar, or click the Text button on the Visual Menu and then choose Insert Text.**

   A Text window appears on the right-hand side of the screen and highlights the string "Your text here," as shown in Figure 26-4.

2. **Type your text.**

   PhotoDraw displays your text in the Text window and on your picture.

3. **Click the close box of the Text window.**

After you type your text, you can format it right away without exiting the Text window. If you prefer, you can exit the Text window and follow the steps in the section "Editing your text."

Editing your text

After you type your text, you can edit or format it later to add fancy formatting or special visual effects:

1. **Double-click the text you want to edit or format.**

   The Text window appears in the right side of the screen (see Figure 26-4).

2. **Choose one of the following in the top half of the Text window:**

   • Click Designer Text and then click a design that you want to use.

   • Click the Format Text so that you can edit your text, choose a font, size, and type style.

   • Click Text Flow (indented underneath Format Text) so that you can define your text alignment, orientation, and whether or not to use smoothing to make your text look less chunky.

   • Click Fill so that you can choose a color for your text.

   • Click Bend Text and then click a bent text shape to use.

   • Click Outline and then click a line type to display within your text characters.

   • Click Settings (indented underneath Outline) to modify the line you chose with the Outline option.

3. **Click the close box of the Text window.**

Text handles   Text rotation handle

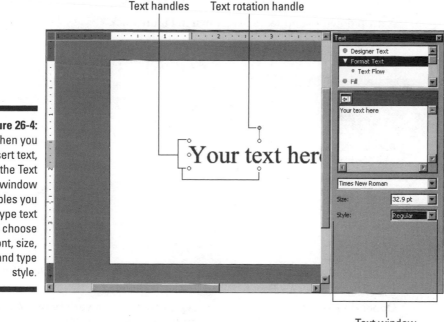

Figure 26-4:
When you insert text, the Text window enables you to type text and choose a font, size, and type style.

Text window

You can also access these text formatting features by clicking the Text button on the Visual Menu.

Drawing and Editing Graphic Images

If you're artistic or don't mind goofing around and trying to make neat graphic effects, PhotoDraw can help you create new graphic images or edit existing ones. Because most people aren't naturally artists, PhotoDraw provides plenty of help in creating good-looking graphic images.

Using templates

The simplest way to create a graphic image is to use a *template,* which is a pre-drawn graphic image that you can modify. To use a template:

1. **Click the Templates button on the Visual Menu.**

   A drop-down list appears, as shown in Figure 26-5.

Figure 26-5: The Templates button provides five different types of templates to choose from.

2. **Click the type of graphic image that you want to create, such as Cards or Business Graphics.**

   Depending on what graphic image type you chose, a variety of images appears on the screen next to a Templates window, as shown in Figure 26-6.

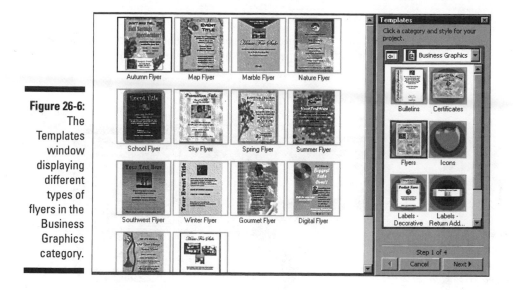

Figure 26-6:
The Templates window displaying different types of flyers in the Business Graphics category.

3. **Click the image that you want to use.**

4. **Click Next and choose from the options available. (Depending on the graphic type you chose, you may have to click Next several times.)**

5. **Click Finish.**

   PhotoDraw displays your final graphic image.

Painting in PhotoDraw

If you can draw decent images with your mouse, you may try the paint feature in PhotoDraw. Just as in real painting, the PhotoDraw paint feature allows you to change the appearance of your brush strokes. To paint:

1. **Click the Draw Paint button on the Visual Menu.**

   A drop-down list appears, as shown in Figure 26-7.

Figure 26-7:
The Draw Paint button provides three ways to create an image.

2. **Click P̲aint.**

   The mouse pointer turns into a crosshair, a Creative Paint floating tool bar and a Paint window appears, as shown in Figure 26-8.

Creative Paint floating toolbar

Figure 26-8:
Creating
artistic
brushstrokes
is easy
with the
PhotoDraw
Paint
feature.

Paint window

3. **Move the mouse where you want to start your brush stroke, hold down the left mouse button, and drag the mouse to draw your brushstroke.**

   If you make a mistake, click the Undo Last command on the Creative Paint toolbar.

4. **Click F̲inish in the Creative Paint toolbar when you're done painting one image.**

   If you want to continue painting, click Paint in the Creative Paint toolbar and repeat Steps 3 and 4.

5. **Click the close box of the Paint window when you're done painting.**

Drawing in PhotoDraw

As an alternative to painting in PhotoDraw, you can also draw lines, geometric objects like circles and squares, or simple objects such as arrows or flowchart symbols. To draw an image in PhotoDraw:

1. **Click the Line, Curve, Arrow, Rectangle, Ellipse, or AutoShapes button on Standard toolbar.**

   Depending on what button you click, the mouse pointer turns into a crosshair, and an AutoShapes toolbar appears along with an Outline window.

2. **Move the mouse where you want to start your drawing, hold down the left mouse button, and drag the mouse to draw.**

   If you're drawing a curve, you have to click the mouse to anchor the curves.

3. **Press Esc.**

Editing an image

After drawing or painting, you may wish to edit an image to change its color, thickness, or borders. To edit an image:

1. **Double-click the image that you want to modify.**

   Handles appear around your chosen graphic object.

2. **Choose one of the following from the Visual Menu:**

   - Click Fill and choose an option such as Texture or Two-Color Gradient.
   - Click Outline and choose an option such as Soft Edges or Photo Brushes.
   - Click Color and choose an option such as Colorize or Tint.
   - Click Touch Up and choose an option such as Clone or Smudge.
   - Click Effects and choose an option such as Shadow or Fade Out.

   Depending on the option you choose, a window appears in the right side of the screen, showing you the different choices available for your chosen options.

3. **Click the close box of the window on the right side of the screen when you're done.**

Moving, Resizing, and Deleting Objects

When you type text or draw a picture, you may later decide it should be larger or in another location. To move a text or graphic object:

1. **Click the object that you want to move.**

   Handles appear around your chosen object.

2. **Move the mouse pointer over the edge of the object until the mouse pointer turns into a four-way pointing arrow at the tip of the normal mouse arrow.**

3. **Hold down the left mouse button and drag the mouse.**

4. **Release the left mouse button when you're happy with the new location of your object.**

To resize an object:

1. **Click the object that you want to resize.**

   Handles appear around your chosen object.

2. **Move the mouse pointer over a handle until the mouse pointer turns into a two-way pointing arrow.**

3. **Hold down the left mouse button and drag the mouse.**

4. **Release the left mouse button when you're happy with the new size of your object.**

To delete an object:

1. **Click the object that you want to delete.**

   Handles appear around your chosen object.

2. **Press Delete.**

Saving Your Stuff

PhotoDraw can save your pictures in a variety of different file formats. That way, you can use your graphics on Web pages, in newsletters, or just to print out all by themselves.

Don't forget to save your work periodically because computer crashes are all too common. If you don't save your work, you can lose it all in an instant.

Saving your picture

Save your picture regularly while you're working, just in case your computer crashes or otherwise ruins your day. To save a picture:

✔ Press Ctrl+S.

✔ Click the Save button on the Standard toolbar (the button that looks like a floppy disk).

✔ Choose File⇨Save.

If you're saving a picture for the first time, a Save As dialog box appears and asks that you type a filename, such as Naughty Picture or Dog Eating Snake.

The longest a filename can be is 255 characters. Filenames cannot include the forward slash (/), backslash (\), greater-than sign (>), less-than sign (<), asterisk (*), period (.), question mark (?), quotation mark ("), pipe symbol (|), colon (:), or semicolon (;).

In the computer world, you can use a variety of silly file formats to store graphic images. In case you're confused by all the weird file format acronyms like GIF, JPEG, or PCX, save your pictures by choosing File⇨Save for Use In. Depending on what option you choose, the Save for Use In Wizard guides you step-by-step to saving your graphic image in the optimum file format.

Saving your pictures under another name and/or file format

You can save any picture you create in PhotoDraw under a variety of different file formats to insure maximum compatibility with other programs. The available file formats are:

- **PhotoDraw:** The default, native file format for PhotoDraw (which is .MIX file format). Use this format unless you have a reason to use a different file format.

- **Picture It 2.0 – 3.0:** Saves pictures in the MIX file format, for use in Versions 2.0 and 3.0 of Microsoft Picture It!

- **GIF:** Saves pictures in the GIF file format, which is a universal file format most often used for Web graphics.

- **JPEG:** Saves pictures in the JPEG file format, a newer universal file format also used for Web graphics.

- **PC Paintbrush:** Saves pictures as PCX files, which can be used by a popular graphics program called (what else?) PC Paintbrush, although fewer people are using this program nowadays.

- **Portable Network Graphics:** Saves pictures as PNG files, which is a newer universal file format for use in Web graphics.

- **Tagged Image File Format:** Saves pictures as TIF files, which are often used in desktop publishing programs.

- **Targa:** Saves pictures as TGA files, called Truevision Targa files.

- **Windows Bitmaps:** Saves pictures as BMP files, which is the file format used by Windows to create background images for your desktop.

To save your picture under a different name or file format:

1. **Choose File⇨Save As.**

   The Save As dialog box appears.

2. **Type a new name for your file in the File Name box.**

3. **(Optional) Click in the Save as Type list box and choose a file format to use, such as GIF or Windows Bitmap.**

4. **Click Save.**

Previewing and Printing Your Masterpiece

Before wasting time and valuable ink or toner printing out your pictures, look at them first through the Print Preview feature.

Putting Print Preview to work

Print Preview lets you see how your picture looks so you can see whether the images are spaced too far apart or too far away from the margins of the page.

To use the Print Preview feature:

1. **Choose File⇨Print Preview.**

   PhotoDraw shows what your picture will look like when printed, and displays the cursor as a magnifying glass.

2. **Move the mouse cursor (the magnifying glass) over the document and click to view your document in its full size.**

3. **Click Close.**

If you like what you see, skip Step 3 and start printing right away by clicking Print.

Defining your pages

Before you actually print your pictures, you may want to define your page margins and paper size. To define your page margins and paper size:

1. **Choose File⇨Picture Setup.**

   The Picture Setup dialog box appears, as shown in Figure 26-9.

2. **Click the Picture Size list box and choose a size to use, such as Business Card or Banner.**

3. **Click the Width and Height text boxes and type a width and height for your picture.**

4. **Click the Color list box and choose a background color for your picture.**

5. **Click the Portrait or Landscape option button in the Orientation group.**

6. **Click OK.**

   After defining the paper you're going to use, you're ready to actually print your PhotoDraw pictures for the whole world (or at least anyone standing near the printer) to see.

Printing your work

It's no fun creating a picture if you can't show it to someone else, either as a printed poster or sign. To print your PhotoDraw pictures:

1. **Choose File⇨Print or press Ctrl+P.**

   The Print dialog box appears.

2. Click in the <u>N</u>ame list box and choose the printer to use.

3. Click in the Number of <u>C</u>opies box and type the number of copies you want.

4. Click in the Print <u>Q</u>uality list box and choose a resolution (such as 150 dpi).

5. Click in the Print <u>W</u>hat list box and choose what you want to print, such as your Document or any comments that you've added to the document.

6. Click in the Por<u>t</u>rait or Lan<u>d</u>scape option buttons in the Orientation group.

7. Click OK.

When you click the Print button on the Standard toolbar, PhotoDraw starts printing your picture immediately, bypassing the Print dialog box.

Part IX
The Part of Tens

The 5th Wave   By Rich Tennant

In this part . . .

After spending your valuable time figuring out the many parts of Microsoft Office 2000, flip through this part of the book to find out the secret shortcuts and hints that can make any of the programs in Microsoft Office 2000 even easier and more effective for your personal or business use.

Just make sure that your family, coworkers, or boss don't catch you reading this part of the book. They may stop thinking that you're a Office 2000 super-guru and realize you're just an ordinary person with a really great book instead.

Then again, why not buy extra copies of this book and give them to your friends, coworkers, and boss so they'll be able to figure out how to use Office 2000 on their own and leave you with enough time to actually do some useful work.

Chapter 27

Ten Common Microsoft Office 2000 Keystrokes

- -

- -

*M*icrosoft Office 2000 consists of several different programs crammed into one convenient package. As a result, the pull-down menus, keystroke commands, and dialog boxes vary from one program to another. Oftentimes you may try a command that works in Word but doesn't work quite the same way in PowerPoint or Access.

Don't worry — blame Microsoft for the inconsistency. Fortunately, each incarnation of Microsoft Office gradually brings the various bundled programs closer together so they work as a unified whole. Although you may need to wait for Microsoft to release Microsoft Office 2001 for further integration among the various programs, check out this chapter for common keystrokes that already work in every Microsoft Office 2000 program.

Creating a New File (Ctrl+N)

Anytime you want to create a new file in any Microsoft Office 2000 program, just press Ctrl+N or click the New button on the Standard toolbar. Office 2000 cheerfully responds by creating an empty file that you can use to start creating anything your heart desires. (Pressing Ctrl+N in Microsoft Outlook can create anything from a new e-mail message to a contact or appointment, depending on what you happen to be doing at the time.)

Opening an Existing File (Ctrl+O)

You often need to open an existing file in order to make changes to it. Whenever you want to open a file, press Ctrl+O or click the Open button on the Standard toolbar to see an Open dialog box, where you can choose the specific file you want to open.

By default, Microsoft Office 2000 looks for existing files in the My Documents folder, which is usually C:\My Documents. Rather than lump all your files in the My Documents folder, create separate subfolders within the My Documents folder. That way, you can prevent files belonging to different projects or programs from getting mixed up.

To create a new folder:

1. **Click the Start button on the Windows taskbar and then choose** **Programs**⇨**Windows Explorer.**

   The Windows Explorer program appears.

2. **Click the My Documents folder.**

3. **Choose File**⇨**New**⇨**Folder.**

   Windows Explorer creates a new folder unimaginatively called New Folder.

4. **Type a new name for your folder and press Enter.**

By default, Word, Excel, PowerPoint, PhotoDraw, and Access always look in the C:\My Documents folder whenever you try to open an existing file. (FrontPage looks in C:\My Webs by default.) To define a different folder for your Office 2000 programs to look in first:

1. **Choose Tools**⇨**Options.**

   An Options dialog box appears.

2. **Click one of the following tabs:**

   If you're using Access, Excel, or Publisher, click the General tab.

   If you're using PowerPoint, click the Save tab.

   If you're using PhotoDraw or Word, click the File Locations tab.

3. **If you're using Excel or PowerPoint, click the <u>D</u>efault File Location text box and type a new directory name (such as C:\My Documents\Useless Work).**

   If you're using Access, click the Default Database Folder text box and type a new directory name (such as C:\My Documents\Secrets).

   If you're using Word, click Documents in the File Types box, click Modify, and then click a folder.

   If you're using Publisher, click Publications in the File Types box, click Modify, and then click a folder.

   If you're using PhotoDraw, click the Look for My Pictures in This Directory text box and type a new directory name (such as C:\My Documents\Stuff).

4. **Click OK.**

Saving Your Work (Ctrl+S)

Save your work often — every ten minutes is good. That way, if the power suddenly goes out, you won't lose all the work you did over the past five hours. Whenever you take a break or walk away from your computer, press Ctrl+S or click the Save button on the Standard toolbar to save your work. This advice can be especially easy to remember after you lose an entire day's work because you forgot to save it to a disk.

Microsoft Word and PowerPoint provide a special AutoRecover feature that automatically saves your work after a specified amount of time. To turn on the AutoRecover feature and specify how often you want to save your work automatically:

1. **Choose <u>T</u>ools⇨<u>O</u>ptions.**

   The Options dialog box appears.

2. **Click the Save tab.**

3. **Click the <u>S</u>ave AutoRecover Info Every check box.**

4. **Click the up or down arrow in the <u>M</u>inutes box to specify how often Word or PowerPoint should save your file.**

5. **Click OK.**

Access 2000 automatically saves your data whether you like it or not, so it doesn't offer an AutoRecover feature that you can change or disable.

Printing Your Work (Ctrl+P)

No matter how often magazines tout the myth of the paperless office, your printer is one of the most important parts of your entire computer system. Whenever you want to print your files, just press Ctrl+P to make the Print dialog box appear. Specify which pages you want to print and how many copies you want, and then click the OK button.

If you're in a hurry to print, just click the Print button on the Standard toolbar. Clicking the Print button automatically sends your entire file to the printer, so make sure that you really do want to print every single page of that document.

Cutting (Ctrl+X), Copying (Ctrl+C), and Pasting (Ctrl+V)

If you want to move data from one place to another, cut and paste the data. If you want your data to appear in the original place as well as another place, copy and paste the data. To cut or copy data to another place:

1. **Select the data that you want to cut or copy.**

2. **Press Ctrl+X or click the Cut button on the Standard toolbar to cut the data. Press Ctrl+C or click the Copy button on the Standard toolbar to copy the data.**

3. **Move the cursor to the location where you want the data to appear.**

4. **Press Ctrl+V or click the Paste button on the Standard toolbar.**

When you cut or copy anything from within any Microsoft Office 2000 program, the cut or copied object gets stored on the Office Clipboard, which can hold up to twelve items at a time. To view the Office Clipboard within Access, Excel, PowerPoint, or Word, choose View➪Toolbars➪Clipboard.

Finding a Word or Phrase (Ctrl+F)

Anytime you want to look for a specific word or number, you can use the fabulous Find command by pressing Ctrl+F. When you use the Find command, Microsoft Office 2000 presents you with the Find dialog box, which gives you the following options:

✔ **Match case:** If you want to find *Bill* but don't want to waste time looking for *bill*.

✔ **Find whole words only:** If you want to find *cat* but not words like *catastrophic* and *catatonic*.

✔ **Use wildcards:** If you want to find parts of a sequence. For example, if you want to find all words that begin with *fail,* tell Microsoft Office 2000 to search for *fail**. (This option is only available in Word.)

✔ **Sounds like:** If you know what you want to find but don't know how to spell it, such as searching for *elefant* when you really want *elephant*. (This option is only available in Word.)

✔ **Find all word forms:** If you want to find all uses of a word, such as *sing, singing,* and *sings*. (This option is only available in Word.)

Finding and Replacing a Word or Phrase (Ctrl+H)

The Find and Replace command lets you look for a word or number and replace it with a different word or number. For example, you may misspell your boss's name as *Frank the Jerk* when his real title should be *Frank the Imbecile*. While you could manually search for *Frank the Jerk* and replace it with *Frank the Imbecile*, it's so much easier to leave mindless, tedious, boring tasks to your computer and Microsoft Office 2000.

Like the Find command — refer to the section "Finding a Word or Phrase (Ctrl+F)" — the Find and Replace command lets you search for specific strings. Unlike the Find command, the Find and Replace command can also automatically replace any text or numbers it finds with a new string of text or numbers.

When you press Ctrl+H to use the Find and Replace command, the Find and Replace dialog box appears and offers two buttons: Replace and Replace All.

The Replace button lets you review each string Microsoft Office 2000 finds so you can make sure that you really want to replace the string. The Replace All button does not give you the chance to review each string found; if you click the Replace All button, you may find Microsoft Office 2000 replacing words that you didn't really want to replace, so be careful.

Checking Your Spelling (F7)

Unfortunately, poor spelling can make even the most brilliantly written paper look amateurish and of low quality. To prevent people from perceiving your writing as moronic, check your spelling before letting anyone see your files.

To check your spelling in a Microsoft Office 2000 document, press F7 or click the Spelling button on the Standard toolbar.

If you don't want Office 2000 to spell-check your entire file, select the text you want to spell-check and then press F7.

Using Undo (Ctrl+Z) and Redo (Ctrl+Y)

Microsoft Office 2000 is a fairly forgiving chunk of software. If you make a mistake at any time, you can undo your last action by clicking the Undo button on the Standard toolbar or by pressing Ctrl+Z.

Not all actions can be undone. When you're about to do something that Microsoft Office 2000 can't undo, a dialog box pops up to warn you that your next action is irreversible.

If you made a mistake undoing an action, click the Redo button on the Standard toolbar or press Ctrl+Y to redo your last undone action.

If you click the down arrow next to the Undo or Redo buttons on the Standard toolbar, a drop-down list of your past actions appears. To undo or redo multiple actions, drag the mouse to highlight the actions you want and click the left mouse button.

Chapter 28

Ten Tips for Using Microsoft Office 2000

. . . .

In This Chapter

▶ Using macros

▶ Keeping up your guard against macro viruses

▶ Clicking the right mouse, when in doubt

▶ Using the What's This? feature

▶ Encrypting your files

▶ Shredding your files

▶ Zooming to avoid eye strain

▶ Making your buttons bigger

▶ Making backup copies

▶ Using Pocket Office

. . . .

*M*icrosoft Office 2000 contains so many features and commands that you should take some time to browse the following tips. See how quickly you can turn yourself from a computer novice to a Office 2000 guru (just as long as you keep a copy of this book with you at all times).

Taking Shortcuts with Macros

While many people dream of the day when they can give orders to their computer by talking to it, the current reality is that you still need to type on a keyboard if you hope to use your computer at all. Because most people would rather avoid typing, Microsoft Office 2000 offers a solution called macros.

Macros don't eliminate typing entirely, but they can reduce the number of keys you need to press to get something done. Basically, a macro enables you to "record" keystrokes that you type. After you record the keystrokes in a macro, whenever you need to use those exact same keystrokes again, you can tell Microsoft Office 2000 to "play back" your recorded keystrokes.

For example, suppose you find yourself typing the name of your company, The Mississippi Mudflat Corporation, over and over again. You can instead type it once and save it as a macro. Then when you need the company name to appear in your document, Office 2000 can automatically type *The Mississippi Mudflat Corporation* for you.

You can create and run macros within Word, Excel, FrontPage, and PowerPoint. Publisher and PhotoDraw don't offer macros.

Access, Outlook, and FrontPage offer macros, but creating macros in all three programs require learning the Visual Basic for Applications (VBA) programming language, which is something most people probably don't want to study.

Recording macros in Word

To record a macro in Word, follow these steps:

1. **Choose Tools⇨Macro⇨Record New Macro.**

   A Record Macro dialog box appears, as shown in Figure 28-1.

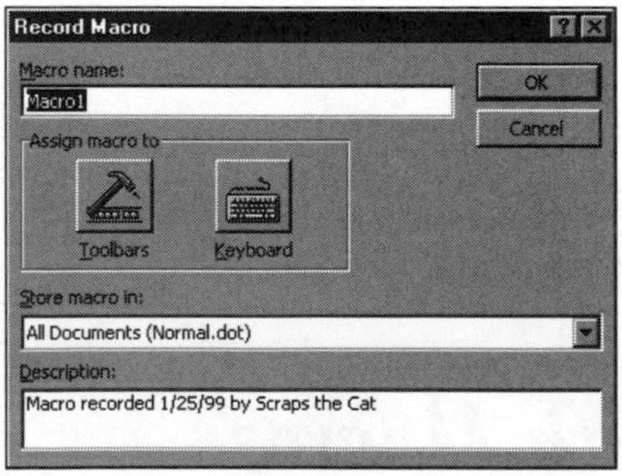

Figure 28-1:
The Record
Macro
dialog box.

2. **Type a name for your macro in the Macro Name box.**
3. **Click the Keyboard button.**

   A Customize Keyboard dialog box appears, as shown in Figure 28-2.

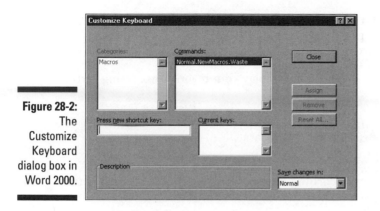

Figure 28-2:
The
Customize
Keyboard
dialog box in
Word 2000.

4. **Press the keystroke that you want to represent your macro (such as Alt+F12).**

5. **Click the Assign button.**

6. **Click the Close button.**

   A Stop Recording toolbar appears, as shown in Figure 28-3.

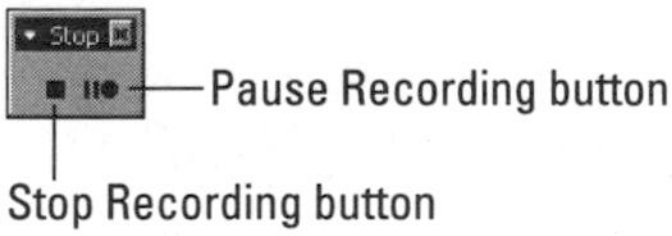

Figure 28-3:
The Stop
Recording
toolbar in
Word 2000.

Pause Recording button

Stop Recording button

7. **Press the keystrokes that you want to record in your macro.**

8. **Click the Stop Recording button when you finish recording the keystokes.**

To run your macro, press the keystroke combination that you chose in Step 4.

Recording macros in Excel

To record a macro in Excel, follow these steps:

1. **Choose Tools⇨Macro⇨Record New Macro.**

   A Record Macro dialog box appears.

2. **Type a name for your macro in the <u>M</u>acro name box.**

3. **Type a letter in the Shortcut <u>K</u>ey box (the one that has Ctrl+ to the left).**

   For example, if you want to replay your macro by pressing Ctrl+W, type **W** in the Shortcut Key box.

4. **Click OK.**

   A Stop Recording toolbar appears.

5. **Press the keystrokes that you want to record in your macro.**

6. **Click the Stop Recording button when you finish recording the keystokes.**

To run a macro, press the keystroke combination that you chose in Step 3.

Recording macros in PowerPoint

To record a macro in PowerPoint 2000, follow these steps:

1. **Choose <u>T</u>ools⇨<u>M</u>acro⇨<u>R</u>ecord New Macro.**

   A Record Macro dialog box appears.

2. **Type a name for your macro in the <u>M</u>acro Name box.**

3. **Click OK.**

   A Stop Recording toolbar appears. (Refer to Figure 28-3.)

4. **Press the keystrokes that you want to record in your macro.**

5. **Click the Stop Recording button when you finish recording the keystokes.**

To run a macro in PowerPoint, follow these steps:

1. **Choose <u>T</u>ool⇨<u>M</u>acro⇨<u>M</u>acros (or press Alt+F8).**

   A macro dialog box appears.

2. **Click the macro name that you want to run.**

3. **Click <u>R</u>un.**

Watching Out for Macro Viruses

Office 2000 gives you two ways to create a macro. The simplest way, as explained in the previous section, is to record your keystrokes and then play them back when you need them. The harder way to create a macro is to use the Microsoft special macro programming language (called Visual Basic for Applications or VBA) to create more powerful and complicated macros.

If the idea of writing your own programs gets you excited, you may be interested in buying the Microsoft special Developer Edition of Microsoft Office 2000. This Developer Edition enables you to use Microsoft Office 2000 to create your own programs by using the Visual Basic language.

While the Microsoft macro programming language gives you the power to create macros of your own, it has also given mischievous programmers the opportunity to write computer viruses.

This new breed of computer viruses, dubbed *macro viruses,* can infect Word documents or Excel worksheets. When you give a copy of a document or worksheet that contains a virus to another person, you risk passing along the macro virus at the same time.

So how can you tell if a macro virus has already infected your Word documents or Excel worksheets? You can't until the macro virus has already attacked your computer and revealed itself or until you run an antivirus program such as McAfee's VirusScan (www.mcafee.com) or Symantec's Norton AntiVirus (www.symantec.com) that can detect and remove macro viruses.

If you want to protect yourself against macro viruses, buy a separate antivirus program and use it regularly. Macro viruses are the fastest-growing threat among computer viruses, so get an antivirus program now before it's too late.

The most common macro viruses infect Word documents. The second most common macro viruses infect Excel worksheets. Macro viruses that attack PowerPoint or Access files have been created, but, so far, none have been able to spread. But make sure you buy an antivirus program and keep it updated regularly, just in case someone eventually figures out how to write PowerPoint or Access macro viruses along with Word and Excel macro viruses.

When in Doubt, Click the Right Mouse Button

When you want to rename, edit, or modify anything in Office 2000, use the handy right mouse button pop-up menu. To use this pop-up menu, follow these steps:

1. **Place the mouse cursor over the item you want to edit.**

2. **Click the right mouse button.**

   The right mouse button pop-up menu appears.

3. **Click a command in the pop-up menu.**

Using the What's This? Feature

Choosing commands from the Microsoft Office pull-down menus can be clumsy, slow, and annoying. To solve this problem, Microsoft put the most commonly used commands on toolbars that appear at the top of the screen.

Unfortunately, toolbars often display cryptic buttons that could confuse even veteran Egyptian hieroglyphic experts. Rather than guess what these toolbar buttons do or waste time experimenting, you can use the Microsoft handy What's This? feature, which offers you a quick explanation of any toolbar button that confuses you.

To use the What's This? feature, follow these steps:

1. **Choose Help⇨What's This?**

   The mouse cursor turns into an arrow with a question mark next to it.

2. **Click a toolbar button that confuses you.**

   A window appears, briefly explaining what commands the button represents.

3. **Click anywhere to remove the explanation from the screen.**

Encrypting Your Files

In case you want to keep your Office 2000 documents private, consider buying an encryption program, which can scramble your data so that no one else but you (and anyone else who steals or figures out your password) can read it.

Two popular encryption programs are Pretty Good Privacy (often called PGP and available from www.mcafee.com) and Norton's Your Eyes Only (www.symantec.com). Both of these programs allow you to encrypt individual files, entire folders, or complete hard disks so only you can access your data (unless you forget your password).

In case you're really paranoid about people peeking at your data, try a bizarre encryption method known as stenography, which can hide data inside sound or graphic files. That way you can transfer innocent looking pictures or sounds, and nobody can tell if you're hiding any data inside those graphic or sound files.

No matter what encryption program you use, just remember that if you pick a simple password, people may be able to guess your password, which makes encryption as effective as locking a bank vault but taping the combination to the front of the door.

Shredding Your Files

Encryption is one way to protect your data. However, when you encrypt a file, you usually wind up with two separate files: the newly encrypted file and the original unencrypted file. If you erase the original unencrypted file, someone can undelete that file and see your documents while avoiding your encrypted files altogether.

The problem stems from the way computers delete files. When you tell your computer to delete a file, it actually plays a trick on you. Instead of physically erasing the file, the computer simply pretends the file doesn't exist. That's why someone can use a utility program, such as The Norton Utilities, and unerase a file that you may have erased several hours, days, weeks, or even months ago.

So if you want to delete a file, don't use the file deletion feature of Windows 98/95/NT. Instead, get a special file shredding program instead. These file shredding programs not only delete a file, but they overwrite that file several times with random bits of data. That way, if someone tries to unerase that file at a later date, all they see is gibberish.

Two popular file shredding programs are Shredder (www.shredder.com) and Nuts & Bolts (www.mcafee.com), which comes with a special file shredding program among its many other features.

If you accidentally delete a file by using a file shredding program, you can never retrieve that file again, so be careful!

Zooming to Avoid Eye Strain

To cram as much text on-screen as possible, Microsoft Office 2000 displays everything in a tiny font size. If you'd rather not strain your eyes, you can zoom in on your screen, blowing up your text so the letters are easier to see.

FrontPage and Outlook don't offer a Zoom feature.

To zoom in (expand) or zoom out (shrink) the appearance of text on-screen:

1. **Choose <u>V</u>iew➪<u>Z</u>oom. (In PhotoDraw, the command is <u>V</u>iew➪Pan and Zoo<u>m</u>.)**

2. **Choose a magnification (such as 200% or 25%) and then click OK. (In Publisher, you don't have to click OK.)**

   Your document appears at the desired magnification for your viewing pleasure.

If you own a mouse with a wheel stuck between the two buttons (such as the Microsoft IntelliMouse), you have another way to zoom in and out. Just hold down the Ctrl key and roll the wheel back and forth.

Enlarging Your Buttons

The Microsoft Office 2000 toolbar buttons can be not only cryptic but hard to even see. Rather than squint and ruin your eyesight, you can enlarge the buttons. To make your toolbar buttons larger in Word, Excel, PowerPoint, Outlook, FrontPage, or Access, follow these steps:

1. **Choose <u>T</u>ools➪<u>C</u>ustomize.**

   The Customize dialog box appears.

2. **Click the <u>O</u>ptions tab.**

3. **Check the <u>L</u>arge icons check box.**

   Microsoft Office 2000 displays your buttons to make them look as if radiation mutated them to three times their normal size.

4. **Click Close.**

To make your toolbar buttons larger in Publisher, follow these steps:

1. **Choose <u>V</u>iew➪<u>T</u>oolbars➪<u>O</u>ptions.**

   The Toolbar Options dialog box appears.

2. **Check the <u>L</u>arge icons check box.**

   Publisher expands your buttons so they gobble up a good chunk of the screen.

3. **Click OK.**

To make your toolbar buttons larger in PhotoDraw, follow these steps:

1. **Choose Tools⇨Customize.**

   The Customize dialog box appears.

2. **Click the Toolbars tab.**

3. **Check the Large icons check box.**

   PhotoDraw blows up your buttons to make them look completely unnatural.

4. **Click OK.**

If you get sick of seeing large buttons staring back at you while you work, just repeat the preceding steps and clear the check mark from the Large icons check box to return the buttons to their normal size.

Backing Up Your Files

You should always keep extra copies of your files in case you accidentally mess up a file by mistake. If you happen to lose or delete a file by mistake, a backup copy of your files enables you to continue working even though your original file may be history.

The simplest way (which is also the easiest to forget) to make backup copies is to do it yourself by using the Windows Explorer to copy files from your hard disk to a floppy disk (or vice versa). Because this method requires conscious effort on your part, it's also the least likely method to rely on when disaster strikes.

As an alternative, get a backup program and a backup device such as a tape drive, ZIP drive, or similar mass storage device. If you can manage to get your backup program configured properly (good luck), the backup program can automatically back up your entire hard disk to your backup drive without any extra effort on your part.

As another way to back up files automatically, Word and Excel have a special backup feature that creates a backup copy of your files each time you save a file. Unfortunately using the Word or Excel backup feature won't protect you in case your entire hard disk crashes, so you may still need to store your backup copies on a floppy disk and keep them separate from your computer.

To turn on this special backup feature in Word or Excel, follow these steps:

1. **Choose File⇨Save As.**

   The Save As dialog box appears.

2. **Click the Tools button.**

   A drop-down list appears.

3. **Click General Options.**

   A Save dialog box appears.

4. **Check the Always Create Backup check box.**

5. **Click OK.**

When you save a file with the backup feature turned on, your backup file has a name like Backup of. For example, if you saved a file called Ransom note, your backup copy would have a name of Backup copy of Ransom note and have a file extension of .WBK (for Word documents) or .XLK (for Excel worksheets).

Using Pocket Office

Laptop computers continue to drop in price and weight, yet increase in power. Some of the latest laptop computers weigh less than three pounds and have enough memory and processing power to run a full-blown copy of Microsoft Office 2000.

But rather than lug a laptop computer around the country, many people are opting for smaller, cheaper, and lighter handheld computers that run a slightly different operating system called Windows CE.

Windows CE comes with a miniature version of Microsoft Office dubbed Pocket Office that includes Pocket Word, Pocket Excel, Pocket PowerPoint, and Pocket Access. (Pocket Access is only available on handheld computers running Windows CE version 2.11.)

These pocket versions of Microsoft Office provide fewer features than the complete Microsoft Office 2000 suite. But Pocket Office can share data with your Microsoft Office 2000 programs, making it perfect for taking your data on the road and viewing or editing it on a handheld computer.

So if you travel frequently but dread breaking your back carrying a heavy and expensive laptop computer, consider buying a handheld Windows CE computer and using Pocket Office instead. For more information about Windows CE, pick up a copy of *Windows CE2 For Dummies,* by Jinjer L. Simon (IDG Books Worldwide, Inc.).

Index

• Q •

Dummies Books™
Bestsellers on Every Topic!

GENERAL INTEREST TITLES

BUSINESS & PERSONAL FINANCE

Accounting For Dummies®	John A. Tracy, CPA	0-7645-5014-4	$19.99 US/$27.99 CAN
Business Plans For Dummies®	Paul Tiffany, Ph.D. & Steven D. Peterson, Ph.D.	1-56884-868-4	$19.99 US/$27.99 CAN
Business Writing For Dummies®	Sheryl Lindsell-Roberts	0-7645-5134-5	$16.99 US/$27.99 CAN
Consulting For Dummies®	Bob Nelson & Peter Economy	0-7645-5034-9	$19.99 US/$27.99 CAN
Customer Service For Dummies®, 2nd Edition	Karen Leland & Keith Bailey	0-7645-5209-0	$19.99 US/$27.99 CAN
Franchising For Dummies®	Dave Thomas & Michael Seid	0-7645-5160-4	$19.99 US/$27.99 CAN
Getting Results For Dummies®	Mark H. McCormack	0-7645-5205-8	$19.99 US/$27.99 CAN
Home Buying For Dummies®	Eric Tyson, MBA & Ray Brown	1-56884-385-2	$16.99 US/$24.99 CAN
House Selling For Dummies®	Eric Tyson, MBA & Ray Brown	0-7645-5038-1	$16.99 US/$24.99 CAN
Human Resources Kit For Dummies®	Max Messmer	0-7645-5131-0	$19.99 US/$27.99 CAN
Investing For Dummies®, 2nd Edition	Eric Tyson, MBA	0-7645-5162-0	$19.99 US/$27.99 CAN
Law For Dummies®	John Ventura	1-56884-860-9	$19.99 US/$27.99 CAN
Leadership For Dummies®	Marshall Loeb & Steven Kindel	0-7645-5176-0	$19.99 US/$27.99 CAN
Managing For Dummies®	Bob Nelson & Peter Economy	1-56884-858-7	$19.99 US/$27.99 CAN
Marketing For Dummies®	Alexander Hiam	1-56884-699-1	$19.99 US/$27.99 CAN
Mutual Funds For Dummies®, 2nd Edition	Eric Tyson, MBA	0-7645-5112-4	$19.99 US/$27.99 CAN
Negotiating For Dummies®	Michael C. Donaldson & Mimi Donaldson	1-56884-867-6	$19.99 US/$27.99 CAN
Personal Finance For Dummies®, 3rd Edition	Eric Tyson, MBA	0-7645-5231-7	$19.99 US/$27.99 CAN
Personal Finance For Dummies® For Canadians, 2nd Edition	Eric Tyson, MBA & Tony Martin	0-7645-5123-X	$19.99 US/$27.99 CAN
Public Speaking For Dummies®	Malcolm Kushner	0-7645-5159-0	$16.99 US/$24.99 CAN
Sales Closing For Dummies®	Tom Hopkins	0-7645-5063-2	$14.99 US/$21.99 CAN
Sales Prospecting For Dummies®	Tom Hopkins	0-7645-5066-7	$14.99 US/$21.99 CAN
Selling For Dummies®	Tom Hopkins	1-56884-389-5	$16.99 US/$24.99 CAN
Small Business For Dummies®	Eric Tyson, MBA & Jim Schell	0-7645-5094-2	$19.99 US/$27.99 CAN
Small Business Kit For Dummies®	Richard D. Harroch	0-7645-5093-4	$24.99 US/$34.99 CAN
Taxes 2001 For Dummies®	Eric Tyson & David J. Silverman	0-7645-5306-2	$15.99 US/$23.99 CAN
Time Management For Dummies®, 2nd Edition	Jeffrey J. Mayer	0-7645-5145-0	$19.99 US/$27.99 CAN
Writing Business Letters For Dummies®	Sheryl Lindsell-Roberts	0-7645-5207-4	$16.99 US/$24.99 CAN

TECHNOLOGY TITLES

INTERNET/ONLINE

America Online® For Dummies®, 6th Edition	John Kaufeld	0-7645-0670-6	$19.99 US/$27.99 CAN
Banking Online Dummies®	Paul Murphy	0-7645-0458-4	$24.99 US/$34.99 CAN
eBay™ For Dummies®, 2nd Edition	Marcia Collier, Roland Woerner, & Stephanie Becker	0-7645-0761-3	$19.99 US/$27.99 CAN
eMail For Dummies®, 2nd Edition	John R. Levine, Carol Baroudi, & Arnold Reinhold	0-7645-0131-3	$24.99 US/$34.99 CAN
Genealogy Online For Dummies®, 2nd Edition	Matthew L. Helm & April Leah Helm	0-7645-0543-2	$24.99 US/$34.99 CAN
Internet Directory For Dummies®, 3rd Edition	Brad Hill	0-7645-0558-2	$24.99 US/$34.99 CAN
Internet Auctions For Dummies®	Greg Holden	0-7645-0578-9	$24.99 US/$34.99 CAN
Internet Explorer 5.5 For Windows® For Dummies®	Doug Lowe	0-7645-0738-9	$19.99 US/$28.99 CAN
Researching Online For Dummies®, 2nd Edition	Mary Ellen Bates & Reva Basch	0-7645-0546-7	$24.99 US/$34.99 CAN
Job Searching Online For Dummies®	Pam Dixon	0-7645-0673-0	$24.99 US/$34.99 CAN
Investing Online For Dummies®, 3rd Edition	Kathleen Sindell, Ph.D.	0-7645-0725-7	$24.99 US/$34.99 CAN
Travel Planning Online For Dummies®, 2nd Edition	Noah Vadnai	0-7645-0438-X	$24.99 US/$34.99 CAN
Internet Searching For Dummies®	Brad Hill	0-7645-0478-9	$24.99 US/$34.99 CAN
Yahoo!® For Dummies®, 2nd Edition	Brad Hill	0-7645-0762-1	$19.99 US/$27.99 CAN
The Internet For Dummies®, 7th Edition	John R. Levine, Carol Baroudi, & Arnold Reinhold	0-7645-0674-9	$19.99 US/$27.99 CAN

OPERATING SYSTEMS

DOS For Dummies®, 3rd Edition	Dan Gookin	0-7645-0361-8	$19.99 US/$27.99 CAN
GNOME For Linux® For Dummies®	David B. Busch	0-7645-0650-1	$24.99 US/$37.99 CAN
LINUX® For Dummies®, 2nd Edition	John Hall, Craig Witherspoon, & Coletta Witherspoon	0-7645-0421-5	$24.99 US/$34.99 CAN
Mac® OS 9 For Dummies®	Bob LeVitus	0-7645-0652-8	$19.99 US/$28.99 CAN
Red Hat® Linux® For Dummies®	Jon "maddog" Hall, Paul Sery	0-7645-0663-3	$24.99 US/$37.99 CAN
Small Business Windows® 98 For Dummies®	Stephen Nelson	0-7645-0425-8	$24.99 US/$34.99 CAN
UNIX® For Dummies®, 4th Edition	John R. Levine & Margaret Levine Young	0-7645-0419-3	$19.99 US/$27.99 CAN
Windows® 95 For Dummies®, 2nd Edition	Andy Rathbone	0-7645-0180-1	$19.99 US/$27.99 CAN
Windows® 98 For Dummies®	Andy Rathbone	0-7645-0261-1	$19.99 US/$27.99 CAN
Windows® 2000 For Dummies®	Andy Rathbone	0-7645-0641-2	$19.99 US/$27.99 CAN
Windows® 2000 Server For Dummies®	Ed Tittel	0-7645-0341-3	$24.99 US/$37.99 CAN
Windows® ME Millennium Edition For Dummies®	Andy Rathbone	0-7645-0735-4	$19.99 US/$27.99 CAN

Dummies Books™
Bestsellers on Every Topic!

 ## GENERAL INTEREST TITLES

FOOD & BEVERAGE/ENTERTAINING

Title	Author	ISBN	Price
Bartending For Dummies®	Ray Foley	0-7645-5051-9	$14.99 US/$21.99 CAN
Cooking For Dummies®, 2nd Edition	Bryan Miller & Marie Rama	0-7645-5250-3	$19.99 US/$27.99 CAN
Entertaining For Dummies®	Suzanne Williamson with Linda Smith	0-7645-5027-6	$19.99 US/$27.99 CAN
Gourmet Cooking For Dummies®	Charlie Trotter	0-7645-5029-2	$19.99 US/$27.99 CAN
Grilling For Dummies®	Marie Rama & John Mariani	0-7645-5076-4	$19.99 US/$27.99 CAN
Italian Cooking For Dummies®	Cesare Casella & Jack Bishop	0-7645-5098-5	$19.99 US/$27.99 CAN
Mexican Cooking For Dummies®	Mary Sue Miliken & Susan Feniger	0-7645-5169-8	$19.99 US/$27.99 CAN
Quick & Healthy Cooking For Dummies®	Lynn Fischer	0-7645-5214-7	$19.99 US/$27.99 CAN
Wine For Dummies®, 2nd Edition	Ed McCarthy & Mary Ewing-Mulligan	0-7645-5114-0	$19.99 US/$27.99 CAN
Chinese Cooking For Dummies®	Martin Yan	0-7645-5247-3	$19.99 US/$27.99 CAN
Etiquette For Dummies®	Sue Fox	0-7645-5170-1	$19.99 US/$27.99 CAN

SPORTS

Baseball For Dummies®, 2nd Edition	Joe Morgan with Richard Lally	0-7645-5234-1	$19.99 US/$27.99 CAN
Golf For Dummies®, 2nd Edition	Gary McCord	0-7645-5146-9	$19.99 US/$27.99 CAN
Fly Fishing For Dummies®	Peter Kaminsky	0-7645-5073-X	$19.99 US/$27.99 CAN
Football For Dummies®	Howie Long with John Czarnecki	0-7645-5054-3	$19.99 US/$27.99 CAN
Hockey For Dummies®	John Davidson with John Steinbreder	0-7645-5045-4	$19.99 US/$27.99 CAN
NASCAR For Dummies®	Mark Martin	0-7645-5219-8	$19.99 US/$27.99 CAN
Tennis For Dummies®	Patrick McEnroe with Peter Bodo	0-7645-5087-X	$19.99 US/$27.99 CAN
Soccer For Dummies®	U.S. Soccer Federation & Michael Lewiss	0-7645-5229-5	$19.99 US/$27.99 CAN

HOME & GARDEN

Annuals For Dummies®	Bill Marken & NGA	0-7645-5056-X	$16.99 US/$24.99 CAN
Container Gardening For Dummies®	Bill Marken & NGA	0-7645-5057-8	$16.99 US/$24.99 CAN
Decks & Patios For Dummies®	Robert J. Beckstrom & NGA	0-7645-5075-6	$16.99 US/$24.99 CAN
Flowering Bulbs For Dummies®	Judy Glattstein & NGA	0-7645-5103-5	$16.99 US/$24.99 CAN
Gardening For Dummies®, 2nd Edition	Michael MacCaskey & NGA	0-7645-5130-2	$16.99 US/$24.99 CAN
Herb Gardening For Dummies®	NGA	0-7645-5200-7	$16.99 US/$24.99 CAN
Home Improvement For Dummies®	Gene & Katie Hamilton & the Editors of HouseNet, Inc.	0-7645-5005-5	$19.99 US/$26.99 CAN
Houseplants For Dummies®	Larry Hodgson & NGA	0-7645-5102-7	$16.99 US/$24.99 CAN
Painting and Wallpapering For Dummies®	Gene Hamilton	0-7645-5150-7	$16.99 US/$24.99 CAN
Perennials For Dummies®	Marcia Tatroe & NGA	0-7645-5030-6	$16.99 US/$24.99 CAN
Roses For Dummies®, 2nd Edition	Lance Walheim	0-7645-5202-3	$16.99 US/$24.99 CAN
Trees and Shrubs For Dummies®	Ann Whitman & NGA	0-7645-5203-1	$16.99 US/$24.99 CAN
Vegetable Gardening For Dummies®	Charlie Nardozzi & NGA	0-7645-5129-9	$16.99 US/$24.99 CAN
Home Cooking For Dummies®	Patricia Hart McMillan & Katharine Kaye McMillan	0-7645-5107-8	$19.99 US/$27.99 CAN

TECHNOLOGY TITLES

WEB DESIGN & PUBLISHING

Active Server Pages For Dummies®, 2nd Edition	Bill Hatfield	0-7645-0603-X	$24.99 US/$37.99 CAN
Cold Fusion 4 For Dummies®	Alexis Gutzman	0-7645-0604-8	$24.99 US/$37.99 CAN
Creating Web Pages For Dummies®, 5th Edition	Bud Smith & Arthur Bebak	0-7645-0733-8	$24.99 US/$34.99 CAN
Dreamweaver™ 3 For Dummies®	Janine Warner & Paul Vachier	0-7645-0669-2	$24.99 US/$34.99 CAN
FrontPage® 2000 For Dummies®	Asha Dornfest	0-7645-0423-1	$24.99 US/$34.99 CAN
HTML 4 For Dummies®, 3rd Edition	Ed Tittel & Natanya Dits	0-7645-0572-6	$24.99 US/$34.99 CAN
Java™ For Dummies®, 3rd Edition	Aaron E. Walsh	0-7645-0417-7	$24.99 US/$34.99 CAN
PageMill™ 2 For Dummies®	Deke McClelland & John San Filippo	0-7645-0028-7	$24.99 US/$34.99 CAN
XML™ For Dummies®	Ed Tittel	0-7645-0692-7	$24.99 US/$37.99 CAN
Javascript For Dummies®, 3rd Edition	Emily Vander Veer	0-7645-0633-1	$24.99 US/$37.99 CAN

DESKTOP PUBLISHING GRAPHICS/MULTIMEDIA

Adobe® In Design™ For Dummies®	Deke McClelland	0-7645-0599-8	$19.99 US/$27.99 CAN
CorelDRAW™ 9 For Dummies®	Deke McClelland	0-7645-0523-8	$19.99 US/$27.99 CAN
Desktop Publishing and Design For Dummies®	Roger C. Parker	1-56884-234-1	$19.99 US/$27.99 CAN
Digital Photography For Dummies®, 3rd Edition	Julie Adair King	0-7645-0646-3	$24.99 US/$37.99 CAN
Microsoft® Publisher 98 For Dummies®	Jim McCarter	0-7645-0395-2	$19.99 US/$27.99 CAN
Visio 2000 For Dummies®	Debbie Walkowski	0-7645-0635-8	$19.99 US/$27.99 CAN
Microsoft® Publisher 2000 For Dummies®	Jim McCarter	0-7645-0525-4	$19.99 US/$27.99 CAN
Windows® Movie Maker For Dummies®	Keith Underdahl	0-7645-0749-1	$19.99 US/$27.99 CAN

Dummies Books™
Bestsellers on Every Topic!

GENERAL INTEREST TITLES

EDUCATION & TEST PREPARATION

Title	Author	ISBN	Price
The ACT For Dummies®	Suzee Vlk	1-56884-387-9	$14.99 US/$21.99 CAN
College Financial Aid For Dummies®	Dr. Herm Davis & Joyce Lain Kennedy	0-7645-5049-7	$19.99 US/$27.99 CAN
College Planning For Dummies®, 2nd Edition	Pat Ordovensky	0-7645-5048-9	$19.99 US/$27.99 CAN
Everyday Math For Dummies®	Charles Seiter, Ph.D.	1-56884-248-1	$14.99 US/$21.99 CAN
The GMAT For Dummies®, 3rd Edition	Suzee Vlk	0-7645-5082-9	$16.99 US/$24.99 CAN
The GRE® For Dummies®, 3rd Edition	Suzee Vlk	0-7645-5083-7	$16.99 US/$24.99 CAN
Politics For Dummies®	Ann DeLaney	1-56884-381-X	$19.99 US/$27.99 CAN
The SAT I For Dummies®, 3rd Edition	Suzee Vlk	0-7645-5044-6	$14.99 US/$21.99 CAN

AUTOMOTIVE

Title	Author	ISBN	Price
Auto Repair For Dummies®	Deanna Sclar	0-7645-5089-6	$19.99 US/$27.99 CAN
Buying A Car For Dummies®	Deanna Sclar	0-7645-5091-8	$16.99 US/$24.99 CAN

LIFESTYLE/SELF-HELP

Title	Author	ISBN	Price
Dating For Dummies®	Dr. Joy Browne	0-7645-5072-1	$19.99 US/$27.99 CAN
Making Marriage Work For Dummies®	Steven Simring, M.D. & Sue Klavans Simring, D.S.W	0-7645-5173-6	$19.99 US/$27.99 CAN
Parenting For Dummies®	Sandra H. Gookin	1-56884-383-6	$16.99 US/$24.99 CAN
Success For Dummies®	Zig Ziglar	0-7645-5061-6	$19.99 US/$27.99 CAN
Weddings For Dummies®	Marcy Blum & Laura Fisher Kaiser	0-7645-5055-1	$19.99 US/$27.99 CAN

TECHNOLOGY TITLES

SUITES

Title	Author	ISBN	Price
Microsoft® Office 2000 For Windows® For Dummies®	Wallace Wang & Roger C. Parker	0-7645-0452-5	$19.99 US/$27.99 CAN
Microsoft® Office 2000 For Windows® For Dummies® Quick Reference	Doug Lowe & Bjoern Hartstvang	0-7645-0453-3	$12.99 US/$17.99 CAN
Microsoft® Office 97 For Windows® For Dummies®	Wallace Wang & Roger C. Parker	0-7645-0050-3	$19.99 US/$27.99 CAN
Microsoft® Office 97 For Windows® For Dummies® Quick Reference	Doug Lowe	0-7645-0062-7	$12.99 US/$17.99 CAN
Microsoft® Office 98 For Macs® For Dummies®	Tom Negrino	0-7645-0229-8	$19.99 US/$27.99 CAN
Microsoft® Office X For Macs For Dummies®	Tom Negrino	0-7645-0702-8	$19.95 US/$27.99 CAN

WORD PROCESSING

Title	Author	ISBN	Price
Word 2000 For Windows® For Dummies® Quick Reference	Peter Weverka	0-7645-0449-5	$12.99 US/$19.99 CAN
Corel® WordPerfect® 8 For Windows® For Dummies®	Margaret Levine Young, David Kay & Jordan Young	0-7645-0186-0	$19.99 US/$27.99 CAN
Word 2000 For Windows® For Dummies®	Dan Gookin	0-7645-0448-7	$19.99 US/$27.99 CAN
Word For Windows® 95 For Dummies®	Dan Gookin	1-56884-932-X	$19.99 US/$27.99 CAN
Word 97 For Windows® For Dummies®	Dan Gookin	0-7645-0052-X	$19.99 US/$27.99 CAN
WordPerfect® 9 For Windows® For Dummies®	Margaret Levine Young	0-7645-0427-4	$19.99 US/$27.99 CAN
WordPerfect® 7 For Windows® 95 For Dummies®	Margaret Levine Young & David Kay	1-56884-949-4	$19.99 US/$27.99 CAN

SPREADSHEET/FINANCE/PROJECT MANAGEMENT

Title	Author	ISBN	Price
Excel For Windows® 95 For Dummies®	Greg Harvey	1-56884-930-3	$19.99 US/$27.99 CAN
Excel 2000 For Windows® For Dummies®	Greg Harvey	0-7645-0446-0	$19.99 US/$27.99 CAN
Excel 2000 For Windows® For Dummies® Quick Reference	John Walkenbach	0-7645-0447-9	$12.99 US/$17.99 CAN
Microsoft® Money 99 For Dummies®	Peter Weverka	0-7645-0433-9	$19.99 US/$27.99 CAN
Microsoft® Project 98 For Dummies®	Martin Doucette	0-7645-0321-9	$24.99 US/$34.99 CAN
Microsoft® Project 2000 For Dummies®	Martin Doucette	0-7645-0517-3	$24.99 US/$37.99 CAN
Microsoft® Money 2000 For Dummies®	Peter Weverka	0-7645-0579-3	$19.99 US/$27.99 CAN
MORE Excel 97 For Windows® For Dummies®	Greg Harvey	0-7645-0138-0	$22.99 US/$32.99 CAN
Quicken® 2000 For Dummies®	Stephen L . Nelson	0-7645-0607-2	$19.99 US/$27.99 CAN
Quicken® 2001 For Dummies®	Stephen L . Nelson	0-7645-0759-1	$19.99 US/$27.99 CAN
Quickbooks® 2000 For Dummies®	Stephen L . Nelson	0-7645-0665-x	$19.99 US/$27.99 CAN

Dummies Books™
Bestsellers on Every Topic!

GENERAL INTEREST TITLES

CAREERS

Cover Letters For Dummies®, 2nd Edition	Joyce Lain Kennedy	0-7645-5224-4	$12.99 US/$17.99 CAN
Cool Careers For Dummies®	Marty Nemko, Paul Edwards, & Sarah Edwards	0-7645-5095-0	$16.99 US/$24.99 CAN
Job Hunting For Dummies®, 2nd Edition	Max Messmer	0-7645-5163-9	$19.99 US/$26.99 CAN
Job Interviews For Dummies®, 2nd Edition	Joyce Lain Kennedy	0-7645-5225-2	$12.99 US/$17.99 CAN
Resumes For Dummies®, 2nd Edition	Joyce Lain Kennedy	0-7645-5113-2	$12.99 US/$17.99 CAN

FITNESS

Fitness Walking For Dummies®	Liz Neporent	0-7645-5192-2	$19.99 US/$27.99 CAN
Fitness For Dummies®, 2nd Edition	Suzanne Schlosberg & Liz Neporent	0-7645-5167-1	$19.99 US/$27.99 CAN
Nutrition For Dummies®, 2nd Edition	Carol Ann Rinzler	0-7645-5180-9	$19.99 US/$27.99 CAN
Running For Dummies®	Florence "Flo-Jo" Griffith Joyner & John Hanc	0-7645-5096-9	$19.99 US/$27.99 CAN

FOREIGN LANGUAGE

Spanish For Dummies®	Susana Wald	0-7645-5194-9	$24.99 US/$34.99 CAN
French For Dummies®	Dodi-Kartrin Schmidt & Michelle W. Willams	0-7645-5193-0	$24.99 US/$34.99 CAN

TECHNOLOGY TITLES

DATABASE

Access 2000 For Windows® For Dummies®	John Kaufeld	0-7645-0444-4	$19.99 US/$27.99 CAN
Access 97 For Windows® For Dummies®	John Kaufeld	0-7645-0048-1	$19.99 US/$27.99 CAN
Access 2000 For Windows For Dummies® Quick Reference	Alison Barrons	0-7645-0445-2	$12.99 US/$17.99 CAN
Approach® 97 For Windows® For Dummies®	Deborah S. Ray & Eric J. Ray	0-7645-0001-5	$19.99 US/$27.99 CAN
Crystal Reports 8 For Dummies®	Douglas J. Wolf	0-7645-0642-0	$24.99 US/$34.99 CAN
Data Warehousing For Dummies®	Alan R. Simon	0-7645-0170-4	$24.99 US/$34.99 CAN
FileMaker® Pro 4 For Dummies®	Tom Maremaa	0-7645-0210-7	$19.99 US/$27.99 CAN

NETWORKING/GROUPWARE

ATM For Dummies®	Cathy Gadecki & Christine Heckart	0-7645-0065-1	$24.99 US/$34.99 CAN
Client/Server Computing For Dummies®, 3rd Edition	Doug Lowe	0-7645-0476-2	$24.99 US/$34.99 CAN
DSL For Dummies®, 2nd Edition	David Angell	0-7645-0715-X	$24.99 US/$35.99 CAN
Lotus Notes® Release 4 For Dummies®	Stephen Londergan & Pat Freeland	1-56884-934-6	$19.99 US/$27.99 CAN
Microsoft® Outlook® 98 For Windows® For Dummies®	Bill Dyszel	0-7645-0393-6	$19.99 US/$28.99 CAN
Microsoft® Outlook® 2000 For Windows® For Dummies®	Bill Dyszel	0-7645-0471-1	$19.99 US/$27.99 CAN
Migrating to Windows® 2000 For Dummies®	Leonard Sterns	0-7645-0459-2	$24.99 US/$37.99 CAN
Networking For Dummies®, 4th Edition	Doug Lowe	0-7645-0498-3	$19.99 US/$27.99 CAN
Networking Home PCs For Dummies®	Kathy Ivens	0-7645-0491-6	$24.99 US/$35.99 CAN
Upgrading & Fixing Networks For Dummies®, 2nd Edition	Bill Camarda	0-7645-0542-4	$29.99 US/$42.99 CAN
TCP/IP For Dummies®, 4th Edition	Candace Leiden & Marshall Wilensky	0-7645-0726-5	$24.99 US/$35.99 CAN
Windows NT® Networking For Dummies®	Ed Tittel, Mary Madden, & Earl Follis	0-7645-0015-5	$24.99 US/$34.99 CAN

PROGRAMMING

Active Server Pages For Dummies®, 2nd Edition	Bill Hatfield	0-7645-0065-1	$24.99 US/$34.99 CAN
Beginning Programming For Dummies®	Wally Wang	0-7645-0596-0	$19.99 US/$29.99 CAN
C++ For Dummies® Quick Reference, 2nd Edition	Namir Shammas	0-7645-0390-1	$14.99 US/$21.99 CAN
Java™ Programming For Dummies®, 3rd Edition	David & Donald Koosis	0-7645-0388-X	$29.99 US/$42.99 CAN
JBuilder™ For Dummies®	Barry A. Burd	0-7645-0567-X	$24.99 US/$34.99 CAN
VBA For Dummies®, 2nd Edition	Steve Cummings	0-7645-0078-3	$24.99 US/$34.99 CAN
Windows® 2000 Programming For Dummies®	Richard Simon	0-7645-0469-X	$24.99 US/$37.99 CAN
XML For Dummies®, 2nd Edition	Ed Tittel	0-7645-0692-7	$24.99 US/$37.99 CAN

Dummies Books™
Bestsellers on Every Topic!

GENERAL INTEREST TITLES

THE ARTS

rt For Dummies®	Thomas Hoving	0-7645-5104-3	$24.99 US/$34.99 CAN
lues For Dummies®	Lonnie Brooks, Cub Koda, & Wayne Baker Brooks	0-7645-5080-2	$24.99 US/$34.99 CAN
lassical Music For Dummies®	David Pogue & Scott Speck	0-7645-5009-8	$24.99 US/$34.99 CAN
uitar For Dummies®	Mark Phillips & Jon Chappell of Cherry Lane Music	0-7645-5106-X	$24.99 US/$34.99 CAN
azz For Dummies®	Dirk Sutro	0-7645-5081-0	$24.99 US/$34.99 CAN
pera For Dummies®	David Pogue & Scott Speck	0-7645-5010-1	$24.99 US/$34.99 CAN
iano For Dummies®	Blake Neely of Cherry Lane Music	0-7645-5105-1	$24.99 US/$34.99 CAN
hakespeare For Dummies®	John Doyle & Ray Lischner	0-7645-5135-3	$19.99 US/$27.99 CAN

HEALTH

llergies and Asthma For Dummies®	William Berger, M.D.	0-7645-5218-X	$19.99 US/$27.99 CAN
lternative Medicine For Dummies®	James Dillard, M.D., D.C., C.A.C., & Terra Ziporyn, Ph.D.	0-7645-5109-4	$19.99 US/$27.99 CAN
eauty Secrets For Dummies®	Stephanie Seymour	0-7645-5078-0	$19.99 US/$27.99 CAN
iabetes For Dummies®	Alan L. Rubin, M.D.	0-7645-5154-X	$19.99 US/$27.99 CAN
ieting For Dummies®	The American Dietetic Society with Jane Kirby, R.D.	0-7645-5126-4	$19.99 US/$27.99 CAN
amily Health For Dummies®	Charles Inlander & Karla Morales	0-7645-5121-3	$19.99 US/$27.99 CAN
rst Aid For Dummies®	Charles B. Inlander & The People's Medical Society	0-7645-5213-9	$19.99 US/$27.99 CAN
tness For Dummies®, 2nd Edition	Suzanne Schlosberg & Liz Neporent, M.A.	0-7645-5167-1	$19.99 US/$27.99 CAN
ealing Foods For Dummies®	Molly Siple, M.S. R.D.	0-7645-5198-1	$19.99 US/$27.99 CAN
ealthy Aging For Dummies®	Walter Bortz, M.D.	0-7645-5233-3	$19.99 US/$27.99 CAN
en's Health For Dummies®	Charles Inlander	0-7645-5120-5	$19.99 US/$27.99 CAN
utrition For Dummies®, 2nd Edition	Carol Ann Rinzler	0-7645-5180-9	$19.99 US/$27.99 CAN
egnancy For Dummies®	Joanne Stone, M.D., Keith Eddleman, M.D., & Mary Murray	0-7645-5074-8	$19.99 US/$27.99 CAN
x For Dummies®	Dr. Ruth K. Westheimer	1-56884-384-4	$16.99 US/$24.99 CAN
ress Management For Dummies®	Allen Elkin, Ph.D.	0-7645-5144-2	$19.99 US/$27.99 CAN
e Healthy Heart For Dummies®	James M. Ripple, M.D.	0-7645-5166-3	$19.99 US/$27.99 CAN
eight Training For Dummies®	Liz Neporent, M.A. & Suzanne Schlosberg	0-7645-5036-5	$19.99 US/$27.99 CAN
omen's Health For Dummies®	Pamela Maraldo, Ph.D., R.N., & The People's Medical Society	0-7645-5119-1	$19.99 US/$27.99 CAN

TECHNOLOGY TITLES

MACINTOSH

acs® For Dummies®, 7th Edition	David Pogue	0-7645-0703-6	$19.99 US/$27.99 CAN
e iBook™ For Dummies®	David Pogue	0-7645-0647-1	$19.99 US/$27.99 CAN
e iMac For Dummies®, 2nd Edition	David Pogue	0-7645-0648-X	$19.99 US/$27.99 CAN
e iMac For Dummies® Quick Reference	Jenifer Watson	0-7645-0648-X	$12.99 US/$19.99 CAN

PC/GENERAL COMPUTING

ilding A PC For Dummies®, 2nd Edition	Mark Chambers	0-7645-0571-8	$24.99 US/$34.99 CAN
ying a Computer For Dummies®	Dan Gookin	0-7645-0632-3	$19.99 US/$27.99 CAN
ustrated Computer Dictionary For Dummies®, 4th Edition	Dan Gookin & Sandra Hardin Gookin	0-7645-0732-X	$19.99 US/$27.99 CAN
lm Computing® For Dummies®	Bill Dyszel	0-7645-0581-5	$24.99 US/$34.99 CAN
s For Dummies®, 7th Edition	Dan Gookin	0-7645-0594-7	$19.99 US/$27.99 CAN
all Business Computing For Dummies®	Brian Underdahl	0-7645-0287-5	$24.99 US/$34.99 CAN
art Homes For Dummies®	Danny Briere	0-7645-0527-0	$19.99 US/$27.99 CAN
grading & Fixing PCs For Dummies®, 5th Edition	Andy Rathbone	0-7645-0719-2	$19.99 US/$27.99 CAN
ndspring Visor For Dummies®	Joe Hubko	0-7645-0724-9	$19.99 US/$27.99 CAN

Notes

Notes